D0914352

DRAMATISTS IN PERSPECTIVE:
SPANISH THEATRE IN THE TWENTIETH CENTURY

Dramatists in Perspective:
Spanish Theatre in the Twentieth Century

GWYNNE EDWARDS

CARDIFF
UNIVERSITY OF WALES PRESS
1985

© University of Wales, 1985

British Library Cataloguing in Publication Data

Edwards, Gwynne
  Dramatists in perspective
  1. Spanish drama — 20th century — History
  and criticism
  I. Title
  862'. 6'09 PQ6115

ISBN 0-7083-0881-3

Typeset in Wales by Afal
Printed in Wales by D. Brown & Sons Ltd.

To my son
GARETH

Contents

Preface

The purpose of this book is two-fold. Firstly, there is not, to the best of my knowledge, a book in English which studies side-by-side the work of the most important Spanish dramatists of the twentieth century. And secondly, there is certainly no study which attempts to consider them within a European context. In seeing these dramatists juxtaposed, students of modern Spanish theatre will be able to compare them more easily and to see too the broad pattern of development in the drama over a long period of time. An awareness of important trends in European theatre enables one, furthermore, to escape the parochialism inherent in any examination of a national theatre, and clarifies both the contribution of major European dramatists to the theatre of Spain and the relationship of playwrights such as Valle-Inclán and Lorca to the European tradition. Given this broader dimension, theatre enthusiasts hitherto unfamiliar with modern Spanish drama may also come to know it better and recognize its importance, for, with the exception of Lorca, the playwrights examined here are largely unknown to British audiences. Thus, it is hoped that this book will have an appeal for students of drama and encourage them to perform some of the plays in question where suitable translations exist. If this study stimulates interest in a theatre which has been for the most part neglected in this country, even by our national theatre companies, its purpose will have been amply justified.

I wish to express my gratitude to the British Academy for a grant which allowed me to visit Madrid in connection with the writing of certain parts of the book, and to Mr John Rhys, Director of the University of Wales Press, for his always helpful advice at various stages of writing.

CHAPTER I

Introduction

For the first three decades of the twentieth century the theatre in Spain was dominated by dramatists who for the most part catered for an unthinking and undiscerning bourgeois public concerned primarily with superficial entertainment. At the turn of the century the favourite of the theatre-going public, distinguished in particular by middle-class and middle-aged women, continued to be the neo-Romantic dramatist, José Echegaray (1832-1916). Though an enthusiastic reader of Ibsen, especially of plays like *Ghosts* and *Brand*, Echegaray invariably took from Ibsen the elements which appealed to his own Romantic disposition — themes of madness, death and fate — and the titles of his plays are a useful pointer to the nature of his theatre: *La esposa del vengador (The Avenger's Wife), En el seno de la muerte (In the Bosom of Death), O locura o santidad (Madness or Saintliness),* and *El hijo de Don Juan (The Son of Don Juan).* The last is concerned with the madness of Lázaro, the son of Don Juan Mejía, a condition which Echegaray presents both as the boy's inheritance and as the punishment of his father's misdemeanours. Echegaray, adhering to a formula characterized by melodramatic subjects, passionate characters and over-inflated language, as well as an advocacy of conventional middle-class morality, had an enormous appeal both for self-indulgent actors and bourgeois audiences who greeted the performance of his plays with wild enthusiasm. That Echegaray was a dramatist not without merit is suggested by the fact that in 1904 he was awarded the Nobel Prize for Literature. Nevertheless, his example was one that was to characterize Spanish theatre for many years to come. In other European countries Ibsen, Chekhov, Shaw, Brecht, Pirandello and others were changing the conventional nature of theatre with their thought-provoking and often experimental plays. Spain, on the other hand, continued to be distinguished by dramatists who gave the public what they wanted and by a public highly resistant to any kind of change. It was a pattern that would prove extremely difficult to break.[1]

Within this pattern, nonetheless, certain changes did take place at the turn of the century, notably in relation to a greater 'realism' in the theatre, and in this context two figures should be mentioned: Galdós and Benavente. Benito Pérez Galdós (1843-1920), Spain's greatest novelist of the second half of the nineteenth century, was also the author of twenty-two plays, many of them adaptations of his novels, and the first of them, *Realidad (Reality)*, was performed in 1892. In his plays Galdós sought to bring to the theatre some of the principal characteristics of his novels, notably a significant degree of realism and a concern with serious issues, both individual and social, that entirely separates his drama from that of Echegaray. The dramatic characters of Galdós are thus very credible, the language unostentatious and the plots well-shaped. *Realidad,* for example, is a play about adultery in which the husband, Orozco, in strict contrast to the avenging husbands of Romantic drama, forgives his erring wife. It suggests too that the theatre of Galdós, far from being a theatre of mere entertainment, is distinguished by its serious themes.

Like Galdós, Jacinto Benavente (1866-1954) represents a movement away from the neo-Romantic overstatement of Echegaray. Moreover, in the sense that Benavente was a more important and accomplished dramatist than Galdós, there can be no doubt that in the first two decades of the century his theatre, with its emphasis on psychologically credible characters and its stylish, easy and 'natural' language, constituted a new art whose effect was far-reaching. Benavente's theatre, broadly speaking, can be divided into four categories. Firstly, there are the so-called 'drawing-room plays' such as *El nido ajeno (Another's Nest)* (1894) and *Gente conocida (Acquaintances)* (1896). Concerned for the most part with the refined society of Benavente's day, they are essentially conversation pieces in which the characters serve to draw attention to their own defects. Secondly, closely linked to the above are those plays with a cosmopolitan setting — *La noche del sábado (Saturday Night)* (1903), *La escuela de las princesas (The School of Princesses)* (1909), *La última carta (The Last Letter)* (1941) — in which English ladies, Italian countesses and exiled princes are used by the dramatist to portray a society in decline. In a third group of plays which have as their settings not urban but Spanish provincial life — *La gobernadora (The Governess)* (1901), *Los malhechores del bien (The Evildoers of Good)* (1905) — Benavente was concerned with the exposure of the self-centredness and hypocrisy of provincial society. And finally, there are the rural dramas — *Señora Ama* (1908) and *La malquerida (The Girl Wrongly Loved)* (1913) — which, for the most part, merely involve the substitution of rural for urban settings. Benavente's finest play, *Los intereses creados (The Bonds of Interest)* really stands on its own. Dealing with the theme that all human beings are capable of hypocrisy and corruption — the theme of so much of his theatre — Benavente drew heavily here on the traditions of the *commedia dell'arte* and Spanish theatre of the sixteenth century and created a work of great pace and vitality, peopled by vigorously drawn and lively characters.[2]

Given the greater realism and social preoccupations of Benavente's theatre, it also has very obvious defects. Firstly, his portrayal of the contemporary scene resulted in plays which are for the most part conversation pieces, in which the characters speak rather than do, and in which genuine dramatic action is subordinated to dialogue. Pérez de Ayala, one of Benavente's severest critics, has described his theatre as being 'sin acción y sin pasión' ('without action and without passion'), and on the latter point Francisco Ruiz Ramón has suggested that Benavente is more the sceptical observer of the social scene of his day than the socially committed dramatist.[3] A final assessment of Benavente must also take into account the fact that his theatre did not evolve and change very much during his long reign as Spain's most popular and thus influential dramatist. In short, he was not part of that revolution in European theatre that became especially prominent after, and largely because of, the First World War. In the sense that he created a dramatic formula which, though different from that of Echegaray, was essentially conservative and unexciting, Benavente did relatively little to advance the cause of the drama of his day.

Much the same can be said of the contribution to the Spanish stage of the two brothers, Serafín and Joaquín Álvarez Quintero (1871-1938 and 1873-1944). Over a period of forty years or so the Quintero brothers exercised an enormous influence on the taste of Spanish theatre-goers, for in those years they produced more than two hundred works consisting of *entremeses* and *sainetes* — short comic pieces with or without music —, *zarzuelas* — musical comedies — and plays ranging from one to four Acts. In this large body of work the Quintero brothers projected a pleasant, rose-coloured vision of Spain, especially of their native Andalusia, and, adapting the tradition of the so-called *género chico* to their own ends, introduced into the idealized world of their plays stock Spanish types and customs. On a superficial level their theatre has the appearance of realism, but it is, of course, a highly stylized form of drama in which the characters are simplified types lacking true individuality and genuine psychological depth. In addition, it is a drama lacking in conflict. Because of this, considerable emphasis is given to the dialogue, and this, devoid of the cut and thrust of true dramatic conflict, is distinguished by its elegance, shapeliness and wit. As well as being masters of entertaining dialogue, the Quintero brothers were highly accomplished craftsmen in relation to plot construction, and their plays were thus invariably well-made. Their theatre was, in short, one which appealed to a bourgeois public seeking a pleasant, escapist, after-dinner entertainment — a public unwilling to be confronted in the theatre with unpleasant or controversial matters. In reality Andalusia during the time of the Quintero brothers' enormous commercial success was a region of Spain plagued by inescapable problems of poverty, hunger and the continued exploitation of the peasant workers by wealthy and often absentee landlords. They were problems which the Quinteros chose to ignore. Having discovered a commercially successful dramatic formula, they adhered rigidly to it. Indeed, in using popular dramatic forms like the *sainete*, which were traditionally distinguished by crude and vulgar elements, the Quinteros stripped them of their grosser features, transforming them into refined and idealized pieces which accorded with their general conception of the theatre.[4]

A number of dramatists, all of them enormously popular in their day, illustrate further the points already made, pointing both to the conventional and the escapist nature of the commercial theatre in Spain. Manuel Linares Rivas (1867-1938), writing in the tradition of Benavente, took the bourgeoisie as the subject matter of his plays and, in criticizing it, employed a largely naturalistic technique. As a dramatist, though, he lacked the qualities of Benavente — the irony, the ability to write amusing and entertaining dialogue and to construct skilful plots. His plays are, indeed, thesis plays. *El abolengo (The Inheritance)* (1904) is a criticism of social climbing. *Maria Victoria* (1904) makes the point that money does not lead to happiness. And *La garra (The Claw)* (1914) argues in favour of divorce. The characters of the plays are merely personifications of different aspects of the thesis, are manipulated by the dramatist and lack a life of their own. Equally, the plot is little more than the elaboration of an argument, the fitting together of its different aspects.[5]

Gregorio Martínez Sierra (1881-1947), a very different dramatist from Linares Rivas, resembles him in the sense that his plays did nothing to advance the cause of the Spanish theatre. In works like *Canción de cuna (Cradle Song)* (1911), *Madame Pepita* (1912), *Mamá* (1912) and *Amanecer (Dawn)* (1915), Martínez Sierra extolled the virtues of family life and domesticity through female characters who are the very epitome of Christian morality and who guide both husbands and sons along the right path. Needless to say, these plays are distinguished by their excessive sentimentality, and it is hard to believe that their author, as will be seen later, made a substantial contribution to the progress of Spanish theatre in his role of producer and translator of significant European dramatists.[6]

Pedro Muñoz Seca (1881-1936) exemplifies perfectly the Spanish theatre-going public's craving for superficial entertainment, as well as its determination to bury its head in the sand. Specializing in short plays known as *astracanadas,* short comic pieces marked by caricature and exaggeration, Muñoz Seca had an enormously successful career over a period of thirty years as either the author or co-author of some three hundred works. The exaggerated popular types, the absurd situations and the far-fetched language of these plays, constantly distinguished by jokes and word play, were intended solely to make the audience laugh, and this they achieved with notable effect. Muñoz Seca's popularity was, though, as Enrique Díez Canedo has correctly pointed out, a measure of the tastes of theatre-goers in the first three decades of the twentieth century.[7]

Mention must be made here too, in relation to this broad picture of theatrical stagnation, of the so-called 'poetic theatre', the *teatro poético*, which began to make its mark toward the end of the first decade of the century. It was in part a reaction against the realistic theatre of Benavente and his school and its sources were thus to be found in Romanticism and the plays of Spain's Golden Age. Within the 'poetic theatre' historical plays figure prominently, their purpose being to present to Spanish audiences conscious of Spain's decline historical figures who epitomized heroism, moral rectitude and other associated qualities. Torrente Ballester has described the 'poetic theatre' as pure nostalgia and escapism, for its picture of Spain's glorious past is idealized and false, lacking historical perspective.

The most important and representative dramatist of the 'poetic theatre' was Eduardo Marquina (1879-1946) whose historical drama falls into two broad periods: the first covering the years 1908 to the outbreak of the First World War, the second beginning in 1930 and ending in 1943. To the first period belong such plays as *Las hijas del Cid (The Daughters of the Cid)* (1908) and *En Flandes se ha puesto el sol (The Sun Has Set in Flanders)* (1910). Heroic in tone, these plays exemplify in their characters such qualities as courage, nobility, loyalty and self-sacrifice, presented as the essence of Spain's glorious past and as a model for the present and the future. But, like the 'poetic theatre' as a whole, their idealized tone inhibits any attempt to present a critical view of the past. The historical plays of the second period, such as *El monje blanco (The White Monk)* (1930) and *Teresa de Jesús* (1933), are much more concerned with religious themes and the exaltation of such virtues as faith and piety. Marquina's real achievement lies, indeed, not in his escapist and over-blown historical drama but in his rural plays — five plays in verse — which are much better written, much more sobre in style and technique, and can be seen as part of the tradition of rural drama which led to the masterpieces of Lorca.[8]

Two famous names who must also be considered under the heading of the 'poetic theatre' are the brothers Antonio and Manuel Machado (1875-1939 and 1874-1947) who between 1926 and 1932 wrote seven plays in collaboration, five of them in verse. The Machado brothers had, in fact, some interesting ideas on theatre, notably on the close integration of action and dialogue and the use of the aside, but in practice their theatre is purely traditional. Instead of using the action of the play to express the motivations of the characters, the Machados did so through over-long stage directions and narrative passages. The subjects of these plays are often set in the past — *Desdichas de la fortuna (Fortune's Blows)* (1926) deals with the illegitimate son of the Count-Duke of Olivares (1587-1645) — and are concerned with tragic or redeeming love. At all events, the 'poetic theatre', be it that of Marquina or the Machados, did nothing to revitalize Spanish drama in the 1920s and early 1930s.

Within this generally depressing history of Spanish drama up to 1936, who, then, were the innovators and writers of real significance? In many respects Carlos Arniches (1866-1943) points the way ahead. He began his career as a dramatist by writing in the tradition of the *género chico* already mentioned in relation to the Quintero brothers, but these short plays, filled with the colourful types and realistic language of low-life Madrid, are far removed from the sugary sentimentality of the Quinteros. Arniches, moreover, succeeded in endowing this traditional form with a greater coherence and introduced into its predominantly comic tone moments of true dramatic conflict and pathos. Subsequently, when the *género chico* began to decline around 1910, Arniches began to develop his dramatic talents in another direction by writing extended *sainetes* and *farsas grotescas* in which he was able to develop much more fully those characteristics already evident in the short plays.

The full-length plays, written between 1915 and 1931, fall into two broad categories. In the first, of which *¡Que viene mi marido! (My Husband is Coming!)* (1918) is a good example, a marked contrast is established between the physical and social appearance of a character and his true nature. In the second, characters who embody particular national vices — ignorance, hypocrisy, cruelty, spiritual emptiness — are counterbalanced by their opposites. To this second category belong the three-act plays, *La señorita de Trévelez* (1916), generally regarded as Arniches's best play, *Los caciques (The Bosses)* (1920), and *La heroica villa (The Heroic Town)* (1921). At the heart of the full-length plays lies Arniches's critical attitude to a highly effective interplay of comic and tragic elements, an awareness of opposites, a sense of contrast between appearance and reality, and a strong suggestion of the absurdity of human life. Quite clearly, in its emphasis on caricature and the grotesque the theatre of Arniches represents a movement away from the realistic bourgeois theatre of Benavente, the Quinteros and their imitators towards the deliberately anti-commercial approach of as innovating a dramatist as Ramón del Valle-Inclán. And, equally importantly, his theatre turns its back on the inward-looking, parochial drama discussed so far and anticipates experiments in the absurd and the grotesque that characterize so much significant European theatre of the twentieth century.[9].

Another important figure in the first thirty years of the century is Miguel de Unamuno (1864-1936). The commercial theatre of the time dismissed Unamuno's theatre, regarding it as strange and problematical, while he in turn remained uncompromising, refusing to conform to the tastes of impresarios and self-indulgent actors. The successful, commercial theatre of dramatists like Benavente and Marquina was thus something which Unamuno despised, and he believed too that the theatre-going public needed to be educated in relation to the true nature of theatre.

Unamuno's own plays may be best described, perhaps, as schematic. The settings are invariably stark and unadorned, corresponding entirely to the requirements of the stage action. The stage action itself is highly concentrated, eliminating unnecessary incident. Characters are few and their feelings are boldly presented. As far as dialogue is concerned, it is spare and to the point. A theatre of this kind, so different from the realistic drama of Benavente with its emphasis on plot, the psychology of the characters, and nicely shaped dialogue, is very striking and anticipates dramatists like Beckett, but in Unamuno's hands it also has its defects. By stripping action and, in particular, character to their very core, Unamuno fails to flesh them out sufficiently to achieve genuine theatrical effectiveness. Instead, his plays tend to become essays, in which the dialogue is often too much of a debate. The characters are, in turn, Unamuno himself expressing his own dilemmas, and the drama, dominated by ideas, rarely converts itself into truly dramatic action.

La venda (The Blindfold) (1898-9), written at a time of religious crisis, is a good example of the way in which Unamuno's theatre exteriorizes his own emotional and intellectual conflicts. María, blind from birth, has recovered her sight through an operation but, without blindfolding herself, cannot find her way to her father's house. When she arrives there, she removes the blindfold, sees her father dead and blindfolds herself again in order not to see reality. In short, the only way to find God is to deny reason and blind oneself with faith. The play is, very clearly, a play of ideas in which the characters are mouthpieces, relationships between individuals are not explored and developed, and genuine dramatic action is largely absent.

Unamuno's theatre as a whole follows the pattern outlined above, though plays like *Fedra* (1910) and *Raquel encadenada (Rachel in Chains)* are more successful in dramatic terms. His best play is often thought to be *El otro (The Other One)*, written in 1926, for here Unamuno succeeds in transforming debate into dramatic action. The theme of the play, typically Unamunian, is one which also dominates *La esfinge (The Sphinx)* (1898-9), *Soledad (Solitude)* (1921-2) and *Sombras de sueño (Dream Shadows)* (1926) — the theme of individual identity. A brother who has killed his identical twin feels he has killed himself and ends by doing so. The question is posed: who is really aware of his true identity? In dramatizing the theme Unamuno eliminates all realistic and extraneous elements. The six characters of the play — echoes, perhaps, of Pirandello — are all closely related to the theme of identity, and the whole of the action and the dialogue is concentrated upon it too, but in a way now which transforms ideas into drama. In general, it can be said of the theatre of Unamuno that, for all its faults, its schematic and intellectual character allows for a comparison with the drama of T.S. Eliot, Cocteau and Giradoux.[10]

While the achievement of Arniches and Unamuno is important in relation to contemporary Spanish theatre, the innovations of Ramón del Valle-Inclán (1866-1936), to whom a subsequent chapter is devoted, must be seen as amongst the most original in European drama in the 1920s. Needless to say, Valle-Inclán's approach to theatre took as its starting point a complete rejection of the naturalistic tradition with its emphasis on particular individuals set in particularized or localized time and space, and advocated in its place a drama which projected a sense of the archetypal, the timeless and the universal. In this sense Unamuno was influenced by European symbolist theatre whose impact, especially that of Maeterlinck, was being felt in Spain in the first decade of the century. In terms of its projection of a timeless, mythical world which suggests the eternal clash of good and evil and man's spiritual redemption, Valle's trilogy, the *Comedias bárbaras (The Savage Dramas)*, is a fine example of symbolist drama. The technique, moreover, achieving a remarkable synthesis of the different elements of dramatic performance — stage settings, costumes, movement, lighting and dialogue — is highly reminiscent of the ideas on theatre of symbolist stage designers and producers such as Adolphe Appia and Edward Gordon Craig in other European countries. Such originality is evident in Valle-Inclán's theatre as a whole, but the years following the First World War saw a greater concern with social issues and with it a shift of emphasis in relation to technique. Elements of social criticism through caricature are evident in earlier plays — *La cabeza del dragón (The Head of the Dragon)* (1900) — but Valle's theory of the grotesque, *esperpentismo*, is clearly expressed in the twelfth scene of *Luces de Bohemia (Bohemian Lights)*, written in 1920. Both here and in *Los cuernos de Don Friolera (The Horns of Don Friolera)* (1921) Valle-Inclán ruthlessly exposes the absurd and inhuman nature of Spanish life and institutions. *Luces de*

Bohemia has as its central character the poor and blind poet, Max Estrella, who, by the end of the play, is reduced by a callous society to the level of a whimpering animal, while *Los cuernos de Don Friolera* pillories the outdated Spanish concept of honour and reputation. If, moreover, Valle's earlier plays reveal the influence of Symbolism, *Luces de Bohemia* has many of the characteristics of Expressionism, while *Los cuernos de Don Friolera*, in reducing human beings to puppet figures, looks forward to the Theatre of the Absurd, to the plays of Ionesco, Beckett and Arrabal. Such comparisons point clearly to the original and forward-looking nature of Valle-Inclán's drama.[11]

In Jacinto Grau (1877-1958) Valle-Inclán had a kindred spirit, for he too believed in a theatre which turned its back on Naturalism in favour of a synthesis of different art forms. The plays written before 1918, including *El hijo pródigo (The Prodigal Son)* (1917) and *El conde Alarcos (Count Alarcos)* (1907) remain somewhat classical in many ways, but at the same time they reveal Grau's use of the different elements of the stage — scenery, costumes and lighting — to achieve a heightened dramatic effect. After 1918, as in Valle-Inclán's case, the nature of Grau's theatre changed somewhat, for his plays began to suggest the sense of the futility of human effort that characterized so much European writing after the First World War. Grau's best and most famous play, *El señor de Pigmalión (Mr Pygmalion)*, was written in 1921, the same year as Pirandello's *Six Characters in Search of an Author* and Karel Capek's *R.U.R.* The play deals with Mr Pygmalion's attempt to create animated life-size puppets with human defects and their final destruction of their creator. In terms of its themes — the true extent of individual freedom, the puppet-like nature of man, the disastrous consequences of human ingenuity — the play expresses many of the most important preoccupations of its time. In its integration of stage settings, costumes, lighting, music, dance and sound effects, it is, moreover, a fine example of non-realistic drama that at this period in time was increasingly making its mark throughout Europe.

Another writer whose aims in the theatre link him with Unamuno, Valle-Inclán and Grau was Ramón Gómez de la Serna (1888-1963). As many of his observations indicate, his purpose was to create a drama totally different from the commercial theatre of his time. His actual achievement did not, however, match his vision and his importance remains largely historical. A sense of the unconventional nature of his plays may be gleaned from their principal concerns, above all from their preoccupation with sexuality. In *El drama del palacio deshabitado, (The Drama of the Uninhabited Palace)*, for instance, Rosa and Juan represent the dramatist's view of the true meaning of life — the triumph of the flesh — in contrast to the dead inhabitants of the palace. Similarly, *Beatriz (Beatrice)* has strongly erotic overtones as Beatriz, in one of the play's most important scenes, bandages the severed head of John the Baptist. As far as technique is concerned, Gómez de la Serna's work as a whole bears witness to his *avant-garde* approach and his plays reveal clear elements of Modernism, Expressionism, and Surrealism.[12]

A similar rejection of the naturalistic tradition is exemplified by Azorín (1873-1967) whose plays were mostly written between 1925 and 1936 and include *Old Spain* (1926), *Brandy, mucho brandy (Brandy, Lots of Brandy)* (1927), *Lo invisible (The Invisible)* (1928) and *Angelita* (1930). An intelligent, sensitive and thoughtful individual, Azorín was much influenced by dramatists like Maeterlinck, Pirandello and Cocteau and was thus concerned both with serious themes and with the projection in his plays of the inner rather than the external reality of his characters' lives. *Old Spain*, for example, embodies in two characters the clash of past and present, tradition and progress. The Marquis of Cilleros lives a life of quiet contemplation in his palace in an old Castillian town, immersed in memories of the past. In contrast, Don Joaquín is a multimillionaire man of action who, though he admires the old traditions, sees the need for change and progress. A reconciliation of the two extremes is achieved through Don Joaquín's marriage to Pepita, the Marquis's daughter, for in the marriage, as well as in the children it will produce, the old and the new will live together, enriching each other.

In *Brandy, mucho brandy* Azorín deals with the themes of happiness and illusion. A middle-class family — mother, father, daughter — hopes for happiness and escape from their present lot. Their illusions seem to be realized when they inherit a substantial sum of money, but instead of happiness it brings them only misery. The daughter, Laura, decides to leave home in search of happiness, but she too fails to find it. Azorín's preoccupation with the exploration of serious issues and the inner lives — the dreams and illusions — of his characters is revealed too in *Angelita*, often regarded as his best play. The heroine, by twisting a ring on her finger, is able to advance in time. In the course of the play she finds herself in a number of different situations — married with a child, later alone in a sanatorium. Interesting as it is in terms of theme, the play's action consists of a series of rather undramatic scenes, and all three plays mentioned above suggest Azorín's weaknesses in this respect. For all the forward-looking nature of his ideas, Azorín lacks the ability to create that tension and conflict which is the very essence of theatre. He remains thus a figure of some importance in the theatre of the 1920s, but his actual achievement is distinctly limited.[13]

In total contrast, Federico García Lorca (1898-1936) is one of the great innovators of the twentieth century, a dramatist whose practice matches his vision of a new kind of theatre. His work will be discussed in detail in Chapter 3. Suffice it to say for the moment that, like Valle-Inclán, Unamuno and a number of dramatists already mentioned, Lorca reacted vigorously against the popular commercial theatre of his day, attributing the poverty of Spanish theatre to the tyranny exercised over aspiring dramatists by commercially-minded theatre impresarios, arrogant actors and a superficial public. His own aim was, quite simply, to save the Spanish theatre both by writing plays with serious themes and by constant experimentation in theatre technique. The themes of Lorca's plays — love, frustration, passing time, and death — have universal relevance. In terms of technique his drama reveals a wide variety of influence, both Spanish and European. Lorca's first play, *El maleficio de la mariposa (The Butterfly's Evil Spell)* (1920), is a play about insects which reveals the clear influence of Symbolism, especially of Maeterlinck. The farces and puppet plays — the form itself is indicative of Lorca's rejection of naturalism — owe much to the traditions of Spanish drama in the sixteenth and seventeenth centuries, but, as in the case of *La zapatera prodigiosa (The Shoemaker's Prodigious Wife)* (1930), he uses the techniques of comic theatre to express serious themes — a materialistic and honour-ridden Spanish society, illusion and frustration — and in the sense that his characters are distinguished by marked elements of dehumanization, this and other plays can also be placed within the context of the theatre of the grotesque in the twentieth century.

A further dimension of Lorca's art is revealed in his experiments with Surrealism in plays like *Así que pasen cinco años (When Five Years Have Passed)* (1930-1) and *El público (The Public)* (1929-30), both of which expose the inner lives of their characters and are quite remarkable works in their brilliant integration of theatrical, balletic and cinematic elements. In the last four years of his life Lorca produced his justly famous tragic trilogy, *Bodas de sangre (Blood Wedding)* (1933), *Yerma* (1934) and *La casa de Bernarda Alba (The House of Bernarda Alba)* (1936). These plays have a social dimension in the sense that they dramatize the inevitable and tragic clash between individual desire and the restrictions of social convention. They are thus a criticism of the narrow-mindedness of the Spanish society of Lorca's day. More important, though, is the universal character of the conflicts they express. To this extent the tragic trilogy has a strongly symbolist character which brings to mind the works of a dramatist such as J.M. Synge. As far as technique is concerned, Lorca is fully in the tradition of such symbolist producers and directors as Adolphe Appia and Edward

Gordon Craig, seeking to integrate into a single powerful image the different aspects of stage performance. Of all the important Spanish dramatists of the twentieth century, Lorca, it seems fair to say, achieved the greatest richness and variety.[14]

Together with Lorca and Valle-Inclán, pride of place must also be given to the theatre of Rafael Alberti (1902-   ). From the very outset Alberti opposed the commercial theatre of his day, appearing on stage at the end of the first performance of *El hombre deshabitado (The Uninhabited Man)* (1929) in order to denounce in the strongest language the state of the Spanish theatre. This play, echoing the concerns of Alberti's poetry, is a work of self-revelation, the dramatization of his loss of religious faith. Employing on the one hand the allegorical techniques of the religious plays of Spain's Golden Age, Alberti was influenced too by the principal features of expressionist drama. Subsequently, the emphasis of his theatre became more political. In 1931 he embarked on a tour of various European countries which brought him into direct contact with the significant changes that were then taking place in the theatre: the expressionist plays of Georg Kaiser and Ivan Goll; the political theatre of Erwin Piscator and the tradition of *agitprop* drama. Involved with his wife, María Teresa, in the activities of the Republic before and during the Civil War, Alberti produced his own *agitprop* plays as a means of arousing Republican fervour. In the year the Civil War ended he and his wife left Spain and, as we shall see, some of his greatest work for the theatre was written in exile.[15]

Another significant name in the period in question is that of Alejandro Casona (1903-65) whose dramatic career really began in 1934 with the performance of *La sirena varada (The Stranded Siren)*. This was followed in the period leading up to the Civil War by *Otra vez, el diablo (The Devil Again)* (1935), and *Nuestra Natacha (Our Natacha)* (1936). During the Civil War itself Casona was in exile but continued to write. 1937 saw the performance in Mexico of *Prohibido suicidarse en primavera (It is Forbidden to Commit Suicide in the Spring)* and 1938 and 1939 the appearance of some lesser pieces. Casona's theatre is without doubt a theatre of serious intention. Under the auspices of the Republic he was, like Lorca, the director of a touring theatre company. As far as his own theatre is concerned, it is characterized very largely by the themes of reality and illusion. In this sense *La sirena varada* is a typical play, for it presents a group of people who, in order to escape the reality of the world in which they live, remove themselves to an island. In so doing they reveal both their fear of reality and their failure to escape it. The play's message is thus the conclusion that man can be true to himself only by accepting reality and learning to live in the world as we know it. Similarly, in *Prohibido suicidarse en primavera* a number of people take refuge in a sanatorium where, in order to escape life's problems, they propose suicide. Once more the point is made that a solution to life's difficulties lies in acceptance of them. Casona's emphasis on the message of his plays is in many instances a source of their weakness, a point which is well illustrated by *Nuestra Natacha*. Set in a reformatory, the action revolves around two opposing attitudes towards the inmates. The directors, believing that their charges are incapable of change for the better, take the view that only authoritarian methods will control them. Natacha and some of her university friends adopt an entirely different approach and seek to rehabilitate the inmates on an abandoned farm. The play is, in fact, an effective piece of theatre, for both characters and situations are presented in truly dramatic terms. On the other hand, its rather sentimental and romantic thesis plays into the hands of those who see Casona's theatre as a kind of self-indulgent intellectual and aesthetic game.[16]

The theatre of Max Aub (1903-72) can be divided into three periods, two of which correspond to the pre-Civil War years and the Civil War itself. Prior to the Civil War, Aub produced plays of an *avante-garde* character and was influenced in this respect by such theatrical visionaries as Edward Gordon Craig. In consequence, his theatre is anti-naturalistic, and its highly stylized techniques are intended to penetrate beneath the surface appearance of things in order to express such universal issues as human isolation and man's inability to communicate with his fellow men. In *La botella (The bottle)* (1924) a bottle dominates the centre of the stage. None of the characters of the play sees the bottle in the same way, for none of them pays really close attention to it. Language becomes not a means of expressing reality but an instrument whereby one individual seeks to impose his viewpoint on another, as a result of which it separates and isolates men instead of helping them understand each other. *Narciso (Narcissus)* (1927) expresses the idea that no one has real knowledge of himself. The technical aspect of the play is interesting in the sense that the sets have a cubist quality and effects of light are particularly sharp and brilliant.

During the Civil War itself, Aub, like Alberti, devoted himself to writing *agitprop* plays in support of the Republican cause. *Pedro López García*, consisting of two Acts, deals with a poor shepherd, Pedro, who, despite the fact that he does not feel himself to be part of the Civil War, is obliged to enrol in the Nationalist army. In a kind of *intermezzo* which links the play's two Acts, the allegorical figure of the Vendedor, the tradesman, is seen selling Spain and its treasure — its land and its rivers — in exchange for weapons. Act Two presents Pedro with a vision of his mother, murdered by the Nationalists, and of Spain, both of whom urge him to switch allegiance to the Republicans. The play ends with Pedro accepting his duty and urging his fellow countrymen to do the same. The importance of this kind of work in relation to Max Aub's theatre as a whole is that it anticipates his mature theatre.[17]

In relation to *agitprop* drama, mention must be made too of Miguel Hernández (1910-42). Though a much better poet than dramatist, Hernández wrote four full-length plays and a number of shorter pieces between 1933 and 1937. Given his uncompromising left-wing stance, Hernández's theatre is inevitably proletarian and anti-bourgeois. *Los hijos de la piedra (Sons of the Rock)* (1935) takes as its subject the miners of the village of Montecabra who are ruthlessly exploited by the mine-owner. Urged on by a shepherd whose wife the mine-owner has raped, the miners finally kill him. The play typifies the weaknesses of Hernández's theatre, for the characters are either black or white and the conflict between them is excessively simplified. In many cases Hernández's debt to Golden Age theatre is very clear— *Los hijos de la piedra* owes much to *Fuenteovejuna* — but the comparison is one which hardly flatters Hernández's dramatic achievement.

Finally, in this discussion of Spanish drama before and during the Civil War the name of Jardiel Poncela (1901-52) merits consideration. Poncela is a significant figure in relation to the comic tradition in the sense that he sought above all to change that tradition. Between 1927 and 1936 he wrote eight plays, the most important being *Cuatro corazones con freno y marcha atrás (Four Hearts with a Brake and Reverse Gear)*. As an innovator, Poncela attempted to avoid the traditional devices of comic drama — linguistic jokes, mistaken identity and the like — and to create instead a comic theatre distinguished by a marked element of fantasy. His plays differ therefore from the comic pieces of such dramatists as Carlos Arniches and Muñoz Seca, for Poncela does not deal with popular types located in a particular time and place, and his language is not regional. The action of Poncela's plays commences with an unlifelike situation and there develops from it a chain of fantastic incidents. His theatre is, in short, a kind of intellectual game and his plots often have the quality of a detective story or an intricate game of chess. The resolution of the comic action is similarly intellectual and gives the impression of being imposed from outside rather than of emerging logically from the events themselves. Nevertheless, Poncela's importance is clear enough, both in relation to his own innovations and the influence he would exercise on future comic dramatists.[18]

* * * * * *

The years of the Spanish Republic, 1931-6, witnessing the flourishing of such outstanding dramatists as Lorca and Alberti, represent, with the exception of Valle-Inclán, the greatest achievement in Spanish theatre in the twentieth century. Here was a time when political freedom had its counterpart in that freedom of thought and expression necessary for the flowering of great works. The years that followed the Civil War marked, in contrast, a period of political repression and artistic censorship which stifled creative activity. Not until the death of Franco in 1975 and the relaxation of the political strictures that characterized his long reign did the circumstances again present themselves in which art might flourish freely. This is not to say, though, that in the intervening thirty-six years dramatists of significance did not appear. But when they did, they were compelled, as we shall see, to work within the limitations of the political system in which they wrote, or, in some cases, to leave Spain altogether.

Of the important dramatists discussed so far, some continued to write after the Civil War, though not in Spain, and a brief account of their work is necessary to complete the picture of their achievement. From 1940 to 1965, when he finally returned to Europe, Rafael Alberti sought refuge in Buenos Aires and continued to write outstanding plays, distinguished now less by their political character than by their consumate artistry. Such are *El trébol florido (The Flowering Clover)* (1940), *El adefesio (The Absurdity)* (1944), *La Gallarda (The Handsome Girl)* (1944-5), and *Noche de guerra en el Museo del Prado (Night of War in the Prado Museum)* (1956). *El adefesio* is a particularly striking play. Through the portrayal of three old crones who victimize their young ward, Altea, Alberti makes a biting comment on the cruelty, narrow-mindedness and hypocrisy of provincial Spanish life. The brilliant technique through which this nightmarish vision of Spain is expressed employs caricature and distortion and fuses into a totally convincing style elements from the later pictures of Goya, the *esperpentos* of Valle-Inclán and Expressionism. *Noche de guerra en el Museo del Prado* is equally striking both in its subject matter and its style, and in the latter respect is influenced by the theatre of Bertolt Brecht. Through the projection on a screen of some of the Prado's finest pictures, especially those of Goya, Alberti establishes a parallel between the violation of Spain by the forces of Napoleon in earlier times and the actions of Franco's fascist troops. The Brechtian technique of distancing and alienation allows the spectator to form a judgement on the events he is asked to observe, though at the same time, as in earlier plays, Alberti's predilection for the exaggeration and distortion of Expressionism also leads to an element of audience involvement and identification. Even a brief summary of Alberti's theatre suggests its exciting, innovating character, its seriousness of purpose, its variety and virtuosity. The detailed examination provided in Chapter 4 will, hopefully, confirm Alberti's importance in twentieth-century Spanish theatre.[19]

Like Alberti, Max Aub left Spain in 1939 and produced his finest work in exile, much of it influenced by his own experience not only of the Civil War but of prison and concentration camps between 1939 and 1942, when he finally settled in Mexico. Special mention must be made here of four plays which have a particular relevance to the European political scene of the 1940s and which fully reveal the relevance and force of Aub's theatre. In *San Juan (St. John)* (1943) Aub portrays a group of Jews, isolated on a ship which no country is willing to accept, and in a series of loosely connected but very moving scenes reveals the range of emotions experienced by them. Powerful in itself, the play acquires an added power through its symbolism, for the particular individuals of the play become all those who endure persecution and are ignored by others who could but do not offer a helping hand. *Morir por cerrar los ojos (To Die for Shutting One's Eyes)*, a two-part work in six Acts, takes as its subject the surrender of France to the Germans in 1940 and depicts a country overwhelmed by fear, loss of pride and conscience. Though the play has three central characters, they become in effect the focal point for the presentation of a vast panorama of French society. In terms of technique Aub is influenced by the perspectivist approach of the novel and the cinema, and the action is thus episodic, fragmented and open-ended, a feature of its style which enhances rather than detracts from the general effect. *El rapto de Europa (The Rape of Europa)* (1941) deals, like *San Juan*, with a group of people fleeing from the Nazis. In the central character, Margarita, who dedicates her life to helping refugees, Aub embodies a compassionate and humanitarian spirit which is his ideal but which, to judge by other works, he finds lacking in political systems and regimes. The faceless and heartless nature of the latter is, indeed, exemplified in *No*. Set in a German town divided by a line which marks the territory commanded by the Americans and the Russians, the play is concerned with the ultimate fate of the town's inhabitants. But the action evidently has a broader meaning, for it suggests the way in which ideologies, whatever their colour, ruthlessly ignore the needs of men as individuals.

In addition to these and other full-length plays, Aub wrote twenty or so one-Act pieces, many of them with similar concerns. *Tránsito (Removal)*, for example, deals with the theme of exile, a situation well understood by Aub himself, and portrays the divided loyalties of a man who has exchanged his country for another, his wife for a mistress, and left behind a family from which he is increasingly estranged. Other one-Act plays deal with the situation of Franco's Spain, as in *La vuelta (The Return)*, in which a female teacher, released from prison, returns to her village only to find everything changed, including the causes for which she fought. Clearly, the theatre of Max Aub is distinguished by its serious and provocative themes, as well as by its European and even universal relevance, and merits more attention than it has hitherto received.[20]

Alejandro Casona (1903-65) whose exile from Spain began in 1937 and ended in 1962, continued to write plays which did not differ greatly in theme and technique from those he had written previously. Casona's concerns, as we have already seen, often involve the interrelationship of reality and illusion, and they are indeed the principal issues of the plays written in exile, including *La dama del alba (Lady of the Dawn)* (1944) and *Los árboles mueren de pie (The Trees Die Standing Up)* (1949). In the former, Ángela, who in years past has abandoned her husband, Martín, for another man, returns home to discover that her infidelity has remained her husband's secret and that everyone, except Martín, believes her to have drowned. Reality has, in effect, given way to the myth of her innocent death. In the meantime her place in Martín's life has been taken by Adela, whom he has saved from drowning and who has since brought him happiness. Ángela, conscious of the fact that her return will destroy both the myth of her innocence and her husband's happiness, transforms the myth into reality by drowning herself. The play undoubtedly gives the impression of being melodramatic and sentimental. In fact it is a highly poetic work in which the different layers of truth and untruth, illusion and reality effectively and subtly overlap. In *Los árboles mueren de pie*, a well-known but less impressive play, the director of an institution, assisted by one of his patients, seeks to bring happiness to an old woman by pretending to be what he is not. The fiction is destroyed when his real nature is made evident, and the theme of the play is, as in so much of Casona's theatre, the theme that salvation can come only from an acceptance of reality.[21]

Finally, in this discussion of exiled writers, some consideration should be given to the plays of Pedro Salinas (1891-1951), who between 1936 and the year of his death wrote fourteen works for the theatre, two full-length and twelve one-Act plays. In comparison with most serious twentieth-century theatre, with its emphasis on the absurd and the grotesque, the drama of Salinas seems somewhat literary and escapist, but, as Francisco Ruiz Ramón has suggested, this is to ignore Salinas's concern with the possibility of love, beauty and harmony in human existence — with man's capacity, in short, to redeem himself from the horrors of existence as in the one-Act *Caín o una gloria científica (Cain or a Scientific Triumph)* in which a scientist who has discovered how to split the atom, but who lives in a military dictatorship, chooses to die rather than place his discovery at the service of his military masters. The two full-length plays are *Judit y el tirano (Judith and the Tyrant)* and *El director*. In the first of these Judit is a revolutionary for whom the tyrant is a diabolical figure. When, however, the occasion to kill him presents itself, she begins to see him as a human being, and in the last Act the tyrant himself abandons and dissociates himself from the role he has adopted for public consumption in order to embrace his real, human self. The principal fault in Salinas's drama, as the play described above suggests, is that ideas, interesting in themselves, are not transformed convincingly enough into dramatic terms.[22]

In contrast to the work of these four dramatists writing in exile, the drama produced in Spain in the years between the end of the Civil War and the 1960s is almost uniformly depressing. This is especially true, of course, of the commercial theatre which, like that of all European countries, was a theatre of and for the middle-classes, with a limited aim and appeal. Many of the old guard — Benavente, Joaquín Álvarez Quintero, Martínez Sierra, Eduardo Marquina — were still alive at the end of the War even if they were not especially productive. The tradition which they stood for was continued now, moreover, by younger men such as José María Pemán, Juan Ignacio Luca de Tena, Joaquín Calvo Sotelo, José López Rubio, and Víctor Ruiz de Iriarte. The principal characteristics of their theatre can be summarized quite easily. Firstly, great importance is placed upon the 'well-made play' with its emphasis on plot, realistic characters and appealing dialogue. Secondly, any social criticism which the plays contain is contained within the bounds of good taste. In the case of comic drama, the emphasis is invariably upon superficial entertainment. And finally, in no way is this kind of theatre noteworthy for its speculation and consideration of man in relation to his circumstances and the problems which preoccupy him most. With the exception of certain technical devices, such as the inevitable influence of the cinema, the theatre outlined above shows little signs of advance in relation to the drama of Benavente and his school and is indicative in every respect of the stagnation that followed the Civil War. As we shall see, only a few writers of foresight and vision had the courage to break the mould.

The plays of José María Pemán, born in 1898, date back to 1933, since which time he has written more than fifty works for the theatre. Many of them are historical plays in verse — *Cisneros* (1934), *Metternich* (1942) — which thus extol traditional virtues and ideals embodied in historical figures. Secondly, Pemán is also a prolific writer of plays with a contemporary setting in which he advances a particular viewpoint which often has a moral character. Typical examples, as their titles indicate, are

Hay siete pecados (There are Seven Sins) (1943) and *Por el camino de la verdad (Along the Road to Truth)* (1950). Skilfully constructed as they are and distinguished too by accomplished dialogue, the message of the plays seems often to outweigh their dramatic quality. As for the message itself, it remains, of course, essentially conservative, and unlikely, therefore, to ruffle its audience's feathers unduly. Pemán's most successful plays are, in fact, not his serious but his comic works, in which he portrays Andalusian types and customs, and in which humour and amusement, devoid of doctrinal overtones, come to the fore.

Juan Ignacio Luca de Tena, born in 1897, provides a good example of the successful, commercial, technically accomplished playwright whose work is entirely conventional both in its themes and technique. *Dos mujeres a las nueve (Two Women at Nine o'Clock)* (1949) is the story of a university professor who is faced with the problem of choosing between two women, the one a traditional Spanish type, the other a modern American. *Don José, Pepe y Pepito* (1952) presents the confrontation of three generations — grandfather, father and son — in relation to an American woman. Otherwise, Luca de Tena produced both historical dramas and farces that were well received by the public. Little more need be said about its taste for a drama that was undemanding or about the willingness of writers like Luca de Tena to provide it with such fare.

Of the group of writers in question, the best-known and one of the most prolific is Joaquín Calvo Sotelo, who for over half a century has written one play per year. The theatre of Calvo Sotelo embraces both comic and serious works. Of his comic plays, some are intended merely to entertain, while others have a more satirical purpose and, without being truly subversive, pinpoint certain bourgeois attitudes. Calvo Sotelo's most important and successful plays are, though, the serious 'thesis' plays in which the dramatist expounds his ideas on certain important issues: *Criminal de guerra (War Criminal)* (1951), *El jefe (The Leader)* (1952), *La muralla (The Wall)* (1954), *La ciudad sin Dios (The Godless City)* (1957), and *El poder (Power)* (1965). *Criminal de guerra* deals with a German general, Hoffman, condemned to death for war crimes, who commits suicide with the aid of poison supplied by an American colonel, Williams. The suicide occurs, however, at the very moment when Williams, who is in love with the general's daughter, discovers documents proving the general's innocence. This brief outline of the plot is sufficient to reveal the nature of the play's conflicts, such as the clash between military duty and personal involvement, and it suggests too Calvo Sotelo's fondness for melodramatic situations.

Calvo Sotelo's *La muralla,* written in 1954, is not only his best-known play but also, extraordinarily, the most successful play in the history of Spanish theatre since the Civil War. Jorge, the protagonist, is a rich landowner from Badajoz who lives in Madrid on the rent from his estate. As a captain on the winning side in the Civil War, he had succeeded in acquiring a property which did not belong to him. Gravely ill and on the point of death, Jorge is faced with a crisis of conscience and wishes to restore his ill-gotten gains to their rightful owner, while his family are opposed to such a plan. As in the case of *Criminal de guerra,* the play is characterized by its somewhat melodramatic situation. It is also, of course, a good example of the well-made play, solidly constructed, and of the play with a moral dimension which, being to do with money and property, is essentially middle-class. As for the kind of dramatic conflict posed and the way in which that conflict is presented, *La muralla* is clearly old-fashioned, not basically different from the plays that commercially successful dramatists were writing fifty years before.

José López Rubio, born in 1903, had written two plays prior to the Civil War but after the War did not begin writing for the stage again until 1949, since when he has produced twenty or so plays, as well as translations of foreign theatre. His most important works are: *Celos del aire (Jealousy in the Wind)* (1950), *Una madeja de lana azul celeste (A Skein of Sky Blue Wool)* (1951), *El remedio en la memoria (The Solution of Memory)* (1952), *La venda en los ojos (The Blindfold)* (1954) and *La otra orilla (The Other Shore)* (1954). In one way or another López Rubio's theatre as a whole focuses on the theme of love and, closely connected with it, on reality and illusion. The interplay of the latter, evident in a play like *La venda en los ojos,* suggests a similarity between the plays of López Rubio and those of Casona, described previously. In *La venda en los ojos,* for instance, Beatriz has been abandoned by her husband and seeks to deny the ugliness of the truth by creating for herself a fictitious world. Using the device of the 'play within a play' in order to juxtapose reality and illusion, López Rubio demonstrates here, as indeed he does in his other plays, his skills in constructing a plot and in writing dialogue, the two qualities for which he is most noted.

Víctor Ruiz de Iriarte, born in 1912, wrote his first play in 1943 and since that time has written more than thirty plays, including *Academia de amor (Academy of Love)* (1946), *Juego de niños (Game for Children)* (1952), *La vida privada de mamá (Mother's Private Life)* (1960), and *La muchacha del sombrerito (The Girl with the Little Hat)* (1967). Like the other dramatists discussed here in relation to the commercial theatre, Ruiz de Iriarte works very much to a proven and tested formula and his theatre is characterized by its skilful craftsmanship, its ingenious plots, and its elegant and witty dialogue.[23]

The years in which the dramatists mentioned above were writing were years in which life in a dictatorship offered themes and issues in abundance, though a harsh and watchful censorship meant, of course, that such issues had to be treated obliquely. In addition, the period in question undoubtedly sharpened the desire of the theatre-going public for escapist entertainment, and this demand in turn created the conditions for a flourishing but ultimately superficial commercial theatre. The dramatists who addressed themselves to the really serious problems were, predictably, few, and when they did so they encountered enormous problems — of expressing their views and of having their plays performed at all. Such are the circumstances that surround the theatre of Antonio Buero Vallejo, Alfonso Sastre, Fernando Arrabal and others. Firstly, though, in discussing the innovators of this period, something needs to be said about the comic theatre of Miguel Mihura.

Miguel Mihura, born in 1905, had written his first play in 1932 and belongs to the generation of Lorca, Casona, Aub, Alberti and Poncela, but the play was not performed until 1952, from which time Mihura's reputation springs. *Tres sombreros de copa (Three Top Hats)* marks, indeed, a break with the Spanish comic tradition. Mihura's comic approach consists quite simply of standing all accepted values and attitudes on their heads by means of a high degree of exaggeration and fantasy in relation both to character and situation, in consequence of which his theatre is reminiscent of that of Ionesco. In *Tres sombreros de copa* the young man, Dionisio, belongs to a way of life characterized by its narrow-minded and repressive provincialism, but in the course of one night in a hotel encounters its opposite in Paula, the young and vivacious member of a music-hall company. In and through both characters Mihura juxtaposes two totally contrasting worlds. Dionisio, though, having fleetingly tasted liberty, rejects it in favour of the absurd and meaningless way of life from which he has come. The comic presentation of that world is matched only by the tragic overtones of Dionisio's acceptance of it. *Ni pobre ni rico, sino todo lo contrario (Neither poor nor rich but the very opposite)* has as its protagonist Abelardo, a wealthy man who decides to ruin himself because Margarita, the girl he loves, despises his wealth. He succeeds in making himself so poor that she then despises him for his poverty. Subsequently, Abelardo becomes rich again through founding a Poor Trust Company but, having done so, renounces his wealth in order to escape from a world ruled by convention. Clearly, Mihura's theatre is distinguished by its exposure of the conventional attitudes of contemporary Spanish society, as well as by its wit and ingenuity, though his later plays largely fail to capture the sparkle of his earlier work.[24]

The best-known and in many ways most accomplished Spanish dramatist of the last thirty years is Antonio Buero Vallejo, whose work will be discussed in Chapter 5. As far as serious drama is concerned, *Historia de una escalera (The Story of a Stairway)*, first performed in 1949, was a landmark in the history of Spanish theatre since the Civil War, for while so many dramatists provided the Spanish public with a diet of well-made but unadventurous plays, Buero Vallejo confronted it with the moral and social problems that afflicted Spain in the years after the War. *Historia de una escalera* is thus concerned with the hopes, the frustrations and the despair of a number of Madrid families who simultaneously symbolize Spaniards as a whole, beset by the economic and psychological aftermath of the late 1930s. *El tragaluz (The Skylight)*, first performed in 1967, takes as its image of a country plagued by poverty and lack of opportunity a claustrophobic basement occupied since the War by a Madrid family, while the son, Vicente, exemplifies the unscrupulous opportunist, the only kind of person able to succeed in a 'dog-eat-dog' society. Given the social relevance of these and other plays with a contemporary Spanish setting, it is important, though, to emphasize as well their universal character, for Buero's concern is invariably as much with man in general as with Spanish man.

In a number of plays — *Las Meninas (The Maids of Honour)* (1960), *El sueño de la razón (The Sleep of Reason)* (1970) — Buero Vallejo uses history as a means of examining, and facilitating the examination of contemporary Spanish issues. *Las Meninas* has as its protagonist Velázquez, the seeker of truth, who exposes the hypocrisy and authoritarianism of a regime, the reign of Philip IV, that parallels in all its implications the Franco dictatorship. Similarly, in *El sueño de la razón* Goya, the champion of liberty, is persecuted by the tyrannical Fernando VII, whose Court is mirrored in the monsters of Goya's nightmares and visions, another image of Franco's Spain. On the other hand, these are highly suggestive and meaningful works in their own right, and their implications extend far beyond their Spanish context.

The searching nature of Buero Vallejo's themes goes hand in hand with a constant search for effective ways of expressing those themes, and in this respect he is obviously very different from the commercial dramatists so far described. Far from following a formula, Buero changes his technique from play to play. *Historia de una escalera*, though in many ways naturalistic, may be more accurately described as an example of symbolic realism and, together with other plays of the 1950s, points to the influence of Ibsen. *Las*

Meninas and *El sueño de la razón*, on the other hand, reveal Buero's interest in the distancing techniques of Brecht whereby the audience is invited to observe and form a judgement on the events placed before it. And in a play like *El tragaluz* where stage and audience mirror each other, establishing a confusion of identity, Pirandello is seen to be a major influence. Buero Vallejo is probably, in relation to stage technique, the major innovator in the Spanish drama of the last thirty years. This aspect of his theatre, together with the searching character of his themes, makes him a truly European dramatist.[25]

A second major figure, though a lesser one than Buero, is Alfonso Sastre, born in 1926. Adopting an attitude of outright rejection to the commercial theatre of the 1940s, Sastre envisaged not merely the need for renovation but for the transformation of drama into an instrument of social reform. In 1950, therefore, Sastre and a group of similarly minded young men attempted to found the Teatro de Agitación Social (Theatre for Social Agitation), setting out their views in a manifesto. Since that time Sastre has expressed his views of the purpose and function of theatre on two fronts: the theoretical and the dramatic. To the former belong his essays, articles and books on the theatre, in all of which he advocates the aim of drama as one of social reform. To the latter belong his plays, most of which put his stated intentions into practice.

Sastre's theatre of the 1940s and early 1950s represents a total break with the soft-centred commercial theatre of those years. In terms of theme this is a drama of protest against injustice and tyranny, its tone aggressive and uncompromising, while the technique is influenced by *avant-garde* movements such as Expressionism and Symbolism. *Escuadra hacia la muerte (The Condemned Squad)* (1952) is, for example, a protest against the catastrophe threatened by a third world war and a denunciation of the inflexible military attitudes which make it possible. The play has as its subject a squadron of five men and an officer sent on a mission which can end only in death. Its first half presents the conflict between the soldiers and the officer — it ends with their killing him, while the second half focuses on their own conflicting emotions in the face of death. *Prólogo patético (Pathetic Prologue)* (1950-3) is a penetrating examination of the morality of terrorist intervention. Set in a dictatorship, the action portrays the attempts of a terrorist group to end that dictatorship and, through the experiences of the central characters, asks to what extent the sacrifice of innocent lives can be justified. The play belongs to the same period as Camus's *Les justes* and valid comparisons can be made between them. In one way or another most of the plays written by Sastre in the 1950s — *La mordaza (The Gag)* (1954), *Guillermo Tell tiene los ojos tristes (William*

Tell Has Sad Eyes) (1955), *Asalto nocturno (Night Assault)* (1959) — are
to do with tyranny or violence in society and can be seen as a comment both
on the Spanish and the world situation.

The plays composed between 1965 and 1972 — six in all — suffered the
fate during the Franco regime of being neither performed nor published,
and appeared therefore in a typed version entitled *Teatro penúltimo
(Penultimate Theatre)*. Sastre defines these plays as 'tragedies complejas'
('complex tragedies'), a complexity which clearly refers to the mixture of
styles, which ranges from Aristotelian tragedy to epic theatre, to
documentary, *esperpento* and farce. The central themes of these plays — as
in *M.S.V.* (1965) and *Crónicas romanas (Roman Chronicles)* (1968) —
are, as in Sastre's theatre of the 1950s, themes of tyranny, violence and
oppression. Technically, they reveal the marked influence of the epic
theatre of Brecht and Piscator, for in the interests of distancing a whole
range of devices is employed: photographs, slogans, loudspeakers, songs,
direct address to the audience. On the other hand, while requiring his
audience's objective judgement, Sastre is also concerned with engaging it
and frequently destroys the separation between stage and auditorium by
allowing his actors to speak from or even invade the auditorium. Given the
provocative nature of his theatre and its declared intention to reform
society, it is hardly surprising that in the years in question Sastre's voice
should have been stifled.[26]

One of the most serious indictments of the Franco years concerns the
theatre of Fernando Arrabal, born in 1932. In 1958 Arrabal's *Los hombres
del triciclo (The Tricycle Men)* was performed in Madrid and rejected in no
uncertain fashion by the Spanish public. Consequently, the plays written by
Arrabal since 1960 or so have been written not in Spanish but in French, for
the intellectual climate of France has proved much more stimulating to a
dramatist of Arrabal's highly original and iconoclastic bent. Moreover, the
plays written since 1960 represent Arrabal's most mature and original
work: *Le grand cérémonial (The Great Ceremonial)* (1963), *Le jardin des
délices (The Garden of Delights)* (1967), *Et ils passèrent des menottes aux
fleurs (And They Handcuffed the Flowers)* (1969). Although in recent
years they have become available in Spanish, it cannot be argued that they
are the product of the Spanish scene. In losing Arrabal to France, Spain has
in effect lost a dramatist who would have placed Spanish theatre at the fore-
front of European experimental theatre.

Together with Buero Vallejo and Alfonso Sastre, a number of dramatists
writing in Spain in similar circumstances in the 1960s and 70s must also be
mentioned, for they illustrate the point that during these years serious
theatre was something marginal, as divorced from the larger theatre-going

public as this was divorced from it. The first dramatist to be considered under this heading is Carlos Muñiz, born in 1926. Broadly speaking, the theatre of Muñiz can be divided into two periods, the first distinguished by its realism, the second by its neo-expressionist style, and both, of course, by their social criticism. *El grillo (Chains)*, written in 1955, belongs to the realist period and has for its protagonist a humble civil servant seen at three critical moments in his life. He is a man continually frustrated in his hopes and ambitions, insignificant as these are, and therefore representative of all those who are the victims of social injustice, and of the society in which they live. While there is no specific criticism of Franco's Spain, the play's implications are very clear, while its realistic style facilitates identification between the audience and the characters on stage.

Muñiz's most effective theatre, on the other hand, is that represented by his neo-expressionist plays, which certainly reveal the influence of Valle-Inclán, and they have sometimes been compared with the work of Ionesco and Beckett. Of these *El tintero (The Ink-Well)* (1960) is a particularly fine example. As in *El grillo*, the protagonist, Crock, is a civil servant, but Muñiz's technique in portraying the society in which Crock lives is now very different. He is seen to be surrounded by individuals who are totally dehumanized and puppet-like, while Crock himself, in order to survive, is obliged to surrender his human qualities. Failing to do so, he is condemned to a life of poverty and ultimately death, for he finally commits suicide. The play is very clearly, in both its themes and technique, a savage indictment of a society in which, for the sake of his own survival, the individual must cease to be a human being. Muñiz's contribution to serious theatre in Spain in the last twenty-five years has justly been acclaimed by Antonio Buero Vallejo, as well as by the critic Francisco Ruiz Ramón.

Another significant figure, Lauro Olmo, born in 1923, has had four plays performed during the Franco years, while permission for the performance of a number of works has been withheld. To the former belong *La camisa (The Shirt)* (1962), *La pechuga de la sardina (The Breast of the Sardine)* (1963), *El cuerpo (The Body)* (1966), and *English Spoken* (1968).*La camisa*, like Carlos Muñiz's *El grillo*, employs an unrelenting realistic approach in order to project in as stark a manner as possible the desperate, inescapable poverty of people like its central character, Juan. His circumstances are precisely those of thousands of other Spaniards beset by a physical adversity which undermines their very being and in many cases forces them to leave the country. Juan, in contrast, recognizes that to emigrate is to accept defeat and failure, and his defiant acceptance of his hunger is thus a protest against the society which inflicts it upon him. *La pechuga de la sardina* is, likewise, a condemnation of a cruel and hypocritical society. To the extent that its characters are drawn from the lower levels of society, including prostitutes, the play is reminiscent of the theatre of Carlos Arniches, as indeed are the elements of the grotesque which characterize its style. The old woman, Doña Elena, typifies the society in which she lives both in her narrow-mindedness and her readiness to condemn, while at the same time she is herself exposed to its viciousness. Olmo's theatre, like Muñiz's, reveals a profound concern wih the ills of the Spain of the 1960s and exposes them in the most uncompromising way.

The theatre of Martín Recuerda, born in 1925, is in many respects reminiscent of that of Lorca, for Recuerda depicts the same kind of Andalusia, governed by narrow-mindedness, cruelty and hypocrisy. His plays can be divided into two broad periods, the first distinguished by individuals who do not rebel against their hostile environment, the second by characters who do. To the former belong *La llanura (The Plain)* (1954), *El payaso y los pueblos del sur (The Clown and the Villages of the South)* (1956), and *El teatrito de Don Ramón (The Little Theatre of Don Ramón)*. In the second category are such plays as *Como las secas cañas del camino (Like the Dry Canes along the Road)* (1965) and *Las salvajes en Puente San Gil (The Savages in Puente San Gil)* (1963). The plays of the second period are particularly impressive, and *Como las secas cañas del camino* is a fine example. It is the dramatization of the experience of a country schoolteacher who is driven from her school and then from her village by its unfeeling and hypocritical inhabitants. In its picture of a narrow-minded and vicious society, savagely exposed by techniques of exaggeration and distortion, the play recalls the *esperpentos* of Valle-Inclán and Alberti's *El adefesio*.

Las salvajes en Puente San Gil is the story of the effect on an Andalusian town of the arrival of a music-hall company, who in different ways become the victims of the townspeople. Firstly, the performance is prevented by the protests of the narrow-minded townswomen. Secondly, the young men of the town assault the girls in the group, in consequence of which one of the girls is killed. And thirdly, the husbands of the townswomen, frustrated by their wives' sexual coldness, avail themselves of the presence of the female music-hall artists. In the end, provoked beyond endurance, the music-hall company vainly appeals to the Church authorities and, when they are arrested, denounces the violence done to them in an aggressive and vulgar song. Recuerda's play, one of the most powerful pieces of the last twenty-five years, is a ferocious attack on the narrow-mindedness of Spanish life, on authority, tradition, the rich and the Church — on all those forces, in short, which condone repression and deny liberty.

Lastly, in this discussion of dramatists in the tradition of Buero Vallejo and Alfonso Sastre, consideration should be given to the theatre of Rodríguez Méndez, born in 1925. *Vagones de madera (The Train)* (1958) looks forward in several respects to Rodríguez Méndez's more mature work, notably in its strongly critical attitude and in its very down-to-earth language. The play presents a group of soldiers on their way to war and underlines their ignorance of the cause of their involvement. The waggon in which they are cooped up is, in effect, part of a convoy, a conveyor-belt system which transports them like unthinking animals to the slaughter-house of war, and the journey to inevitable death is shown to be as senseless as the fights in which they engage during the course of it. *La batalla de Verdún (The Battle of Verdun)* is set in the district of that name in Barcelona and takes for its subject the workers from the south of Spain who vainly seek to find a place for themselves and make a living in the north. Cut off from their roots and exposed to inescapable poverty, the older men search for consolation in such activities as watching football matches, while the younger men, rebelling against their situation, consider the possibility of emigrating to other European countries. The play is a powerful and moving examination of individuals who are constantly oppressed and overwhelmed by their circumstances.

In the plays written since 1965 Rodríguez Méndez's technique has, like that of some of the other dramatists mentioned earlier, moved more towards the kind of grotesque distortion which we associate with Valle-Inclán. The dramatist seeks, in short, to strip away the surface appearance of things in order to expose the true ugliness of Spanish society. An example of a play of this kind is *La mano negra (The Black Hand)*, written in 1965, a play in which Rodríguez Méndez sets the action in the past in an Andalusia dominated by hunger and exploitation — a past, though, whose relevance to the Spain of the 1960s is perfectly clear.[27]

The four dramatists discussed here represent, as the above account suggests, the serious theatre of the 1960s, written in difficult circumstances. To their names can be added others: Antonio Gala, Andrés Ruiz, Luis Matilla, López Mozo and Martínez Ballesteros. In short, the very repression of the Franco years had the effect of producing a number of notable dramatists and notable plays, even if they did not achieve the publicity and exposure which they might have enjoyed in other times. On the other hand, it is equally evident that the circumstances of the dictatorship were in a way necessary for the work of many of the writers mentioned — the infertile soil, as it were, in which they could flourish.

* * * * * *

The Franco period was, then, as far as the theatre is concerned, characterized by two things: firstly, by a commercial theatre that for the most part evaded serious issues; secondly, by a serious theatre which, with very few exceptions, remained marginal or was totally suppressed. Given these circumstances, Franco's death and a subsequent return to a system of democratic government, with all its implications, held out the same promise in 1975 as did the fall of the dictatorship of Primo de Rivera and the beginning of the second Spanish Republic in 1930-1. In that case, as we have seen, newly acquired liberty led to the most dazzling period of Spanish theatre in the twentieth century, witnessing the masterpieces of Lorca and some of Alberti, all, moreover, in a period of five years. What, then, has been achieved in the same period of time since the death of Franco?

The restoration of democracy and the appearance of new political parties have, in the first place, given a new importance to cultural activities of all kinds. One important consequence has been, for example, the creation of the Ministerio de Cultura and, within it, of the Dirección General de Teatro y Espectáculos (General Administration of Theatre and Spectacle). In conjunction with this, a vital step forward has been taken with the abolition of the kind of censorship that proved so daunting during the Franco years. 1 April 1977 witnessed the introduction of a new law relating to freedom of expression, and this was succeeded on 27 January 1978 by a law concerned with freedom in the presentation of plays and theatrical productions. On the other hand, the virtual abolition of censorship has not meant that a new wave of Spanish theatre, especially of serious theatre, has suddenly appeared. Many of the serious dramatists writing during the dictatorship grew so accustomed to writing within the constraints imposed upon them that the sudden acquisition of liberty has proved to be, paradoxically, as much a hindrance as a help.

Another important step was taken in 1978 with the establishment, in conjunction with the Ministerio de Cultura, of the Centro dramático nacional (National Centre of Drama). Operating at two centres in Madrid — the María Guerrero and the Bellas Artes — the organization is composed of a team of professional actors and directors, including Nuria Espert, José Luis Gómez and Ramón Tamayo, and is concerned with the rehearsal and performance of serious drama and the training of actors. In the years since its creation it has performed works from both the classical and modern repertoire: Cervantes's *Los baños de Argel (The Prisons of Algiers)*, Gorki's *The Holidaymakers*, Lorca's *Doña Rosita la soltera (Doña Rosita the Spinster)* and Rodríguez Méndez's *Bodas que fueron famosas del Pingajo y la Fandanga (The Famous Wedding of Pingajo and Fandanga)*.

Clearly, the formation of a company of this kind, reminiscent of some of the ventures that took place during the Republic, holds promise for the future. Under the auspices of the Ministerio de Cultura there has emerged too the Centro de documentación teatral (Centre for Theatre Documentation) under the direction of Professor César Oliva. The aim of the Centro, based in the Escorial, is to research into theatre theory and practice, to bring together for that purpose critics, directors and actors, and to establish a library containing works on theatre, videotapes and film. It is also engaged in publishing texts, and in organizing exhibitions and dramatic performances, and since 1980 has published a monthly journal, the *Boletín de información teatral.*

In the development of theatre in any country, young people have a vital role to play in the sense that they constitute the actors, producers, directors and the public of the future. Youth theatre was, though, one of the areas most neglected in post-Civil War Spain, despite the efforts of dramatists like Lauro Olmo and Luis Matilla to remedy that neglect. In recent years, and especially since 1976, much more attention has been given to this aspect of theatre in Spain, and both professional and semi-professional groups have played their part in this new impetus by performing on a regular basis works suited to and often written for young people. Such groups include 'Libélula', 'Teloncillo', 'Teatro de la Ribera', 'Els Comediants', 'Trabalenguas', and the 'Grupo internacional de Teatro'. They have succeeded both in awakening the interest of young people and in exerting a considerable influence on parents and educationalists in relation to this type of theatre.

In addition to the performance of plays, there have also been important conferences on youth theatre. Thus there took place in Madrid between 30 May and 14 June 1977, the Jornadas de estudio sobre teatro escolar, teatro para niños y teatro de títeres (Study Course on Student, Child and Puppet Theatre) in which the participants included the dramatists, Lauro Olmo and Luis Matilla, the critics Enrique Llovet, Francisco García Pavón and José Monleón, and professors of theatre and education. Similarly, there was held in Madrid in June 1978, the VI Congreso Internacional de teatro para la Infancia y la Juventud (Sixth International Conference on Theatre for Children and Youth), involving thirty countries and more than 350 participants, and in Burgos in March 1980, there occurred the sixth national conference of the Asociación española de teatro para la infancia y la juventud (The Spanish Association of Theatre for Children and Youth). Both conferences were characterized by lectures, discussions and the performance of appropriate plays.

1978 saw too the formation of the Centro nacional de iniciación del niño y el adolescente al teatro (National Centre for the Introduction of Children and Youth to the Theatre). The Centro, possessing a professional company of actors and technicians, has operated in the rural areas of Spain as well as the cities, carrying out a number of important activities, including dramatic performances and theatre workshops for children.

Quite apart from the impetus given to youth theatre, the number of theatre companies and organizations in Spain has grown rapidly in recent years. The activities of the Centro dramático nacional and the Centro de documentación teatral have been accompanied by work presented in Madrid at the Sala Cadarso and the Sala Olimpia. In Barcelona the 'Teatro Lliure', the Regina, the Instituto de Teatro, and the Sala Villaroel have also been extremely active, combining the performance of dramatic works with courses on theatre. In addition, an important contribution has been and is being made by independent groups, both in Madrid and Barcelona and in the provinces. Worth mentioning in this respect are the Catalan groups, 'Els Joglars' and 'Dagoll-Dagon'; in Andalusia 'La Cuadra', 'Esperpento' and 'Teatro de Mediodía'; in the Basque country 'Akelarre'; and in Madrid 'Ditirambo', 'Tábano' and 'Teatro Libre'. Many of these groups, despite limited financial resources, have been motivated purely by love of the theatre and have made a valuable contribution in relation to the performance of experimental plays.

As far as the commercial theatre is concerned, the period immediately following Franco's death saw the performance in quick succession of a cluster of outstanding works, some of them hitherto unperformed in Spain. In 1976 alone the following plays were presented: Valle-Inclán's *Los cuernos de Don Friolera* at the Teatro Bellas Artes; García Lorca's *La casa de Bernarda Alba* at the Teatro Eslava; Rafael Alberti's *El adefesio* at the Teatro Reina Victoria; and Antonio Buero Vallejo's *La doble historia del doctor Valmy (The Double History of Dr Valmy)* at the Teatro Benavente. In 1978 Valle-Inclán's *Las galas del difunto (The Finery of the Deceased)* and *La hija del capitán (The Captain's Daughter)* were performed at the Teatro María Guerrero; Lorca's *Así que pasen cinco años*, his impressive surrealist play, at the Teatro Eslava; and Alberti's *Noche de guerra en el Museo del Prado* at the Teatro María Guerrero. Simply to list these plays is to suggest the feast of theatre with which the Madrid public was presented in a relatively short period of time. The three years that followed Franco's death were evidently richer in the performance of outstanding twentieth-century plays than the forty years which preceded it.

New plays by important dramatists have also been performed. Antonio Buero Vallejo's *La detonación (The Explosion)* received its first performance on 20 November 1977 at the Teatro Lara and *Jueces en la noche (Judges in the Night)* was presented on 2 October at the Teatro Lara. Surprisingly, both plays were received unfavourably by both critics and public, a very unusual occurrence in the extremely successful career of this dramatist. In contrast, Antonio Gala, another dramatist accustomed to working within the constraints of the Franco censorship, achieved a notable success with *Petra Regalada*, performed on 15 February 1979, at the Teatro Príncipe. To the presentation of these plays must be added that of Fernando Arrabal's *Oye, Patria, mi aflicción (My Country, Listen to my Anguish)*, performed on 26 May 1978, at the Teatro Martín, and Rodríguez Méndez's *Bodas que fueron famosas del Pingajo y la Fandanga*, put on, as we have seen, by the Centro Dramático Nacional on 21 November 1978.

The picture may be further filled out by reference to the large number of twentieth-century comic plays that have been presented. In this respect the plays of Jardiel Poncela, Miguel Mihura and Alfonso Paso have proved extremely popular. In addition, Jaime Salom's *La piel de limón (Lemon Peel)* was performed on 10 September 1976, at the Teatro Marquina, Juan José Alonso Millán's *Los viernes a las seis (Fridays at Six)* on 30 September 1976, at the Teatro Club, and the same writer's *Compañero te doy (I give You a Companion)* on 6 December 1978, at the Teatro Barceló.

The changed political climate and the new freedom available to writers have also meant that works with both a political and a sexual emphasis have been very numerous. 1978, in particular, saw the performance of many plays of this kind: *Un cero a la izquierda (Nought to the Left)* by Eloy Herrera; *Lecciones de cama para políticos (Lessons in Bed for Politicians)* by Emilio G. Laygorri; and *Las cien y una noches de boda (A Hundred and One Nights of Marriage)* by Jaime Portillar are some examples. As far as the so-called political plays are concerned, they have generally been of rather poor quality and distinguished by a right wing bias, attributing the evils of Spanish society to left-wing activities or even descending to the level of abusing left-wing politicians. Those plays with a sexual emphasis are, like the soft pornography which has inundated the bookstalls of Spanish cities in recent years, a natural and, it is to be hoped, temporary reaction to the repression of forty years.

Since 1976 there has been very strong evidence of the greater interest and participation in theatre by local authorities and town councils. Many theatrical ventures and activities have had the support of the Dirección General de Teatro of the Ministry of Culture and have also received support of a financial nature from commercial organizations such as banks. One of the best examples is the Centro Cultural de la Villa de Madrid

(Cultural Centre of the City of Madrid) which is financed by the Madrid City Council. In this case, the aim has been to establish a balance, as far as theatre is concerned, between works in a lighter vein and serious *avant-garde* plays performed both by Spanish and foreign companies. The example of the Centro Cultural is not intended to suggest, though, that such activities are confined to Madrid, for both professional and non-professional groups have worked outside the major cities with the kind of assistance described above. What is important is the extent to which such ventures have increased since the advent of democratic government.

Worth mentioning, too, are the theatrical journals that have played an important part in the life of the theatre in Spain both in the course of the last twenty-five years and more recently. The most important of these is *Primer Acto*, and it was therefore a matter of great concern when it ceased to appear in 1975. Fortunately, *Primer Acto* has reappeared in recent years under the editorship of the distinguished Spanish theatre critic, José Monleón, and fears for its existence have to that extent been alleviated. One of the most important contributions of *Primer Acto* has been its publication of the text of plays, many of them previously unpublished, so that the journal has in effect provided the public with the first published version of many plays written during the last quarter of a century. Another important journal, *Pipirijaina*, made its appearance in 1974. Its importance lies in its concern with independent as opposed to commercial theatre and it has thus published many of the plays of Alfonso Sastre, Fernando Arrabal, Angel García Pintado, Jerónimo López Mozo, and Francisco Ors.

In addition to these important journals, which serve to broaden the theatre repetoire and familiarize the public with contemporary plays, mention must be made of the greater representation given to dramatists whose work ran into difficulties in the Franco years in the theatre series published by a number of publishing houses. Thus the 'Colección Austral' now contains many of the plays of Antonio Buero Vallejo, Antonio Gala, Lauro Olmo and Miguel Mihura; 'Letras Hispánicas' has plays by Buero Vallejo, Alfonso Sastre, Martín Recuerda and Rodríguez Méndez; and 'Clásicos Castalia' plays by Buero Vallejo, Alfonso Sastre and Miguel Mihura. In short, dramatists whose work was marginal and often unpublished during the Franco regime are now finding an outlet, and Spanish publishers are playing a vital part in that important process.

In contrast, television, which perhaps more than any other means of communication, has the power to influence public taste, has shown a remarkable lack of interest in promoting the cause of modern Spanish theatre. As might be expected — as indeed is the case in the commercial theatre itself in general — Spanish television channels are dominated by light entertainment, reflecting in that sense what the viewing public wants, but at the same time inculcating in it, by meeting its demands, a feeling that what it wants is good enough. Furthermore, as is so often the case in television, Spanish companies show an increasing tendency to fill their slots with foreign films, and when these are filmed versions of dramatic works they are for the most part by foreign writers. In Great Britain television has produced its own particular brand of drama and developed the talents of many writers. In Spain nothing comparable has happened.

In conclusion, the advent of democracy promises much, but, in terms of the development of Spanish theatre and the appearance of new dramatists, the promise has still to be realized. In this context one is reminded of John Osborne's comment that, as far as Britain is concerned, there are no great causes left to write about. To what extent will this apply to Spain in the years ahead, for the death of Franco has restored the cause, the cause of liberty, for which so many Spaniards fought and in the interests of which much significant theatre has been written? The prospect is intriguing and at the same time worrying. It is to be hoped that Spanish writers will confront the problems posed by democracy as passionately as many of them did the forty years of tyranny now ended.[28]

1 For general studies of twentieth-century Spanish theatre, see G. Torrente Ballester, *Teatro español contemporáneo* (2nd ed.) (Madrid, 1968); Victoria Urbano, *El teatro español y sus directices contemporáneas* (Madrid, 1972); Francisco Ruiz Ramón, *Historia del teatro español, II: Siglo XX* (4th ed.) (Madrid, 1980); L. Rodríguez Alcalde, *Teatro español contemporáneo* (Madrid, 1973).

2 There is a very useful section on the theatre of Benavente in Francisco Ruiz Ramón, *Historia del teatro español...*, 21-38. See too Alfredo Marqueríe, *Benavente y su teatro*, (Madrid, 1960); José Montero Alonso, *Jacinto Benavente. Su vida y su teatro* (Madrid, 1967); Marcelino C. Peñuelas, *Jacinto Benavente*, (New York, 1968); and Julio Mathías, *Benavente* (Madrid, 1969).

3 Pérez de Ayala, *Las máscaras*, in *Obras completas, III* (2nd ed.) (Madrid, 1966), 107; Francisco Ruiz Ramón, *Historia del teatro español...*, 25.

4 On the Quintero brothers see Fransciso Ruiz Ramón, *Historia del teatro español...*, 49-53.

5 Particularly useful on aspects of twentieth-century theatre is the four-volume work by Enrique Díez-Canedo, *Artículos de crítica teatral: el teatro español de 1914 a 1936*, (Mexico, 1968). On Linares Rivas see vol. I, 177-216.

6 For an account of Martínez Sierra's plays, see Enrique Díez-Canedo, *Artículos de crítica teatral...*, vol. I, 293-306; and Patricia Walker O'Connor, *Women in the Theater of Gregorio Martinez Sierra* (New York, 1966).

7 *Artículos de crítica teatral...*, vol, II, 242-324.

8 See Enrique Díez-Canedo, *Artículos de crítica teatral* ..., vol. II, 9-68.

9 On the theatre of Carlos Arniches see the following: Pedro Salinas, 'Del género chico a la tragedia grotesca: Carlos Arniches', in *Literatura española. Siglo XX*, (Mexico, 1949), 129-36; Vicente Ramos, *Vida y teatro de Carlos Arniches* (Madrid, 1966); Francisco Ruiz Ramón, *Historia del teatro español* ..., 38-48.

10 Much has been published on the theatre of Unamuno. See, for example, Andrés Franco, *El teatro de Unamuno* (Madrid, 1971); Lázaro Carreter, 'El teatro de Unamuno', *Cuadernos de la Cátedra Miguel de Unamuno*, VII (1956), 5-29; Iris M. Zavala, *Unamuno y su teatro de conciencia* (Salamanca, 1963); Carlos Clavería, *Temas de Unamuno* (Madrid, 1952).

11 For critical material on Valle-Inclán, see notes to Chapter 2.

12 There is a useful study by Rodolfo Cardona, *Ramón. A study of Gómez de la Serna and His Works* (New York, 1957).

13 On the theatre of Azorín see Enrique Díez-Canedo, *Artículos de crítica teatral* ... vol. IV, 45-62; Guillermo Díaz-Plaja, 'El teatro de Azorín', *Cuadernos de Literatura Contemporánea*, 16-17 (1947), 369-87; Lawrence Anthony Lajohn, *Azorín and the Spanish Stage* (New York, 1961).

14 The critical material on Lorca is mentioned in the notes to Chapter 3.

15 For the critical work on the theatre of Alberti, see the notes to Chapter 4.

16 On the theatre of Casona see J. Rodríquez Richart, *Vida y teatro de Alejandro Casona* (Oviedo, 1963); the introduction by Federico Carlos Sáinz de Robles to the *Obras completas* of Casona, I (Madrid, 1954); Kessel Schwartz, 'Reality in the Works of Alejandro Casona', *Hispania*, XL (1957), 57-61; A. Wallace Woolsey, 'Illusion versus Reality in some of the Plays of Alejandro Casona', *Modern Language Journal*, XXXVIII (1954), 80-4; José Caso González, 'Fantasía y realidad en el teatro de Alejandro Casona', *Archivum*, V, (1955), 304-18.

17 See, in particular, Francisco Ruiz Ramón, *Historia del teatro español* ... 245-69; Ignacio Soldevila Durante, 'El español Max Aub', *La Torre*, 33 (1961), 103-20; Rafael Bosch, 'El teatro de Max Aub', *Hispanófila*, 19 (1963), 25-36.

18 On the theatre of Jardiel Poncela see Francisco García Pavón, 'Inventiva en el teatro de Jardiel Poncela, *Cuatro corazones con freno y marcha atrás*', in *El teatro de humor en España* (Madrid, 1966), and in the same volume, Adolfo Prego, 'Jardiel ante la sociedad', and Alfredo Marqueríe, 'Novedad en el teatro de Jardiel'.

19 See Chapter 4.

20 See note 17 above.

21 See note 16 above.

22 For an account of the theatre of Salinas see Francisco Ruiz Ramón, *Historia del teatro español* ..., 282-93.

23 On Pemán, Luca de Tena, Calvo Sotelo, López Rubio and Ruiz de Iriarte, see the following: Alfredo Marqueríe, *Veinte años de teatro en España* (Madrid, 1959); G. Torrente Ballester, *Teatro español contemporáneo* ...; Victoria Urbano, *El teatro español y sus directrices contemporáneas* ...; L. Rodríguez Alcalde, *Teatro español contemporáneo* ...; Francisco Ruiz Ramón, *Historia del teatro español* ...

24 On the theatre of Mihura see *Miguel Mihura, Teatro* (Madrid, 1965); and in *El teatro de humor en España* (Madrid, 1966), the essays by G. Torrente Ballester, 'El teatro serio de un humorista', 215-30, and Enrique Llovet, 'El humor en el teatro de Mihura', 201-14.

25 For critical studies on the theatre of Buero Vallejo, see the notes to Chapter 5.

26 For critical studies on the theatre of Alfonso Sastre, see the notes to Chapter 6.

27 On the theatre of Muñiz, Olmo, Recuerda and Rodríguez Méndez see: Francisco Ruiz
    Ramón, *Historia del teatro español.* ., 490-516; F. García Pavón, *Teatro social en España*
    (Madrid, 1962). Mention should also be made here of the the regular contributions on the
    work of these writers by José Monleón in the pages of the journal, *Primer Acto,* an
    indispensable aide to the study of modern Spanish theatre.

28 On the post-Franco period see the following: Luciano García Lorenzo, *Documentos sobre
    el teatro español contemporáneo* (Madrid, 1981); *Teatro español actual,* with essays by
    contemporary Spanish dramatists, actors, critics and directors (Madrid, 1977). The reader
    should consult, too, recent issues of *Primer Acto.*

CHAPTER II
Ramón del Valle-Inclán

The previous chapter has revealed that the theatre in Spain at the turn of the century was largely distinguished by its conservatism. While the innovations of Jacinto Benavente served to change the general direction of the Spanish drama by ousting the neo-Romantic plays of Echegaray in favour of a more 'realistic' and socially orientated theatre, he remained for the most part a dramatist whose style and technique changed little during a thirty-year domination of the Spanish stage. The sentimental and somewhat romantic pieces of the Quintero brothers, with their idealized portrayal of Spanish life, offer another, if different, example of the stagnation of the theatre in the early part of the century, while the so-called 'poetic' theatre of Eduardo Marquina and his followers, favouring medieval themes and dialogue in verse, is far more backward than forward looking. For signs of dramatic life and vigour one has to turn to the plays of a less 'commercial' dramatist like Carlos Arniches — to the short pieces in the tradition of the *género chico* and, in particular, to the more extended grotesque farces written after 1910. But the most significant dramatist of the first two decades of the century, in terms both of achievement and influence, is Ramón del Valle-Inclán (1866-1936) whose theatre has recently been described by Francisco Ruiz Ramón as the most original and revolutionary Spanish drama of the twentieth century.[1]

Valle-Inclán's sixteen plays, written over a period of twenty-eight years, constitute a theatre of great variety and constant experiment in total contrast to that of his contemporaries. Consisting of plays which in very general terms may be divided into three broad categories — mythical works, farces and *esperpentos* (the latter distinguished by elements of the grotesque) — , it is a theatre which corresponds in many respects to the most significant advances in the European theatre of our time and which may be profitably examined in relation to Symbolism, Expressionism and the Theatre of the Absurd. In order to illustrate both the intrinsic merits of Valle-Inclán's drama and its European dimension, it is my intention here to avoid too general and diluted a discussion of all the plays by focusing instead on a few highly representative works, each of which marks a significant stage in Valle's dramatic development and is simultaneously part of a broader movement in the theatre.

In the second half of the nineteenth century the commercial theatre in Europe as a whole developed in a way that did not differ significantly from the Spanish pattern. The English drama of the Victorian age, for instance, was distinguished very largely by middle-class respectability, by plays which extolled moral virtue and avoided delicate subjects, and by a general conservatism which did not encourage experiment either in subject matter or dramatic technique. Even towards the end of the century, when dramatists like Wilde and Shaw enlivened the theatre with wit, polemic and their own distinctive personalities, its style remained, broadly speaking, realistic, and there is little in their plays that can be termed modern in any truly revolutionary sense. To perceive a change of direction which would profoundly affect the drama, it is necessary to consider the theory and practice of a few highly significant writers, stage designers and producers, both English and European, who consciously turned their backs on the Naturalism of the nineteenth century. Amongst the dramatists Maeterlinck, amongst the stage designers Adolph Appia, Edward Gordon Craig and Max Reinhardt are some of the best known figures in the so-called symbolist movement that helped transform European theatre in the first decade of this century.

The artistic ideals of the Symbolists had already been anticipated in the course of the nineteenth century in the practice and theory of men such as Richard Wagner and Schopenhauer. What mattered to them was not mundane reality, the province of Naturalism, but the transcendental world, the world of essences which lies beyond the visible and whose existence it is the artist's duty to communicate. To this end Wagner had conceived his music drama which, at the opposite pole from Naturalism, brought together the different arts of music, poetry, acting and stage design in an attempt to stir the imagination and thereby move the observer of the action to the perception of a superior reality. For the performance of Wagner's music dramas with their new demands a new kind of architecture, in the form of the Bayreuth Opera House, was required. Similarly, what has come to be called the New Art of the Theatre could be performed only if old techniques of writing and performing were abandoned.[2]

Although there are elements of Symbolism in many of the plays of Ibsen, it is the Belgian dramatist Maurice Maeterlinck (1862-1949) who is generally regarded as the symbolist dramatist *par excellence*. His best plays — *Les Aveugles, Pelléas et Mélisande, Intérieur, La Mort de Tintagiles*, and *L'Oiseau Bleu* — span the period 1890 to 1910 and in terms of themes and technique perfectly exemplify the predominant concerns of Symbolism. Their themes are the universal themes of birth, the cycle of human existence and death. The characters are not so much individuals set in particularized time and space as archetypal beings who are evocative of man in general. And the action and general stage presentation, far from seeking to imitate reality, are conceived in a style which integrates decor, sound effects, movement and language in a manner which suggests much more than what is actually seen and heard on stage. As far as the broader meaning of Maeterlinck's plays is concerned, it has been said that they present 'man face to face with the universe, looking out into the mysteries of time and death', while their technique, strongly influenced by Maeterlinck's familiarity with European painting, had the effect of giving to the European drama of his time 'a spectacular extension'.[3]

What the New Art of the Theatre signified in terms of stage design can be indicated here by reference to Appia, Craig and Reinhardt. In 1895 Appia published his *La Mise en scène du Drame Wagnérien* and in 1899 his *Die Musik und die Inszenierung (Music and Staging)*. Concerned with the specific problems of staging Wagner's operas, the two books relate also to questions of staging in general and especially to the importance of light and movement. Appia, like Craig, detested realism and its attempt to produce a photographic imitation, favoured suggestion through symbolical representation, and in an attempt to achieve it sought a close-knit harmony between actors, settings, lighting and the other aspects of stage presentation. Craig's views on the theatre were very similar and are lucidly expressed in his influential *The Art of the Theatre*, published in 1905 and quickly translated into German, Dutch and Russian:

> . . . the Art of the Theatre, is neither acting nor the play, it is not scene nor dance, but it consists of all the elements of which these things are composed; action, which is the very spirit of acting; words, which are the body of the play; line and colour, which are the very heart of the scene; rhythm, which is the very essence of dance.[4]   (p.138).

Avoiding the reproduction of realistic details, Craig sought consistently to communicate the essence, mood and atmosphere of a given piece. Max Reinhardt, though not exclusively a Symbolist, for he experimented in many styles in the course of a long career, met Craig in the early years of the century, shared his desire to transform the theatre, and in his own productions of *The Winter's Tale* and *King Lear* employed Craig's methods, using colour, lighting, movement and sound in an integrated way in order to stir the imagination of his audience.

A consideration of Valle-Inclán's *Comedias bárbaras (The Savage Dramas)* reveals important points of contact with the New Art of the Theatre and very substantial differences between Valle and the popular Spanish dramatists of his own time. That Symbolism exercised a profound influence on Valle-Inclán's work in general cannot be doubted, for what has been said already of the philosophy of Wagner and Schopenhauer in terms of the importance of the eternal and the transcendental is reflected in the following lines from *La lámpara maravillosa (The Wonderful Lamp)*, written in 1913 and published three years later:

> La unidad del mundo se quiebra en los ojos, como la unidad de la luz en el prisma triangular de cristal. Es preciso haber contemplado emotivamente la misma imagen desde parajes diversos, para que alumbre en la memoria la ideal mirada fuera de posición geométrica y fuera de posición en el tiempo[5]
>
> The unity of the world is refracted in the eye, as is the unit of light in a triangular prism of glass. It is necessary to have observed the same image emotionally from different angles so that the memory may be illuminated by the ideal vision of things distanced from their geometrical and temporal position.

In practice, moreover, a concern with the timeless essence of things had distinguished Valle's theatre six years earlier. As in the case of those other advocates of the New Art of the Theatre mentioned above, it was an artistic philosophy that both turned Valle away from Naturalism and made his theatre essentially different from that of the Spanish dramatists already mentioned. For dramatists like Benavente and the Quinteros the very nature of their approach placed a particular emphasis on certain aspects of the drama: on the presentation of individualized characters set in specific moments in time, on dialogue whose appeal is intellectual rather than emotional; and on character and dialogue at the expense of settings, movement and lighting. These are, of course, the characteristic of most bourgeois theatre. For Valle, on the other hand, as for the Symbolists in general, a sense of the timeless essence of things could be conveyed only through figures who are archetypal and universal, through settings which create a mood and atmosphere appropriate to those figures, and through language which communicates both basic, timeless emotions and a sense of age-old myth and ritual — in short, through a form of theatre in which the fusion and synthesis of the different dramatic elements create a powerful, imaginative and emotional impact.

One further point needs clarification. Appia, Craig and Reinhardt were men who worked in the theatre. For Craig, for instance, the play was an action to be performed, not words on the printed page. Valle's *Comedias bárbaras* are, in contrast, plays to be read — armchair plays or novels in dialogue — , a fact which poses the question of his right to be regarded as an innovative, experimental dramatist. What matters in the end is Valle's concept of theatre and other, later dramatists' awareness of the nature of that concept. Craig had stressed the omnipotence of the stage director in an effort to place the work of art above the separate and conflicting interests of dramatists, actors and impresarios. In refusing to write the *Comedias bárbaras* for stage performance — possibly after his own unfavourable treatment at the hands of the critics — Valle merely gave himself the kind of total control of the play that Craig always sought, though in Valle's case it would be an ideal rather than a stage performance.[6]

The *Comedias bárbaras* consist of a trilogy — *Aguila de blasón (The Eagle Scutcheon), Romance de lobos (The Ballad of Wolves),*and *Cara de plata (Silver Face)*— of which the first two plays were written in 1907 and the third in 1922, though the events portrayed in *Cara de plata* precede in fact the subject matter of the earlier works. The story of the trilogy, briefly stated, is that of Don Juan Manuel Montenegro, a Galician nobleman, and his six sons. In *Cara de plata* Don Juan Manuel is involved in a conflict with the peasants and with his son Cara de plata (Silver Face), in this case over Sabel, a girl attracted to both men. The discovery that Don Juan Manuel has seduced her leads to Cara de plata's resolve to kill him but the play ends with the father's triumph and an assertion of his daemonic power. *Aguila de blasón* develops the story both in relation to Sabel and to Don Juan Manuel's other sons. He believes them to be the criminals who have robbed him of his gold and is deeply saddened by the embodiment in his children of the passing of true nobility. As for Sabel, she feels obliged to leave Don Juan Manuel when Doña María, his estranged wife, arrives to convince her husband of their sons' innocence. He merely ignores both women and proceeds to indulge his insatiable erotic appetites with the miller's attractive wife. Later Sabel attempts to drown herself, Doña María vows to protect her, and banishes her husband and his new mistress from the house. Don Juan Manuel's story is completed in the magnificent and moving *Romance de lobos.* Learning of Doña María's imminent death, and overcome by feelings of guilt, he sets out through storm and tempest in a last but vain attempt to see her. She dies before his arrival and the children ransack the house. Beset by a sense of the sinfulness of his past life, the futility of human life in general, and the inevitability of death, Don Juan Manuel shuts himself away in readiness for death. Finding no peace, he gives his children their inheritance, leaves the ancestral home and seeks refuge with a madman. He returns finally to chastize his ungrateful children for turning the servants and beggars out of the house, attempts to enter it, and is killed by his eldest son.

This brief account of the trilogy suggests its extraordinary, almost epic character and the larger-than-life nature of its participants. The world of

Valle's *Comedias bárbaras*, totally removed from the bourgeois or aristocratic world of drawing-room comedy, has affinities with the theatre of Shakespeare, with Spanish drama of the seventeenth century, with Romanticism, and with the myths and legends used by Wagner, and by Ibsen in plays liked *Peer Gynt*.[7] In a narrow sense the *Comedias bárbaras* can be said to have their roots in the social reality of Valle-Inclán's time. The growth of the Spanish middle class from the 1830s onwards had a steadily weakening effect on the squirearchy, hitherto strong in Valle's native Galicia, and with which the more traditionalist side of him closely identified. In Don Juan Manuel Montenegro, Valle-Inclán therefore embodied the feudal nobility which he so admired, and in his downfall portrayed with regret the passing of an age. Don Juan Manuel is invariably bold, defiant in adversity, and compassionate to those less fortunate than himself. With his death his virtues are eclipsed, while his childrens' greed, cruelty and malice accentuate the process of rapid and unavoidable decline. Other Galician writers, notably Emilia Pardo Bazán, also dealt with the theme in their works, but if the social dimension of Valle's trilogy is important, it is certainly less important than other things.[8]

On a different level, in accordance with symbolist philosophy, Don Juan Manuel is a truly archetypal, universal, mythical and poetic figure who, in contrast to the majority of puny characters in the realist drama of the period, remains firmly fixed and engraved in the imagination. He is, as his name suggests, Valle's Galician version of the mythical Don Juan, the eternal womanizer who in *Cara de plata* deserts his wife for Sabel; who in *Aguila de blasón* abandons her for the miller's wife; and who in *Romance de lobos* vigorously defends his insatiable erotic appetites:

> Como el hombre necesita muchas mujeres y le dan una sola, tiene que buscarlas fuera.   (p.38).
>
> Since a man needs many women and is given only one, he has to go in search of them.

Like his literary antecedents, and especially Tirso de Molina's seventeenth-century version, Don Juan Manuel is also the very embodiment of courage, a proud, undaunted spirit who dismisses the dangers which surround him, scorns petty authority, and follows unswervingly the dictates of his own fiercely independent spirit. And, like Tirso's protagonist, Valle's heroic figure, brought to account for his sinful past, confronts death with true courage and nobility. Don Juan Manuel Montenegro transcends the Galician background and assumes the proportions of those characters who in their enduring fascination capture the minds and hearts of men across the ages.

The archetypal nature of Don Juan Manuel is also apparent in *Romance de lobos* through a clear association with King Lear. In this play Valle-Inclán, on whom the influence of Shakespeare was very strong, had Shakespeare's tragedy very much in mind. Like the old King, Don Juan Manuel leaves the family home and makes a madman his companion. A growing awareness of his own evil past and of the way in which, through his wife's death and his children's cruelty, he is made to atone for his sins, leads Don Juan Manuel to self-knowledge and, in consequence of his own suffering, to an identification with naked, suffering humanity in the shape of the wretched beggars. By the end of the play the once powerful and magnificent nobleman is very much Shakespeare's 'unaccommodated man', 'a poor, bare, forked animal', stripped of worldly goods, cast Lear-like onto the solitary heath, yet in his acceptance of his fate and his recognition of his nature endowed with a truly inspiring tragic dignity. He is one of the few memorable figures in the otherwise unremarkable drama written in Spain in the first decade of this century.

The stage settings of the *Comedias bárbaras* firmly link Valle to those other exponents of the New Art of the Theatre already mentioned. An impression of the imaginative stylization demanded by them may be formed from the following examples. Maeterlinck's *Les Aveugles* begins with this stage direction:

> *A very old northern forest that seems eternal beneath a starlit sky. In the middle of the stage and outlined against the background of nights is an old priest wrapped in a long black cloak. His head and shoulders, tilted and totally immobile, rest against the trunk of a large, hollow oak. His face is the unchanging colour of wax, his bluish lips half-open. His silent eyes gaze out upon the visible side of eternity and are reddened by unending grief and tears. His hair is very white and falls, stiffly and sparsely around his face . . . To the right, six blind old men are seated on stones, the stumps of trees and dead leaves. To the left, separated from them by a fallen tree and rocks, six women, similarly blind, are seated facing the old men . . . It is extremely dark, despite the moonlight which, here and there, succeeds momentarily in breaking through the darkness of the foliage. . .*[9]

In 1900 and 1901 Edward Gordon Craig staged his performances of Purcell's *Dido and Aeneas* at the Hampstead Conservatoire and the Coronet Theatre. Of one of its central scenes Haldane Macfall observed in 1901:

> That was a splendidly composed scene in which, amidst the mysteries of the night, against a background of moonlight, the Sorceress stands high above her sea-devils, who crawl about her feet, and float and rise and fall, like clouts of raggy seaweed that flap against the rocks at the incoming of the treacherous

tide, as she evilly plots the destruction of the lovers. . . . It was in this scene that Gordon Craig's fine artistic feeling for black and white did him yeoman service. The dim figures, seen in half-light, compelled the imagination.[10]

The initial stage direction for Act One, Scene Three of Valle's *Romance de lobos* is similar in many ways:

> *Noche de tormenta en una playa. Algunas mujerucas apenadas, inmóviles sobre las rocas y cubiertas con negros manteos, esperan el retorno de las barcas pescadoras. El mar ululante y negro, al estrellarse en las restingas, moja aquellos pies descalzos y mendigos. Las gaviotas revolotean en la playa, y su incesante graznar y el lloro de algún niño, que la madre cobija bajo el manto, son voces de susto que agrandan la voz extraordinaria del viento y del mar. Entre las tinieblas brilla la luz de un farol.* DON JUAN MANUEL *y* EL MARINERO *bajan hacia la playa.* (p.20).

> *Stormy night on a beach. A group of grieving women, motionless on the rocks and wrapped in black cloaks, awaits the return of the fishing boats. The black, howling sea, smashing on the rocks, soaks the women's bare feet. The gulls wheel over the sand, and their constant shrieking and the crying of a child, huddled beneath its mother's cloak, are fearful sounds that reinforce the terrible voice of the wind and the sea. The light of a lamp shines in the darkness.* DON JUAN MANUEL *and* THE SAILOR *come down towards the shore.*

Like the scenes in Maeterlinck and Craig, Valle's stage direction is highly stylized. Avoiding the fussy realistic details that characterized the performances of many plays on the stages of Spain and other European countries, he highlights the broad, essential features of the scene — the darkness, the human forms, the sounds, the small light — in order to communicate its dramatic mood and atmosphere. The *Comedias bárbaras* are full of similar scenes portraying the wild Atlantic, expanses of heath, Don Juan Manuel's crumbling house with its vast and gloomy rooms, howling wind, lashing rain, and darkness lit by flashing lightning. They evoke imaginatively the primitive, barbaric world in which the characters move. Conceived in an essentially symbolic manner, Valle's plays, like Wagner's operas, present production problems which in 1910 could hardly have been overcome but which present few problems nowadays. Performed with a multiple set and with all the visual and electronic aids of a modern theatre, *Romance de lobos* would clearly have the dramatic impact that Valle sought and thereby illustrate the far-seeing character of his theatrical vision.[11]

In terms of characterization the simplicity and stylization evident in Valle's stage settings are also to be seen in the presentation of the characters. The naturalistic drama sought to place on the stage men and women who are, as far as possible, copies of their real-life counterparts, as

rounded, solid and palpable as the rooms which they inhabit. Inasmuch as
the symbolist play is not a copy of life but an allegory whereby the dramatic
action reflects a superior reality, its characters lose their individualized and
particularized qualities in favour of the essential and archetypal, which in
turn involves flatness, simplification, exaggeration and distortion. The
characters of the *Comedias bárbaras* have nothing, therefore, of the precise
but small-scale realism of Benavente's men and women. Everything about
Don Juan Manuel Montenegro is heroic and extraordinary, each particular
characteristic heightened as though perceived in a distorting glass or a
magnifying lens. The visual presentation of the man, often in conjunction
with the natural elements, endows him with the majesty of one of those
figures of Blake or Michaelangelo, as in the case of the following example
from *Romance de lobos*:

> *A la luz de los relámpagos se columbra al viejo linajudo erguido sobre las*
> *piedras, con la barba revuelta y tendida sobre un hombro . . .*   (p.23)
>
> *In the flashes of lightning the old nobleman can be seen standing on the rocks,*
> *his great beard flowing over his shoulder . . .*

Facial expressions likewise communicate qualities and emotions that are
consistently on a grand scale. In *Aguila de blasón* Don Juan Manuel has a
'rostro de retrato antiguo' ('face of an ancient portrait') (p.26) and, when in
Romance de lobos he finally confronts his children, *'la altivez de un rey y la*
palidez de un Cristo' ('the haughtiness of a king and the paleness of a
Christ') (p.138). Boldness of gesture, vigour of movement and splendour
of voice further combine to elevate him into the archetypal figure so
characteristic of Valle-Inclán's best theatre.

Archetypal grandeur must, of course, have its opposite, be it in
Wagnerian opera, religious drama, or American western. In the *Comedias*
bárbaras Don Juan Manuel's children are thus, to the exclusion of all
redeeming qualities, the very essence of arrogance, malice, greed and
cruelty, and in *Romance de lobos* physical appearance is the stark,
emblematic image of the man:

> *Los cinco hermanos se parecen: altos, cenceños, apuestos, con los ojos duros y*
> *el corvar de la nariz soberbio.*   (p.25)
>
> *The five brothers are alike: tall, lean, handsome, with hard eyes and proud,*
> *curved noses.*

Concerned more with the generic qualities they embody than with the
differences of dress and manner that differentiate them, Valle further
deepened those universal and archetypal resonances by means of a
consistent pattern of allusions to flesh-eating beasts, especially wolves,

and, even more significantly, to Cain, supreme archetype of greed and murderous intent. The particular characters of the play consistently transcend their circumstances to assume the roles of protagonists locked in the age-old battle of good and evil.

A third group of characters, composed of servants and beggars, offsets the Montenegro family, for in them heroic or daemonic nobility is transformed into images of gargoyle-like monstrosity. Galán, Don Juan Manuel's fool, accompanies his master everywhere, his shadow, his *alter ego*, nobleman reduced to animal. In *Romance de lobos* the blind beggar, El Pobre de San Lázaro, is a huge figure whose eyes are ravaged by disease, while La Rebola, one of Don Juan Manuel's servants, is hideously deformed:

> *Entra otra criada, una moza negra y casi enana, con busto de giganta. Tiene la*
> *fealdad de un idolo y parece que anda sobre las rodillas.*   (p.63)

> *Another servant enters, a dark girl who is almost a dwarf, with a huge head.*
> *She has the ugliness of an idol and seems to walk upon her knees.*

The aristocratic splendour of Don Juan Manuel is matched at the other end of the human scale by human degradation, as though in the world of the play Valle sought to encapsulate the whole range of physical and spiritual beauty and ugliness in an imaginative sweep that echoes Shakespeare, Cervantes and Goya.

In the symbolist theatre in general the presentation of the characters is often dependent on movement and lighting, each of which acquires an importance not accorded it by the naturalistic theatre. Maeterlinck, for example, was familiar with the European painters of his day, especially the pre-Raphaelites, and created in his plays effects of colour and lighting that were directly inspired by painting. Gordon Craig was particularly interested by the way in which painters like Rubens used line as a key component in the creation of a picture's dramatic effect, while his affair with the dancer, Isadora Duncan, which stemmed from 1904, sharpened his awareness of the dramatic significance of pure movement. Writing of Craig's production of Ibsen's *The Vikings* at the Imperial Theatre, London,in 1903, William Rothenstein observed:

> ... never before had we seen such perfect marriage of dramatic suggestions in
> the foreground, background and groupings of the figures, and the actual
> delivery and gesture ...[12]

In an earlier quotation from *The Art of the Theatre* Craig refers to 'rhythm, which is the very essence of dance', while in a later section he describes action as 'both gesture and dancing, the prose and poetry of action' (p.180).

For Valle-Inclán too, as J.E. Lyon has observed, movement on the stage was an integral part of the play, and had a language of its own which harmonized with colour and lighting to enhance the total visual and emotional impact of the play.[13] In this sense the *Comedias bárbaras* possess a discernible and carefully controlled element of gesture, movement and action which, often replacing words, certainly speaks as loudly as them, enhances the archetypal nature of a character, expresses and reveals emotion, or deepens the mood of a given moment. The fifth scene of Act One of *Aguila de blasón* illustrates the point well. In a section without dialogue, almost as in a silent film, the heroic Don Juan Manuel bursts into the room brandishing two pistols, takes the robbers by surprise, and they flee into the darkness:

> *En aquel momento, una puerta se abre con rudo golpe y aparece* DON JUAN MANUEL. *El viejo hidalgo tiene las manos desatadas y empuña dos pistolas de arzón . . . Los ladrones disparan en la oscuridad, y huyen por el huerto . . .* (p.26)

> *At that moment the door flies open and* DON JUAN MANUEL *appears. The old nobleman's hands are no longer tied and he brandishes two large pistols . . . The robbers fire in the darkness and flee through the garden . . .*

Movement and gesture, as stylized as that of opera or ballet, highlight the two extemes of heroism and cowardice, sharpen the sense of an archetypal clash of good and evil, and through their very boldness impress the image upon us. Similarly, in Act One, Scene Four of *Romance de lobos* the violent verbal conflict of the defiant father and his treacherous son becomes the pure language of action:

> *Trémulo, con los ojos ardientes, salta a tierra el primogénito y va contra su padre, que le espera en medio del camino con el bastón enarbolado . . .*(p.57)

> *Quivering, his eyes blazing, the eldest son leaps from his horse and advances towards his father who, with his stick raised, awaits him in the middle of the road . . .*

Examples are innumerable: Don Manuel standing majestically on a rock, boldly descending the great staircase of his house or striding the moonlit countryside. Alternatively, slow movement or immobility are the visual equivalents of despair, as in Act Two, Scene Three, of *Romance de lobos:*

> EL CABALLERO *se sienta solo en un banco que hay frontero al hogar, y permanece abatido y sombrio . . .* (p.65)

> THE NOBLEMAN *sits alone on a bench before the great fireplace, still, bowed, sorrowful . . .*

Haldane Macfall had described Craig's Dido as conveying 'the dignity of her despair, where she reclines miserably at the foot of the great lilac heavens, bowing her head to her destiny . . .'[14]

Some of the examples already quoted suggest very clearly too the key role of lighting. In Maeterlinck's *Pelléas et Mélisande* the lighting of the stage is often symbolic of the psychological states and emotional needs of the characters. In his study of the theatre of Gordon Craig, Denis Bablet observes that '. . . Craig did not think of light and colour as means towards naturalistic description, but as contributions to the dramatic expression, to be used in their own right to act on the sensibilities of the spectator and help convey the central idea of the piece.'[15] Craig's production of *Dido and Aeneas* had made effective use in certain scenes of black and white, in the performance of Handel's *Acis and Galatea* he suggested the fateful approach of the giant Polyphemus by the projection on the stage of a huge shadow, and in Ibsen's *The Vikings* the use of half-light served to evoke the primitive, barbaric setting for the action. Adophe Appia, the stage designer whose name is perhaps most clearly associated with symbolist lighting, devoted much of his artistic career to demonstrating how lighting could be used to enhance dramatic effect both by means of the illumination of the stage in general and by means of particularized, highlighted areas, extending thereby the idea of lighting for mood already familiar to Renaissance designers as a method of deepening the emotional impact of a play.[16]

Valle-Inclán invariably uses lighting effects in a highly dramatic and imaginative way. The example previously quoted from *Romance de lobos* shows how the dramatist highlights Don Juan Manuel's archetypal splendour, emphasizing not detail but an image fleetingly seen:

> *A la luz de los relámpagos se columbra al viejo linajudo erguido sobre las piedras, con la barba revuelta y tendida sobre un hombro . . .*　　　(p.23)

> *In the flashes of lightning the old nobleman can be seen standing on the rocks, his great beard flowing over his shoulder . . .*

On many occasions the intense emotion of a moment is strikingly conveyed by the lighting of the scene. In Act One, Scene Five of *Aguila de blasón* where Don Juan Manuel confronts the robbers, the flash of the pistol spotlights his heroic face and, when he falls wounded, moonlight reveals his still figure, quickly transforming admiration into sudden concern:

> *Levanta la otra pistola, y la azulada vislumbre del fogonazo ilumina un momento aquel rostro de retrato antiguo . . .*　　　(p.26)
> *. . . y la luna, saliendo de entre las nubes, ilumina la sala. En el umbral de la puerta yace DON JUAN MANUEL.*　　　(p.27)

> *He raises the other pistol, and the blue flash of the gunfire illuminates for a*
> *moment that face like an ancient portrait . . .*
> *. . . and the moon, appearing from amongst the clouds, lights up the room.*
> DON JUAN MANUEL *is lying near the door.*

Again, in Act One, Scene Two of *Romance de lobos*, when a sailor brings
news of Doña María's imminent death and he and Don Juan Manuel speak
at the door of the great house, intermittent flashes of lightning pinpoint
their tense expressions:

> DON JUAN MANUEL *le interroga, y de tiempo en tiempo un relámpago les*
> *alumbra y se ven las caras lívidas.*   (p.19)

> DON JUAN MANUEL *questions him, and from time to time a flash of*
> *lightning illuminates them, picking out their white faces.*

Valle consistently captures too the gloom of the vast rooms of Don Juan
Manuel's house, emphasizing it by means of lighting effects that range from
guttering candles to the flickering of the flames in the great fireplace, the
wan light of oil-lamps and the slow approach of dawn. In Act One, Scene
Five of *Romance de lobos* Doña María's corpse is laid out in the bedroom:

> *En la alcoba, la luz del día naciente batalla con la luz de los cirios que arden a*
> *la cabecera de la muerta, y pasa por las paredes de la estancia como la sombra*
> *de un pájaro . . .*   (p.29)

> *In the bedroom the light of approaching day battles with the candles that burn*
> *at the head of the bed where the dead woman lies, and extends along the walls*
> *of the room like the shadow of a bird . . .*

Within the semi-darkness figures are themselves vague and shadowy
forms, often still, images which communicate their own melancholy as well
as that of their surroundings. Thus in Act One, Scene Two of *Aguila de*
blasón:

> *La sala comienza a ser invadida por la oscuridad. Las tres sombras que*
> *ocupan el estrado permanecen mudas bajo el vuelo de un mismo pensamiento*
> *. . .*   (p.15)

> *Darkness begins to fill the room. The three shadowy forms are silent,*
> *engrossed in the same thought . . .*

There is a similar effect in Act Three, Scene Three:

> *Una sala en el caserón. Anochece. Dos mujeres, casi dos sombras, en el*
> *estrado . . .*   (p.81)

> *A room in the great house. It is getting dark. In the drawing-room are two*
> *women, almost two shadows . . .*

The variety of such effects is quite remarkable and points very clearly to Valle's sense of theatre and to what a stage producer of vision and imagination would make of them, given the possibilities of modern theatre technique. Finally, it is important to note the way in which in these early plays the dramatist uses lighting to reinforce aspects of physical distortion, creating Goyaesque images and scenes that anticipate his later plays. In Act One, Scene Six of *Romance de lobos* the huge figure of El Pobre de San Lázaro is seen at daybreak:

> *A la lívida claridad del amanecer, la figura gigantesca del mendigo leproso se destaca en la oquedad de las canteras . . .*   (p.44)

> *In the pale light of dawn, the enormous figure of the diseased beggar is silhouetted in the space between the rocks . . .*

Nothing could be more removed from the techniques of presentation that characterized the commercial theatre in Spain at the time when Valle-Inclán wrote these plays.

As far as the dramatist's use of language is concerned, the dialogue of drawing-room comedy and bourgeois theatre in general serves largely to inform and entertain, and in the latter case tends to be distinguished by its elegance and wit. For Valle-Inclán, on the other hand, language was but a single element, albeit a very important one, in the total emotional and imaginative impact of the play and was divorced from any attempt merely to entertain or, indeed, to imitate the language of real life. He was concerned in particular with the music of language, with its capacity to move the listener, and there are many examples in these plays of the use of language in an essentially non-realistic way. The observations of J.E. Lyon are pertinent in this respect: 'The dialogue does not reason, argue, describe, analyse or relate; it alternates between the expression of spontaneouus emotion and ageless choral feeling: *gritos* and *sentencias*. The presence of ritualistic, choral dialogue is naturally more pronounced in the rural plays where whole scenes are devoted to a choral gloss on the main action (e.g. *Romance de lobos, Jornada III,* Scene Two)'.[17] In the case of Don Juan Manuel in both *Aguila de blasón* and *Romance de lobos*, the marked musical character of many of his lines, reminiscent of the splendour of an Old Testament passage, enhances that archetypal, timeless image already projected in visual terms. The expression of remorse and pity for the beggars in Act One, Scene Six of *Romance de lobos* is a good example:

> . . . ¡Y las mujeres, y los niños, y los viejos, y los enfermos, gritarán entre el fuego, y vosotros cantaréis y yo también, porque seré yo quien os guíe! Nacisteis pobres, y no podréis rebelaros nunca contra vuestro destino. La redención de los humildes hemos de hacerla los que nacimos con ímpetu de señores cuando se haga la luz en nuestras conciencias.   (p.43)

... And the women, and the children, and the old, and the sick, will cry out in the flames, and you will sing and I too, for it is I who will guide you! You were born poor, and you cannot ever struggle against your destiny. The redemption of the humble will be achieved by those of us who were born with the power to command when the light bursts in upon our consciousness.

Later in the play Don Juan prepares for death:

> Cuanto era mío, mañana será vuestro, y el cuerpo, que será de los gusanos, tendrá más noble destino ... No lloréis vosotros, criados y hermanos míos, que estas puertas las hallaréis siempre francas, y aunque fría, siempre sentiréis mi mano tendida hacia vosotros ...   (pp.86-7)

> All that was mine, tomorrow will be yours, and my body, which the worms will have, will find a nobler destiny ... Do not weep, servants and brothers of mine, for these doors you will find forever open, and, you will always find my hand, though cold, extended to you.

Valle uses language in a way which involves us directly, emotionally, for the subject matter in the lines quoted here is something with which we can all identify and draws from us sentiments and responses that are part of a common, universal experience.

In much the same way many of the lines given to the beggars and the servants have a chorus-like, ritualistic effect which not only comments on the action but deepens the emotional impact of a given moment as well as investing it with a much more general significance. In Act One, Scene Six of *Romance de lobos* the beggars lament the death of Doña María in a powerfully elegiac manner:

> ¡Era Doña María la madre de los pobres! ¡Nunca hubo puerta de más caridad! ¡Dios Nuestro Señor la llamó para Sí y la tiene en el Cielo, al lado de la Virgen Santísima! ¡Era la madre de los pobres!   (p.45)

> Doña María was the mother of the poor! Never was there a source of greater charity! God, Our Lord, has called her to him and has her in Heaven, at the side of the Blessed Virgin! She was the mother of the poor!

In the final Act the servants sit in a circle around a basket, dark shapes in the gloom, and their sad chanting anticipates Don Juan Manuel's death:

> ANDREÍÑA: ¡Y así día y noche!
> LA RECOGIDA: ¡No descansa!
> DON GALÁN: ¡Ya tendrá su descanso, y qué luengo será!
> LA RECOGIDA: ¡Para siempre!   (p.106)

> ANDREÍÑA: And so it goes on day and night!
> LA RECOGIDA: He does not rest!
> DON GALÁN: He will have his rest! How long it will be!
> LA RECOGIDA: Forever!

In their incantatory quality these lines are highly reminiscent of those of the blind characters of Maeterlinck's *Les Aveugles:*

> THE YOUNG BLIND WOMEN: I smell a scent of flowers round about us . . .
> FIRST BLIND MAN: I only smell the scent of the earth!
> THE YOUNG BLIND WOMAN: There are flowers, there are flowers near us!
> SECOND BLIND MAN: I only smell the scent of the earth!
> THE OLDEST BLIND WOMAN: I have just smelt the scent of flowers on the wind!
> THIRD BLIND MAN: I only smell the scent of the earth!

The stylization of figures, settings and movement has in the symbolist theatre a parallel in the stylization of language, and visual and aural effects are closely and carefully integrated in order to communicate the feeling, mood and atmosphere of the whole.

Valle's language is also dramatic rather than informative in another way, for he conceives theatre as the direct, head-on clash of individuals and often endows words with the physical force and power of blows. The bitter encounter of father and son in Act Two, Scene Two of *Romance de lobos* begins with a verbal onslaught that quickly becomes a purely physical confrontation:

> EL CABALLERO: A un hijo tan bandido se le abre la cabeza. ¡Se le mata! ¡Se le entierra!
> DON PEDRITO: ¡No me encienda la sangre, que si me vuelvo lobo, lo como!
> EL CABALLERO: Apéate del caballo, y verás quien tiene más fieros dientes.   (p.57)

> THE NOBLEMAN: In the case of a son so wicked, one splits his head in two! Kills him! Buries him!
> DON PEDRITO: Don't make me angry! If I become a wolf, I will devour you!
> THE NOBLEMAN: Get off your horse, and we'll see who has the sharpest teeth . . .

In the course of the *Comedias bárbaras* there are many such exchanges. In addition, in the scenes involving peasants and beggars Valle consistently communicates in incisive, popular and earthy dialogue the vigorous cut and thrust of peasant life. In this respect there is a direct link with the persistent traditional element in Spanish literature that through the centuries has given it its rich and unique flavour, while in its more ritualistic elements Valle's theatre is deeply influenced by forms of communal drama, from Greek tragedy to Church liturgy, which contain deep and often inexplicable resonances, an instinctive feeling of involvement and participation between performers and observers of the action.

Valle-Inclán's innovative spirit can be seen, finally, in the structure of these plays, so different from that of the nicely shaped and proportioned plots of the commercial theatre of his day. With regard to dramatic form in general, it is true to say that the great Spanish dramatists of the late sixteenth and early seventeenth centuries — Lope de Vega, Tirso de Molina, Calderón — had shown a considerable concern with structure, and that the three-Act play of the seventeenth century, with its nicely balanced format of exposition, complication and denouement, had had a decisive and lasting effect on later developments. Two of the plays that comprise the *Comedias bárbaras* are themselves three-Act plays and to that extent traditional, but in other respects they represent a clear break with the earlier close-knit form and a movement towards the altogether looser structure of much twentieth-century drama. Valle's plays are composed of a number of short, self-contained scenes. In *Aguila de blasón*, indeed, the technique has its defects, for there is little sense of the relationship of one scene to another in terms of a steadily developing dramatic rhythm. Sections of the play present bursts of activity which contrast sharply with scenes in which the momentum flags, and the overall effect becomes, therefore, one distinguished by a marked disparity between the dramatic presentation of the characters and settings and the limping pulse of the action. *Romance de lobos*, on the other hand, totally vindicates Valle's method. The series of self-contained scenes, arranged like a series of dramatic pictures, combines incident and powerful emotion, demanding the attention and involvement of the audience. It is not the method of traditional theatre, of building slowly to a single climax, but one in which, through a concentration on the essential moments of conflict, tension and confrontation, climax itself becomes a constant. In short, Valle's central belief that the play should have a direct emotional, not intellectual, impact upon its audience, is seen to determine all the different elements of the play, including the structure itself.

Valle-Inclán's Galician trilogy is in many ways a highly original achievement, while *Romance de lobos* is a remarkable dramatic work by any standards. More than ten years after the appearance of the first two plays of the trilogy Kenneth Macgowan was to describe the symbolist theatre in terms of four main principles: simplification of method and effect, the balanced relationship of actor and stage setting; the power of suggestion; and synthesis, in the form of the close integration of setting, lighting, actors and action.[18] Macgowan's definition, made without any knowledge of Valle-Inclán, might well have been based on Valle's theatre itself and suggests very clearly the Spanish dramatist's close connexion with the experimental European theatre of those years.

* * * * * *

The First World War proved to be a watershed both in relation to European politics and European art. The years that preceded the outbreak of war were already marked by political upheavals and the breaking-up of hitherto accepted values and ideals, most of which were mirrored in the proliferating cultural movements of the time. The cubist revolution had commenced in 1907 with Picasso's *Les Demoiselles d'Avignon* and in its rejection of conventional beauty, imitation of nature and traditional perspective, demanded a new way of looking at the world. In 1909 Futurism made its appearance in Italy, its aim to destroy the inhibiting influence of tradition and high art, as exemplified in Italian museums and libraries, to reject harmony, good taste and the conventional sublimity of the subject, and to attempt to move from the past into the new machine age. Two movements, though, can be associated with the War itself and were either brought about or sharply focused by it: Dada and Expressionism. The Dada movement had its origins in Zurich during the War and involved writers, painters and sculptors. Influenced by earlier iconoclasts like Alfred Jarry, the aim of the Dadaists was nothing less than the destruction of those bourgeois values which they considered to have caused the terrible destruction of War. Dada plays — and it is interesting to note that the first Dada entertainment on 2 February 1916 contained a reading by Hans Arp from Jarry's *Ubu Roi* — were very largely non-plays, for they overturned conventional forms of drama, included nonsensical language and stage business and were, on the whole, designed to shock bourgeois audiences. Those that were more substantial, such as Ribemont-Dessaignes' *L'Empereur de Chine*, dealt with themes of brutality and violence that vividly reflected the atrocities of war. Expressionism, dating from about 1910, was given a particular impulse by the War, but, in contrast to the Dadaists, the exponents of Expressionism were often concerned with positive values — with the ultimate creation, for example, of an ordered society based on social justice, with the rejection of the machine age and a return to a primitive, agricultural society.[19] Expressionist theatre tended, in effect, to be less political than 'Messianic' and few expressionist plays were on a genuinely political plane. In terms of technique they resorted to symbolism in order to communicate their message, transforming characters into idealized abstractions and abandoning psychological characterization in favour of the use of exaggeration and distortion as a means of giving expression to the inner and outward nature of human beings. Yvan Goll, one of the major expressionist dramatists and a fierce opponent of nineteenth-century Naturalism, observed in 1920 that the dramatist of the modern age must abandon naturalistic methods in order to expose the true reality that lies beneath the appearance of things:

> ... It has been completely forgotten that the stage is nothing more than a
> magnifying glass. Great drama has always been aware of this ...
> The stage must not only work with 'real' life; it becomes 'surreal' when it is
> conscious of the things behind the things. Pure realism was the greatest
> mistake in the whole of literature ...[20]

Affirming that the purpose of the theatre is not to comfort but to frighten
the bourgeoisie, Goll suggests an appropriate technique:

> The simplest means is the grotesque, but without inciting to laughter. The
> monotony and stupidity of human beings are so enormous that they can be
> adequately represented only by enormities. Let the new drama be an
> enormity ...[21]

In relation to stage presentation expressionist drama is characterized by
settings in which distortion plays a significant part, by movement of a bold
and exaggerated kind, and by delivery that is often declamatory and
deliberately unlifelike. Resembling in some respects the symbolist drama
previously described, expressionist theatre differed significantly from it in
terms of its much more social and political aims.

The years 1912 to 1919 mark an interim period in Valle-Inclán's literary
career and a significant change in attitude in relation both to life in general
and the function and nature of his art. In 1916 Valle visited the Western
Front and was deeply shocked by his first-hand experience of the horrors of
war. In addition, although Spain was not involved directly in the War, these
were difficult and dangerous years in Spanish political life. The War itself
brought initial prosperity to Spain, for she supplied the allies with many of
their needs, but the boom led in turn to inflation, difficult labour relations,
increasing political unrest, and the ultimate return of the military to
political power. Disillusioned by these events and even more conscious of
the folly of burying his head in an elitist aesthetic sand, Valle-Inclán felt
impelled to turn his attention to the problems of Spain and to expose and
satirize the ills of Spanish society. It was a task which required a style and
technique very different from that of the *Comedias bárbaras,* a technique
more capable of communicating the brutality of the real world. Sensitive to
the efforts of artists and writers elsewhere to express their reaction to a
difficult and often chaotic world through the new movements of Cubism,
Futurism and Expressionism, Valle groped his way to the formulation and
practice of a new aesthetic and technique which, though anticipated in the
plays written in the period 1909-19,[22] finally burst on the scene in 1920 in
the play *Luces de Bohemia (Bohemian Lights).* In Scene Twelve the
protagonist, Max Estrella, denies that the Spanish experience is tragic,
introduces the word *esperpento* to describe it, and proceeds to explain the
meaning of *esperpentismo:*

MAX: . . . El esperpentismo lo ha inventado Goya. Los héroes clásicos han ido a pasearse en el callejón del Gato.
DON LATINO: ¡ estás completamente curda!
MAX: Los héroes clásicos reflejados en los espejos cóncavos dan el Esperpento. El sentido trágico de la vida española sólo puede darse con una estética sistemáticamente deformada.   (p.106)

MAX: . . . *Esperpentismo* was invented by Goya. The classical heroes have gone for a stroll through Cat's Alley.
DON LATINO: You've had too much to drink.
MAX: Classical heroes reflected in distorting mirrors give us the *Esperpento*. The tragic sense of Spanish life can only be suggested by means of an aesthetic based on systematic distortion.

In the ensuing dialogue Max observes that 'España es una deformación grotesca de la civilización europea' ('Spain is a grotesque deformation of European civilization') (p.106), and that 'Las imágenes más bellas en un espejo cóncavo son absurdas' ('The most beautiful images are absurd in a concave mirror') (p.106). He concludes:

Mi estética actual es transformar con matemática de espejo cóncavo las normas clásicas . . .   (p.106)
Latino, deformemos la expresión en el mismo espejo que nos deforma las caras y toda la vida miserable de España.   (p.107)

My present aesthetic is to transform classical norms with the mathematical precision of a concave mirror . . .
Latino, let us distort expression in the same mirror that distorts our faces and the whole wretched existence of Spain.

Esperpentismo, as defined by Max Estrella and exemplified in *Luces de Bohemia,* emphasizes systematic distortion, the reversal through distortion of traditional norms and values — both physical and moral — which will have the effect of portraying Spain as it is. The essential difference between Valle's mirror and the distorting mirrors that lined the Callejón del Gato (Cat's Alley) is that while the latter offer us an optical illusion, Valle is concerned with portraying reality itself.[23]

The transition from the dramatic technique of the *Comedias bárbaras* to the *esperpento* involves a radical change of perspective by the dramatist in relation to his characters. In the former, as in the case of Don Juan Manuel Montenegro, the dramatist's stance is one of awe and reverence as a consequence of which he looks up to and idealizes the dramatic character. In the latter, on the other hand, it is the dramatist and not the character who assumes a position of god-like omnipotence from which he looks down upon his creations, manipulates them like puppets and is thus indifferent to their fate.[24] It would be wrong, though, to assume that the adoption of a new perspective required the total rejection of the dramatic methods described in the preceding pages. In the *esperpentos* the techniques of symbolist theatre are still very much in evidence, though modified and directed to a new end. Experiments in the New Art of the Theatre which initially echo the aesthetic concerns of men like Gordon Craig become in Valle-Inclán's later plays experiments of a different kind which reflect both Expressionism and anticipate the Theatre of the Absurd. It is interesting to note in this respect Martin Esslin's observation: 'Among the younger dramatists of the Absurd, Arrabal acknowledges Valle-Inclán as an important influence on his work.'[25]

Luces de Bohemia has as its central character the blind, ailing and forgotten poet, Max Estrella, who lives in Madrid in a state of acute poverty with his French wife, Madame Collet, and their daughter, Claudinita. In the course of the play's episodic action Max and his friend Don Latino wander through Madrid, Max is arrested for being drunk in the street, shares a prison cell with a Catalan anarchist and is released when his friends plead for his freedom. Later Max visits a café where he meets some of his Bohemian friends — including the great Nicaraguan poet, Rubén Darío — and when he continues his journey through Madrid with Don Latino the atmosphere of political disturbance and repression is once again suggested through his encounter with a woman whose child has been killed in a street riot. After Max and Don Latino have returned to the building where Max lives, Latino goes on his way, Max collapses and dies on the doorstep. Madame Collet and Claudinita commit suicide, and the play ends with an ironic twist when Max's lottery ticket proves to be a winner.

As the *Comedias bárbaras* can be said to reflect social reality in portraying the decline of the Galician nobility, so *Luces de Bohemia* nostalgically recalls Valle's bohemian existence in Madrid around the turn of the century. Many of the play's characters are modelled on real people: Max Estrella on Alejandro Sawa, a figure from the Spanish literary world of the early 1900s who died in great poverty; Dorio de Gadex on the writer Ciro Bayo; and Rubén Darío, of course, on the great champion of *Modernismo*.[26] The element of nostalgia which links *Luces de Bohemia* to the earlier Galician plays is accompanied now, though, by a very different and pressing concern: an evocation throughout the play of the sordid reality of Spain's present, for the events involving Max Estrella have as their background a picture of social unrest and repression. Max is himself arrested for causing a disturbance, the anarchist prisoner is later shot, and a child is accidentally killed in a street riot. Max alludes to the barbarous nature of the Spanish Church: 'España, en su concepción religiosa, es una tribu del Centro de África' ('Spain, in its conception of religion, is a tribe from Central Africa') (p.21). The anarchist speaks of the country's materialism: 'Aquí todo lo manda el dinero' ('Here money rules everything') (p.54). And a newspaper editor gives his view of the freedom of the press: 'Ustedes conocen cómo se hace un periódico. ¡El Director es siempre un tirano! . . .' ('You know how a newspaper is produced. The owner is always a tyrant') (p.61). Inasmuch as the political background against which the individual is presented as a helpless and ultimately crushed figure is so important in *Luces de Bohemia*, it is possible to relate the play to the themes and preoccupations of expressionist drama. It would be misleading to speak of the direct influence on Valle-Inclán of expressionist dramatists like Georg Kaiser and Ernst Toller, many of whose plays preceded *Luces de Bohemia*, but it is true that *Luces de Bohemia* shares the viewpoint and technique of many theatrical works that we would term expressionist. In addition, bearing in mind Esslin's comment on the relationship of Valle and Arrabal, it is always useful in discussing *Luces de Bohemia* to examine its dramatic character in relation to the Theatre of the Absurd. To link Valle too closely to any particular movement is to underestimate his individuality, but to detect in his drama links with the most important trends in modern European theatre is to highlight the progressive and experimental nature of his work.

In terms of characterization, Max Estrella has that expressionist archetypal quality perceived already in his symbolist predecessor, Don Juan Manuel Montenegro. In the first scene of the play he is presented to us with all the majesty of a classical hero:

> MÁXIMO ESTRELLA *se incorpora con un gesto animoso, esparcida sobre el pecho la hermosa barba con mechones de canas. Su cabeza rizada y ciega, de un carácter clásico-arcaico, recuerda los Hermes.* (p.11)

> MÁXIMO ESTRELLA *sits up boldly, his magnificent beard flecked with grey flowing over his breast. His blind and curly head, which has an ancient, classical character, evokes Hermes.*

The Homeric association is a frequent one. In Scene Eight Max describes himself as blind like Homer (p.75), while in Scene One he ascribes to himself the poetic vision that transcends blindness:

> ¡Espera, Collet! ¡He recobrado la vista! ¡Veo! ¡Oh, cómo veo! ¡Magníficamente! (p.11)

> Wait, Collet! I have regained my sight. I see! Oh, how I see! Magnificently!

In the prison cell, which he shares with the Catalan anarchist — himself symbolic of the universal prisoner — the half-darkness serves to create a lack of precision and detail which strips Max of his individuality and thereby deepens his archetypal significance:

> . . . *se sienta con las piernas cruzadas, en una actitud religiosa, de meditación
> asiática. Exprime un gran dolor taciturno el bulto del poeta ciego . . .* (p.58)

> . . . *he sits with his legs crossed, in a religious posture, in the manner of an
> oriental thinker. The shape of the blind poet gives out a great, silent grief. . .*

And in Scene Eight he assumes, as he advances towards the Minister, not
merely an immense dignity but a highly ritualistic, almost Christ-like
significance which anticipates his own crucifixion at the hands of an
unfeeling world:

> MÁXIMO ESTRELLA, *con los brazos abiertos en cruz, la cabeza erguida,
> los ojos parados, trágicos en su ciega quietud, avanza como un fantasma . . .*
> (p.79)

> MÁXIMO ESTRELLA, *with his arms extended sideways, his head held
> high, his eyes closed, tragic in their blind silence, advances like a phantom . . .*

One of the principal features of Expressionism is, indeed, its mystical,
almost religious fervour and its concern with self-sacrifice and human
redemption.[27] The plays of Georg Kaiser present the brutalizing effects of
capitalism and the machine-age, including the horrors of war, and are
concerned with man's redemption either through a rebellion against
society or a conscious sacrifice in the name of his ideal vision. At the end of
Die Bürger von Calais (The Burghers of Calais), written in 1913, Kaiser
draws a parallel between Eustache de Saint-Pierre, who sacrifices himself
for the city, and Christ's sacrifice for mankind. In *Gas I* and *II* Kaiser's new
man, embodied in the characters of the millionaire's son and the
millionaire-worker, are crushed and brushed aside by the social forces
which they fail to stem. In a sense the visionary Max Estrella, destroyed by a
repressive, insensitive and materialistic society, has something of Kaiser's
expressionist martyr about him.

On the other hand, Max is increasingly possessed by a sense of his own
decline and his ultimate insignificance. His opinion of himself is frequently
disparaging and when, after his release from prison, the government
minister gives him some money as compensation, Max accepts it with an
acknowledgement of his own despicable nature:

> Conste que he venido a pedir un desagravio para mi dignidad, y un castigo
> para unos canallas. Conste que no alcanzo ninguna de las dos cosas, y que me
> das dinero, y que lo acepto porque soy un canalla. No me estaba permitido
> irme del mundo sin haber tocado alguna vez el fondo de los reptiles . . .(p.79)

> I came to seek some sort of satisfaction for my dignity, and a punishment for
> those wretches. I have achieved neither, and you give me money, and I accept
> it because I am a wretch. I couldn't leave this world without sinking at some
> time to the level of the reptiles . . .

His Christ-like significance in this scene has its other side, and when in the following episode he takes his farewell of Rubén Darío in a manner reminiscent of the Last Supper — 'Rubén, acuérdate de esta cena' ('Rubén, remember this feast') (p.89) —, the journey on which he embarks is one that takes him through the grotesque experience of suffering and death into a total emptiness:

> Para mí, no hay nada tras la última mueca. Si hay algo, vendré a decírtelo.
> (p.89)
> For me there is nothing after the last grimace. If there is, I will let you know.

It is in Scene Twelve, as he sits cold and shivering on a doorstep, that Max gives, significantly, his definition of *esperpentismo*, for he more than anyone is the classical hero, the blind Homer, transformed in the concave mirror into the grotesque image of mankind. The stray dog that stops in the road to urinate, anticipating perhaps the dog that in Buñuel's *Los olvidados* accompanies Jaibo's wretched death, suggests both the indifference aroused by Max's suffering and his reduction to the undignified level of a whimpering animal. If Max Estrella embodies certain expressionist characteristics, he is also by the end of the play a character who anticipates the Theatre of the Absurd, both in his own exposure of an absurd and grotesque society and in the nature of his own fate. Martin Esslin has defined the Theatre of the Absurd in a way which *Luces de Bohemia* exemplified years before the plays of Beckett, Ionesco, Adamov and Genet:

> This is the experience that Ionesco expresses in plays like *The Bald Soprano* or *The Chairs*, Adamov in *La Parodie*, or N.F. Simpson in *A Resounding Tinkle*. It represents the satirical, parodistic aspect of the Theatre of the Absurd, its social criticism, its pillorying of an inauthentic, potty society. This may be the the most easily accessible, and therefore most widely recognized, message of the Theatre of the Absurd, but it is far from being its most essential or significant feature.
> In its second, more positive aspect, behind the satirical exposure of the absurdity of inauthentic ways of life, the Theatre of the Absurd is facing up to a deeper layer of absurdity — the absurdity of the human condition itself . . .[28]

The grotesque character acquired by Max in the course of the play is evident throughout it in many of the other characters, and there is a consistent emphasis on their less than human nature. In Scene Two the bookseller, Zaratustra, is a hunchback, a man with *'la cara de tocino rancio'* ('a face like rancid bacon') (p.16) and *'con su caracterización de fantoche'* (*'with the manner of a puppet'*) (p.16). In his cave-like hovel, accompanied by a cat, a dog and a parrot, he is little different from them, while the scarf that is wrapped around his neck like a green serpent further underlines the element of dehumanization. In the same scene Max's companion, Don Latino, has about him *'ese matiz del perro cobarde' ('the air of a cowardly dog')* (p.17). The tavern of Pica Lagartos is full of grotesques: the one-eyed girl, Enriqueta La Pisa-Bien, and the tramp known as El Rey de Portugal:

> *Un golfo largo y astroso, que vende periódicos, rie asomado a la puerta, y como perro que se espulga, se sacude con jaleo de hombros, la cara en una risa de viruelas.* (p.30)

> *A tall dirty tramp who sells newspapers appears at the door, laughing, shakes himself like a dog to get rid of fleas, and his face breaks into a small-poxed smile.*

Scene Seven introduces the newspaper editor:

> DON FILIBERTO *suelta la trompetilla del teléfono y viene al centro de la sala, cubriéndose la calva con las manos amarillas y entintadas. ¡Manos de esqueleto memorialista en el día bíblico del Juicio Final!*

> DON FILIBERTO *puts down the telephone and comes to the centre of the room, covering his bald head with his yellow and ink-stained hands. The hands of a skeletal amanuensis on the Day of Judgement!*

In Scene Eight the Government Minister is described as having *'los quevedos pendientes de un cordón, como dos ojos absurdos bailándole sobre la panza' ('spectacles dangling by a cord, like two ridiculous eyes which dance upon his pot-belly')* (p.74). And in Scene Ten the old woman *'bajo la máscara de albayalde, descubre las encías sin dientes, y tienta capciosa a* DON LATINO' *('her face covered with white-lead, she reveals her toothless gums and tempts* DON LATINO') (p.94). The elements of grotesque distortion that in the *Comedias bárbaras* remain subordinate are now predominant, the rule rather than the exception. The world of *Luces de Bohemia*, looking back on the one hand to Quevedo and Goya, looks forward too to Ionesco, Genet and Beckett.

Both Symbolism and Expressionism share a predilection for the anti-naturalistic, the abstract and the archetypal, and the stage settings of *Luces de Bohemia* have much in common with those of the *Comedias bárbaras*, but they have too that extra dimension which is peculiar to Expressionism. Mordecai Gorelik observes that in relation to stage design expressionist dramatists and producers 'developed an hysterical view of environment' and 'gave an unearthly aspect to the once familiar world.'[29] B.J. Kenworthy describes Georg Kaiser's use of stage settings in the following way: 'The settings that Kaiser prescribes in his stage directions reduce the scenery to the minimum essential to his dramatic purpose: like his figures, they, too, are significant abstractions from a wider reality. There is no lavishing of naturalistic detail, nothing to lessen the force of their impact upon the spectator . . .'[30] Many of the stage settings of *Luces de Bohemia* are virtual mirrors of the inner lives of the play's characters. In Scene Four Max and Don Latino, themselves derelict men, stumble drunkenly through dark and empty streets:

> *Noche.* MÁXIMO ESTRELLA *y* DON LATINO DE HISPALIS *tambalean asidos del brazo por una calle enarenada y solitaria. Faroles rotos, cerradas todas, ventanas y puertas. En la llama de los faroles un igual temblor verde y macilento* . . . MAX *y* DON LATINO, *borrachos lunáticos, filósofos peripatéticos, bajo la línea luminosa de los faroles, caminan y tambalean.* (p.36)

> *Night.* MÁXIMO ESTRELLA *and* DON LATINO DE HISPALIS *stumble arm in arm along a sandy, solitary street. There are broken street lamps and doors and windows are closed. The light of the lamps creates a green, wan, trembling effect* . . . MAX *and* DON LATINO, *lunatic drunks, wandering philosophers, advance and stumble beneath the lamplight.*

The green, flickering light suggests very clearly the febrile state of mind of the two men, and the way in which the physical objects in the street move uncertainly in the light evokes the way in which they themselves see those objects. And in addition, of course, the derelict setting is itself an image of and a suitable frame for the derelict men who inhabit it. One of the most effective and evocative settings in the play is, though, the setting for Scene Nine, the Café Colón where the bohemian artists meet:

> Las sombras y la música flotan en el vaho de humo, y en el lívido temblor de los arcos voltaicos. Los espejos multiplicadores están llenos de un interés folletinesco. En su fondo, con una geometría absurda, extravaga el Café. El compás canalla de la música, las luces en el fondo de los espejos, el vaho de humo penetrado del temblor de los arcos voltaicos cifran su diversidad en una sola expresión. (p.83)

> The shadows and the music float in the smoky atmosphere and in the pale trembling light of the lamps. The multiple mirrors are full of anecdotal interest. In them the Café acquires a fantastic and absurd geometry. The harsh rhythm of the music, the lights reflected in the mirrors, the smoke pierced by the flickering light, are fused into a single image.

In the mirrors that line the walls of the café the figures who, as in Max's case, are already grotesque acquire a further element of distortion, an 'absurd geometry', while the dim, smoky light has the added effect of suggesting that the world in general is a place where men like Max grope their way uncertainly.

The importance of lighting is evident in the stage settings already mentioned. It is, of course, an important aspect of expressionist theatre in general and serves to accentuate atmosphere and the archetypal nature of the characters. In relation to Kaiser's use of lighting, B.J. Kenworthy observes that 'the theatrical technique catches in one arresting symbol the essence of the drama'.[31] Much of *Luces de Bohemia* takes place at night as Max Estrella and Don Latino wander through the city. The darkness reflects Max's despair and Spain's unenlightenment, while Zaratustra's bookshop, a place of wisdom and learning, is symbolically engulfed by shadows. In the prison scene subdued lighting is employed in a particularly effective way, firstly to obliterate detail and suggest the universal dimension of the prisoner, secondly to pinpoint his suffering:

> *El calabozo. Sótano mal alumbrado por una candileja. En la sombra se mueve el bulto de un hombre . . . Sale de la tiniebla el bulto del hombre morador del calabozo. Bajo la luz se le ve esposado, con la cara llena de sangre.* (p.53)
>
> *The prison cell. A cellar poorly lit by an oil-lamp. The shape of a man moves in the shadows . . . The shape of the inhabitant of the cell emerges from the shadows. In the light he is seen to be handcuffed, and his face is covered in blood.*

When there is light, as in the tavern of Pica Lagartos, it is the harsh light of an acetylene lamp which accentuates the harshness of the characters' lives. And finally, when Max dies so pathetically and absurdly, the approaching light of day provides an ironic comment on his hopelessness.

Inasmuch as the principal characters of many expressionist plays are fervent, visionary figures, they are often given to declamatory speeches, accompanied by dramatic gestures of an essentially anti-naturalistic kind. There is clearly something of this in the impassioned speeches of Max Estrella, characterized as they are by a high rhetorical style, a powerful surging rhythm and an abundance of strongly visual imagery. The anarchist prisoner notes, indeed, that Max does not speak like other men: 'Su hablar es como de otros tiempos' ('You speak like someone from another age') (p.54). In Scene Two Max launches into a powerful attack on contemporary Spain:

> . . . La miseria del pueblo español, la gran miseria moral, está en su chabacana sensibilidad ante los enigmas de la vida y de la muerte. La Vida es un magro puchero; la Muerte, una carantona ensabanada que enseña los dientes; el Infierno, un calderón de aceite albando donde los pecadores se achicharran como boquerones; el Cielo, una kermés sin obscenidades, a donde, con permiso del párroco, pueden asistir las Hijas de María. Este pueblo miserable transforma todos los grandes conceptos en un cuento de beatas costureras . . . (p.22)

... The wretchedness of the Spanish people, its great moral wretchedness, lies in its crude sensibility in the face of the mystery of life and death. Life is a thin stew. Death a shrouded old hag who bares her teeth. Hell a cauldron of boiling oil where sinners fry like anchovies. Heaven, a garden-party without filth, to which, with the parish priest's permission, the Daughters of Mary may go. The wretched country transforms every grand concept into a tale told by a bunch of pious old women at their sewing.

In Scene Four there is another good example, and on this occasion, as in much expressionist drama, the protagonist's words are given an extra emphasis by the chorus-like agreement of the listeners:

> ... ¡Y soy el primer poeta de España! ¡El primero! ¡El Primero! ¡Y ayuno! ¡Y no me humillo pidiendo limosna! ¡Y no me parte un rayo! ¡Yo soy el verdadero inmortal, y no esos cabrones del cotarro académico! ¡Muera Maura!
> LOS MODERNISTAS: ¡Muera! ¡Muera! ¡Muera!   (pp.40-1)

> ... And I am Spain's best poet! The Best! The Best! And I starve! And I do not degrade myself by begging! And no thunderbolt strikes me down! I am a true immortal, and not these Academy cuckolds. Death to Maura! THE MODERNISTS: Death! Death! Death!

Taken in conjunction with Max's majestic movements, the way he bears himself, gestures, extends his arms, his general presentation accords well with some of Kaiser's characters, as well as with Mordecai Gorelik's observation on expressionist theatre in general: 'Acting ceased almost completely to be "psychological" in the Stanislavsky manner, returning in some degree to the Baroque declamatory style. Kornfeld urged the actor to spread his arms boldly before the audience, to speak as he would not in real life'.[32] In both the *Comedias bárbaras* and *Luces de Bohemia* Valle-Inclán uses language to express emotion and to draw from his audience an emotional response. The essential difference in *Luces de Bohemia* lies in the closer association of the language with political and social themes, which are more the themes of Expressionism than of Symbolism.

In terms of structure *Luces de Bohemia* represents, even more than the *Comedias bárbaras*, Valle's abandonment of traditional structure. The events of the play are, in effect, the accidental consequences of Max's haphazard wanderings through the streets of Madrid, his dropping in at bars and cafes, and his chance encounters with prostitutes, and there is certainly no sense of an arrangement of episodes building steadily to a climax. In its rejection of traditional structure the play is thus a distortion of the classical norm, but it is also in its shapelessness an image of the increasing purposelessness, the drifting, unplanned nature and the absurdity of Max's existence. The *Romance de lobos*, though episodic, presents in Don Juan Manuel Montenegro the heroic spectacle of a man battling against the assault of the natural and the human world. In *Luces de Bohemia*, on the other hand, the battle has been lost from the outset, Max is finally reduced to a helpless puppet figure, and his futile wandering through life is reflected in the structure of the play itself. Although Beckett's plays are different from Valle-Inclán's, their lack of conventional plot is also part of Beckett's purpose to underline the purposelessness of man's existence. In this respect *Luces de Bohemia*, given its clear expressionist elements, can also be said to anticipate the Theatre of the Absurd, and exemplifies in many ways Ionesco's definition, made nearly forty years later: 'Absurd is that which is devoid of purpose . . . Cut off from his religious, metaphysical, and transcendental roots, man is lost; all his actions become senseless, absurd, useless'.[33]

Los cuernos de Don Friolera (The Horns of Don Friolera) belongs to the same time as *Luces de Bohemia*, for it was serialized in the magazine *La Pluma* in 1921, and it is often regarded as Valle-Inclán's finest *esperpento*. The play deals with Don Friolera, a lieutenant in the Spanish army who is informed anonymously of his wife's adultery. Three of Friolera's colleagues, who exemplify the army's intransigence in matters of honour, pass judgement on the innocent Friolera, demanding that he should either resign or cleanse his honour by killing his wife. He attempts to shoot her, but succeeds only in killing his daughter. The action described above is preceded by a prologue in which two Basque intellectuals, Don Manolito and Don Estrafalario, discuss the relationship of a writer to his characters and observe a puppet play in which a deceived husband takes vengeance on his wife. In the epilogue the same two men overhear a romanticized ballad version of Friolera's story in which the brave lieutenant is portrayed as taking appropriate action against his wife and her lover and as going on to perform heroic deeds in battle.

Valle-Inclán's definition of *esperpentismo*, outlined by Max Estrella in *Luces de Bohemia*, is put into practice even more uncompromisingly in *Los cuernos de Don Friolera*. In the former Max often has about him a nobility and dignity that contradict the distortion and grotesque deformation evident in the other characters, but in *Los cuernos* this is everywhere apparent. In this respect the prologue is important, for Valle uses Don Estrafalario to outline the author's standpoint in relation to the play's characters. Stating that he wishes to see 'este mundo con la perspectiva de la otra ribera' ('this world from the perspective of the other shore') (p.69), Estrafalario advocates, in effect, the remoteness, objectivity and indifference to the characters' fate that to a large extent distinguish *Luces de Bohemia* from the *Comedias bárbaras* and which now in *Los cuernos* are taken to their logical conclusion. In the latter part of the prologue the puppet show observed by Estrafalario and his companion puts theory into practice in the sense that Fidel, the puppeteer, manipulates the figures from above with a god-like indifference, and we, the observers of the action, are made to share the sense of distancing. The subsequent action involving Friolera reveals that Valle-Inclán's position in relation to the characters is similar to if not entirely that of Fidel in relation to the puppets.[34] In consequence, the characters are rendered puppet-like, dehumanized, and the comedy associated with them assumes ridiculous, absurd and grotesque overtones, the human characters of the play revealed to us in the distorting mirror of the *esperpento*. In addition, Valle's presentation of his characters as puppets and grotesques is also a way of looking at humanity in general. In *Luces de Bohemia* there still exists the identification between dramatist and protagonist that is evident in many expressionist plays. In *Los cuernos de Don Friolera* it has disappeared and we are offered instead a vision of man and society which makes this play a clear forerunner of the Theatre of the Absurd.

Los cuernos de Don Friolera looks back in one direction to the comic dramatic tradition of sixteenth and seventeenth-century Spain. A comic treatment of the theme of honour, so central to Valle's play, is to be found in the short dramatic pieces of Lope de Rueda and Cervantes. In his eight *entremeses*, published in 1615, Cervantes endowed the tradition of farce with a high degree of artistry and set a pattern involving physical violence, slapstick and grotesque humour that many later dramatists, including Valle-Inclán and Lorca, would adapt to their own ends. There is, though, one dramatist in particular, much closer in time to Valle, who must surely be regarded as a powerful influence and who, more importantly, is generally acknowledged as a true precursor of the Theatre of the Absurd: Alfred Jarry. *Ubu Roi* had been conceived in 1888, when Jarry was only fifteen, as a schoolboy prank directed at one of his teachers, nicknamed Père Héb or Père Hébé and later Ubu. It was initially written as a puppet play and was performed for the amusement of Jarry's schoolboy friends. But when the play was performed on 10 December 1896 at the Theatre de l'Oeuvre, provoking a tremendous scandal, Jarry fully intended it to present to a bourgeois audience a grotesque image of itself:

> I wanted the stage to stand, as soon as the curtain was raised, before the public like a mirror in one of the fairy tales of Madame Leprince de Beaumont in which the vicious villain sees himself with the horns of a bull and the body of a dragon, the exaggerated forms of his own savage nature. It is in no way surprising that the public was astonished by the sight of its own ignoble image, for it had never before been revealed to it in its totality, made up, as M. Catulle

Mendès has finely expressed it, 'of the eternal stupidity of man, his constant lubricity, his perennial gluttony, the baseness of instinct elevated to the status of tyranny; of the coyness, the virtue, the patriotism, and the ideals of people who have filled their stomachs'.[35]

The characters of the play, especially Ubu, were conceived in a highly stylized manner, their physical appearance and costumes designed to communicate in a powerfully symbolic manner their real natures. W.B. Yeats, who attended the first performance, refers to the characters as 'dolls, toys, marionettes . . . hopping like wooden frogs . . .'[36] The decor, echoing and underlining the stylization of the characters, was distinguished by its almost child-like simplicity, its stark and lurid colours. And the actions and language of the characters, often reduced to the fisticuffs and the verbal abuse that we associate with a Punch and Judy show, contributed further to the mood of uncompromising aggression. Martin Esslin makes the important point that Jarry, without knowing it, created both 'a mythical figure and a world of grotesque archetypal images.'[37] In Valle's theatre in general, as the discussion of the earlier plays suggests, the concern with the mythical and the archetypal is central. But the development of Valle's theatre is one in which the archetypes are progressively transformed from the hero of the *Comedias bárbaras* to the grotesques of *Los cuernos de Don Friolera* — to the formulation of an image which, like Jarry's, seems peculiarly of our time.

The puppet play in the prologue to *Los cuernos* is to a large extent the key to the presentation of the characters in the real play.[38] The technique of stylization which in the *Comedias bárbaras* took the form of idealization of Don Juan Manuel is used now for the purposes of parody. Friolera's initial presentation is firmly in the tradition of cartoon or comic strip, while his somewhat impressive name is quickly supplemented by a nickname, Friolera, which in Spanish means a useless trifle:

> . . . *en el marco azul del ventanillo, la gorra de cuartel, una oreja y la pipa del Teniente don Pascual Astete — Don Friolera —.*   (p.77)
>
> . . . *in the blue frame of the window, the forage cap, the ear and the pipe of Lieutenant Don Pascual Astete — Don Friolera —.*

From the outset the wronged husband — the dignified and often tragic protagonist of the honour plays of the seventeenth century is stripped of all his traditional dignity. At the end of the same scene the physical characteristics of the wronged husband merely render him absurd:

> *Los cuatro pelos de su calva bailan un baile fatuo . . . Le tiembla el bigote como a los gatos cuando estornudan.*   (p.80)

The four hairs on his bald crown perform a foolish dance . . . His moustache trembles like the whiskers of a sneezing cat.

It is a far cry from the heroic image of Don Juan Manuel Montenegro, beard and hair flying in the wind. The image has, in effect, been inverted, those bold physical characteristics that ennobled the defiant hero of *Romance de lobos* transformed into physical deficiencies that are synonymous with the hen-pecked or cowardly husband. On the other hand, Friolera,for all his absurdity, does possess one positive characteristic which distinguishes him from the totally dehumanized figures of Fidel's puppet show, for as Francisco Ruiz Ramón has pointed out, he has about him an element of tragedy.[39] In Scene Four, for instance, Friolera is presented as something more than a puppet:

> *Don Friolera, en el reflejo amarillo del quinqué, es un fantoche trágico . . .*   (p.95)
>
> *Don Friolera, in the yellow light of the lamp, is a tragic puppet . . .*

Although his tragic character is not that of the classical tragic hero — of Sophocles, Shakespeare, Racine, or Calderón — for Friolera has no heroism or greatness in him, he is tragic in the sense in which many twentieth-century dramatic characters are tragic — grotesque and absurd in their futile efforts to redeem themselves in a world which mocks them, but at the same time human beneath the comic mask.

Friolera's humanity dashes itself constantly and vainly against a world peopled by unfeeling, superficial and inflexible monsters who, because they are less than human, heighten the absurdity of his predicament. Valle-Inclán's fondness for the essential and the archetypal leads him now away from the heroes of the *Comedias bárbaras* and, to a lesser extent, of *Luces de Bohemia,* to the creation — in Doña Loreta, Friolera's unfaithful wife, Pachequín, her suitor, Doña Tadea, the local gossip, and, in particular, Friolera's military superiors — of grotesques very much in the manner of Jarry. In such cases the puppet or even animal nature of the character is exaggerated to the point where human attributes almost disappear. Doña Tadea, for example, is consistently described in less than human terms:

> *Se desvanece bajo un porche, y a poco, su cabeza de lechuza asoma en el ventano de una guardilla.*   (p.86)
>
> *She disappears through an archway and after a while her owl's head appears in an attic window.*

Valle's dehumanization of the military men is particularly striking, as the following examples indicate:

Conduce la discusión Don LAURO ROVIROSA, *que tiene un ojo de cristal,
y cuando habla, solamente mueve un lado de la cara . . . Don* GABINO
CAMPERO . . . *está en el grupo de los gatos. Don* MATEO CARDONA,
con los ojos saltones y su boca de oreja a oreja, en el de las ranas. (p.129)

The discussion is in the hands of Don LAURO ROVIROSA, *who has a glass
eye, and when he speaks, only one side of his face moves . . . Don* GABINO
CAMPERO . . . belongs to the cat family. Don* MATEO CARDONA, *with
bulging eyes and a mouth that stretches from ear to ear, belongs to the family
of frogs.*

Pachequín, Doña Loreta's suitor, is lame and large-nosed, the grotesque
version of the traditional handsome and dashing lover. Here, in short, are
the puppet equivalents of the characters and values — love, virtue and
honour — which in the honour plays of the seventeenth century, and of
Lorca too, are the stuff of moving and dramatic situations, but which are
rendered farcical in this new form, which is also Valle's new vision of Spain
and of the human condition as a whole. Of his own theatre Eugène Ionesco
was to write:

> I can still remember that as a child my mother could not get me away from the
> puppet-shows in the Luxembourg Gardens. I could have stayed there
> spellbound for days on end. I didn't laugh, though. The spectacles of the
> *guignol* held me there, stupefied by the sight of these puppets who spoke, who
> moved, who bludgeoned each other. It was the spectacle of life itself which,
> strange, improbable, but truer than truth itself, was being presented to me in
> an infinitely simplified and caricatured form, as though to underline the
> grotesque and brutal truth.[40]

Ionesco's first play, *The Bald Prima-Donna*, was first performed in 1950,
thirty years after *Los cuernos de Don Friolera*. In the line that leads from
Jarry to Ionesco and the other dramatists of the Absurd Valle-Inclán
should never be forgotten.

The stage settings of Jarry's *Ubu Roi* were distinguished by their
stylization and naive, child-like simplicity. Those of Valle's play are similar,
far less novelistic than those of the plays examined previously, and highly
characteristic of the puppet tradition. They serve, though, not as mere
decoration but often as a means of heightening the puppet-like appearance
of the characters and of drawing our attention to their less-than-human
nature. And in this respect the effect is often accentuated by Valle's stark
use of lighting. There is a good example in Scene Four involving Friolera
and Doña Tadea. Against the background illuminated by moonlight the
old gossip acquires the stealthy, slinking form of a fox in pursuit of its prey,
while Don Friolera is seen in his room, a still, sad figure silhouetted in the
light of the lamp:

... Arrebujada en su manto de merinillo, pasa fisgona metiendo el hocico por rejas y puertas. En el claro de luna, el garabato de su sombra tiene reminiscencias de vulpeja ... Don Friolera, en el reflejo amarillo del quinqué, es un fantoche trágico ... (p.95)

... Wrapped in her woollen cloak, the nosey old woman passes by, poking her snout into doorways and through the bars of windows. In the light of the moon, the bent form of her shadow brings to mind a fox... Don Friolera, in the yellow light of the lamp, is a tragic puppet ...

In Scene Nine the stylized setting — the white wall, the orange-trees and the oranges touched by the setting sun — throws into absurd relief the seated figure of the brooding Friolera and his daughter whose stockings are around her ankles and who has about her *'la tristeza absurda de esas muñecas emigrades en los desvanes'* (p.138) *(The absurd sadness of those dolls banished to the attic)'* And in Scene Eleven the simple but boldly suggested romantic background of starry sky and moonlight filtering over the garden wall provides an ironic counterpoint to the absurd romantic rendezvous of Loreta and Pachequín. Less complex than the settings of the plays discussed earlier, those of *Los cuernos* are still an integral part of the dramatic action.

In the puppet theatre in general, speed of movement and gesture expresses the basic, uncomplicated feelings of the characters and in reducing to a simple, spontaneous level the complexity of human emotions, renders them comic. Through their simplification and undermining of the complexity and dignity of human behaviour, puppet theatre and farce lie traditionally, therefore, at the opposite end of the scale from tragedy. Valle-Inclán, in bringing together in *Los cuernos* the technique of puppet theatre and the matter of tragedy, strikes the peculiar, disconcerting tragic-comic note described already as being distinctive of much modern drama, and nothing illustrates the point better than his use of movement and gesture in this play. The situations are themselves those of the honour plays of the Golden Age — the dramatic confrontations of husband and wife, the suspicious husband's surprising of his wife and her lover at an unexpected moment—but their subjection to the techniques of the puppet theatre strips them of their seriousness and makes them merely ridiculous.[41] So in Scene Four Friolera accuses and pursues his protesting wife:

Don Friolera y Doña Loreta riñen a gritos, baten las puertas, entran y salen con los brazos abiertos ... (p.97)

Don Friolera and Doña Loreta quarrel at the top of their voices, slam doors, rush in and out with their arms extended ...

When she tries to escape, Friolera grabs her by the hair, and at the end of the scene Loreta *'bate con la frente en la puerta y se desmaya'* (beats her head on

the door and collapses in a faint) (p.102). The climax of the play, when
the husband finds his wife in the garden with her lover, is speeded up, very
much in the manner of a silent film, and in consequence the innate drama of
the situation is wholly undermined:

> *Don Friolera, dando traspiés, irrumpe en el huerto . . . Dispara el pistolón, y*
> *con un grito los fantoches luneros de la tapia se doblan sobre el otro huerto.*
> *Doña Loreta reaparece, los pelos de punta, los brazos levantados.* (p.161)

> *Don Friolera, tripping over himself, rushes into the garden . . . He fires the*
> *pistol, and with a yell the moonlit puppets climbing the wall tumble into the*
> *next-door garden. Doña Loreta reappears, her hair standing on end, her arms*
> *extended . . .*

The language of the play too often subverts tragic implications, for its
character, in accord with the violent and aggressive dialogue of the puppet
theatre in which the words themselves are the equivalent of physical blows,
divests the characters of any dignity. In the prologue to the play the
exchanges of Fidel's puppets are vigorous, colourful and often crude. In the
play itself the confrontation of husband and wife are conducted in a
screaming and hysterical manner which transforms genuine passion and
anger into a childish squabbling:

> DON FRIOLERA: ¡Disipada!
> DOÑA LORETA: ¡Verdugo!
> ....
> DON FRIOLERA: ¡Vas a morir!
> DOÑA LORETA: ¡Asesino!
> DON FRIOLERA: ¡Encomiéndate a Dios!   (p.98)

> DON FRIOLERA: Loose woman!
> DOÑA LORETA: Murderer!
> ....
> DON FRIOLERA: You are going to die!
> DOÑA LORETA: Assassin!
> DON FRIOLERA: Commend yourself to God!

The same transformation and movement away from tragedy to farce are
achieved elsewhere in other ways. Friolera's opening soliloquy is
reminiscent in its general pattern of the soliloquy of a Calderonian husband
beset by doubts, fears and suspicions, and driven, finally, to vengeance, but
Valle divests it of its seriousness by means of repetitions, exaggerations and
popular expressions which are totally incongruous:

... ¡A mis años andar a tiros! . . . ¿Y si cerrase los ojos para ese contrabando? ¿Y si resolviese no saber nada? ¡Este mundo es una solfa! ¿Qué culpa tiene el marido de que la mujer le salga rana? ¡Y no basta una honrosa separación! ¡Friolera! ¡Si bastase! . . . La galería no se conforma con eso. El principio del honor ordena matar. ¡Pim! ¡Pam! ¡Pum! . . .   (p.79)

... To be firing shots at my age! . . . What if I shut my eyes to all this carry-on? What if I decided to ignore it all? This world is a fine song and dance! Is a husband to blame, if his wife turns out a bitch? But an honourable separation is not enough! Friolera! If it were enough . . ! But the public in the gallery won't accept it. The code of honour commands us to kill. Bang! Bang! Bang!

The passage, like much of the play, operates on two levels. It allows us to see the anguish of the man but, as soon as that anguish is perceived, transforms it into the posturing of a puppet — 'Bang! Bang! Bang!' — deflating the tragic image. In terms of its dramatic and direct impact, the language of *Los cuernos* is not unlike the language of the other plays discussed here, but in other respects it reveals clearly the main thrust of Valle-Inclán's development as a dramatist: the movement away from the heroic perspective of the *Comedias bárbaras*, which presents man as a tragic hero, to the viewpoint of the *esperpento* which sees him as a tragic puppet, his humanity glimpsed still but rendered farcical and futile.

Valle-Inclán's contribution to the Spanish theatre of the twentieth century is highly significant in several ways. In turning his back on the conservative trends of the Spanish stage of his own time and refusing to be compromised by its largely commercial interests, he devised a highly personal kind of theatre in which, in terms of theme, a concern with man is ever present, and in which, in terms of technique, a preoccupation with the close integration of the different elements of stage performance is always evident. In both senses Valle is essentially anti-naturalistic, a writer who, in contrast to most Spanish dramatists of his own era, shattered traditional constraints and opened up new vistas in the theatre. In addition, given the innovative nature of his drama generally, it is also in the course of its own development from the *Comedias bárbaras* to the *esperpentos* a drama which constantly renews itself in its search for new forms of dramatic expression. In talking of Valle's theatre in relation to movements of a revolutionary kind that were taking place or would take place in other European countries — Symbolism, Expressionism, the Absurd — we are in effect, talking about artistic liberation. Valle's importance lies very clearly both in the striking originality of his drama and in its liberating influence on future Spanish dramatists.[42]

1 *Historia del teatro español siglo XX* (4th. ed.) (Madrid, 1980), 93.

2 See Mordecai Gorelik, *New Theatres for Old* (London, 1940). Chapters 4, 5 and 6 provide detailed and interesting accounts of Naturalism and Symbolism in the theatre.

3 Katharine Worth, *The Irish Drama of Europe from Yeats to Beckett* (London, 1978), 81, 12. Chapter 3 is devoted to the theatre of Maeterlinck. For a more detailed study of this writer see Bettina Knapp, *Maurice Maeterlinck* (New York, 1975).

4 All page references are to the edition published by Heinemann, 1980. The best study of Craig is by Denis Bablet, *The Theatre of Edward Gordon Craig*, translated by Daphne Woodward (London, 1981).

5 See *La lámpara maravillosa* (Buenos Aires, 1948), 113. Page references in the case of quotations from the plays are to the texts published in Austral as follows: *Romance de lobos* (6th ed.), (1977); *Águila de blasón* (4th ed.) (1976); *Cara de plata* (2nd ed.) (1964); *Luces de Bohemia* (11th ed.) (1980); *Los cuernos de don Friolera* (5th ed.) (1978). The English translations are in every case my own. A useful account of the philosophical and aesthetic background to Valle-Inclán's work is given by Verity Smith, *Ramón del Valle-Inclán* (New York, 1973), chapter 2.

6 Valle expressed his contempt for the contemporary Spanish theatre in an interview published in *A.B.C.* (23 June, 1927).

7 Useful studies of the *Comedias bárbaras* include: Alfredo Matilla, 'Las comedias bárbaras: una sola obra dramática', in *Ramón del Valle-Inclán. An Appraisal of His Life and Works*, ed. A.N. Zahareas (New York, 1968), 289-316; in the same volume, Roberta Salper de Tortella, 'Don Juan Manuel Montenegro: the Fall of a King', 317-32; J.M. Alberich, 'Cara de plata, fuera de serie', *Bulletin of Hispanic Studies*, XLV (1968), 299-308; Alfredo Matilla Rivas, *Las 'Comedias bárbaras'. Historicismo y expresionismo* (Salamanca, 1972). See too Manuel Bermejo Marcos, *Valle-Inclán. Introducción a su obra* (Salamanca, 1971), 120-37.

8 The social aspect of the trilogy is discussed by Verity Smith, *Ramón del Valle-Inclán*, 18. See too J.A. Gómez Marín, *La idea de sociedad en Valle-Inclán* (Madrid, 1967).

9 The translations into English are in every case my own.

10 'Some Thoughts on the Art of Gordon Craig', *The Studio*, XXIII, No.102 (1901), Supplement no: 36, 82.

11 The character of Valle-Inclán's stage directions has been discussed by several critics, notably J.L. Brooks, 'Los dramas de Valle-Inclán, in *Estudios dedicados a Menéndez Pidal* (Madrid, 1957), VII, 182, and Alfredo Matilla, 'Las comedias bárbaras: una sola obra dramática', 294-5.

12 See Denis Bablet, *The Theatre of Edward Gordon Craig*, 57.

13 'Valle-Inclán and the Art of the Theatre', *Bulletin of Hispanic Studies*, XLVI (1969), 139. While this is an excellent study of the various aspects of Valle-Inclán's theatre, Lyon does not examine it in a European context. An attempt of a rather general nature to relate Valle-Inclán and Craig, has been made by Roberto Sánchez, 'Gordon Craig y Valle-Inclán', *Revista de Occidente*, 4 (1976), 27-37.

14 'Some Thoughts on the Art of Gordon Craig', 82.

15 *The Theatre of Edward Gordon Graig*, 42.

16 On stage lighting in the symbolist theatre see Mordecai Gorelik, *New Theatres for Old*, 191-5.

17 'Valle-Inclán and the Art of the Theatre', 144.

18 See Mordecai Gorelik, *New Theatres for Old*, 188.

19 An informative introduction to the subject is provided by R.S. Furness, *Expressionism,* in the series *The Critical Idiom,* ed. John D. Jump (London, 1973).

20 Preface to *Die Unsterblichen,* in *Dichtungen* (Neuwied, 1960), 60-5. The translation into English is my own.

21 Ibid., 65.

22 Elements of distortion and the grotesque are to be found in the whole of Valle-Inclán's theatre, as well as his novels, in varying degrees. For reasons already explained the farces written between 1909 and 1919 in which social concerns and techniques of distortion are very apparent have not been examined here. The reader is referred to the following articles published in *Ramón del Valle-Inclán. An Appraisal of His Life and Works . . .;* Emma Susana Speratti-Piñero, 'La farsa de *La cabeza del dragón,* pre-*esperpento',* 374-85; Sumner Greenfield, *'La reina castiza* and the Esthetics of Deformation', 541-52. See too Manuel Bermejo Marcos, *Valle-Inclán. Introducción a su obra,* 167-85.

23 There are many useful studies of *esperpentismo,* in particular that of Rodolfa Cardona and A.N. Zahareas, *Visión del esperpento* (Madrid, 1970). See too Antonio Risco, *La estética de Valle-Inclán* (Madrid, 1966), 79-109; Alfonso Sastre, *Antomía del realismo* (Barcelona, 1965), 56-67; A.N. Zahareas, 'The Esperpento and Aesthetics of Commitment', *Modern Language Notes, LXXXI* (1966), 159-73; J.L. Brooks, 'Valle-Inclán and the Esperpento', *Bulletin of Hispanic Studies,* XXXIII (1956), 152-64; J. Rea, 'Theatre Done with Mirrors: Valle-Inclán's esperpentos', *Theatre Arts,* XXXVII, (1953), 30-1; María Eugenia March, *Forma e idea de los esperpentos de Valle-Inclán* (Madrid, 1969); Pedro Salinas, 'Significacíon del Esperpento o Valle-Inclán, hijo pródigo del 98', *Cuadernos Americanos,* Mexico, VI, 2 (1947), 218-44; and Francisco Ruiz Ramón, *Historia del teatro español siglo XX . . .,* 118-26.

24 There is a perceptive discussion of the different perspectives of the dramatist in Antonio Buero Vallejo, *Tres maestros ante el público (Valle-Inclán, Velázquez, Lorca)* (Madrid, 1973), 29-54.

25 *The Theatre of the Absurd* (revised ed.) (London, 1969), 346.

26 The relationship of the play's characters to real people is discussed by A. Zamora Vicente, *La realidad esperpéntica. (Aproximación a 'Luces de bohemia')* (Madrid, 1969). See too Allen W. Phillips, 'Sobre *Luces de Bohemia* y su realidad literaria', in *Ramón del Valle-Inclán: An Appraisal . . .,* 601-11.

27 See Mordecai Gorelik, *New Theatres for Old,* 248-54; R.S. Furness, *Expressionism,* 47-75; and B.J. Kenworthy, *Georg Kaiser* (Oxford, 1957).

28 *The Theatre of the Absurd,* 352. There is a useful study of this aspect of *Luces de Bohemia* by Gerald Gillespie and Anthony Zahareas, *'Luces de Bohemia:* Tragedia y esperpento', in *Ramón del Valle-Inclán: An Appraisal . . .,* 615-21.

29 *New Theatres for Old,* 253.

30 *Georg Kaiser,* 195.

31 *Georg Kaiser,* 194.

32 *New Theatres for Old,* 253.

33 'Dans les armes de la ville', *Cahiers de la Compagnie Madeleine Renaud-Jean-Louis Barrault,* XX (Paris, 1957).

34 On the question of the dramatist's perspective see Antonio Buero Vallejo, *Tres maestros ante el público (Valle-Inclán, Velázquez, Lorca),* 29-54, and Francisco Ruiz Ramón, *Historia del teatro español siglo XX,* 122-3. Both writers agree that Valle's perspective differs somewhat in practice from the rather simplified standpoint suggested by his theoretical statements.

35 Alfred Jarry, 'Questions de théâtre', in *Ubu Roi* (Lausanne, 1948), 158.

36 *Autobiographies* (London, 1955), 348-9.

37 *The Theatre of the Absurd*, 309.

38 For studies of the play see Anthony Zahareas, 'Friolera: el héroe visto con "la perspectiva de la ribera"' in *Ramón del Valle-Inclán: An Appraisal*, 630-5, and in the same volume Rodolfo Cardona, '*Los cuernos de Don Friolera:* estructura y sentido', 636-71; Pedro A. González, 'Los cuernos de Don Friolera', *La Torre*, II (1954), no.8, 45-54; and José Francisco Gatti, 'El sentido de *Los cuernos de don Friolera*', in *Ramón María del Valle-Inclán* (Universidad Nacional de la Plata, 1967), 298-313.

39 *Historia del teatro español siglo XX*, 131-4.

40 See Richard N. Coe, *Ionesco, A Study of His Plays* (London, 1971), 40-1.

41 On this aspect of the play see Javier Herrero, 'La sátira del honor en los esperpentos', in *Ramón del Valle-Inclán: An Appraisal*, 672-85.

42 I should like to draw the reader's attention to John Lyon, *The Theatre of Valle-Inclán* (Cambridge, 1983). This is an excellent, wide-ranging study, published since the completion of this book.

CHAPTER III

Federico García Lorca

Lorca completed his first play, *El maleficio de la mariposa (The Butterfly's Evil Spell)*, in 1920, the year of Valle-Inclán's remarkable *Luces de Bohemia*, and his last, *La casa de Bernarda Alba (The House of Bernarda Alba)*, in 1936, the year of his own and Valle-Inclán's death and of the outbreak of the Spanish Civil War. Lorca's greatest and best-known plays — including *Bodas de sangre (Blood Wedding)*, *Yerma (The Barren One)* and *La casa de Bernarda Alba* — were in effect composed a decade or more after Valle's, but in many other respects there is much that links both dramatists. The Spanish stage of Lorca's time continued to be dominated in terms of popular demand by those dramatists mentioned in the previous chapter in relation to Valle-Inclán: Benavente, the Quintero brothers, Eduardo Marquina, Manuel Linares Rivas and others whose conventional pieces kept the theatre on its largely conformist and unexceptional path. Commenting on the Spanish theatre-going public of the period, Leopoldo Rodríguez Alcalde has drawn attention to its lack of aesthetic awareness and intellectual curiosity.[1] The problems that confronted Lorca in relation to theatrical taste and fashion were therefore those that Valle-Inclán had found so daunting: in particular, a commercially orientated theatre governed by bourgeois attitudes and controlled by actors, producers and impresarios whose main concerns were fame and profit. In seeking to rescue the theatre from its deeply entrenched mediocrity, Lorca, following Valle's example, produced a body of work which, though very different from Valle's, was written very much in opposition to the popular drama of the 1920s and 1930s and whose essence lies in its originality and constant experiment.

Lorca's dozen or so plays, written in a mere sixteen years, embrace many traditions and reveal a great variety of influences, dramatic and otherwise, Spanish and foreign.[2] In the years since his death Lorca has become for many the twentieth-century Spanish poet-dramatist 'par excellence', a reputation founded almost entirely on such works as the *Romancero gitano (Gipsy Ballads)*, the *Poema del Cante Jondo (Poem of Deep Song)* and the three rural tragedies, all of which project the mood and atmosphere of southern Spain and serve to colour further foreign preconceptions of the country and the writer. It is an image of Lorca which has spread his fame and popularity throughout the world — a Spanish Dylan Thomas — but which has prevented a true appreciation both of the originality and the European aspect of his work. Against this broader background Lorca's theatre can be constructively examined in relation to those movements — in particular Symbolism and Surrealism — that in the first third of the century sought to liberate artists from the shackles of the past. The following discussion of Lorca's theatre, concentrated for convenience on particular plays, will touch too on other topics, notably the cinema, and will reveal clearly the extent to which the most famous Spanish dramatist of the twentieth century was an important part of the European *avant-garde*.

Lorca's first play, *El maleficio de la mariposa*, was performed at the Teatro Eslava in Madrid on 22 March 1920. Its action portrays the love of a young cockroach, Curianito, for a beautiful wounded butterfly, Mariposa, who becomes the object of his dreams and on whose account he abandons Silvia, a female cockroach wholly devoted to him. Fascinated by the world of light and beauty evoked by the lovely, shimmering, fragile butterfly, Curianito aspires to something beyond the limitations of his own humble and constricting sphere of activity, but in the end his hopes are ruthlessly dashed when Mariposa recovers from her injuries and flies away. For the young dramatist venturing onto the Spanish stage, the performance of his first play proved to be disastrous. A public accustomed to the 'bourgeois interiors' of Benavente with their 'realistic' characters and elegant language reacted sharply to a play in which the characters were cockroaches. But although it received only two performances *El maleficio de la mariposa* is a very important play in relation to the rest of Lorca's theatre, for in its largely symbolist character it has distinctive features that are everywhere apparent in the later works.

Lorca's familiarity with progressive movements in the arts can be related to his stay at the Residencia de Estudiantes in Madrid, which he entered in 1919, a year before the performance of *El maleficio de la mariposa*. The Residencia was a famous institution where students lived while following courses there or elsewhere in the capital and it was distinguished in particular by a liberal intellectual atmosphere, which encouraged them to exchange ideas and develop their own creative talent. Here it was that the young and receptive Federico encountered such talented young men as the poet, Juan Ramón Jiménez, the future champions of Surrealism, Salvador Dalí and Luis Buñuel, the playwright and director, Gregorio Martínez Sierra, and, amongst foreign guests, G.K. Chesterton, H.G. Wells, François Mauriac and Igor Stravinsky. Of these gifted individuals it was Martínez Sierra who was to exercise the greatest influence on Lorca's first dramatic venture. From 1917 to 1925 Martínez Sierra was director of the Teatro Eslava where he developed his interest in modern theatre techniques and produced plays by modern Spanish and foreign writers, including Carlos Arniches, Eduardo Marquina, Bernard Shaw and James Barrie. In terms of stage design Martínez Sierra's contribution to the Spanish theatre was essentially forward-looking and has been described as decisive by the Spanish critic, Enrique Díez-Canedo.[3] Secondly, his work as a translator was important, for he brought to the attention of educated Spaniards the plays of contemporary foreign dramatists, including Barrie, Courteline, Tristan Bernard and Maurice Maeterlinck. As far as the origin of *El maleficio de la mariposa* is concerned, José Mora Guarnido has observed that Martínez Sierra heard Lorca recite some poems about insect life, one of which dealt with the love of a young cockroach for an injured butterfly, and suggested that he write a play on the subject, to be performed at the Teatro Eslava.[4] Given the director's interest in Lorca's work and his championing of a dramatist like Maeterlinck, there can surely be no doubt that the influence of the Belgian symbolist playwright is considerable in relation to *El maleficio*. Maeterlinck's *L'Oiseau Bleu*, written in 1905, is a clear point of connexion both in subject matter and technique. Lorca's predilection for themes that are universal in their relevance, for the creation of generic characters, and for a means of expression that rejected realism in favour of a more poetic style, would in any case have attracted him to the symbolist theatre. The circumstances in which he found himself in 1919 made that likelihood a certainty.

The prologue to Lorca's play indicates both his anti-Naturalism and his belief that a public accustomed to Benavente and his school would accept only reluctantly a different kind of drama. In a somewhat defensive manner the young dramatist argues that human experiences, be they of love, despair or death, may be convincingly communicated in a story whose characters are insects, for an old wood sylph has instructed him to say that such experiences are universal:

> . . . di, poeta, a los hombres que el amor nace con la misma intensidad en todos los planos de la vida; que el mismo ritmo que tiene la hoja mecida por el aire tiene la estrella lejana, y que las mismas palabras que dice la fuente en la umbría las repite con el mismo tono el mar; dile al hombre que sea humilde, ¡todo es igual en la Naturaleza![5]   (II., pp.6-7)

> . . . Poet, inform men that love is born with the same intensity in all levels of life; that the movement of a leaf blown by the wind is the same as that of a distant star, and that the words uttered by the fountain in a shady spot are repeated by the sea in the same tones; tell men to be humble, for in Nature all things are equal!

Lorca's symbolist preoccupation with the expression of universal truths and with the revelation in his drama of the true, unadorned essence of things is revealed constantly both in his statements and his plays. In *El público (The Public)*, written in 1930, his stated aim was to penetrate beneath the appearance of things to reveal the true passions that link all men — 'el perfil de una fuerza oculta' ('the profile of a hidden force') (p.155).[6] Just as W.B. Yeats had set himself the task of exploring the 'interior' and Maeterlinck of suggesting much more than is seen on stage, so Lorca's concerns involved the mysteries that confront man both within and outside himself, even if the characters of his first play were insects.

Maeterlinck's *L'Oiseau Bleu* focuses on the quest of two children, Tyltyl and Mytyl, for the Blue Bird which, they have been told, will cure the sick child of a neighbour. The play, as Bettina Knapp has shown, has a precise symbolic meaning which derives from Maeterlinck's philosophical and metaphysical interests, and each stage of the children's journey can be interpreted accordingly.[7] For audiences in general, though, and for Lorca in particular, it was the play's broader symbolic meaning which made more impact. The two children in search of the Blue Bird assume universal qualities of innocence, dream and fantasy. When Night obstructs them, Light guards them, and the Blue Bird escapes. Their experience captures the very essence of human aspiration, disappointment and ultimate failure.

The general symbolism of *El maleficio de la mariposa* is clearly in the tradition of Maeterlinck, for while the characters are cockroaches, glow-worms and a butterfly, they are essentially generic figures, the embodiment of universal experiences, attitudes and feelings which anticipate the human characters of Lorca's mature drama. The protagonist, Curianito el Nene (young boybeetle) is the very epitome of youth, the insect equivalent of the young men who in the later plays are often designated by symbolic names — el Joven (the young man) of *Así que pasen cinco años (When Five Years Have Passed)* and el Novio (the bridegroom) of *Bodas de sangre*. Curianito is endowed, indeed, in a highly stylized manner, with the essential qualities of youth, as in Act Two, Scene Six, where vibrant colouring reinforces the effect of youthfulness:

> *Aparece* CURIANITO EL NENE, *pintado graciosísimamente de amarillo*
> . . .   (II., p.54)

> THE YOUNG BOYBEETLE *appears, painted a most charming yellow* . . .

On an emotional level, moreover, he possesses the archetypal, poetic and romantic nature of all young men.

Curianito's female counterpart, Curianita Silvia (girlbeetle Sylvia) embodies the beauty and the illusions that in Lorca's later drama are embodied in characters as clearly symbolic as la Novia (the bride) in both *Así que pasen cinco años* and *Bodas de sangre*, and Yerma in the play of the same name. In addition, in the insect world of the play, youth, love and illusions are counterbalanced by images of destruction, age, disillusionment and death. Alacranito El Corta-Mimbres (little scorpion the reed-cutter), constantly threatening with his pincers the fragile limbs of the young lovers, anticipates the sinister Leñadores (the woodcutters) of *Bodas de sangre*. The three Gusanos (the glow-worms), whose beauty is already fading, are the symbols both of beauty and of age, to be paralleled later by el Viejo (the old man) of *Así que pasen cinco años*, the ageing Rosita of *Doña Rosita la soltera*, and the fading daughters of Bernarda Alba.

Mariposa, the butterfly, is, like Maeterlinck's Blue Bird, the embodiment of illusion, her wings a perfect image of fragile beauty, her flight an effective equivalent for the elusive nature of human happiness. The image is one which Lorca was to use again both in *El paseo de Buster Keaton (Buster Keaton's Spin)* and *La zapatera prodigiosa (The Shoemaker's Prodigious Wife)*. In his very first play it is clear that Lorca dramatized thus not merely the particular loves, hopes, disappointment and despair of individual characters, but the passions and concerns that are common to us all.

In terms of dramatic style and technique, *El maleficio* reveals already Lorca's fondness for that integration of different art forms so revered by the Symbolists. Both Maeterlinck and Gordon Craig were deeply influenced in relation to their appreciation of the visual impact of the theatre by their knowledge of painting, and both were responsive too to the expressive power of music and dance.[8] Of W.B. Yeats, Katherine Worth has observed: 'He had an exceptionally lively visual imagination, not surprisingly, coming as he did from a family of talented painters. He himself trained at an art school for two years. He was acutely sensitive to the power of stage pictures, knew how they could enhance the spoken word or distract from it, by wrong grouping, perhaps, or by dim lighting which put a strain on the eye . . .'[9] Lorca's own interest in drawing and painting similarly explains the powerful visual impact of his plays, and it is not without significance that in 1933 he designed the costumes and sets for the performance of Manuel de Falla's ballet suite, *El amor brujo (Love the Magician)*. Mention of Falla points too not only to Lorca's friendship with him, which dated from the years preceding the composition of *El maleficio*, but also draws attention to the dramatist's love of music, both Spanish and classical, and of song and ballet. Lorca's development as a dramatist was one in which the concept of total theatre became increasingly important, and in that development *El maleficio* is a significant and anti-naturalist beginning.

The stage directions call, as in Maeterlinck's *L'Oiseau Bleu*, for stylized settings which capture the essence of a scene. Thus, the opening scene symbolizes the fresh, unspoilt beauty of dawn:

> *La escena representa un prado verde y humilde bajo la sombra densa de un gran ciprés . . . Más allá del pradito, una pequeña charca rodeada de espléndidas azucenas y unas piedras azules . . . Es la hora casta del amanecer. Y todo el prado está cubierto de rocío . . .*   (II.,p.9)

> *The stage represents a humble green meadow beneath the deep shade of a large cypress. Beyond the meadow is a small pond surrounded by magnificent lilies and blue stones . . . It is the pure hour of dawn. And the whole of the meadow is bathed in dew.*

The physical setting has here a Garden of Eden purity and perfection which becomes a frame for the dreams and illusions of the characters, and, ceasing to be merely a piece of decoration, it functions as an image of emotional experience. Conversely, for both Lorca and Maeterlinck darkness signifies both the destruction of hope and the extinction of life. In Act Two the beautiful setting of *El maleficio* is already touched by twilight, presaging Curianito's anguish:

> *. . . Todas las plantas están pintadas con luz suave del crepúsculo maduro.*
>   (II., p.39)

> *. . . All the plants are bathed in the soft light of deep twilight.*

Shortly afterwards twilight has become the darkness of night. Within the stage settings lighting is, indeed, particularly important throughout the play, an integral part of the stage design, serving to add emphasis to images both of beauty and illusion as well as of death and destruction.

The movements and postures of the characters have their own expressive power. In Act One, Scene Four the romantic Curianito sits dreamily on a stone:

> CURIANITO *se sienta en una piedrecita blanca y mueve las antenas con lentitud.*   (II., p.23)

> THE YOUNG BOY BEETLE *sits on a small white stone and slowly waves his antennae.*

By the end of the Act stillness and immobility have become the expression not of daydream but of despair, a recurring physical motif in Lorca's theatre:

> *Se sienta en la piedra y llora con la cabecita entre las manos.*   (II.,p.38)

> *He sits on the stone and weeps, his little head held in his hands.*

The influence of the language of ballet is prominent in Act Two, Scene Seven when the butterfly attempts to rise and dance, falls to the ground, is embraced by Curianito, withdraws from him and begins to dance again. At the other extreme the gross, insensitive and dangerous presence of Alacranito is effectively conveyed, from the moment of his first appearance, in lumbering, staggering movements, vigorous leaps and the axe-like swing of his pincer.

The language of *El maleficio* is typically symbolist. It is no accident that Lorca should make his characters speak poetry, for poetry has the dual effect of universalizing, by means of its allusive nature, the particular incidents of the play, and of accentuating, in consequence of its musicality, the difference between the characters. As to the first point, Curianito's final words, expressing his own anguish, encapsulate the anguish of all men:

> ¿Quién me puso estos ojos que no quiero
> y estas manos que tratan
> de prender un amor que no comprendo?
> ¡Y con mi vida acaba! (II., p.57)

> Who gave me these eyes I do not want
> and these hands that seek
> to grasp a love beyond my understanding?
> A love that ends my life!

Moreover, the yearnings and sorrows of Curianito, Sylvia and the glow-worms, expressed in rhythms which convey those feelings, contrast markedly with the jerky, loud and uncouth utterances of the greedy Alacranito:

> Tenía una pata rota
> y yo me la comí.
> Era una hermosa araña.
> *(Riendo a cacajadas.)* (II., p.33)

> She had a broken leg
> and I ate her up.
> She was a lovely spider.
> *(Cackling with laughter.)*

In short, the language of Lorca's first play, expressing universal experiences and emotions, is fully within the tradition of the Symbolists mentioned previously. In howling down *El maleficio de la mariposa*, the audiences who attended its two performances revealed very clearly both their allegiance to the naturalist theatre and their failure to understand Lorca's intentions.

* * * * * *

After the disappointing public reception of *El maleficio de la mariposa,*
Lorca did not write another play for five years, completing *Mariana Pineda*
in 1925. Performed first at the Teatro Goya in Barcelona in June 1927, and
later in the year at the Teatro Fontalba in Madrid, the play received
considerable public and critical acclaim, and its success more than
compensated Lorca for the failure of his first venture on the commercial
stage. In *Mariana Pineda* he had hit on a subject with which, given its
historical and Spanish background and thus its greater realism, theatre-
goers were able to identify more easily.[10]

The action of the play, set in the reign of Ferdinand VII (1808-33), deals
with Mariana's involvement in the republican opposition to the King and
with her love for Pedro, one of the republican leaders. In order to avoid
capture by Pedrosa, the King's harsh and brutal representative, Pedro is
obliged to flee to safety and Mariana, the object of Pedrosa's desires and
the means of luring Pedro back, is arrested. The final Act presents Mariana
awaiting execution. She clings still to the hope that Pedro will return to
rescue her, but her hopes are dashed when news arrives that he has left
Spain. The play ends with Mariana's execution and her defiant assertion of
the ideal of freedom.

As far as sources are concerned, the story of Mariana Pineda was a very
well-known one in Granada. Local archives contained many documents
relating to her trial and execution and there were many popular ballads too
which celebrated her heroism. Lorca was, indeed, confronted by an
abundance of material on which to base his play. As a dramatist, though, he
was less interested in the historical details of Mariana's story than in the
possibilities it offered him of exploring those themes already evident in *El
maleficio de la mariposa.* The theme of passion, symbolized in the earlier
play in the insect lovers, is exemplified now in Mariana and Pedro. Passion,
moreover, as is ever the case in Lorca's theatre, is closely linked to
frustration. Mariana, waiting in vain for Pedro, is its most eloquent
expression, but Pedro too is frustrated in his love of her, and so is Fernando
whose love for Mariana is unrequited. In addition, the play is dominated
from the very outset by the imminence of death, so often connected in
Lorca's work to passion and frustration. In the very first scene the red
thread with which Mariana sews the republican flag is a portent of her
death. Later, destroyed by Pedro's abandonment of her even before her
execution, she shares the fate of Curianito in *El maleficio* and anticipates
many of Lorca's later heroines, especially Doña Rosita in *Doña Rosita la
soltera (Doña Rosita the Spinster).* The instrument of death here, the evil
Pedrosa, is the human form of the scorpion of *El maleficio,* constantly
threatening Mariana in the way that the scorpion threatens the insect

lovers. He embodies, moreover, the sense of fatality that runs through the play, anticipating such deadly figures as the fatal Jugadores, the cardplayers, of *Así que pasen cinco años,* and the Leñadores, the woodcutters, and la Mendiga, the beggar woman symbolic of death, of *Bodas de sangre.* Lorca's achievement in *Mariana Pineda* is to have transformed the insects of *El maleficio de la mariposa* into human beings and, secondly, to have invested the human characters with archetypal, universal dimensions. In the sense that *Mariana Pineda* suggests eternal concerns and conflicts, it is as symbolist in character as *El maleficio de la mariposa.*

To all appearances, *Mariana Pineda* is from the point of view of technique a more realistic play than *El maleficio.* The prologue, taking the form of a ballad which recounts Mariana's tragedy, suggests a sense of history, of distancing, which is reinforced by Lorca's description of each Act as an 'estampa', a print or engraving. In addition, a realistic background is created by the political background against which the action is set, while the characters are, of course, historical figures. Nevertheless, the play's realism is, in the last resort, less important than its poetic and symbolic qualities, for, as in *El maleficio,* both action and characters function on a poetic and universal level to which the play's technique makes a vital contribution.

The settings are in one sense realistic. The opening stage direction of the estampa primera — the first Act — presents, for example, a room in Mariana's house with various items of furniture:

> ... *Sobre una mesa, un frutero de cristal lleno de membrillos... Encima de la cómoda, grandes ramos de rosas de seda ...* (II., p.123)

> ... *On a table, a glass fruit bowl filled with quinces... On a chest of drawers, large bouquets of roses of silk ...*

On the other hand, allusions to the white walls of the room, to the red of the roses, and the dark dress of Doña Angustias, Mariana's adoptive mother, already introduce a strongly symbolic element, for they foreshadow Mariana's paleness, the spilling of her blood and the blackness of despair that overtakes her. Similarly, in Act Two the rain and the wind which buffet the house suggest the greater conflicts and storms to which Mariana and Pedro are exposed. And in Act Three the convent where Mariana is imprisoned until her death is more than a physical prison, for its silence and its sense of emptiness point to Mariana's emotional desolation.

Costume, lighting, movement and language are also used by Lorca to create a stylized and poetic effect. The black clothes of Pedrosa, framing his white face, become an image of evil, while in Act Three Mariana's

'esplendido traje blanco' ('magnificent white dress') (II., p.202) is the very
embodiment of purity, innocence and fragility that are always threatened
by the powers of darkness. In terms of lighting, the play is, indeed, a journey
into a darkness whose physical manifestation, as in the case of *El maleficio
de la mariposa*, is the outward representation of inner states, a favourite
symbolist technique. The onset of night in the closing scenes accompanies
and echoes Mariana's sense of abandonment and the imminence of her
death. As far as movement is concerned, the earlier agitation of the play,
reflecting conflict and tension, has subsided into a stillness and immobility
evocative of hopelessness:

> *Se sienta en un banco y apoya la cabeza sobre sus manos . . .*   (II., p.209)
>
> *She sits on a bench and rests her head in her hands . . .*

In terms of language, the verse of *Mariana Pineda* functions for most of the
time as dialogue and has much of the character of prose. On the other hand,
there are many passages in which the allusive nature of poetry extends the
range of meaning, universalizing the particular experience of the
characters. In the end the apparent realism of the play dissolves before its
poetic and symbolic qualities in a way which, as we shall see, would
characterize Lorca's later drama.

Lorca's opposition to the naturalistic theatre is reflected too in his
allegiance to the traditions and techniques of puppet-theatre and farce.[11]
Even as a child he had entertained the members of his family, the servants
of the household and their children with the performance of plays in the
little puppet-theatre bought for him by his parents. On 6 January 1923,
Lorca and Manuel de Falla organized a children's festival at the Lorca
household in Granada which included his own puppet-play, *La niña que
riega la albahaca (The Girl who Waters the Basil Plant)*. Lorca himself
designed the sets and the small stage and worked the puppet figures. A
second puppet-play, *Tragicomedia de Don Cristóbal y la señá Rosita
(Tragicomedy of Don Cristóbal and Miss Rosita)*, may have been written
even earlier, and in 1931 he wrote a third, *El retablillo de Don Cristóbal
(The 'retablillo' of Don Cristóbal)*. In 1926 he had commenced work on
his most famous farce, *La zapatera prodigiosa (The Shoemaker's
Prodigious Wife)*, completed and premiered in 1930 and performed in a
revised and expanded form in 1933, and in 1928 he completed *Amor de
Don Perlimplín con Belisa en su jardín (The Love of Don Perlimplín for
Belisa in the Garden)*. In the 1920s, with the exception of *El maleficio* and
Mariana Pineda, puppet-plays and farces evidently preoccupied the
developing dramatist. In the 1930s he would turn his attention to other
forms of drama, but in the surrealist plays and the rural tragedies of those

later years the imprint of the puppet-plays and farces is still clearly visible in the human characters.

Lorca's interest in this kind of theatre is simply explained. In the first place tradition occupies a very important place in Lorca's work in general, be it theatre or poetry, and the puppet-theatre itself has been popular in Spain for centuries. Cervantes had introduced a puppet show — *El retablo de Maese Pedro (Master Peter's Puppet Show)* — into the second part of *Don Quixote*. In the Madrid of Lorca's time there were frequent puppet-shows and while at the Residencia de Estudiantes Lorca, together with Juan Chabas and Luis Buñuel, had become acquainted with a puppeteer called Mayeu who mounted performances for children in the Retiro Park. They helped him in the preparation of more ambitious puppet-shows which were also given at the Residencia itself. The tradition of farce was also an old one in Spanish literary history. In the late fifteenth and early sixteenth centuries Gil Vicente, Juan del Encina and Torres Naharro had written comic plays which contain the stock types and the stylized situations of the Italian *commedia dell'arte*. In the mid-sixteenth century Lope de Rueda composed his short comic sketches, the *pasos*, which were distinguished by their boldly drawn comic characters, amusing situations and down-to-earth language. And finally there was Cervantes himself, a master of comic theatre and a constant source of inspiration to future Spanish writers. Cervantes's *entremeses*, short comic pieces to be performed between the acts of full-length plays, were published in 1615. Full of ingenious situations and comic but human characters, they were a model of their kind. Lorca's admiration for Cervantes is reflected in the fact that in the childrens' festival at his home in 1923 Lorca included Cervantes's comic play, *Los dos habladores (The Two Gossips)* in the programme.

In addition to these models from the past, contemporary Spanish dramatists also provided Lorca with notable examples of puppet-plays and farces. Both Valle-Inclán and Jacinto Grau are important influences, while Carlos Arniches cannot be ignored. Arniches was, as has already been observed, the master of the *género chico*, short comic pieces portraying popular types and customs which he developed into full-length plays — the *tragedias grotescas (grotesque tragedies)*. In these plays stock comic characters and situations acquire serious overtones, are presented as both amusing and absurd, and the play itself becomes an instrument of social satire and criticism. In the hands of Valle-Inclán puppet characters and farcical techniques serve to amuse and to ridicule in a manner much more cutting than that employed by Arniches. *Farsa y licencia de la reina castiza (Farce and Licentiousness of the Pure Queen)*, written in 1919 and described as a 'farsa para muñecos' ('a farce for dolls'), is above all a savage parody of the nineteenth-century Spanish monarch, Isabel III, its characters grotesque caricatures, its laughter bitter. But puppets could also be used for more than social criticism, and the previous chapter has suggested that in *Los cuernos de Don Friolera* the characters suggest the absurdity and the futility of the human condition itself. It was this theme that was developed by Jacinto Grau in *El señor de Pigmalión (Mr Pygmalion)*, written in 1921, for in this play Mr Pygmalion creates a number of mechanical life-size puppets only to become in the end a puppet in their hands, a man ruled by the machines of his own creation. During the 1920s the view of man as a puppet figure manipulated by the harsh, unfeeling nature of the world in which he finds himself was, of course, a very prevalent one. Virginia Higginbotham has drawn attention to the Italian dramatists of the *teatro del grottesco (theatre of the grotesque)* who 'frequently dramatized the helplessness of man by use of puppets'.[12] Similarly, many of Pirandello's characters are puppet-like figures, worked upon by forces they cannot control. In the European theatre of more recent times, dramatists like Ionesco and Arrabal have made telling use of the traditions and techniques of puppetry and farce to project their own particular view of the absurdity of human life. In short, in twentieth-century theatre in general, playwrights of vision and imagination have invested the comic tradition with a new seriousness, employing it both as an instrument for social criticism and as a comment on the human predicament.

Quite apart from the new possibilities afforded by the puppet farce in terms of theme, its inherent characteristics provided dramatists with the opportunity of escaping from the strictures of the commercial and the naturalistic theatre in both an economic and artistic sense. As to the first point, both Gordon Craig and Valle-Inclán sought in their different ways control of their work that the economic pressures of the commercial stage would have otherwise denied them. Lorca directed his own anger against the tyranny of economic factors:

> Eso de que un señor, por el mero hecho de disponer de unos millones, se erija en censor de obras y definidor del teatro, es intolerable y vergonzoso. Es una tiranía que, como todas, sólo conduce al desastre.   (II., pp.972-3)

> That a man, by the mere fact of availing himself of a few millions, should set himself up as a censor of plays and arbiter of the theatre is intolerable and shameful. It is a tyranny that, like any other tyranny, can lead us only to disaster.

The puppet-theatre, in which the dramatist himself controlled the whole performance, effectively freed him from the commercial concerns of impresarios and the artistic vanity of actors and directors. But it also did more than that, for in the puppet figure Lorca saw an opportunity for that freedom of expression, spontaneity and vitality which he felt to be the vital ingredients of a living theatre. The puppets could, in short, express action and emotion in a simple, bold, direct and dramatic manner that for Lorca was the very essence of theatre. In the prologue to the *Retablillo de Don Cristóbal* he has the poet refer to 'el delicioso y duro lenguaje de los muñecos' ('the delicious and hard language of the puppets') (II., p.491). And when, at the end of the play, the director gathers in the puppets, he draws a revealing distinction between the liveliness of puppet-theatre and the stale Naturalism of contemporary Spanish theatre:

> Las malas palabras adquieren ingenuidad y frescura dichas por muñecos . . . Llenemos el teatro de espigas frescas, debajo de las cuales vayan palabrotas que luchen en la escena con el tedio y la vulgaridad a que la tenemos condenada . . . (II., p.513)

> Bad words acquire frankness and freshness when they are spoken by puppets . . . Let us fill the theatre with fresh wheat and from it let there spring the bold words that will confront the tediousness and vulgarity to which we have condemned the theatre. . .

It is interesting to note in this connexion Gordon Craig's preoccupation with the puppet figure, expressed originally in 1905 in his famous essay, *The Actor and the Über-Marionette*.[13] Craig fully recognized the marionette's expressive power and he saw too its capacity to convey in bold movement and gesture not the fussy details of Naturalism but the symbolism and ritual that in his view constituted the art of the theatre. And, like Lorca, Craig was constantly aware of the extent to which the commercial interests of the theatre, including the star system which regarded the actor as more important than the work, militated against the creation of true art. A consideration of *La zapatera prodigiosa* shows quite clearly that Lorca, like many significant dramatists of the twentieth century, employed the traditions and techniques of puppet-theatre and farce both for serious purposes and as a means of escape from the confines of Naturalism.[14]

The plot of *La zapatera prodigiosa* focuses on the marriage of the old Zapatero, the shoemaker, to the young and spirited Zapatera and on the consequences of their marriage, in particular their own mutual disappointment and the villagers' mockery of them. In taking a theme which from classical times had been the subject of innumerable comic works, Lorca did not, of course, neglect its comic possibilities, and the swiftly moving action, the often grotesque characters, the use of disguise and the colourful and earthy language all combine to produce many moments of great hilarity. At the same time, the simplified, even symbolical figures of the play — in line with Ortega y Gasset's theories on dehumanized art, expressed in 1925 in *La deshumanización del arte* — allowed Lorca to confront his audience with serious problems without shocking it unduly, for the play's characters, though played by actors, are puppets who require relatively little human sympathy. Above all, *La zapatera* ruthlessly exposes, beneath the guise of laughter, particular social attitudes. In particular, Lorca gives expression here to a theme which in the later rural tragedies — *Bodas de sangre, Yerma* and *La casa de Bernarda Alba* — becomes part of the tragic conflict and which even in this lively farce is already a powerful factor in the unhappiness of the married couple: the theme of social honour and reputation, so deeply ingrained in the Spanish temperament. In the play's first Act the old man and his wife are already the object of the villagers' mockery and scorn, for in a society in which the man must wear the trousers and the wife must bear his children the hen-pecked Zapatero and his childless wife invite only ridicule. Inasmuch as they are from the outset the prisoners of a community ruled by traditional views, the Zapatero and his wife react to public mockery, he by pleading with her that she should not provoke a scandal, she by taunting him in flirting with her numerous admirers. When in sheer frustration the Zapatero abandons his wife, he brings upon himself the dishonour he sought to avoid and exposes her to further vilification, while she, defying conventional attitudes by turning her shop into a public tavern, invites further criticism. On the other hand, throughout Act Three the Zapatera retains her virtue and integrity, rejects her various suitors, and in so doing embodies a concept of honour as personal goodness that fully rejects and positively answers the traditional view of honour as public image. Acknowledging her goodness, the Zapatero returns and, united with his good if sharp-tongued wife, resolves to defy the future gossip of the villagers.

The play touches too on other social themes. The Zapatero's sister, concerned for his future in the event of her own death, has pushed him into a marriage of convenience. The arranged marriage, so common in Spain and a source of much unhappiness, is a topic that Lorca would return to again and again in his later plays. And secondly, in the Zapatera's ludicrous suitors he embodies the Spanish male's ambivalent, hypocritical attitude to women, for while they condemn her for her lack of seemliness, men like the Alcalde, the mayor of the village, attempt to obtain her for their own pleasure. For all its high spirits, *La zapatera prodigiosa* is thus a play of social comment, and is in that respect in the tradition of much comic theatre, both Spanish and European, of the twentieth century. In *Amor de*

Don Perlimplín, which is almost contemporary with *La zapatera*, the topics of honour and the arranged marriage also provided Lorca with opportunities for combining humour with social criticism, and by the end of the play the central character has taken on a comic-tragic character, a multifaceted identity that is virtually Pirandellian. Lorca's comic plays, for all their serious implications, are never, though, as bitter as Valle-Inclán's. Of *La zapatera* it has rightly been said that 'he works along the same lines as Valle-Inclán, but in a more humorous way and without reaching the extremes of his satire'.[15]

While the social implications of the play are important, they never obscure its broader, more universal meaning, emphasized by Lorca himself in various observations regarding its essentially poetic character:

> *La zapatera* es una farsa, más bien un ejemplo poético del alma humana y es
> ella sola la que tiene importancia en la obra . . .   (II., p.907)

> *La zapatera* is a farce, but more than that it is a poem about the human spirit
> and the latter is the only really important character in the play . . .

> Desde luego la zapatera no es una mujer en particular sino todas las mujeres
> . . . Todos los espectadores llevan una zapatera volando por el pecho.
>   (II., p.907)
> After all, the shoemaker's wife is not a particular woman but all women . . .
> The whole audience has a shoemaker's wife within its bosom.

The young woman, whose generic name points to her symbolic meaning, embodies a universal conflict between illusion and reality, dream and disillusionment, dramatized already in *El maleficio de la mariposa* but given expression now in a figure that, for all its puppet features, is much more recognizably human. When she pursues the butterfly and fails to catch it, she is in effect another form of the dreaming Curianito vainly dreaming impossible dreams. But she is not the only dreamer in the play, for the Zapatero has his dreams, if not of love at least of kindness and companionship. The frustration embodied in both of them is the frustration of dashed hopes and illusions that to a greater or lesser degree is expressed by Lorca in so many of his characters, male and female, comic and tragic. In addition, the Zapatero exemplifies the theme of advancing years and passing time, for when his wife alludes to one of her young suitors he angrily and nostalgically comments that he too was once young:

> ZAPATERA: . . . Aquél era medio señorito . . ., tendría dieciocho años, ¡se
> dice muy pronto! ¡Dieciocho años!
> (El ZAPATERO *se revuelve inquieto*.)   (II.,p.262)
> ZAPATERO: También los tuve yo.

WIFE:. . .He was quite a smart chap . . ., about eighteen, you can say it so
quickly! Eighteen!
(*The* SHOEMAKER *turns uncomfortably.*)
SHOEMAKER: I was eighteen once.

Looking back on the one hand to the Gusanos, the glow-worms, who in *El
maleficio* lament their fading youth and beauty, the Zapatero anticipates
the anguish of many future Lorquian characters: the old man of *Así que
pasen cinco años,* Doña Rosita who waits in vain for love as the years slip
by, and the daughters of Bernarda Alba whose youth is slowly withered by
the passing years. To this extent, the puppet figures of *La zapatera* are
more than puppets. Their broad, simplified and stylized character is
certainly a source of humour, but it also transforms them into universal
images, suggesting that in his exploitation of the comic tradition Lorca still
remained very much a Symbolist.

The play's technique is striking for a variety of reasons.[16] As in the rest of
his theatre Lorca abandons realism in order to arrest the attention and
imagination of his audience, and in the prologue to the play he condemns
the fact that a constant diet of realistic plays had dulled the sensibilities of
the theatre-going public:

> . . . la poesía se retira de la escena en busca de otros ambientes donde la gente
> no se asuste de que un árbol, por ejemplo, se convierta en una bola de humo o
> de que tres peces, por amor de una mano y una palabra, se conviertan en tres
> millones de peces para calmar el hambre de una multitud . . .(II., pp.255-6)

> . . . poetry withdraws from the theatre in search of other areas where people
> will not be surprised when, for example, a tree is transformed into a puff of
> smoke or three fishes, through a loving word and gesture, become three
> million to satisfy the hunger of the multitude.

What has not, though, been generally appreciated is the clever and original
integration in *La zapatera* of the stylistic features of Symbolism and
puppet traditions which are the source of the play's poetic and comic
qualities and which, with a shift of emphasis, came to distinguish Lorca's
future dramatic works.

A consideration of certain aspects of the play's technique reveals the
overlapping of the two traditions. In terms of stage settings, the stage
direction for Act One is a good example:

> . . . *Habitación completamente blanca. Gran ventana y puerta. El foro es una
> calle también blanca, con algunas puertecitas y ventanas en gris. A la derecha
> e izquierda, puertas. Toda la escena tendrá un aire de optimismo y alegría,
> exaltada en los más pequeños detalles. Una suave luz naranja de media tarde
> invade la escena.*   (II., p.257)

. . . A completely white room. A large window and door. The back-cloth is a street which is also white, with cheerful little doors and windows in grey. To the right and left, doors. The whole scene is one of optimism and joy, heightened in the smallest details. The soft orange light of mid afternoon floods the stage.

The bold and simplified character of the setting owes much to the puppet-play tradition and is thus appropriate to the puppet figures to be set within its frame. On the other hand, the evocation of mood and atmosphere, through a careful integration of colour and lighting is not, on the whole, something we would normally associate with the puppet-play. The lyrical effect is typically symbolist and there are many other examples in the play where the fusion of setting, character and lighting produces moments of a deeply emotional nature. When towards the end of Act One the butterfly enters the Zapatera's room and she and the child pursue it, shadows are descending, the room itself is in semi-darkness, and the Zapatera and the child speak in whispers:

> NIÑO *(Enérgico)*: Cállate y habla en voz baja, ¿no ves que se espanta si no? ¡Ay! ¡Dáme tu pañuelo!
> ZAPATERA *(Intrigada ya en la caza)*: Tómalo.
> NIÑO: ¡Chist!. . . No pises fuerte. (II., p.280)

> CHILD *(Firmly)*: Be quiet, speak softly. If you don't you'll frighten it. Give me your handkerchief!
> WIFE: *(Fascinated now by the chase)*: Here, take it!
> CHILD: Shh! . . . Move quietly.

The interplay of lighting and movement and the music of the language bring to mind the poetic atmosphere of scenes from Maeterlinck or Craig, as well as from Lorca's own *El maleficio de la mariposa*. And the magical mood is deepened and intensified by the child's song to the butterfly — a song which, distinguished by its repetitions and simple yet effective images, goes far beyond the context in which it is sung to evoke a world of dream and illusion that is beautiful, fragile and unattainable:

> Mariposa del aire,
> qué hermosa eres,
> mariposa del aire
> dorada y verde.
> Luz del candil,
> mariposa del aire,
> ¡quédate ahí, ahí, ahí! . . . (II., p.280)

> Butterfly of the breezes,
> how lovely you are;
> butterfly of the breezes,
> golden and green.
> Light of a candle,
> butterfly of the breeze,
> stay, stay, stay!

In its poetic mood the scene looks forward to certain episodes in *Yerma* and *La casa de Bernarda Alba* where the female characters dream impossible dreams. As in the case of the final scenes of *Amor de Don Perlimplín*, where symbolist effects of lighting are also prominent, Lorca invests the tradition of the puppet-play with a new depth and richness.

At the same time, it would be wrong to underemphasize the puppet features of the play and their contribution to its dramatic impact. Costume, movement, gesture and language are all, for the most part, distinguished by the boldness and exaggeration that we associate with marionettes.[17] In Act One the Zapatera wears *'un traje verde rabioso'* (*'a dress of angry green'*) (II., p.257), and in Act Two *'un traje rojo encendido'* (*'a dress of burning red'*) (II., p.284). The costume is itself a visual statement of the youth and aggression of the character. La Vecina, the neighbour in Act One, is dressed in a vivid red which embodies her fiery and spiteful nature, and in Act Two she is joined by another neighbour dressed in yellow who proceeds to vent her spleen on the Zapatera. The dark blue of the Mayor's suit, his great cape and his silver-tipped stick personify both his authority and his high opinion of himself, while in the Zapatera's other suitors, Don Mirlo and el Mozo, the sad young man, Lorca expresses in the physical language of costume and appearance the respective absurdity and romantic anguish of the two characters.

Similarly, in true puppet fashion, the characters express themselves in word and action with enormous boldness and immediacy. The Zapatero vents his anger on the shoes, hammering them furiously, while the Zapatera beats her head with her hands, stamps her feet, rages at the gossiping neighbours and slams the window shut. The exchanges of husband and wife often take the form of the slanging matches that characterize the Punch and Judy show, the language distinguished by its vigorous, repeated patterns:

> Yo me he rebajado. ¡Tonta, tonta, tonta! Maldito sea mi compadre Manuel, melditos sean los vecinos, tonta, tonta, tonta.   (II., p.263)

> I've lowered myself. Fool, fool, fool! Damn my friend Manuel, damn the neighbours! Fool, fool, fool.

When the neighbours mock the Zapatera as Act One concludes, they do so in a manner which reduces to the level of the puppet-play the solemn chorus of Greek tragedy:

VECINA AMARILLA: Un refresco.
VECINA ROJA: Un refresquito.
VECINA VERDE: Para la sangre.
VECINA NEGRA: De limón.
VECINA MORADA: De zarzaparilla.
VECINA ROJA: La menta es mejor.
VECINA MORADA: Vecina.
VECINA VERDE: Vecinita.
VECINA NEGRA: Zapatera.
VECINA ROJA: Zapaterita.   (II., pp.282-83)

YELLOW NEIGHBOUR: A cool drink.
RED NEIGHBOUR: A little cool drink.
GREEN NEIGHBOUR: To cool the blood.
BLACK NEIGHBOUR: Of lemon.
PURPLE NEIGHBOUR: Sarsparilla.
RED NEIGHBOUR: Mint is better.
PURPLE NEIGHBOUR: Neighbour.
GREEN NEIGHBOUR: Little neighbour.
BLACK NEIGHBOUR: Shoemaker's wife.
RED NEIGHBOUR: Shoemaker's little wife.

The effects are comic, but there is, for all the pace and liveliness of the play, an underlying seriousness evident in Lorca's use of symbolist techniques and evident too in the comedy itself. Lacking Valle-Inclán's savage bite, Lorca nevertheless presents us in *La zapatera prodigiosa* with characters and situations that are more than merely funny. The prejudices of the villagers, the scathing and scornful neighbours, and the hapless married couple at the centre of their mockery, all have about them a human dimension which brings their experience uncomfortably close to ours. In a play like the *Tragedia de Don Cristóbal y la señá Rosita* the puppet characters always remain puppets, distanced from us and therefore objects of our laughter. In *La zapatera*, in contrast, the puppets have become more human and the idea of manipulation has acquired resonances beyond the traditions of the puppet-theatre, touching instead on the nature of human life itself and on the theme of man manipulated by his nature and his circumstances. In this particular sense the step from puppet-play and farce to tragedy is not very great.

* * * * * *

Surrealism proved to be another significant influence in Lorca's theatre. It is exemplified in particular in *El público (The Public)* and *Así que pasen cinco años (When Five Years Have Passed)*, written respectively in 1930 and 1931, but it is evident too in his earlier writings. The Residencia de Estudiantes, as we have seen, exposed its inhabitants to *avant-garde* movements as a whole, and, as far as Lorca is concerned, to Surrealism in particular, for Luis Buñuel and Salvador Dalí, two of the movement's greatest champions of the future, were amongst his greatest friends.[18] From the end of the first World War both Madrid and Barcelona had responded to the emergence of revolutionary cultural movements in the rest of Europe. In 1917 the first four numbers of the Dada magazine, *391*, were published in Barcelona by Francis Picabia who in 1922 was acclaimed by André Breton as an important figure in the early stages of Spanish Surrealism. From 1915 one of the most significant figures in Madrid literary circles was Ramón Gómez de la Serna who encouraged his friends and associates to experiment in new art forms and whose personal lifestyle, characterized by such eccentricities as the delivery of a lecture from a trapeze, anticipated in many respects the outrageous, deliberately shocking, anti-bourgeois extravagances of Dalí himself. In these years Spanish writers were also increasingly familiar with the works of the Comte de Lautréamont, Rimbaud, the Marquis de Sade and others who exemplified the love of the erotic, the horrific, the illogical and the irrational, so revered in the years ahead by 'official' Surrealists like Breton, Eluard and Aragon. In addition, Spanish literary tradition from the Golden Age to modern times provided many of the ingredients associated with the writers mentioned above, for in the picaresque novel, the prose writings of Quevedo — especially *Los sueños (The Visions)* — , the excesses of the Romantics, and, above all, in the later nightmarish pictures of Goya, greatly admired by Lorca, are to be found those very elements of horror, cruelty and fantasy that distinguished Surrealism itself. Finally, no discussion of the movement can omit the influence of Freud. For the students at the Residencia the works of Freud were a source of constant fascination. Luis Buñuel has observed that in 1921 he read Freud's *Psychoanalysis of Daily Life* in a Spanish translation by José Ortega y Gasset. Between 1922 and 1934 the Biblioteca Nueva translated many of Freud's important scientific studies and there can be no doubt that throughout the 1920s his investigations into the unconscious proved to be an inspiration to many Spanish writers.[19]

Lorca's association with Buñuel and Dalí proved crucial. In 1926 Lorca referred to Dalí as his friend and inseparable companion, in 1927 he planned to write an opera with him, and in 1925 and 1928 he stayed with

Dalí at his home in Cadaqués. As far as Buñuel is concerned, Lorca had established a friendship with him in the early days at the Residencia, and both of them took part in the annual student production of Zorrilla's Romantic play, *Don Juan Tenorio*. As early as 1921 Lorca expressed his affection for and admiration of Buñuel in the dedication to him of eleven poems. In 1925 Buñuel left Madrid for Paris, but physical distance did not terminate either his Spanish friendships or his continuing influence on Spanish *avant-garde* movements. Between 1927 and 1932 he contributed surrealist pieces and articles on the cinema to the Spanish literary magazines, *Hélix* and *La gaceta literaria*. Moreover, in 1928, Ernesto Giménez Caballero, the director of *La gaceta literaria*, founded the Cineclub Español and invited Buñuel to become the director of the cinema section of his magazine. From Paris Buñuel transmitted to Madrid not merely information and opinion about new developments in the cinema but examples of surrealist films such as René Clair's *Entr'acte*, distinguished by its flow of images without anecdotal argument. Buñuel also returned to Madrid on numerous occasions and refers to having met Lorca there in September 1928. But his greatest impact on the Cineclub and its members was achieved by the presentation on 8 December 1929 of *Un Chien andalou* which earlier that year had achieved a notable success in Paris. It is the influence of this film that is particularly evident in Lorca's surrealist phase.

Surrealism provided Lorca with the kind of artistic liberty encountered already in Symbolism and the tradition of the puppet-play. In a lecture entitled 'Sketch de la pintura moderna' ('Outline of Modern Painting'), given in 1928, Lorca referred to the way in which surrealist painters, shaking off the constricting techniques of the past, had discovered the freedom to express the inexpressible, the inner recesses of the mind and soul:

> Empiezan a surgir los sobrerrealistas, que se entregan a los latidos últimos del alma. Ya la pintura libertada por las abstracciones disciplinadas del cubismo, dueña de una inmensa técnica de siglos, entra en un período místico, incontrolado, de suprema belleza. Se empieza a expresar lo inexpresable. El mar cabe dentro de una naranja y un insecto pequeñito puede asombrar a todo el ritmo planetario donde un caballo tendido lleva una inquietante huella de pie en sus ojos finos y fuera de lo mortal.   (I., pp.1041-2)

> The Surrealists begin to emerge, giving themselves to the deepest throbbings of the soul. Now painting has been freed by the disciplined abstractions of Cubism and, mistress of techniques that are centuries old, enters a mystical, uncontrolled period of supreme beauty. The inexpressible begins to be expressed. The sea is contained within an orange and a small insect can astonish the entire rhythm of the universe where a horse lies and bears in its fine animal eyes a disturbing imprint.

The paintings of Miró which Lorca used to illustrate the lecture showed, as did the pictures of Dalí, that unconscious urges and desires could be projected onto canvas, a process which he sought to emulate in drawings like 'Manos cortadas' ('Severed Hands'). But it was the cinema, more than painting, that in its capacity to display on the screen a succession of emotive and unrelated images came closest to expressing the chaotic and often frightening character of the unconscious mind, and it was in this respect that Buñuel's astonishing *Un Chien andalou* influenced Lorca so profoundly.

His debt to Buñuel's film is expressed in *Viaje a la luna (Trip to the Moon)*, a screenplay which he wrote in New York in late 1929 and early 1930 after discussing Buñuel's film with Emilio Amero, a Mexican friend.[20] Consisting of seventy-eight scenes, *Viaje a la luna* is characterized by precisely those things that make *Un Chien andalou* so distinctively surrealist: a lack of narrative sequence in favour of images which, in C.B. Morris's words, 'flow with hypnotic speed and change with magical ease';[21] an emphasis on cinematic techniques such as fade-out, fade-in, transpositions and transformations which convey the chaotic and illogical processes of the unconscious mind; and, above all, the importance given to sexual fears and obsessions which in Buñuel's film are transposed to the screen with a force and frankness that shocked the audience of the late 20s. Lorca's Scene 49, for example, is described thus:

> on the screen a moon appears, outlined on a white background that fades into a male sex organ and then into a screaming mouth.

Towards the end of the screenplay a violent sexual encounter takes place between a boy and a woman who meet in a lift:

> 62 The harlequin boy and the nude woman ascend in the elevator.
> 63 They embrace.
> 64 A view of the sensual kiss.
> 65 The boy bites the girl on the neck and violently pulls her hair.

But if the technique owes much to Buñuel, the preoccupations of *Viaje a la luna* are very much those of Lorca himself, and the obsession with sexuality, violence and cruelty reflect both his disturbed state of mind at the time in question — which led to his leaving Spain — and the profound effect which his experience of New York had upon him. In the difficult poem *Poeta en Nueva York (Poet in New York)* Lorca also expressed in a series of violent and disturbing images his highly emotional reaction to a place that was a source of excitement and of outrage. In short, as is the case in all his creative work, *Viaje a la luna* is a projection of Lorca's personal anguish, expressed now in surrealist language.[22]

As far as European theatre is concerned, Surrealism had its manifestation there, principally in Paris in the plays of Apollinaire and Cocteau.[23] Apollinaire's *Les Mamelles de Tirésias (The Breasts of Tiresias)* and Cocteau's *Parade* were both performed in 1917 and marked the beginning of a ten-year period of surrealist theatre in France. Owing a considerable debt to Alfred Jarry's *Ubu* and to the Dadaists, Apollinaire and Cocteau set out to undermine the realism of the well-made play in an attempt to draw the attention of the audience to the existence and importance of another kind of reality, be it that of the unconscious mind or the truth that lies beneath the appearance of things. Apollinaire's *Les Mamelles de Tirésias* assaults the naturalistic tradition in almost every way. The Tiresias of the title is initially a woman who, in consequence of her wish to enter the male preserves of politics and the arts, is transformed into a man — she releases her breasts which are merely toy balloons — while her husband becomes his wife and in Act Two gives birth to forty thousand and forty-nine children merely by wanting them. The action of the play takes place in Zanzibar, whose people are represented by a single actor who produces a variety of sound effects by banging pots and pans. At the heart of the play lie serious themes — the emancipation of women and the depopulation of France in consequence of the Great War — to which the dramatist draws attention by means of a technique designed to shock his audience.

Cocteau's *Parade* and, to an even greater extent, his *Les Mariés de la Tour Eiffel (The Wedding on the Eiffel Tower)* both outraged their audiences. *Parade* was a highly visual piece, danced by Diaghilev's Russian Ballet and decorated by a Cubist set by Picasso. The action, presenting a side-show outside a circus tent, depicted amongst other things two acrobats, a Chinese juggler and three managers encased in scenery, and in its bizarre nature sought to make the spectators aware of their own grotesque nature, the true reality beneath the surface of things. Similarly, *Les Mariés de la Tour Eiffel* presents a bird's-eye view of Paris whose unreality serves to emphasize the truth that the play exposes. In the preface to the 1922 text Cocteau declared that he was seeking 'to paint more truly than the truth'. In the play itself, whenever a photographer attempts to photograph the wedding party, various creatures leap from the camera, including a lion, an ostrich and a bathing beauty, as though underlining the absurd and even nightmarish nature of life itself.

Although Lorca's *Así que pasen cinco años* shares many of the aims of the plays described above, its direct source was clearly Buñuel's *Un Chien andalou*, and many points of contact can be discerned between the film and the play in relation both to theme and technique. C.B. Morris has observed that certain details in Lorca's play reflect his interest in the cinema, notably the ace of hearts projected on the bookcase in the last act.[24] Virginia Higginbotham, as well as describing the cinematic character of particular incidents in Lorca's theatre in general, has stated that in *Así que pasen cinco años* there are scenes which seem to have been conceived more with the cinema than the theatre in mind.[25] The influence is, though, more widespread and more Buñuelian than has been suggested. As we have seen, *Un Chien andalou* inspired Lorca to devise his own screenplay, *Viaje a la luna*, which, had it been filmed, would certainly have been most striking. In *El público*, too, Lorca's principal concern was to expose in a manner that is often extremely visual the unconscious and unspoken urges which motivate the characters. The themes of both *El público* and of *Así que pasen cinco años* are typically Lorquian — the characteristic themes of passion, frustration, passing time and death — but a knowledge of Surrealism and of Buñuel's film in particular allowed Lorca to express those themes in an altogether freer and more fluid manner.

Un Chien andalou presents in its initial sequences the listless, passive figure of the young man who falls from his bicycle into the gutter and who, though kissed passionately by a young woman, merely stares at her without response. Subsequently they are seen in the girl's room looking down upon a woman in the street who prods a dismembered hand with a stick. The young man, aroused from his passivity, advances on his female companion, reaches out to squeeze her breasts, and she, frightened by his ardour, rushes into another room. He reverts to his passive role and in another sequence in which he lies on his bed another young man appears, a vibrant, energetic figure who vigorously rings the doorbell, pulls the young man to his feet and seeks to arouse him from his lethargy. Instead the young man shoots him, and the newcomer, a younger, romantic form of him, is seen falling in a park, his fingers brushing the back of a naked female. In the film's final sequences the young man — or another version of him — and the girl are seen on a beach, happily embracing, but in a sudden transformation the beach becomes a desert in which the couple are buried in sand and are slowly eaten by insects.[26]

Así que pasen cinco años has for its protagonist el Joven (the young man). In Act One he indulges in a day-dream of his sweetheart, imagining her return in five years' time and rejecting the love of la Mecanógrafa (the secretary). In the course of the act he is confronted by various characters who are other forms of himself both in the future and in the past — el Viejo (the old man), el Amigo (the friend), and el Amigo Segundo (the second friend) — , is brought face to face with the inevitability of passing time in a nightmarish scene involving a dead boy and a dead cat, but is seen at the end of the act to cling still to his passive dream of love. Act Two is to a large extent el Joven's dream of his reunion with his sweetheart, for in its opening scenes she is visited in her room by the vigorous and forceful Jugador de Rugby (the rugby player), evidently el Joven's idealized vision of himself. When el Joven appears, the girl rejects him for his lack of passion, and he is then confronted by another female figure, el Maniquí (the mannequin), a dream-like character who accuses him of sexual passivity. Responding to her words, he is transformed into a much more positive individual and begins his search for la Mecanógrafa who had earlier sought him. In Act Three the search is seen to be in vain, for the girl's feelings have changed, and human aspiration is encountered first by failure and then by death. Initially thwarted by the mocking figures of Arlequín (Harlequin) and el Payaso (the clown), el Joven is visited in the play's concluding scene by the three Jugadores (the cardplayers), the agents of death. He dies alone on an empty stage as darkness descends, listening to the echo of his own futile cries.

Lorca's el Joven is very similar to Buñuel's young man. They embody initially the theme of sexual immaturity and emotional paralysis and in both young men the idea is largely conveyed through physical inaction. So in Act One of *Así que pasen cinco años* el Joven *'está sentado' 'is seated'* (II., p.363), and is unresponsive to la Mecanógrafa, echoing the listlessness of Buñuel's young man as the girl embraces him. Later both individuals undergo a total transformation and aggressively pursue the young women, Buñuel's cinematic images of naked breasts and buttocks finding their counterpart in el Joven's verbal pictures of his lover's naked body:

> traeré temblando de amor
> mi propia mujer desnuda. (II., p.421)
>
> I will bear my naked lover
> trembling with love.

Secondly, in film and play the sexually passive protagonists are contrasted with dynamic and passionate figures who are imagined projections of themselves. Buñuel's energetic young man vigorously rings the doorbell while Lorca's el Jugador de Rugby blasts the horn of his car:

> *Se oye un claxon de automóvil que toca con furia.* (II., p.396)
> *There is heard the horn of a car, blaring furiously.*

The influence of film is also suggested by the fact that el Jugador's significance is conveyed in visual terms — in pure movement and gesture — for he does not speak a word.

There are parallels too between the female characters.Buñuel's young woman passes from sexual aggression to sexual inertia. In Lorca's plays la Mecanógrafa undergoes the same experience, for the woman who initially loves el Joven later fails to respond to him. In addition, in an early sequence of the film the woman who prods the hand with the stick serves to arouse the passive young man into vigorous sexual action. She has her counterpart in the play in the two female figures of Act Two, la Novia and el Maniquí, both of whom stir el Joven into a new and vital amorous activity. In film and play, indeed, both male and female characters constantly duplicate, parallel and reflect each other.

A second linking theme is that of frustration. In *Un Chien andalou* the young man's sexual advance upon the girl is impeded by his inhibitions — represented visually in pianos, priests and dead mules (the dead weight of culture and religion) — and by the girl's sudden attack of conscience. The energetic young man of the film is frustrated in his pursuit of life's enjoyment when he is killed and, as he falls, his fingers merely brush the back of the woman in the park. Lorca's el Joven is equally frustrated, both by his own passivity, by la Novia's rejection of him, and by la Mecanógrafa's change of heart, though it is true to say that Buñuel gives greater emphasis to the inhibiting influence of social, educational and religious institutions. And finally, although the endings of the film and the play are different in terms of detail, they are both distinguished by a mood of total desolation and a terrible sense of human isolation.

In terms of technique *Un Chien andalou* conveys the shifting, confused pattern of thoughts and desires through a succession of flowing visual images. It has no narrative or action of the traditional kind, nor indeed are its 'events' subject to the logic of time. The characters who appear on the screen — both male and female — are, with the exception of the young man himself, the projections of his imaginings, the different facets of himself, past, present and future, and the woman in his life. And if the action of the film is the 'exteriorization' of his mental processes, there are also within it further 'exteriorizations' — imaginings by the characters who are themselves the young man's imaginings. Such is the scene in which, visualizing himself in the girl's bedroom, he looks down at the woman prodding the hand with the stick — a moment which, two stages removed from reality, is presented as a kind of film within a film. And finally, since *Un Chien andalou* is a silent film, dress, gesture and movement become, as in a ballet, the key to its meaning and its impact.

The action of Lorca's play, like that of Buñuel's film, depicts to a very large extent the inner life of its central character. R.G. Knight has observed:

The play is in fact a day-dream, that is, the only action is that which occurs in the Joven's mind, and the changes of scene are not physical, but symbolic of the various stages of his inner debate.[27]

To this extent the characters who appear throughout Act One — el Viejo, el Amigo, el Amigo Segundo — are el Joven's imaginings of different forms of himself, and the action of the play, true to the tenets of Surrealism, lacks both a conventional story-line and a sense of logic. Act Two, which portrays el Joven's visit to la Novia, is in effect a day-dream, the girl his idealized vision of her, and el Jugador de Rugby his romanticized vision of himself. Similarly, the terrifying figures of Act Three — the shapes in the wood, the three Jugadores — can be seen as the physical projections of el Joven's fears, the characters of nightmare:

> ... *cruzan entre los troncos dos figuras vestidas de negro, con las caras blancas de yeso y las manos también blancas.* (II., p.424)

> ... *there move between the tree-trunks two figures dressed in black, their faces as white as plaster and their hands white too.*

By the end of the play six hours have elapsed, but within that time there has occurred a mental action whose duration cannot be clearly defined.

While the plot of *Así que pasen cinco años* is the 'exteriorization' of el Joven's thoughts, it also contains those further 'exteriorizations' of the kind described in relation to *Un Chien andalou.* Thus in Act One the scene involving the dead child and the dead cat is witnessed not merely by el Joven but also by el Viejo, el Amigo and el Amigo Segundo — by figures who are already 'exteriorizations' of him and who here witness an 'exteriorization' of their own terrors. The scene, bathed in an eerie blue light, is a kind of 'play with a play', paralleling the 'film within a film' technique of *Un Chien andalou,* and it is repeated in Act Two when el Joven is confronted by the haunting, 'unreal' figure of el Maniquí with her grey face and golden lips and eyebrows, the embodiment of el Joven's accusations against himself.

The influence of film, and in particular of silent film, is particularly evident in Lorca's play in the highly visual presentation of the characters. In *Un Chien andalou* the meaning of characters and incidents is suggested entirely through their physical appearance and movements. From the outset, when the young man appears on his bicycle, his lifeless expression and his mechanical movements, the frills on his head and around his waist and shoulders, convey both his passivity and his infantile sexuality. Subsequently, the facial expressions, the general appearance, and the highly expressive gestures of the figures on the screen constitute the language of the film. Lorca's use of costume, gesture and movement as a self-explanatory image owes much, as we have seen already, to the traditions of Symbolism, puppetry and farce, but there can be no doubt that the impact of cinema made a further contribution to the development of his markedly visual technique. In the first scene of the play costume differentiates youth and age when el Joven appears in his *pijama azul (blue pyjamas)* and el Viejo is *de chaqué (in a grey morning-coat)* (II., p.363) In Act One the white suit of el Amigo Segundo suggests the unspoilt innocence of childhood, and in Act Two la Novia, dressed in a splendid dressing gown adorned with lace and rose-coloured bows, is the very embodiment of romantic love. In terms of movement about the stage, el Jugador de Rugby expresses all the vitality of youthful passion without speaking a word:

> *El* JUGADOR DE RUGBY *no habla, sólo fuma y aplasta en el piso el cigarro. Da muestras de gran vitalidad y abraza con ímpetu a la* NOVIA. (II., p.396)
>
> *The* RUGBY PLAYER *does not speak, he merely smokes cigars and puts them out by stamping on them. He suggests great vitality and embraces the* BRIDE *passionately.*

Similarly, although he has lines to speak, el Amigo's restless pursuit of life's enjoyment is communicated to us in an almost continuous flow of physical movement as he rushes about the stage, drinking cocktails, throwing cushions in the air, and flinging himself on the sofa. In contrast, despair and anguish, as in the case of el Joven, el Amigo Segundo and el Maniquí, are conveyed in images of physical prostration, reminiscent of the manner in which in *Un Chien andalou* the young man lies on his bed, staring blankly into space. In conclusion, it can be said of *Así que pasen cinco años* that if its themes and general dramatic technique are already present in Lorca's earlier drama, a knowledge of Surrealism and of Buñuel's film allowed him to express those themes in a new and altogether freer manner. In none of Lorca's plays, either before or after *Así que pasen cinco años*, is the action a projection of the protagonist's thoughts and emotions, nor is the technique so exclusively concerned with communicating the fluid, illogical and often obsessive nature of the unconscious mind.[28]

* * * * * *

Bodas de sangre (Blood Wedding), the first of the three tragic plays written in the dramatist's last years, was completed in 1932 and received its triumphant première at the Teatro Beatriz in Madrid in March 1933. The subjects and themes of Lorca's theatre in general have a tragic dimension, and even the boisterous fun of *La zapatera prodigiosa* does not conceal its sadness, but in the years that saw the completion of *Bodas de sangre, Yerma* (1934), and *La casa de Bernarda Alba* (1936), he was more explicitly concerned with writing tragedies. Thus in an interview in 1934 Lorca observed:

> Estoy trabajando mucho. Ahora voy a terminar *Yerma*, una segunda tragedia mía. La primera fue *Bodas de sangre*. *Yerma* será la tragedia de la mujer estéril. El tema, como usted sabe, es clásico. Pero yo quiero que tenga un desarrollo y una intención nuevos. Una tragedia con cuatro personajes principales y coros, como han de ser las tragedias. Hay que volver a la tragedia. Nos obliga a ello la tradición de nuestro teatro dramático.(II., p.964)

> I am working hard. Now I shall finish *Yerma*, a second tragedy. The first was *Bodas de sangre*. *Yerma* will be the tragedy of the barren woman. The theme, as you know, is a classical one. But I want to develop it in a new way. A tragedy with four main characters and a chorus, as tragedies should be. It is necessary to return to tragedy. The tradition of our theatre compels us to do so.

Lorca's reference here to the need to return to tragedy because it is the 'tradition of our theatre' is interesting in several ways, for it suggests that even if his preoccupation with tragic themes in the years preceding his murder in 1936 was born of a growing pessimism and apprehension, it also had something to do with other factors of a much more literary kind. These, as we shall now see, also help to explain Lorca's return in *Bodas de sangre* to a largely symbolist mode of expression, even though in Act Three in particular surrealist influence is still apparent. In relation to the importance of *Bodas de sangre* within the symbolist tradition, it is worth noting the observation of a critic as important as J. L. Styan:

> He worked outside the mainstream of European symbolist drama, but his contribution to this genre is in many ways the most accomplished and exciting we have . . . It is as if he were the one playwright born to give theatrical life to the theories of Appia and Craig, those which held that all the arts should combine in the art of drama . . .[29]

One of the key factors in relation to both the subject matter and the dramatic technique of the tragic trilogy is Lorca's assumption in 1931 of the directorship of the touring theatre group, the Teatro universitario (The University Theatre), a group more commonly known as *La barraca*. Organized under the auspices of the new Republican Government, the company's task was largely educational — to travel the length and breadth of Spain and perform in a portable theatre — la barraca — for the benefit of the ordinary people the plays of the great Spanish dramatists of the sixteenth and seventeenth centuries: Cervantes, Lope de Vega, Tirso de Molina and Calderón. A glance at the repertoire of the plays performed by *La barraca* under Lorca's direction between 1931 and 1935 reveals that it included a number of very significant works of a serious and even tragic nature, in particular Tirso de Molina's *El burlador de Sevilla (The Trickster of Seville)* and Lope de Vega's *Fuenteovejuna* and *El caballero de Olmedo (The Knight of Olmedo)*. Performed respectively in 1934, 1933, and 1935, they postdate the writing of *Bodas de sangre* itself, but more significant than this is the fact that from 1931, the year of his appointment to the company, Lorca's thoughts turned in a very concrete and specific manner to those plays which in the next few years would be included in its programme. In addition, from 1933 the Ministry of Education organized in various Spanish towns and cities spectacular outdoor performances of classical tragedies. In 1933 Seneca's *Medea* was presented in the Roman amphitheatre in Mérida, and later in the year was performed in Barcelona and Madrid. In 1934 Mérida saw performances of both *Medea* and *Elektra, Medea* was presented again in Salamanca, and *Ifigenia* in the Greek theatre at Ampurias. To this extent classical tragedy was very much part of the Spanish theatrical scene at the very time when Lorca was involved in the writing of his tragedies. Moreover, the actress who played the tragic heroine in those notable classical performances was Margarita Xirgu, who was closely connected with the performance of Lorca's plays in the 1930s.[30]

The experience of directing plays with *La barraca* had important repercussions in relation to Lorca's dramatic technique, for he quickly realized that plays of the sixteenth and seventeenth century could only be meaningful for a modern and largely uncultured audience if they were performed in a lively and imaginative manner, unencumbered by the traditional, suffocating realism and heavy-handedness which was generally associated with the presentation of the Spanish 'classics'. In the plays staged by *La barraca* and directed by Lorca himself the style of performance was thus essentially modern, blending settings, dialogue, dances, songs, costume and movement into an effective and absorbing whole. Thus, *Fuenteovejuna* was presented in 1933 in modern dress, and in order to update and enliven its peasant setting and characters Lorca made liberal use of traditional Spanish songs and dances, the former sung by a chorus, the latter directed by Pilar López. Similarly, in the 1934 performance of *El burlador de Sevilla* Spanish dancers performed a ballet during the play's wedding scenes and in the 1935 production of *El caballero de Olmedo* a sense of continuity, simplicity and directness was achieved by the use of a plain black curtain and portable folding-screens, as well as by focusing the lighting on the characters themselves. In such productions Lorca had ample opportunities to develop a style and technique which both broke with the traditions of the commercial theatre and allowed him to treat traditional subjects in a new and invigorating manner which, paradoxically, he was able to turn to his own advantage in the commercial productions of *Bodas de sangre* and *Yerma*.

While these factors played their part in the composition of *Bodas de sangre*, mention must also be made of the influence of particular European dramatists. Many critics have commented on the similarities between Lorca's play and J.M.Synge's *Riders to the Sea*.[31] That Lorca knew the play there can be no doubt, for Juan Ramón Jiménez had translated it into Spanish and in 1920 or 1921 Lorca read and discussed the play with his friend, Miguel Cerón. In terms of setting, nothing could be more different than the coast of Ireland, exposed to the wild Atlantic, and the sun-bleached villages of Andalusia, but in many other ways Synge and Lorca are kindred spirits. Ronald Gaskell has observed of Synge that he is 'a dramatist of passion', that his characters 'are defined by their emotional life', that they possess 'a vivid awareness through their senses of the world about them', and that both the action and the characters of *Riders to the Sea* become 'an image of human life'.[32] Synge's Maurya, whose sons are taken from her by the sea, has her counterpart in Lorca's la Madre (the mother), whose husband and elder son are already dead and whose fears for her younger son become inevitably her final lament over his dead body. They are less individualized characters than the voice of universal woman, and in the same way the ordinary, concrete objects of their existence — water, stones, nails, the spinning wheel — assume in the course of the action a much more symbolic meaning which allows the play to work on both a particular and a metaphorical level. In reading *Riders to the Sea* Lorca undoubtedly recognized a voice and a vision of the world which in many ways resembled his own.

Amongst other modern influences Ibsen's *Peer Gynt* has also been mentioned. Its story resembles that of *Bodas de sangre* in the sense that, as la Novia (the bride) and Leonardo run off together after her marriage to el Novio (the bridegroom), so Peer Gynt abducts Ingrid after her wedding. Moreover, *Peer Gynt* is Ibsen's most overtly symbolist play, even though its composition preceded the symbolist movement in the theatre as such, and contains precisely those elements of universality and poetic symbolism to which Lorca would have responded. But if these modern, non-Spanish dramatists influenced Lorca in any way, the all-pervading influence of Shakespeare, already mentioned in relation to *El maleficio de la mariposa*, should never be forgotten. In *El público* the characters of Romeo and Juliet figure prominently. There are also numerous allusions to the two lovers in Lorca's poetry. As far as *Bodas de sangre* is concerned, both the irresistible attraction of la Novia and Leonardo to each other and the family feud that dominates the action bring *Romeo and Juliet* to mind.[33] And in

Shakespeare, as in Synge and Ibsen, Lorca found, of course, both a sense of the universality and the timelessness of things, as well as a tragic vision with which he could identify.

Lorca's tragic vision is both ancient and modern. C.B. Morris has stated that 'Lorca clearly shared with Shakespeare — and with Sophocles — a tragic perception of events: the conviction that a single circumstance, or a human weakness, can — as in the case of King Oedipus — motivate a pattern of events which can be resolved only in death'.[34] Ronald Gaskell suggests that in order to find a true comparison to Lorca's tragedies, 'we have to go beyond Synge to *The Bacchae* to find it; for in Lorca, as in Euripides, the driving force of the play is an energy fiercer than anything we are accustomed to recognise as human feeling.'[35] On the other hand, if the primitive passions that drive the characters of *Bodas de sangre* and the sense of inevitability that hangs over them suggest a vision of the world which is alien to us and to that extent more ancient than modern, Lorca's tragedy is essentially of our time in its evocation of the helplessness and the smallness of human beings. Throughout his life the sense of ultimate individual insignificance was forcefully borne in upon him — by society's treatment of 'outsiders', especially homosexuals in the Granada of his youth; by his experience of New York and its horrific spectacle of human beings crushed by their environment; and by his own poignant awareness of the gulf between reality and human aspiration. In *Bodas de sangre,* as in *Yerma* and *La casa de Bernarda Alba,* Lorca gives particularly powerful expression to the conflict between the individual — in this case la Novia and Leonardo — who follow the dictates of their natures and their instincts, and the forces of tradition and convention — parental and social obligation, honour and family reputation — which obstruct them and finally destroy them or those close to them. The clash is, of course, that of *La zapatera prodigiosa* raised to a tragic level, but the clash itself, for all its primitive violence, is as modern as it is ancient.

Despite the fact that *Bodas de sangre* was based on a newspaper account of a real event which involved the flight of a newly-married woman with her former lover, it is one of Lorca's least realistic and most poetic plays, and certainly the most poetic of the three rural tragedies. The human characters, though differentiated from each other, have an archetypal and symbolic quality indicated in the first place by their generic names: la Madre (the mother), el Padre (the father), la Novia (the bride), el Novio (the bridegroom). Only Leonardo has a real name, but even in his case it is a name which evokes the lion ('león' in Spanish) and fiery passion ('ardo', 'I burn') and embodies both strength and physical beauty. La Madre, in her concern for those near to her — her dead husband and son and her one remaining child — expresses the instinctive possessiveness of all mothers. In the play's first scene, moreover, she is linked by her grief — and the link is reinforced by the black of mourning — to la Vecina (the neighbour), and both of them are linked to another neighbour whose son has beeen mutilated in a recent accident. By the end of the play la Madre's loneliness and isolation is shared by both la Novia and Leonardo's wife, and their lamentation has its echo in the grieving, weeping neighbours. Furthermore, la Madre is linked to Mother Earth itself, to the natural world which is the source of life and death:

> . . . Hemos de pasar días terribles. No quiero ver a nadie.
> La tierra y yo. Mi llanto y yo . . .   (II., p.610)

> . . . We must endure days of suffering. I wish to see no one.
> The earth and myself. My tears and myself.

To this extent, the human characters, though retaining their humanity and thus their capacity to move us, are part of and subordinated to a greater reality, the tides and currents, the remorseless and inevitable rhythms of nature itself. Throughout the play the inextricable relationship between the lives of men and women and the elemental forces, creative and destructive, which constitute the vitality and tension of existence, is established through a network of motifs and images — allusions to flowers, crops, horses, rivers, climate — whose innate allusive and evocative capacity constantly extends and broadens the frame of reference, transforming the particular detail or episode into something of much greater significance.[36]

While the human characters are thus absorbed into larger patterns, the final Act of *Bodas de sangre* personifies in the figures of la Luna (the moon) and la Mendiga (the beggar woman) the destructive forces to which in Acts One and Two there has been frequent reference. The great dark wood into which the lovers flee, the three woodcutters, the cold, white moon, the old beggar woman whose face can barely be discerned, is the lovers' encounter with death presented in a heightened, symbolic manner. But the symbolism of the scene, which universalizes it, extends the range of reference to embrace us all as we, the spectators of the action, witness, as it were, our own deaths and see on stage the projection of our own fears, terrors and nightmares. In *Bodas de sangre* Lorca had not forgotten the lessons of Surrealism rehearsed already in *Así que pasen cinco años*. The terrifying figures in the wood are derived from the last Act of the earlier play where el Joven is first confronted by the taunting, mocking figures of Arlequín and el Payaso, the latter's skull-like head evocative of death, and then by the impassive and ruthless Jugadores, the card players whose cloaks of smooth white satin have that icy coldness embodied in the figure of la Luna in the later play. This remarkable scene in *Bodas de sangre*, perhaps the most memorable in the whole of Lorca's theatre, works in effect on two levels. In the sense that it captures in its stylized figures enormously suggestive and powerful images of death, it has that monumental, archetypal quality so typical of Symbolism. On the other hand, insomuch as the frightening darkness of the wood and its menacing inhabitants are both the projection of the lovers' and our own terrors, the scene is highly surrealist. Both levels complement each other. The sense of distance and unnerving proximity, functioning simultaneously, reveals the extent to which Lorca mastered the techniques of two of the twentieth century's most significant movements and put them to the service of his own highly individual art.[37]

The dramatic technique of *Bodas de sangre* is perfectly designed to express its dominant concerns, reveals the benefits of Lorca's experience as director of *La barraca*, and marks the flowering of the constant experiment essayed in his own dramatic work. The stage settings, for example, like Craig's, Maeterlinck's and Valle-Inclán's, are images which both convey the feeling of a scene and extend its implications, suggesting the universal nature of the particular experience.[38] Thus the simplicity of the opening stage direction creates the mood of the ensuing action — the expression of la Madre's grief and fear — and gives it a monumentality which transforms a single woman into a universal symbol of grieving motherhood:

Habitación pintada de amarillo.   (II., p.517)

A room painted yellow.

Within the scene itself the stark symbolism of the setting is expanded in the black of la Madre's costume and her static, seated posture, the whole a closely integrated image of dark, brooding melancholy. In contrast, in Act One, Scene Three, the stylized setting for la Novia's home with its white walls and colourful flowers, jars and ribbons, reflects her father's positive and constructive efforts to shape his life into something meaningful, as well as his optimism for his daughter's future, while his silver hair is an image less of old age than of his pride in his life's achievement and the respect accorded him by society at large. The tension of the play is, indeed, as the preceding remarks suggest, one composed of the accumulating and accelerating clash of opposites — pessimism/optimism, harmony/discord, aspiration/frustration —, and the stage settings are themselves an integral part of that tension. Thus, throughout Act Two, Scene One, the setting of la Novia's house is increasingly filled with light and colour, in the flowers, costumes and songs of the wedding guests and in the splendid appearance of la Novia herself. On the other hand, the mood of optimism is dispelled by the cold starkness of the setting for Scene Two:

Exterior de la cueva de la novia. Entonación en blancos grises y azules fríos.
Grandes chumberas. Tonos sombríos y plateados . . . (II., p.569)

Exterior of the bride's cave. Colouring of whitish grey and cold blues. Great
cacti. Dark and silvery shadows . . .

It anticipates the pessimistic ending of the scene when la Novia and Leonardo run off together, and leads as well into the scene in the wood where the chill of the moon creates the atmosphere for the appearance of death. In the final scene, whose colouring is dominated by the black of mourning, tonality has come full circle, echoing and underlining the emotional experience of la Madre.

The play's conflicts are also powerfully expressed in its music, both in song and the rhythms of poetry. As the wedding guests approach la Novia's house, their song in celebration of marriage assumes a sustained momentum, embraces the central characters in its optimistic and joyful cadences, and, through its evocative images, places the action of the play on an altogether different level that is both poetic and archetypal — the level of myth and ritual in which the celebration of the marriage is a celebration of life and all its creative energy:

> Despierte la novia,
> que por los campos viene
> rondando la boda,
> con bandejas de dalias
> y panes de gloria. (II., p.561)

> May the bride awaken,
> for through the fields
> the wedding-guests approach,
> with trays of dahlias
> and cakes of puff-pastry.

On the other hand, these surging harmonies which convey the greater harmony of life dissolve inevitably into the discordant cries of individuals venting their anguish or their anger, as at the end of the second Act where the voices of el Padre and la Madre are raised acrimoniously against each other, suggesting both their bitterness and their awareness of inevitable tragedy. In the final Act that sense of doom and inescapable sorrow is expressed ritualistically in the lines of la Luna and la Mendiga and in the final chorus of grief:

> Vecinas: con un cuchillo,
> con un cuchillito,
> en un día señalado, entre las dos y las tres,
> se mataron los dos hombres del amor.

Con un cuchillo,
con un cuchillito
que apenas cabe en la mano,
pero que penetra fino
por las carnes asombradas
y que se para en el sitio
donde tiembla enmarañada
la oscura raíz del grito.   (II., p.614)

Neighbours: with a knife,
with a little knife,
on an allotted day, between two and three,
two men killed each other for love.
With a knife,
with a little knife
that barely fits in the hand,
but which slides in deep
in the startled flesh
and stops at the spot
where there trembles the twisted
dark root of a scream.

Lorca's conception of *Bodas de sangre* is to a large extent operatic, and, as in the case of genuine music drama, possesses that magical power to evoke through sound and rhythm those deeper resonances that lie beyond what is actually seen on stage.

Lighting too has a crucial role to play. Darkness in Acts One and Two is associated with the blind, irrational passions of la Madre, la Novia and Leonardo. Thus, when Leonardo visits la Novia before the wedding, the darkness of night is a fitting background to their bitter confrontation. Conversely, the arrival of the wedding guests is accompanied by daylight and the mood of growing optimism is reflected in the lively interplay of colour on the stage. Act Three, Scene One, returns to darkness, the darkness of the wood that is at once the chaotic darkness of passion, the blackness of dishonour, and the engulfing shadows of death. And when light penetrates that darkness, it is no longer the warm, optimistic light of the wedding celebrations but the icy blue light of death. The effects, in terms of their power to convey the mood and the deeper resonances of individual scenes and of a developing pattern, are masterly.[39]

Bodas de sangre was followed in quick succession by three more plays: *Yerma*, completed in 1934, *Doña Rosita la soltera (Doña Rosita the Spinster)* in 1935, and *La casa de Bernarda Alba* in 1936. The last three years of Lorca's life witnessed, then, a flowering of true genius, for in their different ways all these plays are master works. They reveal too Lorca's continuing concern with experimentation and new techniques, for in this

·respect each of the plays is different from the others. On the one hand, the symbolic and poetic qualities of *Bodas de sangre* remain an important distinguishing feature of all three works. On the other, they are characterized by a greater sobriety, by a paring away of the kind of symbolism that marks Act Three of *Bodas de sangre*, and, to a certain degree, by a gradual movement towards a greater realism. The following discussion, considering all three plays but focusing in particular on *La casa de Bernarda Alba*, is intended to illustrate these points.

In terms of its principal themes, *Yerma* is closely related to *Bodas de sangre*, as it is, indeed, to the major preoccupations of the whole of Lorca's poetry and drama. Yerma, the childless wife, is, like la Novia in the earlier play, caught in a loveless marriage to a farmer, Juan, a man more interested in his fields than in his wife. Her longing for a child, and thus her frustration, grows in proportion to Juan's increasing indifference to her pleas. At the same time Yerma is instinctively drawn to another man, Víctor, the shepherd, for whom she feels a much greater natural affinity. But, as in *Bodas de sangre*, instinct and passion come into conflict with honour, for Yerma's sense of her own reputation, worth and integrity will not allow her to take a lover. On the other hand, the very fact of her childlessness makes her an object of scorn and mockery, and when, in desperation, she seeks the advice of a local sorceress on the subject of her infertility, her actions expose her further both to public suspicion and her husband's accusations. In the end, realizing that he does not want a child and that perhaps he cannot give her one, Yerma murders him, condemning herself to a childless, empty and tragic future. The similarities between *Bodas de sangre* and *Yerma* in relation to the themes of instinct and passion, frustration, honour, and the clash whose outcome is inevitably tragic, are very clear.

As far as Lorca's treatment of the subject is concerned, it is clear that *Yerma* has none of the highly poetic symbolism or the supernatural figures of the final act of *Bodas*. Nor, indeed, does it have the amount of poetry, be it in the form of songs or carefully structured prose dialogue, which distinguishes that play. Francisco García Lorca has noted that in *Yerma* his brother sought a greater simplicity, for he felt that his theatre 'would benefit by a more austere technique'.[40] The characters of the play are, without exception, human characters, and there are fewer of them. As for the poetry, it takes for the most part the form of songs, five of them short songs sung by Yerma herself. If, though, the greater sobriety and austerity of the play give the impression that *Yerma* is a more 'realistic' play than *Bodas de sangre*, nothing could be further from the truth. Francisco García Lorca has, indeed, observed of the rural tragedies that 'Yerma is the play which has the smallest number of elements inspired by reality', while Mildred Adams has drawn attention to its essentially poetic qualities.[41]

As is the case in *Bodas*, the characters of *Yerma*, and especially Yerma herself, have an archetypal and symbolic significance. Yerma's name is not in fact a real name but an adjective — 'barren', 'empty' — which, normally applied to the land, describes here the barrenness of a woman and, inasmuch as that state is not necessarily peculiar to her, the state, both physical and emotional, of all women similarly afflicted. The two men with whom she is involved have real names — Juan and Víctor — but they too, contrasting markedly with each other, are the embodiment of universal masculine attributes or defects: in Víctor's case virility, in Juan's case the lack of it. The other characters of the play, grouped around these central figures, are linked to them in the sense that they too are the personification of fertility and fecundity which in a positive or negative sense the central trio represent. Such is the significance of María, la Vieja (the old woman), and the Muchacha Primera (first girl) and the Muchacha Segunda (second girl). In addition, as in *Bodas de sangre*, the human characters are constantly placed within the context of the natural world and related to the cycles of birth and death, fertility and barrenness in nature itself. In short, the close interweaving of the human and non-human elements of *Yerma* continually broadens and extends its frame of reference, investing it with a truly universal and even mythical quality.[42]

The dramatic technique of the play is distinguished by a stylization which transforms individual objects, episodes and figures into archetypes. A consideration of the settings, for example, reveals that they are notable not for their detail but for their starkness, simplicity and an emphasis on particular, isolated concrete objects which are full of highly suggestive resonances. Thus, in the play's first scene the concentration on a single object — Yerma's embroidery frame — is sufficient to underline the inescapable reality of her domestic tasks, her wifely duties, while its solidity contrasts with the fragile, insubstantial nature of her dream of a child. Later, in Act Two, Scene Two, two pitchers of water, constantly present throughout a scene whose setting is simply and briefly described, serve to remind us and Yerma herself of her own dryness. As to the characters of the play, they too have a simple starkness, often communicated in strongly visual terms, which is immensely evocative. Juan's lack of vitality is conveyed by his thinness and his pallor; Víctor's vitality by his strong physical presence; the stifling, deadening impact of Juan's sisters by their withered, lizard-like skin and the black clothes that they wear like shrouds; and Yerma's final despair by her immobility, the outward manifestation of her emotional numbness.

In relation to the presentation of the figures, movement and lighting are, of course, highly significant, creating throughout the play visual patterns which are, in effect, emotional graphs. At the outset Yerma's dream of Víctor and a child is presented in a white light that symbolizes hope and aspiration. Later, both in Act Two, Scene One and Act Three, Scene Two, vibrant colour and vigorous physical movement — the village women washing the clothes and the enactment of a fertility rite — again evoke a world of passion and procreation for which Yerma longs. It is, though, the scenes of twilight and of darkness, deepening throughout the action, that reflect her actual situation as she advances step by step into the blackness of total despair.

The language of the play, far from being realistic, corresponds to the characters' obsessions and is distinguished throughout by its highly patterned and structured character. Quite apart from the songs, which occur at moments of great emotional intensity, the prose dialogue itself often has the rhythm and the emotional quality of music, as much expressive of Yerma's joy and enthusiasm as of her despair. Indeed, in its closely integrated pattern of stage settings, costumes, movement, lighting, dialogue and music, Yerma illustrates supremely well the theory and practice of European symbolist producers and writers like Craig, Appia, Maeterlinck, Yeats and Wilde. It is surely no coincidence that when the play was presented in Madrid in December 1934, it was directed by Cipriano Rivas Cherif, who had studied the work of Gordon Craig in Italy.[43]

Doña Rosita la soltera, first performed in Barcelona in December 1935, is concerned with the protagonist's prolonged and vain wait for her suitor's return from South America. In the sense that the play portrays the heroine's anguished frustration, its links with Yerma are clear enough, but Lorca himself observed that the idea for the play was first conceived in 1924 when he was in the process of writing Mariana Pineda.[44] Although the latter had been a public success, Lorca was evidently disappointed with it, and Francisco García Lorca has observed that 'with Doña Rosita, written with great care, he overcame the private failure of Mariana Pineda'.[45] The play must also be seen, though, in relation to Bodas de sangre and La casa de Bernarda Alba. In some respects Lorca seems to have returned in Doña Rosita to the lyricism of Bodas de sangre while, on the other hand, the play has elements of realism which anticipate aspects of La casa de Bernanda Alba. The mixture of these two apparently contradictory styles accounts in no small measure for the particular flavour of the play.

The realism of *Doña Rosita* is suggested by its settings, for the stark simplicity of *Bodas de sangre* and *Yerma* becomes here, in a manner reminiscent of Chekhov, the representation of real rooms, complete with chairs, sideboard, table, sofa, curtains and so on. The directions for the costumes of the characters are detailed and precise, locating them, as in Rosita's case, in a specific period in time:

> ... *Viene vestida de rosa con un traje del novecientos, mangas de jamón y adornos de cintas.*   (II., p.701)

> ... *She is dressed in pink, in the style of 1900, with leg-of-mutton sleeves and ribbon trimmings.*

In many respects the dialogue matches the settings and costumes in its greater realism, for, to a greater extent than in the other plays, it focuses on the ordinary day-to-day concerns of the characters' existence: the uncle's preoccupation with his greenhouse; the aunt's and the housekeeper's concern with domestic matters; the importance given by Rosita and her friends to largely frivolous topics. In short, as in a play like *The Cherry Orchard*, the desultory, commonplace conversations of everyday life account for much of the dialogue of *Doña Rosita*, and it has too a certain flatness which enhances the effect of realism.

On the other hand, the play's realism, far from diminishing its poetic qualities, has the effect of enhancing them. While, for example, the setting for each Act is in itself a realistic picture, the three Acts, juxtaposed, evoke in a highly effective manner, as does the changing style of costume, the relentless march of time. The realism of settings and costumes is seen to be, on closer analysis, a clever stylization, a creation of images whose effect goes beyond realism. In the course of the play Rosita's costume, changing stage by stage from pink to white, is less important in a literal than symbolic sense and points, through its association with the beautiful but fading rose, to broader themes and concerns of which the particular action of the play is itself but an image: fading beauty, dreams and disillusionment, passing time, human helplessness. By Act Three Rosita's dialogue is itself more poetic, not only in the sense that its patterns are more rhythmic and stylized, but in the sense that its concerns are now with her inner life and, by extension, with the lives of all similarly despairing and abandoned women. And then, of course, there are the specifically poetic sections of the play, of which the best example is the poem to the rose that opens in the morning, blooms at midday and dies with the onset of night:

Cuando se abre en la mañana,
roja como sangre está.
El rocío no la toca
porque se teme quemar.
Abierta en el mediodía
es dura como el coral.
El sol se asoma a los vidrios
para verla relumbrar.
Cuando en la ramas empiezan
los pájaros a cantar
y se desmaya la tarde
en las violetas del mar,
se pone blanca, con blanco
de una mejilla de sal.
Y cuando toca la noche
blanco cuerno de metal
y las estrellas avanzan
mientras los aires se van,
en la raya de lo oscuro,
se comienza a deshojar.   (II., pp.704-5)

When she opens in the morning,
she is red as blood.
The dew does not touch her
for fear of burning.
Open at noon
she is as firm as coral.
The sun appears at the window
to see her glow.
When the birds in the trees
begin to sing
and evening sinks
into the violet sea,
she grows pale, with the paleness
of a cheek of salt.
And when night blows
on its white metallic horn,
and the stars advance,
and the wind drops,
on the edge of darkness
her petals begin to fall.

This poem, a beautifully expressive piece, striking in its visual impact and moving in its emotional effect, is recited on three occasions, each corresponding to a stage in Rosita's emotional life. In the final Act a haunting interplay of motifs — the white petals of the rose, Rosita's white dress, and the white curtains blown by the wind — suggests Rosita's emotional death and her empty future, as well as, of course, the continuing sadness of other abandoned women. In *Doña Rosita la soltera* Lorca achieved a particularly striking blend of realism and symbolism and in this respect the play marks a clear step forward to the technique of his last tragedy, *La casa de Bernarda Alba.*

La casa de Bernarda Alba, completed in June 1936, only two months before Lorca's death, has as its principal character the tyrannical widow, Bernarda Alba, who rules her five spinster daughters with a rod of iron. Reflecting the puritanical and narrow-minded values of the village where she lives — and, above all, a concern with family name and reputation — Bernarda is, in effect, her daughters' keeper and the house a prison where they, aged from twenty to forty, age and grow increasingly embittered, their future reflected for them in María Josefa, the demented grandmother. For Angustias, the eldest daughter, the chance of escape presents itself in the form of a marriage of convenience to Pepe el Romano, a man much younger than herself. As for the other women, they are either resigned to their fate, as in Magdalena's case, or unwilling to accept it, an attitude best exemplified in Adela, the youngest of the five. A spirited and rebellious girl, she expresses her opposition to her mother in a secret affair with Pepe el Romano. Martirio, suspecting the relationship and jealous of her sister, confronts Adela with the truth and their argument informs Bernarda of what she had not suspected. After a scene of bitter exchanges, Bernarda cruelly tricks Adela into believing that Pepe has been shot and killed, and Adela, seeing no future, hangs herself. In an attempt to avoid a scandal, Bernarda reasserts her authority, forcing her remaining daughters to declare that Adela died a virgin.

As far as influences are concerned, Lorca had observed to a friend, Carlos Morla Lynch, that life itself provided him with a model for Bernarda, for in a village not far from Granada he had known a woman like her:

> En la casa vecina y colindante a la nuestra vivía 'doña Bernarda', una viuda de muchos años que ejercía una inexorable y tiránica vigilancia sobre sus hijas solteras. Prisioneras privadas de todo albedrío, jamás hablé con ellas; pero las veía pasar como sombras, siempre silenciosas y siempre de negro vestidas . . .[46]

> In the house immediately next to ours lived 'Doña Bernarda', a very old widow who kept over her spinster daughters an inexorable and tyrannical watch. They were prisoners deprived of all freedom of choice and I never spoke with them; but I saw them pass like shadows, always silent and always dressed in black . . .

In addition, Adela's lover, Pepe el Romano, is said to have been based on Pepe de la Romilla, the real-life lover of one of the girls. The situation of the play, though heightened for dramatic effect, is certainly of the kind one might expect to find in a small provincial Spanish town in the first decades of the century. The general impression that Lorca intended the play to approximate to real life is further strengthened both by his reference to it as a 'documental fotográfico' ('a photographic documentary') and by his choice of sub-title: *Drama de mujeres en los pueblos de España (A Play about Women in the Villages of Spain)*. If the source of *Bodas de sangre* was a newspaper report, that of *La casa de Bernarda Alba* seems to have been at least a stage nearer real life.

On the other hand, the influence of literary sources and traditions is equally apparent. While *Bodas de sangre* is indebted in certain respects to some of the plays of Lope de Vega, *La casa de Bernarda Alba* owes much in terms of its presentation of the theme of honour to the immensely powerful honour plays of Calderón. Although they did not figure in the repertoire of *La barraca* — pride of place being given to Calderón's *auto sacramental, La vida es sueño (Life is a Dream)* Lorca's familiarity with the honour plays cannot be doubted, and in relation to *La casa de Bernarda Alba* the general influence of Calderón's *El médico de su honra (The Surgeon of His Honour)* certainly suggests itself. The play's protagonist, Don Gutierre Solís, is highly reminiscent of Bernarda in the sense that his obsession with his own good name and reputation fills him with fear at the merest prospect of any slight upon it. In consequence, Gutierre's wife, Mencía, is, like Bernarda's daughters, the prisoner of an unbending code. In the end, though innocent, she is suspected by her husband of a secret affair, and he, as obedient as Bernarda to a system whose demands are ruthless, has her secretly put to death while publicly proclaiming her death an accident. Throughout *El médico de su honra* there is, moreover, the terrible sense of claustrophobia that is so much a feature of Lorca's play. The image of Gutierre's house as a place of confinement is very strong. Much of the action takes place at night, the characters enveloped in a physical darkness that is the visible counterpart of their fears. In the play's concluding scenes Mencía is kept by Gutierre in her bedroom whose locked door and barred window evoke the prison world of the work as a whole. While there are many differences between *La casa de Bernarda Alba* and *El médico de su honra*, the latter comes very close in spirit to Lorca's play. Given his knowledge of the literature of the Golden Age, it would be surprising indeed if the honour plays of that period left no clear imprint on his theatre.

Another Spanish work whose influence suggests itself is *Doña Perfecta*, a novel by the nineteenth-century novelist, Benito Pérez Galdós. The action of the novel — and it is interesting to note that Galdós later transformed it into a play — focuses on the clash between Doña Perfecta, a wealthy, narrow-minded, intolerant woman typical in her attitudes of the small provincial town of Orbajosa, and Pepe Rey, a young engineer from the city who embodies the progressive ideas of the modern world. Bitterly opposing Pepe Rey's general beliefs, Doña Perfecta opposes too his desire to marry her daughter, Rosario, from whom she demands unswerving obedience. When she discovers the lovers' plans to elope, Doña Perfecta arranges Pepe's murder and in consequence of his death Rosario loses her sanity.

Doña Perfecta herself is remarkably like Bernarda Alba in terms of her intolerant and inflexible attitudes, and even if honour itself is not the central issue of the novel it is certainly part of the oppressive and claustrophobic world of Orbajosa. The clash between Rosario and her mother over Pepe Rey brings to mind Adela's conflict with Bernarda, while Pepe Rey's name is curiously similar to that of Pepe el Romano. In novel and play too there is a shooting incident, and in both the presentation of the central characters — especially Doña Perfecta and Bernarda — in bold outline has itself that symbolic and archetypal quality which is a hallmark of Lorca's theatre.

La casa de Bernarda Alba suggests too, as do Bodas de sangre and Yerma, the very marked influence of classical tragedy. The point has been made already that in 1933 and 1934 Medea, Elektra and Ifigenia were all presented in spectacular performances in different towns and cities of Spain, including Madrid and Barcelona. It is, perhaps, more than a coincidence that the tragic characters of Lorca's last three plays should thus be women. Moreover, La casa de Bernarda Alba is reminiscent of Greek tragedy in the sense that its very title suggests a household or a lineage whose fall we are to witness. In Aristotelian terms the tragic 'error' can be seen both in Bernarda's pride and obsessive concern with her honour, which leads her to tyrannize her children, and in Adela's persistent defiance of her mother. Bernarda's attempt to avert disaster, which resides in her attempted domination of her daughters, merely brings it about, thereby according with the Greek 'reversal of intention'. Throughout the play there is too a strong sense of fatality and of human beings manipulated by irresistible forces, as much outside as inside themselves. And finally, the spectacle of Bernarda's tyranny and its terrible consequences is evidently one that awakens the classical tragic emotions of pity and terror. It is interesting to note in relation to the first performance of La casa de Bernarda Alba in Buenos Aires in 1945 that the role of Bernarda was taken by Margarita Xirgu, who in the performances of the classical tragedies in Spain in the 1930s had played the tragic heroines.

In terms of its themes, *La casa de Bernarda Alba* is in many ways a fitting climax to Lorca's dramatic writing. Bernarda herself is, perhaps, his most powerful expression of the inflexible and destructive forces of social convention and tradition, notably honour, that in *Bodas de sangre* and *Yerma* are exemplified in la Madre and in Yerma's husband, Juan. In both those plays unbending social values clash with instinct and passion. In *La casa de Bernarda Alba* Adela, in particular, is the equivalent in her embracing of passion of la Novia in *Bodas de sangre*, while the bitter frustration encountered in a household which stifles her spirit links her to Yerma. The clash of opposites — of yearning and denial, of aspiration and failure — is, indeed, embodied in all the characters and invests the play with an impressive sense of cohesion and totality of vision. The village girl, Paca la Roseta, the harvesters, Pepe el Romano, all personify passion and vitality. Its denial, on the other hand, finds expression in Bernarda's daughters, the grandmother and, beyond the family, in the village girls who are either hounded for their so-called immorality or punished by their father for disobedience. The world of the play, in which character echoes character, is thus a microcosm, the particular world of Bernarda's village an image of other similar worlds and identical conflicts. In this sense the ultimate value of Lorca's rural tragedies, as well as his theatre as a whole, lies in the fact that, in typical symbolist fashion, they suggest much more than is actually seen on stage.

As far as the play's technique is concerned, Lorca, as we have seen, had spoken of his intention to produce a 'documental fotográfico'. This, together with the play's real-life source, has suggested to many critics that, of the last four plays, *La casa de Bernarda Alba* is the most realistic, the culmination of a process already evident in *Yerma* and *Doña Rosita la soltera*. In *Yerma* Lorca had already abandoned the poetic symbolism of the final Act of *Bodas de sangre*. In *La casa de Bernarda Alba* he goes further, reducing the seven examples of song in *Yerma* to only two. Furthermore, as in *Doña Rosita la soltera*, the settings of the play and the exchanges of the characters seem closer to the texture of real life. *Doña Rosita*, though, has already revealed that its surface realism conceals a high degree of symbolism, and *La casa de Bernarda Alba* is in that sense very similar. It is worth noting Francisco García Lorca's observation:

> The House of Bernarda Alba, of these plays, is the one which has the most direct inspiration in reality . . . And in spite of this basic reality, I would say that this is his most artful play and the one which is most disciplined in technique . . .[47]

The stage settings represent two rooms and the patio of Bernarda's house and are, indeed, in terms of detail, suggestive of real locations. The opening stage direction reads:

> *Habitación blanquísima del interior de la casa de Bernarda. Muros gruesos. Puertas en arco con cortinas de yute rematadas con madroños y volantes. Sillas de anea. Cuadros con paisajes inverosímiles de ninfas o reyes de leyenda...* (II., p.789)

> *A very white room in the house of Bernarda. Thick walls. Arched doorways with jute curtains tied back with tassels and ruffles. Wicker chairs. Pictures of fantastic landscapes with nymphs or legendary kings...*

In the setting for Act Two there is less detail but the room is still a real room, with doors leading off and chairs. The patio setting of Act Three presents Bernarda and her daughters seated at a table eating their meal, the noise of plates and silverware, and light flooding from inside the house. If the schematic and stark settings of *Bodas de sangre* are borne in mind, it is difficult to dispute the fact that the settings of *La casa de Bernarda Alba* are indicative of a greater realism.

Given this fact, even a glance at the stage directions suggests that the realistic elements also have a metaphorical significance. The whiteness of the walls, linking all three settings, points to a monotony and a sameness that is true not only of the physical character of the house but also of the lives of the people who live in it. That sameness is echoed too in other features of the rooms, as in the case of the arched doorways which parallel each other. In addition, the visual impact of the settings is accompanied by suggestive non-visual elements. The initial stage direction provides a good example:

> *... Un gran silencio umbroso se extiende por la escena. Al levantarse el telón está la escena sola. Se oyen doblar las campanas.* (II., p.789)

> *... A great brooding silence fills the stage. When the curtain rises the stage is empty. The tolling of bells can be heard.*

The whole becomes, in short, an image of imprisonment and oppression. Furthermore, Bernarda's house, far from being unique, is merely one house in a village where other houses and other households seem to be the same, and the village itself is an image of other villages. Not without cause did Lorca sub-title his play *Drama de mujeres en los pueblos de España (A Play about Women in the Villages of Spain)*.

The characters' names, given that some of them — Martirio, Angustias — are suggestive of emotional and spiritual states, are generally typical of the names to be found in the kind of society represented in the play and therefore reinforce its realism: Bernarda, Adela, Amelia, Magdalena, La

Poncia, Paca la Roseta, Pepe el Romano. The characters themselves, though, both in their appearance and in their manner, are clearly archetypal. Bernarda, dressed in black throughout the play — an ironic contrast to the implications of her surname, Alba (Dawn) — is the very essence of a narrow-mindedness and a joylessness that stifles life and gaiety, while her daughters, also dressed in black, their beauty fading, bear further witness to that fact. Adela, on the other hand, is the epitome of youth and vitality, and her dress, linked to the green of nature, is a dazzling image of life and vigour. The characters as a whole fall, in effect, into two broad categories, the one symbolic of the life of instinct and passion, the other of the repressive influence of social convention. Bernarda has her counterpart in many of the other villagers, Adela hers in the lively figures of Paca la Roseta and the harvesters. They evoke, in short, those universal and eternal conflicts that distinguish *Bodas de sangre* and *Yerma*.

The dialogue of the play, almost entirely in prose, has a deceptive air of realism, for it is seen on close examination to be stripped of the clutter of the language of daily life and to be shaped in a way which reveals the essence of each character. Bernarda's dialogue, reflecting her harshness, is extremely forceful, her words the equivalent of blows that seek to dominate those around her, assaulting them, bending them to her will. The end of the play, following Adela's suicide, provides a good example:

> Y no quiero llantos. La muerte hay que mirarla cara a cara. ¡Silencio! (*A otra* HIJA.)¡A callar he dicho! (*A otra* HIJA.) ¡Las lágrimas cuando estés sola! Nos hundiremos todas en un mar de luto. Ella, la hija menor de Bernarda Alba, ha muerto virgen. ¿Me habéis oído? ¡Silencio, silencio he dicho! ¡Silencio!   (II., p.882)

> And I want no weeping. Death must be looked at face to face. Silence! (To *another* DAUGHTER.) I said, be quiet! (To *another* DAUGHTER.) You can cry when you're alone! We'll drown ourselves in a sea of mourning. She, the youngest daughter of Bernarda Alba, has died a virgin. Do you hear me? Silence, silence, I said! Silence!

As evidence of Bernarda's success, the language of Magdalena and Martirio is heavy with the dragging weight of despair, while Adela's dialogue has the spring and vitality of rebellion, echoes the forcefulness of her mother but is at the same time different from it. In short, the language of the play, deceptively naturalistic, has the quality of music and goes beyond the literal meaning of words to suggest clashes and conflicts that are universal.

Poetry, in the form of songs, is used on only two occasions. Firstly, in Act Two Bernarda's daughters, standing at a window which is only partly open, observe the harvesters passing by outside and listen to their song of love:

> Ya salen los segadores
> en busca de las espigas;
> se llevan los corazones
> de las muchachas que miran.   (II., p.836)

> The reapers set out
> in search of the wheat;
> they bear away with them the hearts
> of the girls whom they see.

The spring and vibrancy of the lines, contrasting with the flat and leaden dialogue of the women, are immensely effective, like an oasis in the surrounding prose, and expressive, of course, of a world of energy and passion totally outside the experience of the women. Secondly, in Act Three María Josefa, the crazed grandmother, sings a lullaby which expresses both her own longings and aspirations and those of her grand-daughters:

> Ovejita, niño mío,
> vámonos a la orilla del mar . . .
> y en la playa nos meteremos
> en una choza de coral.   (II., p.872)

> Little lamb, my baby,
> let's go to the sea-shore
> and on the beach we'll hide
> in a coral cabin.

There is, though, a terrible contrast between the sentiments of the song and the mad woman who sings it, and she, of course, represents the reality that may well confront Bernarda's spinster daughters — the gulf between their dreams and the ultimate actuality of their lives. The two examples of poetry occur, thus, at crucial moments in the play and are strikingly and tellingly situated.

The lighting of the play, like so many of its other features, has a deceptive naturalness. In the stage directions for Acts One and Two there are no specific references to the lighting of the stage, but the overall effect is clearly one of dullness, lit principally by the sunlight that succeeds in penetrating the closed shutters, or in some cases the partially opened shutters, as in the scene where the women observe the harvesters. In addition, especially in Act One, the opening and shutting of doors allows light to flood into the house momentarily. The effect, natural and realistic as it is, is to suggest the enormous difference between the world of Bernarda's house and the world outside it — between a world of claustrophobic repression and inhibition and a world of joy and spontaneously expressed feeling. In short, the naturalistic lighting of the stage is used in a highly symbolist manner, and the evocation of two different worlds is further heightened by those elements of brightness or darkness suggested by the costumes themselves, be it the black of the women's clothes or the vivid green of Adela's dress in Act One. As the play unfolds, moreover, the lighting of the stage suggests the emotional journey of Bernarda's daughters into the darkness of despair and also into the dark world of their chaotic passions. For all its simplicity and apparent naturalness, lighting in *La casa de Bernarda Alba*, interwoven with stage settings, costumes and the movements of the characters, contributes enormously to the overall impact of the play, especially in the sense that the stage picture becomes an image whose resonances and implications extend far beyond the picture itself.[48]

Lorca's theatre as a whole, like that of Valle-Inclán, is one in which deeply serious themes are expressed in a great variety of ways, in which highly personal issues acquire a dramatic form and technique very different from that of the popular, commercial theatre of Lorca's time. Both dramatists, as the preceding discussion suggests, employed traditional forms — notably the puppet-play — in a new way, and both responded too to new movements in European art and culture which gives to their own work a truly European character. As far as Lorca is concerned, nothing illustrates better his European dimension than *El público* and *Así que pasen cinco años*, two of the boldest experiments in surrealist theatre. And the rural tragedies — *Bodas de sangre*, *Yerma* and *La casa de Bernarda Alba*— far from being, as many would have it, essentially Spanish plays, are amongst the most striking examples of symbolist theatre in the twentieth century. Lorca wrote in an effort to save the Spanish theatre from its stifling mediocrity. His achievement lies not only in saving it but in transforming it into a theatre of universal relevance.

---

1 *Teatro español contemporáneo* (Madrid, 1973), 25.

2 There are a number of useful studies of Lorca's theatre in general. See, for example, Robert Lima, *The Theater of García Lorca* (New York, 1963); Edwin Honig, *García Lorca* (New York, 1963); Virginia Higginbotham, *The Comic Spirit of Federico García Lorca* (Austin, 1976); and Gwynne Edwards, *Lorca: The Theatre Beneath the Sand* (London and Boston, 1980). There is also much useful information in Alfredo de la Guardia, *García Lorca: persona y creación* (Buenos Aires, 1944).

3 *Artículos de crítica teatral: el teatro español de 1914 a 1936* (Mexico, 1968), I, 28-9.

4 On this point see Robert Lima, *The Theater of García Lorca*, 56-7.

5 All page references, unless stated otherwise, are to *Federico García Lorca, Obras completas*, ed. Arturo del Hoyo, (19th ed.) (Madrid, 1974). In all cases the English translations are my own.

6 Page references to *El público* are to the edition of R. Martínez Nadal, *Federico García Lorca, 'El público' y 'Comedia sin título', Dos obras teatrales póstumas* (Barcelona, 1978).

7 *Maurice Maeterlinck* (New York, 1975), 119-27.

8 See Katherine Worth, *The Irish Drama of Europe from Yeats to Beckett* (London, 1978), 29-31, 41-7.

9 *The Irish Drama of Europe from Yeats to Beckett*, 23.

10 For studies of *Mariana Pineda* see Sumner M. Greenfield, 'The Problem of *Mariana Pineda*', *Massachusetts Review*, 1 (1960), 751-63; and Ricardo Doménech, 'A propósito de *Mariana Pineda*', *Cuadernos Hispano-americanos*, LXX (1967), 608-13.

11 On Lorca's puppet-plays and farces see, in particular, William I. Oliver, 'Lorca: The Puppets and the Artist', *Tulane Drama Review*, VII (1962), 76-95, and the relevant sections in the books by Lima, Honig, Higginbotham and Edwards mentioned in note 2.

12 *The Comic Spirit of Federico García Lorca*, 73.

13 See Edward Gordon Craig, *The Art of the Theatre*, in the edition published by Heinemann, London and New York, 1980, 54-94 and Denis Bablet, *The Theatre of Edward Gordon Craig*, translated by Daphne Woodward (London, 1981), 93-116.

14 There is an informative essay on the themes and dramatic technique of *La zapatera prodigiosa* by John and Florence Street in their edition of the play published by Harrap, London, 1962. See too Carlos Rincón, '*La zapatera prodigiosa* de Federico García Lorca', *Ibero-Romania*, IV (1970), 290-313.

15 John and Florence Street, in the introduction to *La zapatera prodigiosa*, 17.

16 The dramatic technique of *La zapatera* has not been examined in detail by many critics. On this aspect of the play see John and Florence Street and the appropriate sections in the books by Higginbotham and Edwards.

17 Lorca called the play a 'farsa violenta'. The phrase is intended to describe not any physical violence perpetrated by the characters upon each other but rather the speed and pace of the action and the vigour of the characters' movements and gestures.

18 The most comprehensive study of the impact of Surrealism in Spain is that by C.B. Morris, *Surrealism and Spain, 1920-1936* (Cambridge, 1972). On the influence of Surrealism on Spanish theatre see Barbara Sheklin Davis, 'El teatro surrealista español', *Revista Hispánica Moderna*, XXXIII (1967), 309-29.

19 Much useful information on the Residencia and its response to foreign cultural movements, including Freud, is contained in Franciso Aranda, *Luis Buñuel: A Critical Biography*, translated by David Robinson (London, 1975). See 22-9.

20 Lorca, '*Trip to the Moon. A Filmscript*', translated by Bernice G. Duncan, *New Directions*, vol. 18 (1964), 35-41. This translation is the only available version of Lorca's filmscript. The original Spanish version remains in the hands of Emilio Amero.

21 *The Dream-House (Silent Films and Spanish Poets)* (Hull, 1977), 16.

22 For a longer discussion of the influence of cinema on Lorca see C.B. Morris, *This Loving Darkness: The Cinema and Spanish Writers, 1920-1936* (Oxford, 1980), 121-39.

23 See in this respect J.L. Styan, *Modern Drama in Theory and Practice, II, Symbolism, Surrealism and the Absurd* (Cambridge, 1981), 54-60.

24 *Surrealism and Spain, 1920-1936*, 48; *The Dream-House*, 15; *This Loving Darkness*, 125.

25 'Lorca y el cine', *García Lorca Review*, VI (1978), 90.

26 There is a detailed study of *Un Chien andalou* in Gwynne Edwards, *The Discreet Art of Luis Buñuel* (London and Boston, 1982). See Chapter I.

27 'Federico García Lorca's *Así que pasen cinco años'*, *Bulletin of Hispanic Studies*, XLII (1966), 33.

28 On Lorca's play see the relevant sections in the books by Lima, Honig, Higginbotham and Edwards.

29 *Modern Drama in Theory and Practice; II . . .*, 85-6.

30 A very informative account both of the activities of *La barraca* and of the performances of classical tragedies in Spain is given by Suzanne Byrd, *'La Barraca' and the Spanish National Theatre* (New York, 1975). See too Luis Sáenz de la Calzada, *'La Barraca: teatro universitario'* (Madrid, 1976).

31 The most detailed study is that by Jean J. Smoot, *A Comparison of Plays by John Millington Synge and Federico Garcia Lorca: The Poets and Time* (Madrid, 1978). See Chapter 2.

32 *Drama and Reality: the European theatre since Ibsen* (London, 1972), 99-105. Gaskell's chapter on Synge, which focuses on *Riders to the Sea,* is followed by a chapter on Lorca, with particular emphasis on *Blood Wedding.* The author makes some interesting comparisons between the two dramatists.

33 See C.B. Morris, *Garcia Lorca: Bodas de sangre, Critical Guides to Spanish Texts* (London, 1980), 23-4.

34 *Garcia Lorca: Bodas de sangre . . .*, 25.

35 *Drama and Reality . . .*, 107.

36 For a perceptive study of the nature and effect of the play's imagery, see *Federico Garcia Lorca: Bodas de sangre,* edited with introduction, notes and vocabularly by H. Ramsden, (Manchester, 1980). The relationship between Man and Nature has been analysed by Gustavo Correa, *La poesia mitica de Federico Garcia Lorca* (2nd ed.) (Madrid, 1975). See 82-116.

37 For some critics the last Act of the play is a discordant element within it, at odds with the heightened realism of Acts I and II. This view has been forcefully expressed by William I. Oliver, 'The trouble with Lorca', *Modern Drama,* VII (1964), 2-15.

38 It is worth noting that Cipriano Rivas Cherif, a very significant figure in Madrid theatrical life from about 1928, had earlier studied in Italy and had absorbed there many of the production ideas of Edward Gordon Craig. Given Lorca's contact with Rivas Cherif, who directed *Yerma* in 1934 and *Doña Rosita la soltera* in 1935, there can be no doubt that he was familiar with Craig's ideas on the theatre.

39 Few critics have written at any length on the staging of *Bodas de sangre.* For a discussion of settings, costumes, lighting, music, etc., see Gwynne Edwards, *Lorca: The Theatre Beneath the Sand,* and C.B. Morris, *Garcia Lorca: Bodas de sangre . . .*

40 See the introduction to *Three Tragedies: Blood Wedding, Yerma, Bernarda Alba,* translated by James Graham-Luján and Richard L. O'Connell (Penguin, 1961), 25.

41 *Garcia Lorca: Playwright and Poet* (New York, 1977), 198-9.

42 On this aspect of the play see the relevant chapter in Gustavo Correa, *La poesia mitica de Federico Garcia Lorca,* (2nd ed.) (Madrid, 1975).

43 Enrique Díez-Canedo, *Articulos de critica teatral: el teatro español de 1914 a 1936* (Mexico, 1968), I, 57-59.

44 See Robert Lima, *The Theater of García Lorca,* 243.

45 *Three Tragedies . . .*, 22-3.

46 Carlos Morla Lynch, *En España con Federico García Lorca: Páginas de un diario íntimo, 1928-36,* (Madrid, 1958), 488-9.

47 *Three Tragedies . . .*, 28.

48 For a more detailed study of the play's themes and technique, see Gwynne Edwards, *Lorca: The Theatre Beneath the Sand,* 234-76.

CHAPTER IV
Rafael Alberti

Alberti's literary reputation rests more on his poetry than his drama, yet he has written plays for more than thirty years, from the first full-length *El hombre deshabitado (The Uninhabited Man)* of 1929, to *La lozana andaluza (The Voluptuous Andalusian)* of 1963. Furthermore, Alberti's theatre, like Valle-Inclán's and Lorca's, is a theatre both of serious intention and constant experiment. From the outset Alberti expressed his violent opposition to the popular commercial theatre that dominated the Spanish stages of the 1920s. When the curtain fell on the first performance of *El hombre deshabitado* on 26 February 1931, Alberti made a sensational appearance on the stage, roundly declaring:

> ¡Viva el exterminio! ¡Muera la podredumbre de la actual escena española!

> Long live death! Let us put an end to the rotteness of the present-day Spanish theatre![1]

He has described in the following way the reaction to the play and to his provocative outburst:

> El teatro, de arriba abajo, se dividió en dos bandos. Podridos y no podridos se insultaban amenazándose. Estudiantes y jóvenes escritores, subidos en las sillas, armaban la gran batahola, viéndose a Benavente y los Quintero abandonar la sala, en medio de una larga rechifla. (p.309)

> The theatre was divided from top to bottom into two groups. The rotten and the unrotten threatened and insulted each other. Students and young writers, standing on their seats, created a great uproar, and Benavente and the Quintero brothers were seen to leave the theatre accompanied by sustained catcalls.

The dramatist's initial opposition to a theatrical tradition devoid of intellectual stimulus and technical innovation has been sustained in eight major plays and half a dozen shorter pieces in which he has turned both to the drama of Spain's Golden Age and to significant forms of twentieth-century European theatre: Expressionism, *agitprop* and political theatre, and the epic theatre of Brecht and Piscator. In the following pages, Alberti's development as a dramatist and his efforts to revitalize Spanish theatre are considered in relation to four representative plays: *El hombre deshabitado* (1929), *Radio Sevilla* (1937), *El adefesio (The Absurdity)* (1944), and *Noche de guerra en el Museo del Prado (Night of War in the*

Prado Museum) (1956). In addition, some attention will be given to his interesting adaptation of Cervantes's *Numancia*.

As a key to the understanding of Alberti's theatre, certain aspects of his background are of great importance.[2] In his autobiography he provides a vivid account of the bourgeois, Catholic environment in which he grew up. Happy recollections of his mother and his brothers and sisters combine with bitter references to aunts and uncles and to his teachers. Their narrow-mindedness, hypocrisy and prejudice, as well as their ostentatious flaunting of Christian virtues, embodied for Alberti the repressive, traditionalist Andalusia of his childhood and explain in no small measure his subsequent anti-bourgeois attitudes, his anti-clericalism, his rejection of the Catholic faith and his embracing of Communism. The vision of Andalusia which Alberti would present in *El adefesio* is reminiscent in many respects of that of Lorca's *La casa de Bernarda Alba* and suggests that in their reaction to the world of their childhood and adolescence both dramatists shared a similar response.

Alberti's early enthusiasms were less for literature than for painting, an interest which had important consequences for his theatre. The family move from El Puerto de Santa María to Madrid in 1917, when Alberti was fifteen, brought him into decisive contact with the galleries and museums of the capital city and, above all, with the paintings of the Prado. There the boy from the provinces stood in wonder before the masterpieces of Velázquez, Titian, Tintoretto, Rubens, El Greco and Goya. The encounter with Goya was especially important in the sense that the happy face of Spain presented in Goya's cartoons had its opposite in the bitter and biting drawings and paintings of the later period, a dualistic vision of Spanish life which accorded perfectly with Alberti's own experience:

> Las salas de Goya, en las que se colgaban todos sus cartones para la Real Fábrica de Tapices, me abrían cada mañana los ojos a una fiesta . . . Mas para cruel contraste, no lejos . . . se hallaban los dibujos y parte, si no recuerdo mal, de los feroces muros de la Quinta del Sordo . . . definiendo así lo que Goya y toda la España que le tocó representar eran realmente: un inmenso ruedo taurino partido con violencia en dos colores: negro y blanco . . .(pp.110-11)

> The Goya rooms, which contained all his cartoons for the Royal Tapestry Factory, opened my eyes each morning to a true delight . . . But as a cruel contrast, not far from there . . ., were the drawings and, if I remember correctly, some of the savage murals from the Quinta del Sordo . . . which defined the true reality of Goya and the Spain which he depicted: a great bullring violently split into two colours: black and white.

In a more general sense Alberti's interest in painting, as practitioner and observer, would also contribute, of course, to the strong visual impact of his

theatre. Like so many exponents of the new drama of the twentieth century
— Craig, Yeats, Lorca — Alberti's familiarity with another art form allowed
him to achieve more easily the integration of dramatic and plastic elements
that has come to be known as total theatre.

The stimulus of painting was accompanied in Alberti's late teens by a
growing interest in poetry, while a serious illness in these years allowed him
the necessary time to extend his knowledge of literature: of contemporary
and Golden Age Spanish poets, as well as of Russian writers like Chekhov,
Dostoyevsky and Tolstoy, whose works were then being published in
Spain. In addition, through Spanish literary journals ranging from the
deliberately provocative *Ultra* to more restrained and broadly-based
magazines like *Horizonte* and *Alfar* Alberti became familiar with Spanish
and European *avant-garde* movements. In his autobiography he refers on
the one hand to Azorín, Machado, Unamuno, Gómez de la Serna, Gerardo
Diego and Guillermo de Torre, and on the other to Apollinaire, Jules
Romains and Ivan Goll. At all events Alberti began to devote himself more
and more to writing. His first book of poems, *Marinero en tierra (Sailor
Ashore)*, appeared in 1923 and was followed in the course of the decade by
other volumes of verse: in 1925 *La amante (The Beloved)*, in 1926 *El alba
del alhelí (The Dawn of the Wallflower)*, in 1927 *Cal y canto (Lime and
Stone)*, and in 1929 *Sobre los ángeles (Concerning the Angels)*.

Alberti's artistic formation during these years was greatly influenced by
his contact with the Residencia de Estudiantes, whose influence on Lorca
has been described in the previous chapter. Unlike Lorca, Alberti was not a
student at the Residencia but he has provided us with a detailed enough
account both of its activities and of his friendships. He describes his initial
meeting with Lorca as unforgettable, refers to the increasing frequency of
his visits to the Residencia, and lists the individuals he met and came to
know there: in addition to Lorca, Luis Buñuel, Salvador Dalí, Pepín Bello,
Moreno Villa, and many others. It was not until the end of the decade that
Alberti's visits, like Lorca's, became infrequent, but during those years his
contact with the institution, as well as with the cultural life of Madrid in
general, served to deepen and enrich his knowledge of the most modern
trends in art. Quite apart from his involvement in the activities of the
Residencia, Alberti attended performances of both ballet and opera, and it
is clear that if painting had its effect on his sense of the visual impact of stage
pictures, costumes and the grouping of figures, so his experience of ballet
showed him the expressive power of pure movement and the effects that
could be achieved through the harmonious integration of movement and
setting. In this respect Alberti was impressed as early as 1920 or 1921 by
Diaghilev's productions of Manuel de Falla's *El sombrero de tres picos*

(The Three-Cornered Hat), the Rossini-Respighi *La Boutique Fantasque,* and the Rimsky-Korsakov *Scheherazade* and *Tamar.* His reaction to the performances is worth noting, for it suggests that his response to a style of production that explored new and exciting possibilities was very much that of men like Gordon Craig and Lorca, a response to 'toda aquella simple y cálida geometría que se abrazaba fusionándose al quiebro colorido de los bailarines' ('that simple and warm geometry which fused and blended with the colourful movements of the dancers') (p.130) and to 'el más nuevo lenguaje, la más audaz expresión del nuevo ritmo corporal, musical y pictórico que inauguraba el siglo veinte' ('the new language, the boldest expression of physical, musical and pictorial rhythms that ushered in the twentieth century'). In addition, — and the similarity to Lorca is again apparent — Alberti embraced with enthusiasm the advent of the cinema in the Madrid of the 1920s. In his autobiography he refers to expressionist and surrealist films that impressed him greatly: *The Cabinet of Doctor Caligari,* Fritz Lang's *Metropolis,* Eisenstein's *The Battleship Potemkin,* and, in 1929, Luis Buñuel's *Un chien andalou.* These, as well as the comic films of Chaplin, Keaton, Langdon, Laurel and Hardy and others, contributed greatly to Alberti's visual sense. C.B. Morris has observed:

> ... films did not merely furnish what Alberti termed 'a new vision', but encouraged him to take a fresh look at commonplace events, to see things in a new light. Alberti thus paid tribute to the cinema for increasing his and everyone else's frame of visual references, for enriching the mind with new sets of pictures and scenes as colourful and as varied as the paintings he contemplated and copied in the Prado.[3]

Alberti's view of the kind of theatre that dominated the Spain of the 1920s has been noted in his remarks to the audience at the end of *El hombre deshabitado,* and the autobiographical account of the experimental films to which he responded with enthusiasm is followed immediately by a disparaging reference to the artistic poverty of the Madrid stage:

> Nuestra escena, invadida aún . . . por Benavente, los Quintero, Arniches, Muñoz Seca . . . nada podía darme . . .   (p.285)

> Our theatre, occupied still, . . . by Benavente, the Quintero brothers, Arniches, Muñoz Seca . . . could give me nothing . . .

On the other hand, there was, as the previous chapters have suggested, an experimental drama, growing throughout the twenties, in which Alberti certainly found inspiration. Valle-Inclán's highly original works, *Luces de Bohemia* and *Los cuernos de don Friolera* belong to this time, as do Jacinto Grau's *El señor de Pigmalión* and many of Lorca's early masterpieces. In the smaller, non-commercial theatres there were performances of plays by Baroja, Valle-Inclán, Azorín, Unamuno and Cipriano Rivas Cherif. Alberti himself recalls being impressed by Claudio de la Torre's *Tic-Tac* of 1926 and Azorín's *Brandy, mucho brandy (Brandy, Lots of Brandy)* of 1927, as well as by Gómez de la Serna's *Los medios seres (Partial Beings)* of 1929. From 1917 to 1925 Martínez Sierra, director of the Teatro Eslava in Madrid, produced both foreign and Spanish plays in a new, forward-looking style that echoed the advances being made in theatrical production in other European countries. Of the other directors, Cipriano Rivas Cherif, who had absorbed the ideas of Edward Gordon Craig in Italy, became advisor from 1928 to Margarita Xirgu, Spain's leading actress, at the Teatro Español in Madrid. The dreary spectacle of a sterile commercial theatre had its counterpart, then, in an experimental theatre of considerable vision and vitality. Alberti's first play, *La pájara pinta (The Painted Bird)*, written in 1925, is a short piece for puppets, its characters and language largely drawn from the world of children's nonsense rhymes. Its significance lies in the fact that in its highly stylized manner it reflects very clearly Alberti's rejection of naturalistic theatre and his enthusiastic response to the new, if minority, Spanish theatre of that time.

Alberti's first full-length play, *El hombre deshabitado*, sub-titled *Auto en un prólogo, un acto y un epílogo (Auto with prologue, act and epilogue)*, was premièred at the Teatro de la Zarzuela in Madrid on February 26 1931, to the protests of the traditionalists and the acclamation of the supporters of the *avant-garde*. Alberti himself, as we have seen, appeared on stage at the final curtain, urging the demise of the traditional theatre. In the days that followed the extraordinary performance, the newspapers voiced either their support or condemnation of the play, particularly in relation to its exposition of religious themes and doctrines. Thus, for Jorge de la Cueva, writing in *El Debate,* the work was immoral in its frank portrayal of passion and irreverent in its religious unorthodoxy.[4] Other critics, in contrast, recognized the seriousness of Alberti's purpose and the ambitious nature of the play's technique. Of these Enrique Díez-Canedo observed perceptively that the imperfections of the production should not be allowed to obscure the play's qualities. *El hombre deshabitado,* drawing on the great theatre of Spain's Golden Age, is also, he argues, an essentially modern and forward-looking work, a play which in its very qualities is far more effective than Alberti's hysterical outburst against a decadent theatre.[5]

El hombre deshabitado has for its protagonist el Hombre (man), and the action of the play presents his emergence into the world, his journey through it, and his final return to the point from whence he came. In the first section of the play — the prologue — el Hombre is a man who emerges from the subterranean depths, a being who dwells in darkness and who is therefore equipped by el Vigilante nocturno (The Nightwatchman), a magician-like character, with a soul and the five senses in order to embark upon his journey in the world. In the central section of the play el Hombre, now called el Caballero, has a wife, la Mujer, for his companion, and they live happily and innocently in a beautiful garden. When he encounters a woman who has been injured, el Hombre and la Mujer too feel only pity for her, but el Hombre is deceived by his innocence and fails to exercise his will in the face of the advances of the strange and beautiful woman, whom he finally recognizes as temptation. He is persuaded by her to murder his wife, but the latter's death leads only to his own unhappiness and he is killed finally by a figure who is the personification of his own remorse. In the epilogue el Hombre bitterly accuses el Vigilante Nocturno of deceiving him with false promises of happiness. He has been transformed in consequence of his experiences from the innocent into the rebel who knows that, for all his protestations, paradise cannot be achieved. The enigmatic statements of el Vigilante reduce el Hombre to a final state of anguished hopelessness.

In terms of theme and technique Alberti's play owes much to the tradition of the Spanish *autos sacramentales,* the religious plays which flourished in the sixteenth and seventeenth centuries and of which Calderón became the master exponent.[6] Alberti himself has referred to the influence of the Spanish-Portuguese dramatist, Gil Vicente, whose *autos* belong to the first two decades of the sixteenth century, but it is clearly the *autos* of Calderón whose impact is most clearly seen in *El hombre deshabitado.* It is, indeed, worth noting that Calderón's *autos* were very much in vogue in Spain in the 1920s. In 1926 the great German theatre director, Max Reinhardt, planned a performance of a Calderón *auto* — probably of Calderón's *Los encantos de la culpa (The Attractions of Wrong-Doing)* — in collaboration with the Spanish painter, José María Sert, and the composer, Manuel de Falla. The performance did not take place, but in 1927 Calderón's famous *auto, El gran teatro del mundo (The Great Theatre of the World),* with music by Falla, was presented in the Alhambra in Granada. Furthermore, in 1930 Margarita Xirgu, Spain's leading actress, performed *El gran teatro del mundo* at the Teatro Español in Madrid. At the time when Alberti was writing *El hombre deshabitado* — it was still not finished at the beginning of February 1931 — the theatrical climate in Spain was thus one in which the *auto,* and especially the *autos* of Calderón, had achieved a new popularity. It explains, at least in part, why Alberti chose the form of the *auto* for his own play.

The traditional *autos sacramentales* were invariably, whatever the differences between them, celebrations of the Christian faith, performed for that purpose on the day of Corpus Christi. For Lope de Vega the mere dramatization of religious stories, *historias divinas*, was an acceptable way of praising the Catholic faith, and his *autos* are not always distinguished, therefore, by a religious exposition of doctrine. In the *autos* of Calderón, on the other hand, the doctrine of Christ's sacrifice for mankind is always central, and the dramatic action, whatever form it takes, invariably illustrates that point. As A.A. Parker has observed: 'The *asunto* (theme) of every *auto* is therefore the Eucharist, but the *argumento* (plot) can vary from one to another: it can be any "historia divina" — historical, legendary or fictitious — provided that it throws some light on some aspect of the *asunto*.'[7] Calderón's *El gran teatro del mundo* illustrates the point well. At the outset the characters of the play — the king, the rich man, the poor man, the peasant, beauty, and discretion — are given the parts they have to play and the costumes and accessories appropriate to them. While each is different from the other in the social hierarchy, each has a common purpose — to work out his or her salvation and to achieve that end by fulfilling their obligations both to their fellows and to God. In the course of their exposure to the world, the characters are, of course, misled by their own self-centredness, as a consequence of which they are forgetful of the true end of life. By the end of the play all, except the rich man, come to recognize their errors, and inequality is seen to lie not in material or social differences but in the extent to which each individual is aware of the life of the spirit. In its celebration of God's purpose and man's salvation through his recognition of it, *El gran teatro del mundo* comes to a triumphant conclusion.

As Theodore Beardsley has indicated, the prologue and the Acto of Alberti's play derive from Calderón in several respects.[8] The prologue combines elements from *El gran teatro del mundo*, *La vida es sueño (Life is a Dream)* and *Los encantos de la culpa*. When, for example, el Vigilante Nocturno endows el Hombre with a soul and the five senses, the episode recalls the beginning of *El gran teatro del mundo*. On the other hand, the prologue also owes something to the beginning of *Los encantos de la culpa* where Ulysses is seen upon a stormy sea accompanied by the five senses. The influence of this *auto* is evident too in Alberti's Acto, for el Hombre's seduction by la Tentación (temptation) recalls the surrender of Ulysses to the fatal charms of Circe, while in *La vida es sueño* Adam likewise abandons la Luz de Gracia (light of grace) in favour of la Sombra (ignorance). The prologue and the acto of *El hombre deshabitado* are thus, as Beardsley indicates, indebted in terms of detail and general development to the *autos* of Calderón in particular.

Nevertheless, as Louise Popkin suggests, the borrowings do not conceal important differences, notably in Alberti's presentation of el Hombre.[9] In the traditional *auto* man can avail himself of various allies, especially reason and understanding, in order to defeat temptation. In contrast, Alberti's el Hombre is a defenceless innocent, naively aspiring to happiness and destroyed by that very innocence. In the course of the prologue and the Acto he is led, not like Calderón's man, to knowledge of how to combat and surmount evil, but to the final realization that his destruction is preordained. Alberti's epilogue is, in the light of this, the traditional ending to the *auto* completely overturned. El Hombre accuses el Vigilante nocturno of cruelly deceiving him and demands an explanation. He is denied it and left with a sense both of his own hopelessness and the meaninglessness of life. The traditional *auto's* celebration of man's salvation through God has thus become a twentieth-century affirmation of spiritual emptiness and the absurdity of human aspiration.

In terms of its pessimism *El hombre deshabitado* is, of course, a powerful personal statement rooted in the circumstances of Alberti's life at the time of the play's composition. Between 1928 and 1931 he found himself, for a variety of reasons, in a state of spiritual torment. On the one hand, an unhappy love affair and the suicide of a friend, on the other feelings of guilt and fear connected with his loss of religious faith. In his autobiography Alberti provides a vivid picture of the spiritual crisis of this period in his life:

> ¿Qué espadazo de sombra me separó casi insensiblemente de la luz, de la forma marmórea de mis poemas inmediatos, del canto aún no lejano de las fuentes populares, de mis barcos, esteros y salinas, para arrojarme en aquel pozo de tinieblas, aquel agujero de oscuridad, en el que bracearía casi en estado agónico, pero violentamente, por encontrar una salida a las superficies habitadas, al puro aire de la vida?   (p.268)

> What shadowy sword cut me off almost insensibly from the light, from the marmoreal form of my poems written shortly before, from the songs still quite close to their popular origins, from my ships, my inlets, and my salt flats, only to throw me into that pit of darkness, that black void in which I would struggle in agony and desperation in search of escape to habitable regions, to the pure, fresh air of life?

The struggle with the dark forces of despair is forcefully expressed in *Sobre los ángeles (Concerning the Angels)*, Alberti's complex and difficult poem of 1929. Of this poem C.B. Morris has written:

> In *Sobre los ángeles* Alberti is his own theme; he himself is the object of his attention. Previously he was not interested in introspection . . . [10]

During the composition of the poem he seems too to have commenced work on *El hombre deshabitado*, although he did not complete it until

1931. The similarities between the poem and the play in terms of the theme of spiritual desolation have been noted by Richard Cardwell when he suggests that the play is 'a journey of self-discovery that accompanies the presentation of the autobiographical hero . . . '[11] The personal dimension assumes, though, a wider relevance, for Alberti's spiritual 'malaise' is also in many ways that of his time. As we have already seen in relation to Valle-Inclán, the circumstances of the First World War, the terrible events that characterized it and the sense of anguish that followed it, all served to deepen throughout Europe that sense of disillusionment, of disorientation, of individual insignificance whose presence was already strongly felt. Even before the War, and unconnected with it, the breakdown of accepted values and traditions was manifest in the new movements of Cubism and Futurism. Afterwards, nourished by the War, Dadaism and Expressionism communicated the destructiveness of a machine-dominated, war-torn Europe. The advent of Freud and Jung, emphasizing man's unconscious, further undermined his sense of certainty. In the maelstrom of events that questioned all that had gone before, it is little wonder that a man as sensitive as Alberti was to the world around him should see his own spiritual crisis as part of a greater whole. Nor is it surprising that, having availed himself of the traditional form of the *auto sacramental* to communicate his strongly personal viewpoint, he should also have availed himself of a technique highly suited to the expression of subjective feeling: the technique of Expressionism.

It is interesting to note that both the forerunners of Expressionism and the Expressionists themselves produced a number of works in which, as in *El hombre deshabitado*, the influence of the morality play is much in evidence. Strindberg's trilogy *To Damascus*, written in 1898, evokes the Biblical story of Saul's journey to Damascus and his conversion to Christianity, but is otherwise strongly autobiographical in character. The character called 'The Unkown' is Strindberg himself, 'The Lady' his wife or wives, the journey of the play Strindberg's own journey through the various stages of guilt and sin, and the other characters of the play — a beggar, a madman, a confessor — extensions of the dramatist. The more famous *A Dream Play*, written in 1902, has similar characteristics and its personages are both Strindberg himself and mankind in general. As for the later Expressionists, Georg Kaiser's *The Burghers of Calais* (1913) and *From Morn to Midnight* (1916) can both be regarded as morality plays. The former embodies the virtues of self-sacrifice, and the latter, its structure suggesting the stations of the cross, follows the journey of the cashier through a materialistic world to his suicide, the symbol of his own spiritual regeneration in a world otherwise bent on its own destruction. Even if

Alberti's play is a statement not of spiritual renewal but of emptiness, the parallel with some of the major works of Expressionism is clearly illuminating. In a study of *El hombre deshabitado* Louise B. Popkin has noted that 'Alberti undoubtedly echoes the German Expressionist playwrights', though it is important to bear in mind that Alberti's trip to Europe, which would take him to Paris, Germany, Holland, Belgium, Scandinavia and Russia, did not take place until 1931-2, after the composition of the play.[12] On the other hand, it cannot be denied that *El hombre deshabitado* reveals in terms of its settings, its characterization, its dialogue and its plot, characteristics that, whatever Alberti's direct contact with expressionist theatre, are essential features of that movement. To a certain extent they are also features of the traditional *auto sacramental*, for this was distinguished by its use of symbolism and allegory, which in turn influenced staging and characterization. But reference to Spanish tradition is not enough to explain the striking modernity of Alberti's dramatic technique. This, like the spirit of the play itself, is very much of our time.

As far as stage settings are concerned, the *auto sacramental* was distinguished by its emphasis on the symbolic and the archetypal. Of the settings of expressionist plays it has been noted, and the earlier consideration of *Luces de Bohemia* has confirmed, that they too are starkly simplified images, often abstract and unlocalized, which express in themselves the play's principal concerns.[13] When the curtain rises on the prologue to *El hombre deshabitado,* we are presented with an urban landscape, a scene of dereliction composed of a pile of bricks, pieces of twisted metal, a fallen telegraph pole, and various heaps of rubbish:

> *En el centro de la escena, y en primer término, la gran boca cerrada de una alcantarilla. A su derecha, y al borde, clavados en la tierra, tres hierros retorcidos, unidos por un cordel . . . Al lado izquierdo de la escena, sobre una plancha de acero con ruedas, un gran cono de carbón . . . Contra el fondo negro, un poste medio tumbado, de luz eléctrica, del que pende un largo cable roto.[14]*   (p.9)

> *In the centre of the stage, to the front, the large, closed entrance to a sewer. To the far right, fixed in the ground, three twisted metal stakes, joined by a rope . . . To the left of the stage, on a flat metal dray a pile of coal . . . Against the dark background, a lamp-post at an angle, and a long piece of broken cable hanging from it.*

The setting is less precise and realistic than a highly stylized, archetypal image of the modern, urban world. But it is also more than that, for it evokes not simply the desolation of a physical setting but the spiritual emptiness of modern man, symbolized in the play's protagonist. Indeed,

the darkness of the stage is significantly echoed by el Hombre's very first
words as he emerges from the sewer:

> ¡Sombras, sombras, sombras por todas partes! Arriba y abajo. Oscuridades
> llenas de aguas corrompidas . . .   (p.9)

> Shadows, shadows, shadows everywhere! Above and below. Darkness full of
> stinking water . . .

In truly expressionist manner the play's settings mirror the protagonist's
inner, subjective state.

Similarly, the setting for the Acto, the central section of the play, is an
image of el Hombre's spiritual journey from innocence to sin. To the right is
a garden:

> *Es la primavera. Cuatro árboles en los extremos y uno en medio, al pie de un
> estanque bajo, redondo, sobre un plano inclinado hacia los espectadores. Al
> fondo, muro blanco de casa.*   (p.20)

> *It is Spring. Four trees at the sides and one in the middle, at the edge of a round
> shallow pool, which is tilted towards the audience. At the back, the white wall
> of a house.*

The stylized perfection of the setting, with its emphasis on symmetry and
unblemished colour, evokes both paradise, as in a Bosch painting, and el
Hombre's untarnished innocence. On the other hand, in the centre of the
stage, linked to the garden by an archway, there are signs of dereliction in
the shape of broken tiles and a mound of sulphur:

> *Ante ella [la tapia], un montón de azufre y tejas rotas.*   (p.20)

> *In front of it [the wall], a pile of sulphur and broken tiles.*

Stage-left is dominated by a dark barn, reached from centre-stage by a
door, and is distinguished by ominous and disturbing signs:

> *Haces de trigo por el suelo. Toneles altos y bajos, llenos de enormes escobas y
> varas de bambú. Un carrillo volcado. Y grandes telarañas pintadas por las
> paredes.*   (p.20)

> *Bundles of wheat on the floor. Tall and low barrels, full of huge brooms and
> bamboo canes. An overturned cart. And great spider-webs painted on the
> walls.*

As the eye traverses the stage it moves from Paradise to darkness, observing
the physical representation of el Hombre's journey into spiritual darkness.
Alberti's stage pictures may be compared both in their imagistic function
and in their emotional impact upon the spectator to those of Kaiser. Act
One of *GAS II* begins with the following stage direction:

> *Concrete hall. Light cascading from arc-lamps. From the hazy height of the*
> *dome a cluster of wires vertically down to the iron platform and thence*
> *distributed to small iron tables — three right, three left. At each table a BLUE*
> *FIGURE — sitting stiffly in uniform staring at a glass panel in the table...*[15]
>
> (p.245)

Kaiser's picture is one of a modern, machine-dominated age and of man reduced physically and spiritually to the level of an automaton. It is stylized and archetypal, as well as emotive. In essence Alberti's method is very similar.

The characters of expressionist drama are, like the settings in which they move, stripped of realistic detail, less individuals than symbolic types. R.S. Furness has drawn attention to Expressionism's 'concern for the typical and essential rather than the purely personal and individual',[16] while J.L. Styan observes of German Expressionism that the 'characters for the most part remain nameless and impersonal ... , their characteristics being emphasized by costume, mask or make-up ...'[17] Allegory, symbolism and abstraction were traditional features too, of course, of the *auto sacramental,* and Alberti's characters have their counterpart there. The overlapping of both traditions is reflected in the generic names of the characters of Alberti's play: el Hombre (the man), la Mujer (the woman), el Vigilante nocturno (the nightwatchman), la Tentación (temptation), los Cinco Sentidos (the five senses). Costume or mask or both are used by Alberti, moreover, to underline both the archetypal, eternal significance of his characters and in many cases to make the point that the figures on the stage are, indeed, facets, aspects and 'exteriorizations' of the principal participants of the drama. When el Hombre first emerges from his subterranean dwelling, he wears a diver's suit and a mask:

> ... *asciende, torpe, inflada hasta la exageración su máscara de buzo,* EL
> HOMBRE DESHABITADO.
>
> ... THE UNINHABITED MAN *appears, moving awkwardly, the diver's*
> *helmet grossly swollen.*

Costume and movement are used to suggest the idea of a formless creature, of a figure in search of his true identity. Shortly afterwards he vigorously rejects the accusation made by el Vigilante nocturno that he is 'un pellejo sin aire' 'an airless bladder', (p.10) but the verbal image indicates very clearly the extent to which the figure on the stage is the physical manifestation of a spiritual state. Man is, indeed, anatomized in the course of the action, his inner self revealed to himself and to the audience of the play. His five senses are thus paraded before him, each a self-explanatory visual image whose striking character resides in its simplicity:

... los cinco sentidos asoman las cabezas. LA VISTA *es un monstruo todo lleno de ojos;* EL OÍDO, *todo lleno de orejas;* EL OLFATO, *de narices;* EL GUSTO, *de bocas, y* EL TACTO, *de manos.* (p.14)

... the five senses poke out their heads. SIGHT *is a monster covered with eyes;* HEARING, *all ears;* SMELL, *all noses;* TASTE, *all mouths, and* TOUCH, *all hands.*

Quite apart from their appearance, the senses respond, moreover, in a manner which, appropriate to their natures, is necessarily one-dimensional — sight to the purely visual impact of la Tentación, hearing to her voice, smell to her scent. Inasmuch as the characters on the stage act out a drama which is universal and spiritual, they can be seen within the context and the technique of the *auto sacramental.* On the other hand, the stage action of the Golden Age *auto* is not the dramatization of the dramatist's personal, subjective crisis. It is this subjective element, the anguished baring of his own soul, which in Alberti's play places it firmly within the context of Expressionism.

Movement in the play, much more akin to that of ballet than of naturalistic drama, is highly expressive of inner states. At the beginning of the Acto, before a word is spoken, the static poses and the slow, dream-like movements of the figures in the garden communicate the magical, unruffled calm of Paradise. Thus, el Hombre is seen seated:

> *... EL HOMBRE, soñoliento ... se halla sentado ...* (p.20)
> *... THE MAN, drowsy ... is seen seated ...*

Similarly, the senses:

> LOS CINCO SENTIDOS, *aletargados, también están en el jardín.* (p.20)
> THE FIVE SENSES, *sleepy, are also in the garden.*

Slowly, the static, dreamy figures come to life, their stylized, balletic movements — which bring to mind the slow-motion sequences of silent films — expressing their awakening by means of pure physical action:

> EL OÍDO *despierta, atiende, balanceando los pies en la escalera.* EL HOMBRE *vuelve a desperezarse, aspirando con fuerza el aire del jardín.* (p.21)
> HEARING *awakens, listens, swinging his feet on the stairs.* THE MAN *stretches again, breathing in deeply the air of the garden.*

Later, the elaborate dance of the senses, an intricate interplay of movement reminiscent in some respects of the dance of the various characters in Calderón's *No hay más fortuna que Dios (There is No Greater Fortune than God),* is highly expressive of their delight in their new awareness of their and el Hombre's powers, music and words combining here in a powerfully suggestive ritual:

> LA VISTA *(avanzando un paso):* Yo soy ver. Todo lo veo. *(Retrocede).*
> EL GUSTO *(lo mismo):* Yo, gustar. Yo todo lo gusto. *(Retrocede)*
> EL OLFATO *(lo mismo):* Yo, oler. Yo todo lo huelo. *(Retrocede)*
> EL OÍDO *(lo mismo):* Y yo, oír. Todo lo escucho. *(Retrocede)*
>
> SIGHT *(Taking a step forward):* I am sight. I see everything. *(Steps back).*
> TASTE *(steps forward):* I am taste. I taste everything. *(Steps back).*
> SMELL *(steps forward):* I am smell. I smell everything. *(Steps back).*
> HEARING *(steps forward):* I am hearing. I hear everything *(Steps back).*

As the dance progresses — the lines quoted are only a small sample — it acquires an insistent, sustained momentum, an ecstatic frenzy which is the very essence of sensual pleasure. Another example occurs in the Acto when the senses, surrendering to the attractions of temptation, rush to and surround el Hombre, the physical movement on the stage a perfect exteriorization of the assault that is taking place within el Hombre's spirit:

> (LOS CINCO SENTIDOS *le rodean, encendiendo cada uno su linterna.)*

> (THE FIVE SENSES *surround him, each lighting his lantern).*

The examples quoted suggest that in Alberti's play there are extremes of movement, from the static postures of the figures in the garden, to the senses' hysterical attack upon el Hombre. Rhythmic movement and a style of acting which in its often intense and impassioned manner invariably expresses inner states is, of course, a feature of Expressionism. It is interesting to note too in this respect that, as the discussion of Valle-Inclán's *Luces de Bohemia* has suggested, the Expressionists favoured a bold, Baroque style of acting. From that point of view the technique of the Baroque *auto sacramental* lent itself extremely well to Alberti's purpose.

The dialogue of *El hombre deshabitado* is especially noteworthy. J.L. Styan has referred to the dialogue of expressionist drama as a whole as being 'poetical, febrile, rhapsodic' and as often distinguished by its 'staccato telegraphese — made up of phrases of one or two words or expletives'.[18] Bearing this in mind we can consider some examples from Alberti's play that are not exceptional but highly characteristic, and which, in Styan's words, 'evoke sympathetic feeling directly'.[19] When, in the prologue, el Hombre sees the stars for the first time his reaction is highly emotional:

> ¡Oh! ¡Oh! ¡Oh!   (p.14)

Shortly afterwards he is enraptured by the scent of a rose:

¡Oh! ¡Oh! ¡Oh! ¡Una rosa, una rosa!

Oh! Oh! Oh! A rose, a rose!

And again:

¡Una rosa blanca, una rosa blanca! La quiero. Démela.
(Subrayando las palabras como un niño.)
Yo quie-ro una ro-sa blan-ca. (p.15)

A white rose, a white rose! I want it.
Give it to me *(emphasizing the words like a child).*
I wa-nt a wh-ite ro-se.

Exclamations and repetitions, employed to transform the language of everyday speech into a form of expression which instantly reveals strong emotion, are a constant feature of the play. In the earlier discussion of the importance of movement, reference was made to the interaction of words and movement in relation to the creation of a mood of growing ecstasy. At the climax of the dance a piercing shriek is heard from the middle of the stage and the atmosphere is totally and violently changed:

VOZ DE MUJER *(en la playa)*: ¡Socorrooooo! *(Tumulto y golpes tras la puerta de la tapia, en la parte central de la escena.* LOS CINCO SENTIDOS *interrumpen el juego y escuchan asustados.)*
VOCES DISTINTAS: ¡Aquí, aquí! ¡Ésta es la casa! ¡Auxilioooo! (p.16)

A WOMAN'S VOICE *(on the beach)*: He-e-e-e-e-e-lp!
(Commotion and noise behind the door in the wall, in the centre of the stage.
THE FIVE SENSES *stop their game and listen in fright.)*
DIFFERENT VOICES: Over here, over here! This is the house! He-e-e-e-lp!

Another example of the way in which the language of the play, often through its sheer musicality, reveals inner conflict occurs when the senses whisper into the ear of el Hombre the irresistible attractions of la Tentación:

EL OÍDO *(a media voz)*: Dime. ¿Cuando escuchaste otra voz como la suya? ¿Quién en el mundo te encolerizó, te suplicó y acarició con ese timbre? No permitas que suene para otros oídos.
....

EL OLFATO *(a media voz)*: Huele a sol, a ola, a cielo, a viento libre. Si la dejas marchar, será como quedarte sin aire. (p.28)

HEARING *(whispering)*: Tell me. When did you hear a voice like hers? Who else in the whole world could provoke you, appeal to you and caress you with such a tone of voice? Don't let her speak to anyone else.
....

SMELL *(whispering)*: She smells of the sun, the waves, the sky, the breeze. If you let her escape, it will be as though you cannot breathe.

Finally, the language captures el Hombre's changing moods, effectively tracing his increasing anguish not merely in the rhythm of his lines but in phrases and images which have a marked visual and graphic character. His desperate attempt to avoid temptation is a good example:

> No me hables de ver. Arráncame los ojos y déjame sin luz, antes de que otras sombras entenebrezcan mi alma. Arroja mis pupilas al mar. Que los salitres más hondos me las quemen . . .   (p.38)

> Don't speak to me about seeing. Tear out my eyes and leave me in darkness, before other shadows darken my soul. Throw my eyes into the sea. Let the salt of the deepest water burn them . . .

El hombre deshabitado is in many ways a very fine dramatic work, and certainly one of great originality. In its splitting of a single character into different facets, it brings to mind the expressionist plays of Strindberg; in its integration of sets, lighting and movement, as well as in the emotional impact of its language, it has powerful echoes of the German Expressionists. Louise Popkin points to the play's faults, listing among them diffuseness, prolixity and a failure to integrate dialogue and visual effects.[20] On the contrary, it seems perfectly clear that a producer of vision and ability could make much of this play. In 1931 its impact on an audience largely accustomed to an altogether more conventional drama was very great indeed.

1931 was an important year for Alberti not merely because it saw the performance of his first full-length play but also because it marked his and his wife's departure for Paris. In the course of a tour of various European countries, including Belgium, Germany, Holland, Scandinavia and the Soviet Union, Alberti and María Teresa — herself a woman of the theatre — had the opportunity of observing and studying at first hand the work of significant European dramatists and directors who were seeking, like Alberti, to change the direction of the drama. Above all he seems to have been attracted by the methods and the political approach to theatre of Erwin Piscator; by the didacticism and the anti-realism of Bertolt Brecht; by the experiments in production techniques of the Austrian, Max Reinhardt, who seemed equally at ease in realistic or non-realistic plays and who gave an added impulse to Expressionism and the concept of 'total theatre'; and, finally, by the Russian directors, Vsevolod Meyerhold and Alexander Tairov, both products of the Moscow Art Theatre and revolutionaries in the drama, be it in relation to their efforts to destroy the tradition of the theatre as illusion or to endow it with a social dimension.[21] If in *El hombre deshabitado* there are clear expressionist tendencies, the European tour brought Alberti into direct contact with some of its major exponents. Furthermore, the experience of the early 1930s, both inside and outside Spain, had the important effect of shifting the emphasis of Alberti's theatre away from introspection and self-analysis to social commitment. The dramatist's formative years, as we have seen, instilled in him both anti-clerical and anti-bourgeois sentiments, while the spiritual crisis reflected in *Sobre los ángeles* and *El hombre deshabitado* points clearly to the search for a new purpose and direction, as much ideological as artistic. In the course of his European trip Alberti was made aware of the controversies taking place amongst intellectuals in relation to the role of the artist and the function of art, a debate which centred very largely on the relative importance of formal experimentation in drama championed by the Formalists and the need for a theatre of ideas and social commitment advocated by the Realists and, of course, the Communists. At all events, in an interview of 1933 Alberti declared unequivocally his changed attitude to the theatre:

> ... No creo en eso que llaman teatro experimental y de minorías. Desde mi particular punto de vista, no veo otra [solución] más que la de organizar tropas o grupos de agitación, para crear el teatro de masas.
> ... El teatro, aunque se crea lo contrario, tiene que ser tendencioso y volver a su fuente natural: el pueblo.[22]

> ... I don't believe in the thing they call experimental, minority theatre. From my own point of view, the only solution is to organize companies and groups who will agitate, who will create a theatre of the people.
> ... The theatre, though the opposite might be thought true, must be tendentious and return to its natural roots: the people.

When he returned to Spain he was able to declare that, in terms of his art and its aims, he was indeed a new man whose personal spiritual crisis had been resolved by a growing awareness of the importance of commitment to causes greater than himself.

As far as the Spanish situation of the early 1930s was concerned, political events matched and evidently fired Alberti's new social and ideological preoccupations. The dictatorship of Don Miguel Primo de Rivera, which had come into being in a single day in 1923, ended on 28 January 1930, and the following year saw the inauguration of the Second Spanish Republic and, in conjunction with it, the promise of a new era of liberty. Alberti, together with many other intellectuals and creative writers such as García Lorca, Machado, Ortega y Gasset, Pérez de Ayala, Unamuno and Valle-Inclán, aligned himself with the aims and aspirations of the Republic. Both he and María Teresa worked on behalf of the Republican cause and Alberti himself gave recitals of his poetry at political meetings. They founded the revolutionary magazine, *Octubre,* and in 1934 went to Moscow to attend the First Congress of Soviet Writers. The Asturian rebellion in October

1934, news of which reached Alberti in Moscow, led him in the following year to undertake a tour of America where lectures and poetry recitals provided financial assistance for the Asturian victims, and in 1936 he returned to Spain to give his support to the Popular Front which, under Azaña, came to power in February of that momentous year.

During the Civil War Alberti and María Teresa worked for the Republic in a variety of ways. Alberti was secretary to the Alianza de Intelectuales Antifascistas (the Alliance of Antifascist Intellectuals) which he had helped to found in 1936, and he was also one of the founders and guiding spirits of the newspaper, *El Mono Azul,* which between 1936 and 1938 was circulated amongst Republican supporters. In 1937 he attended in Paris the Second Congress of International Writers and in the same year became a member of the Arma de Aviación. In addition, Alberti's involvement with the *agitprop* theatre groups that flourished on the Republican side for the purpose of political propaganda was particularly important. He and María Teresa were prominent in 'Nueva Escena' (New Theatre) which operated in the Teatro Español in Madrid and was part of the Alianza mentioned above. At the same time María Teresa directed the 'Teatro de Arte y Propaganda'(The Theatre of Art and Propaganda) at the Teatro de la Zarzuela, and both she and Alberti joined in 1937 the Consejo Nacional de Teatro, formed to co-ordinate the theatrical activities of the Republicans. With the theatre group, 'Guerrillas del Teatro' (Guerrillas of the Theatre), they visited the Republican front, performing short plays for the troops which served both to entertain them and boost their morale. In 1936 and 1937 Alberti himself wrote two plays, *Los salvadores de España* (The Saviours of Spain) and *Radio Sevilla,* both of which were in all probability in the repertoire of 'Nueva Escena' and the second of which was published in 1938 in *El Mono Azul.* Alberti has described the nature of this 'teatro de urgencia' ('theatre of commitment') in the following way:

Hacen falta . . . obritas rápidas, intensas — dramáticas, satíricas, didácticas . . . — que se adapten técnicamente a la composición específica de los grupos teatrales. Una pieza de este tipo no puede plantear dificultades de montaje ni exigir gran número de actores. Su duración no debe sobrepasar la media hora. En 20 minutos escasos, si el tema está bien planteado y resuelto, se puede producir en los espectadores el efecto de un fulminante.[23]

What we need are . . . short, powerful plays — dramatic, satirical, didactic . . . — that lend themselves technically to the precise size of theatre groups. A piece of this kind cannot pose problems of staging or demand a large number of actors. It should not last for more than half an hour. In twenty minutes, if the argument is effectively stated and expressed, the effect upon the spectators can be that of an explosive.

In addition to the two plays already mentioned, the *Dos farsas revolucionarias (Two Revolutionary Farces)* of 1934 are also characteristic of Alberti's theatre of these years: an ideological theatre whose message is conveyed through an essentially non-realistic style involving caricature, distortion and the broad effects of puppet-theatre. It is worth noting in relation to Alberti's 'teatro de urgencia' the general development of *agitprop* theatre in Europe from the time of the Russian Revolution and, in particular, its importance in the work of Erwin Piscator, already mentioned in connection with Alberti's European tour of 1932.[24] The first genuine *agitprop* troupe had been founded in Moscow in 1923 and its function was to tour the country, taking as its material current events and news reports considered harmful to the party and transforming them, mainly through caricature, into political satire. In Germany Piscator's first theatre, Das Tribunal, founded in 1919, was concerned more with the performances of expressionist plays, whose message was often that of self-sacrifice and martyrdom rather than the use of force to overthrow existing institutions, but in 1920 his founding of the Proletarisches Theater, as the name suggests, marked the beginning of a much more politically activist role. Piscator's group, performing not in traditional theatres but in beer-halls and workers' meeting-rooms, played to the proletariat, uneducated and totally ignorant of traditional, bourgeois drama. The actors were usually amateurs and lacked professional training. The stage equipment was portable and thus basic. The scripts, given the nature of the actors, had to be easy to learn, the content easy to assimilate, the characters of the plays uncomplicated, and their message politically unambiguous. In short, this was a kind of theatre that was in every sense crude. A typical piece — indeed, the only one to have survived from the Proletarisches Theater — is the short sketch entitled *Russia's Day*, which was staged in 1920. Against a simple backcloth depicting a map of Europe are presented the representatives of different political attitudes; a professor who advocates parliamentary democracy; the Establishment embodied in caricatured figures of a diplomat, an officer and a priest; war widows and the wounded who blame capitalism for their fate; two Hungarians whose account of indescribable horrors denounces the Hungarian counter-revolution; and the German workers who finally invade the stage, proclaiming the victory of the proletariat and driving out the symbolic figures, capital, the Church, learning, the military and diplomacy. Of such plays C.D. Innes has observed:

> Ideology as such is simplistic and encourages emotionalism. Appeals to the emotions tend to reduce subtleties of feeling to a common denominator, and the vulgarisation of sentiment in turn leads to the adoption of oversimplified positions and artificial expression. All didactic art is liable to this danger.[25]

In order to escape the limitations of the *agitprop* movement, Piscator was soon to discover that he would have to return to the professional theatre. *Radio Sevilla* is based on the radio broadcasts given every night during the Civil War by the Falangist general, Queipo de Llano. The play begins with a prologue in which a Nationalist soldier and a young woman whose father and brother have been killed by the Nationalist forces decide to escape to the Republican side. The prologue then gives way to the play itself as the curtain is drawn aside to reveal a large matchbox — the studio from which Queipo de Llano makes his broadcasts. He is seen seated, with a girl, Clavelona, on his lap, and surrounded by an adoring group of Falangists arranged in the manner of a flamenco tableau. Urged to begin his broadcast, Queipo imitates a horse and is joined by the other characters in a series of animal impersonations which leads in turn to a mock bullfight in which Clavelona plays the bull. The bullfight is interrupted by the arrival of two of Franco's allies — a German and an Italian officer — who seek to order the Spaniards about, are in turn frightened by their bravado, threaten to return home but are finally persuaded to stay by the pleading, fawning Queipo who is clearly afraid to fight his own battles. The appearance of three Italian and three German soldiers signals the reconciliation of the allies. Finally, as the figures on stage are frozen into a static tableau, the matchbox closes, trapping Queipo's neck. The soldier of the prologue addresses the audience, inviting them to take advantage of the situation, and the stage is filled with people armed with sticks and brooms who proceed to beat Queipo's protruding head.

In terms of technique, Alberti's sketch is distinguished by those characteristics essential to *agitprop* theatre; non-representational sets, simplified characters, vigorous action and language, and a strong element of parody. Thus, as far as the setting of the play is concerned, the action involving Queipo and his followers takes place within a studio represented not realistically but by a large, gaudy matchbox:

> *Al descorrerse las cortinas, surge, abriéndose lentamente, dentro de una gran caja de cerillas de la época monárquica, la sala de la emisora sevillana. Un micrófono. Adornando las paredes: carteles taurinos, una cabeza de toro de cartón, banderillas, dos capotes extendidos y un gran rejón de lujo . . .* [26]
> (p.6, col.3)
> *The curtain is drawn back and there appears, opening slowly within a large matchbox in the style of the period of the monarchy, the studio of Radio Seville. A microphone. On the walls posters of bull-fighters, the cardboard head of a bull, 'banderillas', two cloaks spread out, and a splendid spear.*

The stylized setting suggests at once the traditions of the puppet-play. The matchbox, both in its shape and in its colouring, brings to mind the traditional Punch and Judy theatre. Within this setting the characters are themselves simplified types, their physical features exaggerated and heightened into visual, self-explanatory images which bring to mind the technique of Alfred Jarry's *Ubu Roi* and Valle-Inclán's *Los cuernos de don Friolera*. Thus Queipo's bravado and virility are embodied in his full, bristling moustache at the sight of which women swoon:

> CLAVELONA: Queipo. Requeipo
> Queipo, Queipillo,
> me tiene muerta tu bigotillo.   (p.6, col 3. . .)

> CLAVELONA: Queipo, Queipo,
> twice over, dear little Queipo,
> I am overcome by your dear little moustache.

In the studio his imitation of a horse precipitates a mock bullfight in which he is ridden by Catite, an aide, while Clavelona dons the cardboard head of a bull. The characters are literally reduced to the level of animals and Queipo's actions, intended by him to display his physical strength and courage, have the effect of exposing his brutish, insensitive and less-than-human mentality. Similarly, the physical appearance of the Italian and German soldiers is pure caricature, designed to suggest particular national characteristics:

> *Entran tres* SOLDADOS ITALIANOS, *de negro, facinerosos, bigotudos, llenos de plumas los sombreros, pistolones al cinto y un inmenso sable desenvainado. Van seguidos por tres* SOLDADOS NAZIS, *finos, rubios, afeminados, despiladas las cejas, pintados los labios, etc . . .*   (p.8, col.4)

> *Three* ITALIAN SOLDIERS *appear, dressed in black, criminal types, big moustaches, their hats full of feathers, pistols at their waist, and a huge, unsheathed sabre. They are followed by three* NAZI SOLDIERS, *slim, fair, effeminate, their eyebrows plucked, their lips painted, etc. . .*

From the strutting Spaniards to the swaggering Italians and the dandyish Germans, the stage is filled with grotesques.

The action of the play, in accordance with its puppet character, is distinguished by a strong element of slapstick and by the bold, exaggerated movements of the characters. When the curtain opens, it reveals a tableau composed of Queipo and his followers. The poses of the individuals, highly stylized, have the effect of underlining their puppet nature and when, in total contrast, they come to life in the mock bullfight, charging violently about the stage, the idea of characters jerked suddenly into life is reinforced, as well as their absurdity. Thus Clavelona seizes the bull's head, advancing on Catite, Queipo himself, displaying his 'machismo', charges the foreign invaders and they retreat in terror before him. Queipo and his adoring followers indulge in a suitably exaggerated pasadoble in which they strut about the stage to the accompaniment of vulgar guitar-music. And at the end of the play the people, urged on by the soldier, rush onto the stage and proceed to belabour Queipo's head with sticks and brooms in true puppet manner. In consistently exaggerating the gestures and physical movements of the characters Alberti has made them more than comic — he has transformed them into overblown, grotesque monsters who are as inhuman as they are absurd. We are made to laugh at them, but inasmuch as they themselves are blind to their absurdity and treat seriously the very things that render them absurd, there is also something dangerous and threatening in these figures. As in the case of the ranting Ubu of Jarry's play, the comic mask does not conceal the monster.

Louise Popkin has observed quite rightly that *Radio Sevilla* has a subtlety and sophistication not found for the most part in *agitprop* plays.[27] Above all, Alberti develops in the studio sequence, through the mock bullfight and the pasadoble episode, a theme which is central both to his view of life and his drama: the theme of role-playing, of appearance, of life as a play or a game. The prologue and the epilogue to *Radio Sevilla*, reminiscent of the structure of *El hombre deshabitado,* frame the central action, creating the effect of a 'play within a play'. Within the central action the idea of people playing parts is, moreover, heightened by the framing effect of the matchbox, the static flamenco tableau, the props that lie at hand — from the microphone to the cardboard head of the bull — and the theatrical games in which the characters participate, as well as by their exaggerated gestures and language. In short, Alberti makes us aware that in their assumption of roles Queipo and his cronies are merely indulging in an activity — pretence and sham — which is consistent with the everyday reality of their lives. In *El hombre deshabitado* the idea of life as a play or game had more to do with man's manipulation in an empty, cruel and meaningless world and stemmed from Alberti's personal crisis. In *Radio Sevilla* and later plays the focus is different, for Alberti looks not inwards but outwards on a world in which men conceal or try to conceal their real natures beneath the mask of appearance, thereby deceiving and deluding both others and themselves.

Apart from Alberti's original *agitprop* pieces, his adaptation of Cervantes' famous play, *Numancia,* affords a very interesting example of the kind of work performed by the Teatro de Arte y Propaganda during the years in question.[28] Cervantes' play, a full-length work in four Acts, has as its subject the siege of the old Iberian city of Numancia by the army of the Roman general, Scipio, and depicts the heroic resitance and ultimate self-sacrifice of the beleagured Spaniards. At the time of its composition,

Numancia was certainly a source of inspiration and nationalistic fervour to a proud and confident people, and it is easy to imagine that Alberti's version of it, performed before the Republican defenders of Madrid, fired them to an even firmer resistance of the besieging Nationalist army. María Teresa, who directed the performances of her husband's *versión libre* at the Teatro de la Zarzuela in December 1937, commented on its effect:

> Nunca hubo mayor correspondencia entre una sala y un escenario. Allí los numantinos, aquí los madrileños. Cervantes nos resultó el mejor sostenedor de nuestra causa . . . Luego, llegaban los aplausos . . . Saludábamos los vivos y los muertos al pueblo de Madrid que teníamos delante. Se abrían de par en par las puertas del Teatro de la Zarzuela y todos un instante escuchábamos los duelos de la artillería, el bombardeo de la aviación . . . [29]

> Never was there a greater rapport between an auditorium and a stage. There the people of Numancia, here the people of Madrid. Cervantes proved to be the strongest supporter of our cause . . . Then, the applause . . . The living and the dead hailed the people of Madrid there before us. The doors of the Teatro de la Zarzuela were opened wide and for a moment we could hear the screech of gunfire, the thump of aerial bombing . . .

Given the demands of *teatro de urgencia*, Alberti's adaptation of *Numancia* is characterized in particular by compression and condensation. The four Acts of Cervantes' play were, in the interests of simplicity, directness and a more tightly knit structure, reduced to three, and throughout Alberti's version, whose overall length is a little more than a half of the original, the emphasis is placed very firmly on those aspects of the play which underline heroic resistance. A significant omission is, for example, the long scene in Cervantes' second act where the priests appear to seek through religious rites and offerings to discover Numancia's ultimate fate. Both the length of the scene, which slows the action, and the presence of priests, offensive to an audience which was strongly anti-clerical, led to Alberti's decision to remove what in Cervantes' play is a highly atmospheric episode. Other cuts, also intended to add greater pace, involve the reduction by almost a half of the speeches spoken by the two symbolic figures of España (Spain) and the river Duero at the end of Act One. Similarly, with an eye to a less static presentation, Alberti redistributed the lines of some of the longer speeches of Cervantes' play. While Golden Age audiences were quite accustomed to extended passages in verse, Alberti's modern and in some respects less sophisticated public was much happier if the same speech were divided up amongst three or four characters.

Alberti's changes to the original also involved certain additions, especially in relation to the need to establish a clear parallel between the

events on stage and the contemporary situation. One example of this, in the
Duero's prophecy at the end of Act One, is the allusion to the involvement
in Spanish affairs of another ambitious Roman — not Scipio, but Mussolini:

> ... los malos españoles que te entreguen
> a otro romano de ambición sombría,
> haciendo que tus hijos se subleven.   (p.26)
>
> ... The treacherous Spaniards who offer you
> to another Roman full of dark ambition,
> forcing your sons to take up arms.

In addition, Scipio's exhortation to his army in Act One for a restoration of
strict discipline can be seen to be a plea on Alberti's part for the need for
discipline amongst Republican forces, and, equally, a comment on the lack
of it on the Nationalist side.

There are some additions of a comic and even slapstick kind which can be
related to the satirical, parodying elements seen already in *Radio Sevilla*.
The two Roman characters, Macus and Buco, who appear at the beginning
of Alberti's version, are portrayed as buffoons, and, since the purpose of
the scene is to ridicule the Nationalists, they are used to that end. When a
pregnant woman appears on stage, surrounded by drunken Roman
soldiers, and is revealed to be Macus with a pig's bladder stuffed inside his
clothing, a suitably absurd note is struck and the enemy is shown to consist
of characters who seem more fitted to the world of pantomime. In addition,
when a soldier dressed as a woman sings a song which portrays as
effeminate those who have no wish to fight, the song at once becomes a
comment on and a parody of the singer and, by extension, of the
Nationalists. If Alberti's larger purpose is to inspire the Republican allies to
heroic resistance, he does so to some extent by portraying the enemy as
incompetent fools.

The heroic note was struck in particular in the staging of the play. The
resistance of the Numantinos to the Romans and of the Republicans to the
Nationalists was effectively symbolized in a wall, which represented the city
of Numancia and which covered the entire width of the stage. In contrast to
those *agitprop* plays which were performed in beer-halls and workers'
meeting-rooms with a minimum of stage furniture, the performance of
Numancia at the Teatro de la Zarzuela was clearly distinguished by its
splendour. The set was, indeed, designed by Santiago Ontañón who a few
years earlier had worked with Lorca on the productions of *La barraca* and
who in 1933 designed the sets and costumes for the professional
performance of *Bodas de sangre*. Music too played its part, for the moving
final moments of the play involved an orchestra, which played solemn

music, and a choir, which sang verses written by Alberti. His aim, clearly, was to give to the ending of the play a note not merely of heroism but also of redemption through sacrifice.[30]

Alberti's free version of Cervantes' play is, as the above account suggests, highly interesting for a variety of reasons. Above all, it shows how Alberti, as is the case in so much of his work, avails himself of traditional forms and subject matter — from the Golden Age to Goya — to create something new that is also vital and relevant to the audiences of his time. To that extent, his stated aim of seeking to revitalize the Spanish theatre was something that had real meaning, for his drama, in the process of reinvigorating itself, also became a source of inspiration for real people.

During the last year of the Civil War, with the Republican defeat imminent, Alberti and María Teresa left Spain and made their way to Paris. A year later, in February 1940, the events of the Second World War compelled them to abandon Europe altogether and seek refuge in Buenos Aires where they would live for the next twenty-five years. Here, between 1940 and 1946, Alberti composed his so-called neo-popular trilogy of plays: *El trébol florido (The Flowering Clover)* (1940), *El adefesio (The Absurdity)* (1944), and *La Gallarda (The Handsome Girl)* (1944-5). To a large extent the ideological and political emphasis of Alberti's work of the 1930s gives way now to a greater concern with the craft of the playwright and the art of the theatre, though it is also true to say that in matters of technique the imprint of the earlier plays is still clearly discernible. *El adefesio,* generally regarded as one of Alberti's most original and strikingly theatrical works, is a good example of his development as a dramatist.

El adefesio focuses on three old maids, Gorgo, Uva and Aulaga, and on their relationship towards each other, a beggar, Bión and the young and beautiful girl, Altea, for whom they are responsible since the death of her father, Don Dino. In the first Act the three old women bicker over the dirty, ragged Bión and then, when Altea is brought into their presence from the tower where she is kept a prisoner, Gorgo, the most authoritarian of the three old women, slowly turns on her and, failing to discover the identity of Altea's suitor, cruelly abuses her, tears her clothes and forces her to wear a black dress. In Act Two Gorgo succeeds in prising from Bión a letter for Altea from her suitor, Castor, with which she confronts the girl, destroying it in her presence while she berates her for her deceitfulness. Finally, in Act Three, Gorgo succeeds in making Altea believe that Castor has committed suicide, as a consequence of which the girl throws herself from the tower. Gorgo explains that her efforts to terminate the relationship of the young couple stem from the fact that they, without knowing it, were half-brother and sister, in which case their marriage would have been incestuous.

The sources of *El adefesio* are both personal and literary. Firstly, in the mid 1920s, twenty years before the composition of the play, Alberti had travelled through Andalusia and stayed with a married sister in the small town of Rute. In his autobiography he refers to the claustrophobic, inhibiting atmosphere of this typical Andalusian town:

> ... aquel dramático pueblo andaluz al pie del Monte de las Cruces ... saturado de terror religioso, entrecruzado de viejas supersticiones populares ...   (p.189)

> ... that dramatic Andalusian town at the foot of the Mount of the Cross ... impregnated with religious fanaticism, riddled with old popular superstitions ...

In particular he gives an account of a young and beautiful girl known as 'La encerrada' (The prisoner), who lived in seclusion in the highest part of the town, guarded by her mother and her aunts. Desired by the young men yet never seen by them except briefly at early morning Mass, 'La encerrada' eventually committed suicide, and Alberti, fascinated by her circumstances and her fate, observes that two decades later he was to try to recreate the sense of physical and moral horror prompted by the incident in his 'fábula del amor y las viejas' ('fable of love and old women') — *El adefesio*. Of the other personal experiences which find an echo in the play, mention might be made of the stifling narrow-mindedness and oppressive religiosity, together with an appropriate measure of prejudice and hypocrisy, which Alberti encountered as a young boy both in his family and his teachers. In his autobiography (p.14) he refers to the monotonous tolling of a church bell — an important element in Act Two of *El adefesio* — and speaks too of his mother's interest in flowers and plants with strange and exotic names — the source perhaps of the names of two of the old maids of *El adefesio*. In 1944 Alberti, far from his native land, distanced from it in more ways than one, sifted through the memories of his childhood, weaving them in his imagination into an artistic vision of what seemed to him to be most typical of southern Spain.

The literary and cultural influences evident in *El adefesio* are both Spanish and European. As to the former, the element of grotesque distortion which is suggested by the title of Alberti's play and which is so marked in the presentation of the characters may owe something to the comic dramatic tradition of the Golden Age, to the farces of Lope de Rueda and Cervantes, but if there is one Golden Age writer whose influence is clearer in the play than any other it is that of Quevedo — the Quevedo of *Los sueños (The Visions)* and *La vida del buscón (The Life of the Swindler)* whose often one-dimensional and savagely dehumanized caricatures are strongly reminiscent of the three old hags and the beggar of

El adefesio. In relation to the grotesque, another clear source of inspiration was the painter Goya, so much admired and studied by Alberti during his many visits to the Prada. One of Goya's last pictures, *The Old Women Gazing into the Looking Glass*, captures the very essence of Alberti's play. Firstly, Goya distorts the physical features of the two old women in order to suggest non-physical characteristics — the dark, twisted souls of these creatures who clearly see themselves as beautiful. Secondly, their failure to perceive their own ugliness powerfully conveys the theme of humanity blind to its own faults and both absurd and dangerous in consequence of that blindness. And thirdly, the mirror theme is important in the sense that while within the picture the old women see themselves in the mirror in the way they want, Goya allows us to see the horrific image, duly exaggerated, that the mirror actually reflects. In Act One of *El adefesio* the three old women, Gorgo, Uva and Aulaga, parade in front of the mirror, but although Gorgo, in recognizing her physical ugliness, seems to perceive herself as she is, none of the women are really ever aware of their moral and spiritual defects. The stage action itself becomes in Alberti's hands the mirror in which we see them for what they are — monsters beneath a mask of compassion and charity. Furthermore, there are many allusions in the play — to animals, birds, bats — which have the effect of transforming the characters into figures that are less than human and which bring to mind those pictures of Goya in which men fly through the air or carry donkeys on their back.

Mention of Goya and the technique of distortion in relation to *El adefesio* leads inevitably to the positing of Valle-Inclán as another strong influence upon Alberti. In the earlier discussion of *esperpentismo*, whose invention Valle-Inclán interestingly attributes to Goya, the idea of the concave or distorting mirror which renders human beings absurd and transforms beautiful images into grotesque deformities has been seen to be central to the dramatist's intention in *Luces de Bohemia* and *Los cuernos de Don Friolera* to portray the reality of Spanish life and attitudes as 'una deformación grotesca de la civilización europea'. In *Los cuernos*, in particular, the process of distortion is one which, as in many of Goya's dark and pessimistic paintings, not merely divests the characters of their human characteristics, both physical and moral, but transforms them into animals or birds — Doña Tadea's appearance brings to mind a fox, while her head is that of an owl; the two military men, Don Gabino Campero and Don Mateo Cardona belong respectively to the cat and the frog family. Alberti, in calling his play *El adefesio* — a word whose meaning ranges from 'grotesquerie' to 'extravagance', 'absurdity' and 'nonsense' — doubtless wished to establish in the mind of his audience a direct parallel with Valle-

Inclán's *esperpento* — 'absurdity', 'nonsense', 'grotesque tale', 'scarecrow'. Of the other twentieth-century writers whom Alberti may have had in mind, but not to the same extent as Valle-Inclán, both Carlos Arniches and Lorca should at least be mentioned. Arniches' *tragedias grotescas (grostesque tragedies)* in some cases precede Valle-Inclán's *esperpentos* and, as the phrase suggests, contain that element of distortion and dehumanization that became the hallmark of Valle's later style. As far as Lorca is concerned, his puppet-plays and farces, though not as savage as Valle's, were particularly popular in Spain and their influence was great. In addition, certain features of *El adefesio* — the tyrannical Gorgo, her deception of Altea in relation to her suitor's death, and Altea's suicide, as well as the claustrophobic atmosphere of the play — bring to mind parallel situations in Lorca's last play, *La casa de Bernarda Alba*. Lorca sub-titled the work, completed over a decade before Alberti's, *Drama de mujeres en los pueblos de España (A Play About Women in the Villages of Spain)*, while Alberti described *El adefesio* as a story set in *uno de esos pueblos fanáticos caidos entre las serranias del Sur de España (one of those fanatical villages set in the mountains of the South of Spain)*. The point remains, though, that even if Lorca's play was completed in 1936, it was not performed until 1945, albeit in Buenos Aires, and was certainly not in print until the same year. The similarity between the two plays, which is less than the considerable differences between them, may merely be due to the fact that both dramatists shared a similar vision of provincial Spanish life.[31]

As far as European movements are concerned, *El adefesio* can in some respects be related to the political theatre which influenced Alberti so strongly in the 1930s in the sense that its characters are the bold, simplified, caricatured figures of the *agitprop* plays. On the other hand, as the discussion of Valle-Inclán has already suggested, this was also a feature of expressionist drama which, diminishing a genuinely political emphasis, used exaggeration and distortion to communicate both the inner and the outer nature of the characters. Yvan Goll's statement on the purpose of expressionist drama, with its important allusion to the magnifying glass, is worth repeating, for it applies as much to Alberti's 'grotesquerie' as it does to Valle-Inclán's 'scarecrow' technique:

> ... It has been completely forgotten that the stage is nothing more than a magnifying glass. Great drama has always been aware of this ...
> ... Pure realism was the greatest mistake in the whole of literature ... The simplest means is the grotesque ... The monotony and stupidity of human beings are so enormous that they can be adequately represented only by enormities. Let the new drama be an enormity ...[32]

The point has already been made that in *El hombre deshabitado* there are many clear echoes of Expressionism. In the years that separate that play and *El adefesio*, Alberti's knowledge of Expressionism was reinforced both by direct contact with European drama and, clearly, by an even greater exposure to and familiarity with painting and cinema. As far as the latter is concerned, Alberti had been fascinated by both comic and serious films from the late 1920s, and his imagination, as C.B. Morris has suggested, was greatly stimulated by the highly evocative techniques of films such as *La Chute de la Maison Usher, The Cabinet of Dr. Caligari* and *Nosferatu*, all of which he would have been able to see in Madrid in the late 20s and for much of the 30s.[33]

Finally, what of the connections between *El adefesio* and the Theatre of the Absurd? From the plays of Jarry to those of Ionesco and Adamov the element of satire, parody and social criticism, aimed at the exposure of, as Martin Esslin puts it, 'an inauthentic, petty society' can be seen to constitute one important strand of the so-called Theatre of the Absurd.[34] To the extent that the grotesque characters of *El adefesio* represent Alberti's scathing observation of the narrow-mindedness and intolerance of southern Spain, the play belongs clearly to the tradition described above. On the other hand, it does not, as do Valle-Inclán's *Luces de Bohemia* and *Los cuernos de Don Friolera*, leave us with that sense of the absurdity of the human condition itself, which is the most important characteristic of the Theatre of the Absurd. The latter is suggested much more strongly by *El hombre deshabitado*.

The stage settings of the play, often reminiscent of paintings in their general stylization and arrangement of figures, frame the characters, and in that sense, as in the case of *Radio Sevilla*, give to the play that sense of distance, even of puppet-show, that is the province of *esperpentismo*. Thus, when the curtain rises, Aulaga, Uva and Bión are seen in static poses, arranged on different levels in the centre of the stage, as in a picture:

Sala de una casa rica. Puertas laterales. Puerta al fondo. Un gran espejo portátil. UVA y AULAGA *arreglan a* BIÓN, *mendigo pelirrojo, subido en un taburete, al centro de la escena.* UVA, *de rodillas, le remienda un pernil del pantalón.* AULAGA, *en lo alto de una silla, le peina y tijeretea las espesas barbas. Es de noche. Silencio.* (p.115)

A room in a fine house. Doors at the sides. A door at the back. A large, portable mirror. UVA *and* AULAGA *tidy up* BIÓN, *a red-headed beggar who is placed on a stool in the centre of the stage.* UVA, *kneeling, mends one of his trouser legs.* AULAGA, *standing on a chair, combs and snips his thick beard. It is night. Silence.*

The framing effect is then reinforced by the appearance of Gorgo in the doorway at the back of the stage:

> ... *Iluminada por una palmatoria, Doña* GORGO *aparece en el marco de la puerta del fondo* ...   (p.115)
>
> ... *In the candlelight Doña* GORGO *appears in the doorway at the back* ...

Lighting here, as in the plays of Valle-Inclán, silhouettes the human figures, eliminating detail in favour of a stark, stylized image. The effect is illustrated perfectly by another example from Act One when the three old women mock Altea:

> *Como tres sombras, como tres rebujos siniestros, riendo, burlonas, hirientes, van y vienen alrededor de* ALTEA *que llora, baja, cubierta la cara por sus cabellos.*   (p.129)
>
> *Like three spectres, like three sinister shapes, laughing, mocking, wounding, they move around* ALTEA *who weeps, cowering, her face covered by her hair.*

The figures are, moreover, grotesque silhouettes, as both appearance and, in particular, movement suggest throughout the play. When the curtain rises on Act One, the arrangement of the three figures brings to mind the formal harmony of a classical painting, while the characters are themselves in their physical appearance the very opposite of their classical counterparts. In the spectacle of the ragged, red-haired beggar solicitously attended by the two old hags, Alberti captures perfectly Valle-Inclán's intention of depicting in the *esperpento*, 'héroes clásicos reflejados en los espejos cóncavos' ('classical heroes reflected in distorting mirrors'). When Gorgo appears in the doorway, she is seen to be wearing a beard:

> ... *Trae barbas de hombre. Aire de abatimiento.*   (p.115)
>
> ... *She wears a man's beard. Her manner is dejected.*

In a sense we are in the world of puppet-play, farce and pantomime, the principal difference being that, as the action unfolds, any initial suggestion of light-hearted humour is transformed into an altogether grimmer and darker mood.

If the settings and the lighting serve to emphasize the less-than-human aspect of the characters, this is further underlined by Alberti's suggestions for the way in which they move. In Act One Gorgo and Aulaga accuse Uva of secretly meeting Bión and begin to move around her, circling in opposite directions:

GORGO *(girando alrededor de* UVA): Lo has visto, Lo has visto. Lo has visto. *(Deteniéndose, seca). ¿*Y qué más, Uva? ¿Y qué más?
AULAGA *(girando en sentido contrario):* ¡Lo vio! ¡Lo vio!   (p.121)
GORGO *(Circling around* UVA): You have seen him. You have seen him. You have seen him. *(Stopping, abruptly).* And what else is there, UVA? What else?
AULAGA *(circling in the other direction):* She saw him! She saw him!

The circling movement is a key motif in the play. Gorgo and Aulaga's circling of Uva becomes later in Act One the three old women's circling of Altea:

> ... *van y vienen alrededor de* ALTEA *que llora, baja, cubierta la cara por sus cabellos.*   (p.129)

> ... *they move around* ALTEA *who weeps, cowering, her face covered by her hair.*

In Act Two Gorgo and Bión circle each other in turn, Gorgo adopting an exaggerated, fawning manner, Bión pretending to be the devil. And in the final scene of Act Two, as Altea is made to watch them, the three old women re-enact a bat-hunt in which they once participated and in which now a black rag tied to the end of a long stick represents the bat:

> *Las van girando rítmicamente, mientras suena lejano aún y triste el toque de Oración.*   (p.149)

> *They move them* [the sticks] *in a circular movement, rhythmically, while in the distance the church-bell tolls, sadly announcing evening prayer.*

The circling movement is meaningful in several ways. It suggests, firstly, the idea of preying animals. Secondly, in the sense that the movement is repeated, repetition indicates the extent to which the characters, in terms of behaviour, conform to certain set, unchanging patterns. To that extent they are, indeed, puppet-like, manipulated both by others and by their own limited natures, and the idea is reinforced by physical movements and gestures which bring to mind the world of puppets. So in Act One Gorgo shakes Aulaga like a rag-doll:

> GORGO: ¡No, no! Mírame bien. Estás ciega. Abre los ojos. *(Zamarreándola).*   (p.118)

> GORGO: No, no! Look at me. You aren't looking. Open your eyes. *(Shaking her).*

The analogy is clearer still later in the Act when Gorgo confronts Altea:

> *La zamarrea por los hombros, al par que* ALTEA, *como un pelele, vuelve a mover afirmativamente la cabeza.*   (p.129)

> *She shakes her by the shoulders, while* ALTEA, *like a puppet, moves her head once more in agreement.*

Dominated by the authoritarian Gorgo, a Punch-like figure, Altea has no will of her own:

GORGO *(amenazante con su bastón)*: ¿Es, es, es?

GORGO *(threatening with her stick)*: Is it him? Is it him? Is it him?

In addition, the characters often move jerkily, or in an exaggerated manner which points to their less-than-human nature. In Act One Gorgo's slow movement explodes into violent action:

... GORGO *se vuelve, grave, hacia* UVA *y* AULAGA, *pero de pronto corre hacia la puerta, gritando* ...   (p.123)

... GORGO *turns slowly, towards* UVA *and* AULAGA, *but suddenly she runs towards the door, shouting* ...

In Act Two Uva responds violently to Gorgo's insinuations:

UVA *(con asombro, saltando, inquieta):* El!

UVA *(with a start, leaping up, agitated):* Him!

Alberti's stage directions both for the settings and the movements of the characters on the stage point very clearly to the influence of Expressionism. Of the expressionist style of acting J. L. Styan has observed that it 'was a deliberate departure from the realism of Stanislavsky. Moreover, in avoiding the detail of human behaviour, a player might appear to be overacting, and adopting the broad, mechanical movements of a puppet.'[35] In addition, Styan makes the point that the style of performance 'was intense and violent, and expressed tormented emotions. Actors might erupt in sudden passion and attack each other physically. Speech was rapid, breathless and staccato, with gesture and movement urgent and energetic ... '[36] In the sense that Alberti communicates through the stage action the inner lives of the characters, *El adefesio* is clearly expressionist.

The dialogue is particularly interesting. In the first place it has, like the dialogue of *El hombre deshabitado*, that febrile, intense character that is a feature of the language of expressionist drama. The action is thus punctuated constantly by explosive outbursts, as in the confrontation involving the three old women in Act One:

UVA: ¡No tengo a nadie! ¡Sola! ¡Sola!
GORGO: ¡Uva de perro! ¡Uva de gato!
AULAGA: ¡Corre!
UVA: ¡Matadme! ¡Matadme! ¡Furias, furias! ¡Arpías!   (p.121)

UVA: There's no one! I'm alone! Alone!
GORGO: Uva is a dog! Uva is a cat!
AULAGE: Run!
UVA: Kill me! Kill me! Furies, furies! Harpies!

When the servant, Ánimas, enters at this point, there is an abrupt change of mood:

GORGO *(con tono suave)*: ¿Qué quieres, Ánimas? ...   (p.122)

GORGO *(in a gentle manner)*: What do you want, Ánimas?

It is the kind of violent contrast that can be seen throughout the play. Later in Act One Gorgo's flattery of Altea, expressed in almost rhapsodic terms, explodes into a violent denunciation of the girl, and in Act II the pattern is repeated in relation both to her and to Bión. Through the dialogue, which is thus consistently distorted and pulled into a shape which corresponds to the emotions of the characters, Alberti reveals their motives, their inner self, as effectively as he does through other aspects of stage performance. In particular, the dialogue, distinguished by a consistent pattern of animal allusions, lays bare the predatory nature of the three old women as vividly as do their movements and their general appearance. Gorgo refers to her two companions as 'comadrejillas' (little weasels') (p.119), and she commands Uva to bark and howl:

... ¡Ladra, Uva, confiesa! ¡Aúlla que sí, anda, aúlla que sí!   (p.121)

... Bark, Uva, confess! Howl the truth, come on, howl the truth!

In a similar episode Uva confronts Bión:

... Escupe, larga tu saliva, sapejo ... ¡Cuác-cuác! Babea por esa lengua ...
(p.143)

... Spit, spit out your spittle, toad ... Croak, croak! Drivel ...

She commands him to bark and howl in harmony with her:

¡Pues a morder, a ladrar libre! ¡Venga! ¡Ladra! ¡Guau, guau! ¡Aúlla, Bión, aúlla largo! ¡Uuuuh! (BIÓN *lanza al par que* UVA *aullidos y risotadas grotescas.)*   (p.144)

Bite, then, and bark as much as you can! Come on! Bark! Bow, wow! Howl, Bión, howl loud and long! Oooooo! (BIÓN *makes howling noises and grotesque cackles along with* UVA).

The sounds made by the characters, reinforcing the meaning of their words, serve to project their real natures, shattering whatever masks of kindness and compassion they employ in order to disguise themselves.

Louise Popkin offers the opinion that in *El adefesio* Alberti surpassed the satiric achievements of his plays of the 1930s in the sense that in the terrible figures of the three old women and their young victim he succeeded in creating an image that is concise, terryifying and memorable, particular and universal.[37] To this assessment of Alberti's play might be added the opinion that *El adefesio* is a significant work within the European theatrical tradition. Its expressionist characteristics have been described, but it is evident too that in many respects it looks forward, as do Valle-Inclán's *esperpentos,* to the Theatre of the Absurd. The grotesque characters, stripped of all physical and moral dignity, taunting and abusing each other, are strongly reminiscent of characters and situations in plays such as *Waiting for Godot* and *The Birthday Party.* Alberti's particular achievement, though, is not merely to have anticipated those plays in kind but to have done so in terms of artistic excellence.

Noche de guerra en el Museo del Prado (Night Attack on the Prado Museum) was written in 1956, twenty years after the outbreak of the Spanish Civil War and is one of Alberti's very finest plays. Its action takes place during the first aerial attack on Madrid. The prologue consists of an evocation by a character designated as el Autor of some of the Prado's greatest paintings. He is interrupted by a group of soldiers who wish to remove the paintings from the building in order to save them from destruction. In the course of the action the figures of a number of paintings come to life and join the soldiers in their efforts to defend the Prado. In particular, characters from the paintings of Goya serve to establish a relationship between the terrible events of the Napoleonic invasion, depicted so vividly by the Spanish painter, and the atrocities of the Spanish Civil War itself. In both instances Alberti is concerned with the struggle against tyranny, embodied for him as much by the supporters of Franco as by their foreign predecessors. The play ends with a mock trial in which the ruling class is accused of treachery, reminiscent of the ending of *Radio Sevilla* where the people belabour Queipo, the Falangist general.

As far as sources are concerned, Alberti had to look no further than his own experience. The members of the Alianza de Intelectuales Antifascistas, which Alberti and his wife had helped to found in 1936, were concerned during the years of the Civil War with the safety of the national art treasures, and in November of 1936, as bombs were falling on the Spanish capital, they oversaw the removal to Valencia of the paintings housed in the Prado.[38] The event is the direct source of *Noche de guerra.* As for theatrical influences, Brecht is the most important. During his European tour of 1932 Alberti, as has been mentioned already, had come into direct contact with the dramatic theory and didactic techniques of both Brecht and Piscator. In the mid 1950s he made a trip to eastern Europe, visiting Czechoslovakia, East Germany, Poland, Rumania, the U.S.S.R. and Communist China too, and in January 1956, met Brecht in Berlin. It was the intention of the German dramatist and director to perform *Noche de guerra* with the Berliner Ensemble in November of that year, and

Alberti, having already commenced work on the play, promised to complete and deliver it by May. The promised performance did not take place, for Brecht died in the meantime, but the play itself bears the unmistakable imprint of Brechtian epic theatre.[39]

Epic theatre — 'episches Theater' — developed in Germany in the 1920s where Erwin Piscator, working at first with Bertolt Brecht, sought to create a form of drama suited to the public discussion of political and social issues.[40] For Piscator the stage was, or should be, a political platform and the function of the play should be, as it had been in times past, both to entertain and teach. Given the importance of its doctrinal purpose, the drama should thus be rational rather than empathetic and the style of performance should therefore aim at objectivity: not at drawing the audience emotionally into the events presented to it on the stage but at distancing it in a way which allowed its members to contemplate and ponder on the action, its meaning and its relevance. In consequence, Piscator abandoned a naturalistic style of production, which blurred the distinction between the stage and the audience, and employed a technique which emphasized the play's message. Objectivity was sought by the use of such devices as placards, signboards, photographs and sequences of film, which could be employed both to break the sense of theatrical illusion and to provide a commentary upon the stage action. Piscator's dramatization of Jaroslav Haček's comic novel, *The Good Soldier Schweik*, produced at the Theater am Nollendorfplatz in 1928, proved to be one of the landmarks of twentieth-century theatre. In order to tell this story of a simple Czech soldier who is conscripted into the Austrian army in 1914, Piscator availed himself of various mechanical devices which enabled him to suggest a great variety of settings, to comment upon the events, and to present them in a way which maintained the necessary objectivity between the action and the audience. Prominent amongst these mechanical aids were two moving platforms or conveyor belts which allowed for quick changes of scene. The backcloth served as a screen against which line-drawings by the cartoonist George Grosz were projected — satirical drawings of Austrian officers which underlined the play's anti-war theme. The screen was also used to display military propaganda, and at one point a map of a town appeared on it to show how Schweik evaded the police. Piscator's fascination with machinery was, as his many productions suggest, less a concern with technical ingenuity than with the function of the theatre as education and in that context with the creation of an objective, documentary manner.[41]

Brecht worked with Piscator in Berlin between 1919 and 1930 and therefore shared many of his ideas on epic theatre. For Brecht the Aristotelian theatre, with its emphasis on the emotional involvement of the audience in the events presented to it, was something to be avoided. Instead, the idea of 'distancing' the audience in order to allow it to adopt a true critical attitude towards the stage action came to be central to Brecht's theory and practice. As far as the actor was concerned, Brecht required that he avoid impersonation or total indentification with a role and seek to stand outside it, reminding the observer that he is playing a part and performing actions and speaking lines prescribed for him. As for settings, every effort should be made to destroy the theatrical illusion: by the use of a stage with a minimum of furniture; by scene changes in full view of the audience. In terms of structure, the play should consist of a series of episodes, each preceded by a title which would underline the 'historical' character of the piece and underscore the sense of distancing. Similarly, the lighting of the stage should not have the effect of immersing the audience in a magical world of make-believe but should present the stage starkly and clearly, as a stage. In plays that range from *The Threepenny Opera* (1928) to *Mother Courage* (1939) and *The Caucasian Chalk Circle* (1943-5) Brecht put into practice with brilliance and imagination his concept of a dialectical theatre that would also entertain.

Noche de guerra is described by Alberti as an 'aguafuerte, en un prólogo y un acto' ('an etching, consisting of a prologue and one Act'). The stage-action is thus not merely about the pictures in the Prado; rather it is itself a picture, with the sense of distancing that the observation of a picture implies. The conception of the play in terms of the etching, and in particular of the etchings of Goya, gives it, moreover, both a certain starkness and austerity, a sharpness of line, and a sense of historical perspective. The prologue is particularly important in this respect. The curtain acts as a cinema screen on which is outlined at the outset the main gallery of the Prado:

DECORACIÓN: *En penumbra, un gran telón blanco, a modo de pantalla cinematográfica, diseñada en él con líneas negras la perspectiva de la sala central del Museo del Prado . . .* [42]

THE SETTING: *In shadow, a great white curtain, like a cinema screen, and outlined on it in black lines is the shape of the main gallery of the Prado Museum . . .*

On the screen are projected throughout the prologue slides of paintings and etchings by Rubens, Titian, Velázquez, Fra Angelico and, above all, Goya. As far as the latter is concerned, *The Executions of the Third of May, The Pilgrimage to San Isidro, The Old Women Gazing into the Looking Glass,* and individual items from *The Disasters of War,* establish with their dark colouring and their terrible images of death and human degradation the dominant tone of the prologue. The Autor, moreover, appearing before

RAFAEL ALBERTI 163

the screen in order to comment on the paintings, proceeds to instruct the audience in relation to their meaning, establishing the play's strongly didactic tone. A series of imperatives maintains the sense of distance between the observer and the object observed:

... ¡Miradlo! Uno de tantos héroes de nuestra guerra de independencia. *(Desaparece.)* También entre los frailes hubo buenos patriotas. *(Aparece el aguafuerte número 38, también de 'Los desastres de la guerra'.)* ¡Bárbaros!, exclama el propio Goya al pie de este aguafuerte. *(Desaparece.)* Cosas más duras vio el pintor. Nadie se atrevió nunca, hasta que él lo hizo, a dejarlas grabadas en el acero. *(Aparece la lámina 39 del mismo álbum.)* Mirad. Se diría que la cabeza cortada de ese hombre va a romper a gritar reclamando justicia. (p.163)

... Look at this one! One of the many heroes of our War of Independence. *(It disappears).* There were good patriots amongst the clergy too. *(There appears etching No.38, also from 'The Disasters of War').* 'Savages!', says Goya himself at the foot of this etching. *(It disappears.)* The painter saw still darker things. No one dared, until he did, to etch them on steel. *(There appears plate 39 from the same series.)* Look! It's as if that man's severed head is about to call out for justice.

The voice of the commentator, in conjunction with the rapidity with which the pictures succeed each other, ensures in the audience less an emotional involvement than an intellectual curiosity and attention cleverly sustained. The distancing effect is consolidated too by the movement in relation to the paintings shown on the screen from one historical and cultural moment to another — a movement into the past from Goya to Velázquez to Fra Angelico and Titian which gives to the events set before us both a panoramic quality and a sense of universality. In addition, between the Autor, standing in front of the screen, the projected pictures appearing behind him, and the audience, seated in front of him, there is a spatial distance, as opposed to the temporal distance between the painters represented. And finally, when at the end of the prologue the Autor announces himself as the dramatist whose play is about to be represented in the Acto, the distancing effect already achieved in the prologue is extended, flowing over into the main action. It is appropriate that at that point the screen on which the paintings have been shown should rise, allowing us to see beyond it, as through a frame, into the world of the paintings now suddenly brought to life:

... Perdonad un olvido involuntario. No les dije mi nombre. Por si acaso les interesa, podrán hallarlo en el cartel, en el programa, dando título al acto que van a ver representar dentro de unos segundos. Y ahora, sí: Buenas noches, señoras y señores. *(Se va levantando el telón.)* (pp.165-6)

... Forgive an unintentional slip. I didn't tell you my name. If you are interested by any chance, you will find it on the poster, in the programme, preceding the play that in a few seconds you will see performed. And now you have it: Good night, ladies and gentlemen. *(The curtain rises)*.

In the sense that the prologue to *Noche de guerra* acts as a framing device to the subsequent action, Alberti's technique recalls *Radio Sevilla*, though it now has a greater sophistication.

The Acto itself, developing and expanding the threads and ideas of the prologue, is a brilliantly executed example of the techniques of epic theatre combined with Alberti's individual style and manner. On the one hand, the characters and situations are filled out, endowed with life and dramatic tension, yet on the other hand, despite the attendant dangers of greater audience involvement, a remarkable sense of distance and objective appraisal of the action is achieved. In this sense Alberti succeeds in enjoying in *Noche de guerra* the best of both worlds. The events of the Spanish Civil War, like the horrors of the Napoleonic invasion, demand a reaction involving outrage, shock and profound horror. If such emotions were not aroused, Alberti's condemnation of those atrocities could hardly be conveyed. On the other hand, they are events which, for the epic dramatist, equally require critical appraisal and a cool judgement. The emotional and intellectual balance required firstly of the dramatist, then of the observer of the play, is something which Alberti achieves here with very considerable artistry through practice of a highly controlled dramatic technique in which distancing effects are always to the fore.

The characters most prominent in the Acto are those based on Goya's paintings and etchings of the Napoleonic invasions: El Fusilado (The Executed Man), El Manco (The Maimed Man), El Amolador (The Grinder). Inasmuch as these figures describe the terrible events which have overtaken them, they are highly sympathetic figures who awaken our sympathies. Thus el Fusilado movingly describes his fate:

> Las mujeres son fieras. Y dan valor. A mí me fusilaron con la mía. ¡Las cosas que gritaba! La tuvieron que amarrar a un árbol. Luego, la desnudaron. Le cortaron los brazos a machete y los clavaron en las ramas.   (p.170)

> Women are fierce. And they inspire courage. They shot me with my wife. The things she shouted! They had to tie her to a tree. Then they stripped her. They cut off her arms with a knife and nailed them to the branches.

If, though, the event is horrific, the manner of its telling is controlled, as though el Fusilado is describing a stranger's fate, and a sense of distance is thus created, both between him and the incident in question and between him and our emotional involvement with him. In addition, although the human dimension of the characters is frequently to the fore, it is balanced by Alberti's insistence on the extent to which they are also puppet-like and thus dehumanized. Thus, when el Amolador makes his first appearance, the dagger protruding from his back reminds us of many a puppet character who, though mortally wounded, has not succumbed:

AMOLADOR *(intenta andar, pero cae de rodillas):* Sacadme antes esta navaja de los huesos. No puedo casi respirar. *(Rueda por el entarimado.)*
(p.168)

THE GRINDER *(trying to walk, but he falls on his knees):* First pull this knife out of my ribs. I can hardly breathe. *(He rolls to the floor).*

As they come on stage the various characters are also given names and identities, which draws attention to the fact of role-playing, while the generic nature of the names creates a further sense both of universality and of distance. And if a number of the characters are still deeply human in their plight, they have their counterpart in others who are almost totally dehumanized. At the beginning of the Acto, Vieja I (first old woman) is described in a way which brings to mind the *esperpento* figures both of *Radio Sevilla* and *El adefesio:*

Espantajo de negro con ojos de lechuza, bigotes y verruga con pelos.
(p.167)

A black scarecrow with the eyes of a bat, a moustache and a wart with hairs.

Later, in a sequence based on a painting by Velázquez, Philip IV is presented as a puppet both in appearance and action:

Ha terminado, mientras, de salir por el escotillón una alta figura de espantajo, cubierta totalmente por un fláccido sudario negro. Se yergue un instante, para dejar caer el brazo con la luz, desmoronándose toda, silenciosamente, en el suelo.
(pp.178-9)

Meanwhile, from a trapdoor there has emerged a tall, scarecrow figure, completely covered by a loose black shroud. It stands erect for a moment, only for the arm holding the candle to fall, whereupon the figure itself collapses in a heap, sinking silently to the floor.

The extent of the dehumanizing process is linked to and controlled by, as this example shows, the degree of Alberti's satirical intention, and it reaches its climax in the final presentation of Queen María Luisa, wife of Charles IV, as a *pelele de cara amarillenta (doll with a yellow face)* (p.192), and her lover, Manuel Godoy, as an *enorme SAPO, de ojos saltones y rasgos humanos (a huge TOAD, with bulging eyes and human features)* (p.193). Even so, to a greater or lesser degree, all the characters of the play have a puppet quality which allows us to view them more objectively.

The effect is also achieved, as is the case in the prologue, by the sharp divisions established between different parts of the stage action. While most of the Acto is devoted to the actions and conversations of the characters based on the paintings of Goya, there are also important scenes involving well-known pictures by Titian, Velázquez and Fra Angelico. Clearly, the costumes of the characters, corresponding to the style of the different painters and pictures, mark off one section from another. For the Goya characters Alberti has the following instruction in relation to the costumes:

> *Estos personajes han de vestir como a comienzos del siglo XIX: unos, en colores vivos, pero opacos, y otros en grises, sepias, blancos y negros, buscando el claroscuro de los dibujos y aguafuertes.* (p.159)

> *These characters should be dressed in the manner of the beginning of the nineteenth century: some in lively but dull colours, and others in greys, sepias, whites and blacks, in an effort to suggest the 'chiaroscuro' of the drawings and etchings.*

The indications for Titian's Venus and Adonis could not be more different:

> VENUS *ha de ir casi desnuda, con un color blanquecino de estatua.* ADONIS, *con túnica color vino granate, muslos desnudos y sandalias.* MARTE, *primero, con piel y máscara de jabalí. Luego, casi desnudo, con casco de acero.* (p.159)

> VENUS *should be almost nude, with the whitish colouring of a statue.* ADONIS *has a tunic the colour of red wine, bare legs and sandals.* MARS *is first seen with the skin and mask of a wild boar. Subsequently, he is almost naked and wears a helmet of steel.*

While colours establish a clear line of demarcation, this is further reinforced by Alberti's use of lighting, which has a discernible framing effect. The transition from an episode involving the Goya characters to the mythological figures of Venus and Adonis is thus marked off in the following way:

> *En vez de la [luz] de los faroles, cae de lo alto, sobre el lateral izquierda del salón, un opaco rayo del luz que deja en una total penumbra a la barricada. El cañoneo se va alejando. Volcados en el suelo, medio desnudos, están* VENUS *y* ADONIS. (p.172)

> *Instead of that [the light] from the lanterns, there comes from above, falling on the left-hand side of the room, an opaque light which leaves the barricade in total darkness. The sound of cannons grows faint. Reclining on the floor, half nude, are* VENUS *and* ADONIS.

The audience is, in effect, made to look into the world of Titian's painting, which is to be sharply distingushed from that of the episodes based on the works of the other painters.

The language of each episode is also important as a distancing instrument. Nothing could be more different, for example, than the vigorous, popular, down-to-earth and often crude language of the Goya characters and the highly literary and poetic exchanges of Venus and Adonis. With regard to the former, the vulgar comments of the Vieja are worth noting:

¡Napoleón! ¡Napoladrón! Yo guardo su retrato . . . Al fondo de un bacín . . .
¡Ji, ji! ¡Como lo pongo al pobre todas las mañanas!   (p.168)

Napoleon the lion! Napoleon the thief! I've got his picture . . . In the bottom of a piss-pot . . . Hee, hee! The poor soul has a terrible time in the mornings!

In contrast, Venus and Adonis express all the rapture and idealization of love:

VENUS: Nada podrán contra nosotros sus rayos ni sus truenos, Adonis. Las armas del amor son más potentes que las suyas. Tú y yo somos la paz, el ramo del olivo, el arrullo de las palomas, el florecer de los jardines en cada primavera. Llévame pronto de este sitio . . .   (p.173)

VENUS: His thunder and lightning cannot harm us, Adonis. The weapons of love are stronger than his. You and I are peace, the olive branch, the music of doves, the flowering of gardens in spring. Take me quickly from this place . . .

The stylization of language, like the stylization of characters, effectively engages a critical rather than emotional response. Having said that, it is also necessary, though, to draw attention to the highly expressionist character of the Venus-Adonis scene. Throughout, the characters express themselves in that fervent and rapturous manner that we have already seen to be a characteristic of many of Alberti's earlier plays. The death of Adonis draws from Venus a powerful emotional reaction:

¡Ira y celos de Marte! Despecho cruel de un triste dios enceguecido! ¡Miserable venganza que me hunde en la más negra de las noches! ¡Adonis! ¡Mi Adonis!   (p.173)

The anger and jealousy of Mars! The cruel spite of a sad, blind god! A despicable vengeance that plunges me into the darkest of nights! Adonis! My Adonis!

Equally intense episodes are to be found elsewhere in the play, when, for example, the victims accuse the perpetrators of their ills:

FUSILADO: Tú trajiste a la gente que me fusiló. ¡Tú!
AMOLADOR: Tú me clavaste la navaja en el pecho. ¡Tú!
MAJA: ¡Tú! Tú me rajaste con tu sable el costado. ¡Tú!
MANCO: ¿Ves este brazo? Míralo. Ya no está. Tú me lo arrancaste de cuajo con tu ciega metralla. ¡Tú!
TORERO: ¡Traidor! ¡Asesino! ¡Ladrón de nuestro suelo! ¡Tú!   (p.182)

THE EXECUTED MAN: You brought the people who shot me. You!
THE GRINDER: You stuck the knife in my chest. You!
MAJA: You! You cut my side with your sword. You!
THE MAIMED MAN: Do you see this arm? Look at it! No longer there. You tore it out from the socket with your shrapnel! You!
THE BULLFIGHTER: Traitor! Murderer! Pilferer of our land! You!

The emotional power of such passages engages our feelings and threatens to overwhelm our critical faculties, drawing us into the scene. On the other hand, Alberti succeeds in retaining the necessary sense of distance and detachment: firstly, through the framing device previously mentioned, which makes the scenes in question a play within a play; and secondly, through the stylization of language in those scenes — as in the Venus-Adonis episode — which has the effect of moving the action away from a realistic plane and drawing attention to its literary character.

Finally, in relation to the technique of distancing it is important to note the balancing effect of tragic and comic elements. Such a moment occurs when el Descabezado (the beheaded man) climbs onto the barricade and in a fit of anger and outrage hurls his severed head at the enemy:

DESCABEZADO *(subido en lo más alto, mostrando, asida de los pelos, su cabeza)*: Ésta sí es buena bala. ¡La mejor! Cien mil rayos de odio lleva dentro. No vais a resistirla. *(La lanza fuertemente hacia donde se supone la puerta alta del museo, cayendo exánime su cuerpo desde la cima de la barricada.)*(p.183)

THE BEHEADED MAN *(he has climbed to the highest point and he displays his head, holding it up by the hair)*: This will make a fine bullet. The best of all! It contains an enormous explosive charge. You will not be able to survive it. *(He throws it violently towards where we imagine the main door of the museum to be, and his lifeless body crashes down from the top of the barricade).*

Just afterwards the high tension and emotion of the episode dissolve completely into comic crudity as the Vieja, the old woman, is overcome by the fear of the moment in the most physical manner:

FUSILADO: ¿Qué te sucede, vieja bruja?
VIEJA I: Que estoy de parto . . . Pero por otra parte. No por la delantera. ¡Ay!   (p.184)

THE EXECUTED MAN: What's the matter, you old witch?
FIRST OLD WOMAN: I'm going to give birth . . . But by the back end. Not the front. Oh!

The outrageous comments of the Vieja, her cackling laughter, the down-to-earth language of many of the Goya characters, and the often almost slapstick, puppet-like nature of their actions, all these are strategically interwoven with heroic and tragic incidents throughout the play. The effect is, of course, to offset too close an involvement with those moving events and to burst the emotional bubble in the course of its formation. Like the other techniques employed by Alberti in *Noche de guerra*, it can be seen to assist the dramatist greatly in that delicate juggling act which in this play allows him to pay worthy homage to Brecht, true master of the *verfremdungseffeckt*, and in so doing to write one of his finest works.[43]

Of Alberti's achievement as a dramatist there can be no doubt. It is clear from the preceding discussion that Alberti, like Valle-Inclán and Lorca, reacted against the commerically successful theatre of his time and sought through constant and bold experiment to rejuvenate the Spanish stage. In one direction the process of experiment took the form of looking backwards to traditional Spanish forms — the *auto sacramental*, the puppet-play — and of injecting them with new life and meaning. In another it embraces contemporary trends and movements in European theatre, from Expressionism to the political theatre of Brecht and Piscator. But whatever the degree and the nature of experiment, the achievement of any dramatist is determined in the end by the extent to which his theatre can be said to have its own individual voice, and by the extent to which that voice has something to say that is worth saying. On the first point, it is impossible to mistake Alberti's theatre for any other. On the second, his message embraces some of the most important issues, both individual and social, of our time. In every sense Alberti is to be grouped, as a dramatist, with Valle-Inclán and Lorca.

1 See Alberti's *La arboleda perdida*, I and II (Buenos Aires, 1959). All subsequent page references are to this edition. The translations into English are my own but the reader is also recommended to the translation by Gabriel Berns, *The Lost Grove* (University of California Press, 1976).

2 For an account of Alberti's life and background the interested reader may consult *La arboleda perdida*; Claude Couffon, *Rafael Alberti* (Paris, 1966); María Teresa León, *Memoria de la melancolía* (Buenos Aires, 1970); and Louise B. Popkin, *The Theatre of Rafael Alberti* (London, 1975).

3 C.B. Morris, *This Loving Darkness: The Cinema and Spanish Writers, 1920-1936* (Oxford, 1980), 86.

4 *El Debate*, (27 February 1931).

5 *Artículos de crítica teatral: el teatro español de 1914 a 1946*, V (Mexico, 1968), 113-17.

6 There is an interesting article on the relationship between Alberti's play and the Golden Age *autos* by Theodore S. Beardsley, Jr., 'El Sacramento desautorizado: *El hombre deshabitado* de Alberti y los autos sacramentales de Calderón', in *Studia Iberia: Festschrift für Hans Flasche* (Bern and Munich, 1973), 93-104. See too Robert Marrast, *Aspects du Théâtre de Rafael Alberti* (Paris, 1967), 29-31; and Louise B. Popkin, *The Theatre of Rafael Alberti*, 57-8.

7   *The Allegorical Drama of Calderón* (Oxford and London, 1943), 59.

8   'El Sacramento desautorizado . . . ', 94-6.

9   *The Theatre of Rafael Alberti*, 55-6

10 *Rafael Alberti's 'Sobre los ángeles': Four Major Themes* (Hull, 1966), 11.

11 'Rafael Alberti's *El hombre deshabitado'*, *Ibero-romansch*, Munich, 2, 122-33.

12 *The Theatre of Rafael Alberti*, 59, n.3.

13 In this context see J.L. Styan, *Modern Drama in Theory and Practice, III, Expressionism and Epic Theatre* (Cambridge, 1981), 4, 53.

14 All pages references are to the edition published by Losada, Buenos Aires, 1959. Translations into English are my own. This is, in fact, a revised version of the work performed in 1931, though the revisions, made in 1950, reinforce the meaning rather than alter them and are not in any case extensive.

15 See *Georg Kaiser, Five Plays*, translated from the German by B.J. Kenworthy, Rex Last and J.M. Ritchie (London, 1971).

16 *Expressionism* (London, 1973), 21.

17 *Modern Drama in Theory and Practice*, III, 53.

18 *Modern Drama in Theory and Practice*, III, 5.

19 *Modern Drama in Theory and Practice*, III, 5.

20 *The Theatre of Rafael Alberti*, 61-2.

21 See Louise B. Popkin, *The Theatre of Rafael Alberti*, 21.

22 In an interview with J. Pérez Domenech in *El Imparcial*, (23 April, 1933).

23 In 'Teatro de urgencia', *Boletin de Orientación Teatral*, (15 February 1938), 5.

24 For a very informative account of *agitprop* theatre and its development in the hands of Piscator, see J.L. Styan, *Modern Drama in Theory and Practice*, III, 128-39; and C.D. Innes, *Erwin Piscator's Political Theatre: The Development of Modern German Drama* (Cambridge, 1972).

25 *Erwin Piscator's Political Theatre . . .* , 33.

26 All references are to the text published in *El Mono Azul*, No.45 (May 1938), 6-8.

27 *The Theatre of Rafael Alberti*, 92.

28 See *Numancia*, ed. Rafael Alberti (Madrid, 1937); also Rafael Alberti, *Numancia* (Madrid, 1975). References are to the latter.

29 María Teresa León, *Memoria de la melancolia*, 52-4.

30 For a recent study of Alberti's adaptation, see J. McCarthy, 'The Republican Theatre During the Spanish Civil War: Rafael Alberti's *Numancia'*, *Theatre Research International*, V, No.3 (1980), 193-205.

31 Alberti has himself denied the influence on *El adefesio* of *La casa de Bernarda Alba*, noting that when he was writing his own play Lorca's was in the hands of the Lorca family. In a letter to Robert Marrast, 2 May 1954, Alberti stated that 'el clima de mi obra es más tenso y raro que el de la pieza de Federico' ('the climax of my play is more tense and unusual than that of Federico's piece'), and he also pointed to other differences between the two works. Louise B. Popkin, *The Theatre of Rafael Alberti*, 149, n.25, suggests that 'the striking similarities between *El adefesio* and Lorca's tragedy result from shared experience and common inspiration'.

32 Preface to *Die Unsterblichen,* in *Dichtungen* (Neuwied, 1960), 60-5. The translation into English is my own.

33 See C.B. Morris, *This Loving Darkness* . . . , 13, 83.

34 Martin Esslin, *The Theatre of the Absurd,* 352

35 *Modern Drama in Theory and Practice,* III, 5.

36 *Modern Drama in Theory and Practice,* III, 54.

37 See Louise B. Popkin's analysis of the play, *The Theatre of Rafael Alberti,* 116-30.

38 For an account of this, see María Teresa León, *Memoria de la melancolía,* 202-4.

39 María Teresa León, *Memoria de la melancolía,* 269.

40 For a detailed account of 'epic theatre' and its development in the hands of both Piscator and Brecht, the reader is recommended to J.L. Styan, *Modern Drama in Theory and Practice,* III, 128-64

41 On the 1928 production of *The Good Soldier Schwiek,* see C.D. Innes, *Erwin Piscator's Political Theatre,* 4-6, 58-9, 81-3.

42 Page references are to the edition published by Losada, Buenos Aires, 1964. There is a more recent, revised version of the play, but the main difference involves a scene between Goya and Picasso in which they lament Spain's tragic fate. All translations into English are my own.

43 On *Noche de guerra* see Louise B. Popkin, *The Theatre of Rafael Alberti,* 154-63. The reader is also recommended to R. Domenech, 'Introducción al teatro de Rafael Alberti', *Cuadernos Hispanoamericanos,* 259 (1972), 96-126; and to R. Marrast, *Le théâtre de Rafael Alberti,* Unpublished Mémoire de Diplôme d'Etudes Supérieures (University of Bordeaux, 1954); 'Essai de bibliographie de Rafael', *Bulletin Hispanique,* 57 (1955), 147-77; 'Essai de bibliographie de Rafael Alberti (addenda et corrigenda)', *Bulletin Hispanique,* 59 (1957), 430-5; 'L'esthétique théâtrale de Rafael Alberti', *La mise en scène des oeuvres du passé,* ed. Jean Jacquot and André Veinstein (Paris, 1957); 'Situation du théâtre espagnol contemporain', *Théâtre Populaire,* 13 (1955), 15-23; and 'Le théâtre à Madrid pendant la guerre civile', *Le théâtre moderne: hommes et tendances,* ed. Jean Jaquot (2nd ed.) (Paris, 1965).

CHAPTER V

Antonio Buero Vallejo

Antonio Buero Vallejo (born 1916) is the best-known, the most productive and, in the opinion of many, the most interesting contemporary Spanish dramatist. The celebrated Spanish critic, Francisco Ruiz Ramón, has observed that the performance in 1949 of Buero Vallejo's *Historia de una escalera (The Story of a Stairway)* marked the beginning not merely of a single dramatic career but of the new Spanish drama.[1] In the thirty or so years since that notable event, Buero has written approximately twenty plays, in all of which he has shown himself to be a consistently serious dramatist in terms of theme, and a constant experimenter in terms of dramatic technique. In this sense he is to be grouped with Valle-Inclán, Lorca and Alberti, even though his theatre is in many respects very different from theirs. Like them, regardless of his own commercial success, he has written plays in opposition to the kind of theatre which has dominated the commercial stages of Spain for many years. The theatre that immediately preceded him was, in part, the very theatre against which Lorca and Alberti had themselves reacted: the theatre of Benavente, the Quinteros, Marquina. There were, in addition, the dramatists who echoed Benavente — Pemán, Luca de Tena — and there were also the dramatists of the so-called 'teatro de evasión' ('theatre of evasion'), the effect of whose plays was less to confront the theatre-going public with the moral and social problems posed by post-war Spain than to encourage them to avoid the consideration of serious issues. In plays like *Historia de una escalera, Las Meninas (The Maids of Honour)* (1960), *El tragaluz (The Skylight)* (1967), and *El sueño de la razón (The Sleep of Reason)* (1970), Buero Vallejo has fashioned a post-war theatre that has restored to the Spanish stage a note of true seriousness and dignity and simultaneously invested it with a truly European dimension.[2]

It need hardly be said that the theatre of Buero Vallejo has to be considered within the context and the consequences of the Spanish Civil War. Twenty years old when the War began, Buero served on the Republican side and, when hostilities ended, he was detained, tried and sentenced to death for his allegiance to that cause. The sentence was commuted to imprisonment and, in 1946, to a conditional discharge. For the duration of the Franco dictatorship Buero was for obvious reasons obliged to work within the limitations imposed by a keen and watchful censorship. As Robert L. Nicholas has observed, 'Spain's contemporary political reality forces continuing concessions by the playwright'.[3] Many of Buero's plays are thus to be seen as powerful but oblique comments on the post-War Spanish situation. Ricardo Doménech advances the convincing argument that for the audience of *Historia de una escalera* in 1949 the hopes and frustrations of the play's characters had a particular poignancy.[4] In *Las Meninas* Velázquez's conflict with the Inquisition — the clash of progress and tradition, of truth and the forces that oppose it — has powerful contemporary implications, the lesson of history made meaningful for another generation. And similar too in its relevance is the powerful *El sueño de la razón* in which the figure of Goya, the champion of liberty, is exposed to the hypocrisy, the prejudice and the tyranny of a heartless regime. Buero's theatre thus has a clear message, shaped by the circumstances of its time. On the other hand, the particularized level of his drama is never allowed to obscure its broader significance, and Francisco Ruiz Ramón, a powerful advocate of the importance of Buero's work, has emphasized the way in which in play after play the characters and situations have posed 'unas interrogaciones fundamentales, esenciales' ('fundamental and essential questions').[5] The here and now of the dramatic action consistently opens out to reveal that Buero's real concern is man himself, in relation both to his social problems and his ultimate destiny. The issues of his plays are, in short, those that have preoccupied truly serious dramatists throughout the ages.

Given Buero's commitment to a serious theatre, it is hardly surprising that tragic drama should have had a particular fascination for him. He has written many tragic plays and he has written too on the question of tragedy itself. Robert L. Nicholas notes: 'The most basic common denominator of all Buero's plays is . . . their tragic conception.'[6] His concept of tragedy is, to put the matter simply, Aristotelian, for at its core lies the Aristotelian idea of catharsis, of the releasing in the spectator of the emotions of fear and terror, with its attendant effects of purification and spiritual elevation. In this sense the idea of audience involvement in the dramatic action is clearly central to Buero's theatre. In addition, the awakening and purging of strong emotions, of concern for man's predicament, reject explicit moralizing in favour of a spiritual and aesthetic response. Buero has spoken in the following way of the aim of his tragic drama:

> . . . por directa impresión estética y no discusión . . . [porque] la belleza estética es un hallazgo . . . supremo del hombre que, con su sola presencia, puede expresarlo todo sin decir nada.[7]

. . . by means of a direct aesthetic impact and not discourse . . . [for] aesthetic beauty is a discovery . . . of supreme human significance and by itself can express everything without stating anything.

Another important point to bear in mind is that Buero's tragic theatre is, despite its frequently dark and apparently pessimistic tone, a theatre of hope, a point which the dramatist himself has emphasized on many occasions. A world that seems to be chaotic and devoid of purpose may thus in the end have meaning:

> El último y mayor efecto moral de la tragedia es un acto de fe. Consiste en llevarnos a creer que la catástrofe está justificada y tiene un sentido, aunque no podamos conocer su justificación ni entender su sentido.[8]

> The ultimate and deepest moral effect of tragedy is an act of faith. It consists of leading us to believe that the catastrophe is justified and has meaning, though we cannot comprehend its justification nor understand its meaning.

As a dramatist Buero feels impelled to assert that, notwithstanding the darkest moments of doubt and despair and the daunting spectacle of man's inhumanity to man, his faith in man and his hope for man remain unshaken:

> Esta fe última late tras las dudas y los fracasos que en las escenas se muestran; esa esperanza mueve a las plumas que describen las situaciones más desesperadas. Se escribe porque se espera, pese a toda duda. Pese a toda duda, creo y espero en el hombre, como espero y creo en otras cosas: en la verdad, en la belleza, en la rectitud, en la libertad . . .[9]

> This ultimate faith lies behind the doubts and the failures that are shown on stage; that hope moves the pens which describe the most desperate situations. One writes because one hopes, despite all doubts. Despite all doubts, I believe in and hope for man, as I hope for and believe in other things: in the truth, in beauty, in decency, in freedom . . .

Buero's continuing hope in the ultimate meaning of events and man's salvation can be said to separate him from the other dramatists studied here. They are distinguished for the most part by their pessimism. He, in contrast, can be linked with those dramatists, especially Shakespeare and Ibsen, who suggest in the darkest moments of their theatre a compensating hope for suffering humanity.

In terms of style and technique, Buero Vallejo's theatre embraces in the course of its long development naturalistic, symbolist, historical and epic drama. Ramón del Valle-Inclán, Lorca and Alberti were all, as we have seen, dramatists who constantly sought new methods of expression whereby to communicate more effectively their particular point of view, and the influences upon them were varied and important, Spanish and European. As far as Buero is concerned, his early theatre is strongly, though not exclusively, naturalistic, and in its settings, characters and language reveals the imprint both of the Spanish naturalistic tradition and, in a broader context, of Ibsen. Ibsen is, indeed, an enormous influence on Buero, and the development of his drama is one in which the symbolic realism so closely associated with the Norwegian dramatist in plays like *The Doll's House* is very marked. *Historia de una escalera* and *En la ardiente oscuridad* are important plays in this respect. In the later historical drama, on the other hand — as in the case of *Las meninas* — the illusion of a realistic-naturalistic theatre is less, and the stage is acknowledged as stage, with important repercussions on the technique and stage presentation. The change in approach is related, in effect, to Buero's increasing familiarity in the late fifties with the dramatic theories of Brecht and implies, in terms of technique, a breaking of the theatrical illusion in favour of a greater sense of critical distance between the audience and the stage. This, on the other hand, conflicts with Buero's wish to involve the observer of the action emotionally, and means that in practice the Brechtian effect of alienation is only partially achieved, as, of course, is often the case in the theatre of Brecht itself.[10] Indeed, as will be seen later, alienation often gives way in Buero to what has been called the 'immersion' effect, a technique whereby the audience in the theatre is made to share in as full a sense as possible the experience of a character on stage, be it the blindness of the characters of *En la ardiente oscuridad* or the deafness of Goya in *El sueño de la razón*.[11] The development of Buero's theatre, given its steady shift away from the naturalism of *La historia de una escalera*, is therefore one in which the dramatist never loses sight of the 'directa impresión estética' to which in his theoretical writings he attributes such importance.

As to the visual impact of Buero's theatre, his interest in painting, which links him to Lorca and Alberti, is clearly important. As a young man Buero had left his native town of Guadalajara to study painting at the Escuela de Bellas Artes in Madrid. His studies were interrupted by the outbreak of the Civil War and he did not return to them subsequently, though he continued to paint while he turned his attention to writing. Buero's plays about Velázquez and Goya are a clear pointer to his interest in those painters, while his technique is often an attempt to create on stage — as in the case of the multiple-scene, impressionistic style of *Las meninas* — aspects of their method. But in a general sense too the influence of painting is important in Buero's theatre in relation to the interplay of settings, characters, movement and lighting. In the sense that many modern dramatists and stage designers — Maeterlinck, Craig, Yeats, Lorca, Alberti — have been affected by the dramatic qualities of painting, Buero is one of a long line.

Historia de una escalera was first performed on 14 October 1949, at the Teatro Español in Madrid, directed by Cayetano Luca de Tena. Its success was immediate and resounding, for the play received 187 consecutive performances, one unusual consequence being that for the first time in its history the National Theatre company was obliged to forgo its annual performance of José Zorrilla's *Don Juan Tenorio*. It was, indeed, awarded the 'Lope de Vega' prize which had not been given for fifteen years. Public and critical acclaim indicates the extent to which Buero's play was a landmark in his theatre and in the history of Spanish drama in the twentieth century.

The action, to describe it very briefly, portrays the lives of four Madrid families over a period of thirty years. The setting for their activities — their conversations, arguments, love-affairs, ambitions and failures — is the stairway of a tenement building, the stairway of the play's title, where their paths constantly meet. The principal characters, Fernando and Urbano, are at the outset full of dreams and aspirations. Fernando, the handsome gallant, longs to escape from the wretched surroundings of the tenement. Urbano, the committed Union man, aspires to improve his own and his comrades' lot. In the course of the action Fernando marries Elvira, not for love but in the hope that her father's money will help him fulfill his ambitions. Urbano marries Carmina whom Fernando has rejected. In the event both marriages prove disastrous, and Fernando and Urbano, thirty years on, are exactly what and where they were. At the end of the play their children, Fernando and Carmina, resolve to marry and avoid their parents' unhappy fate.

The predominant theme of *Historia de una escalera*, which suggests both its seriousness and its tragic character, is the theme of frustration — a frustration which affects individuals and the society to which they belong. It is embodied in different degrees in most of, if not all, the characters, and is expressed with particular power and sharpness in Fernando and Urbano, as the preceding summary suggests. Rejecting the society in which they live and reacting to it in different ways, both men dream of a happy future — Fernando of a future which concerns only his own interests; Urbano of a future which links his own success to that of others. By the end of the third Act both individuals have failed to realize their dreams, for they live still in the same shabby tenement and occupy the same social position. Their marriages to Elvira and Carmina respectively are as much prisons as their physical surroundings. Their frustration is a deeply personal one, the negation of all their deepest longings, but it has too a clear social dimension, not merely in the sense that Urbano's dream and thus his failure is that of those he fights for, but in the wider sense that Fernando and Urbano are also in their aspirations and disappointments mirrors in which the other

ANTONIO BUERO VALLEJO 177

characters of the play, men and women of similar social standing, are clearly reflected.

Inasmuch as the play concerns frustration, it has a tragic dimension, though not one that involves death. As far as the causes of tragedy are concerned, the failure of Urbano and Fernando resides, it can be argued, in a kind of moral error on account of which both men suffer.¹² According to this argument, Fernando's error lies in the betrayal of his feelings for Carmina in favour of a marriage to Elvira for largely financial motives. Similarly, Urbano persists in marrying Carmina even though he knows that she loves Fernando. In both cases an unhappy marriage is seen to be the outcome of self-interested action. On the other hand, while Fernando and Urbano are individuals who shape their destiny by their own actions, they are also part of the society of post-Civil War Spain and in that sense personify the hopes and frustrations of others like them. The circumstances of the time, including poor economic conditions and the lack of opportunity, drive men like Fernando to think only of themselves, or oblige men like Urbano to sacrifice himself in the interests of others. In both cases the aspiration is either distorted or negated by the end it seeks and Fernando and Urbano point to the fact that many other young men in similar circumstances carry the seeds of failure in the very extent of their dreams and ambitions.

Despite the tragic character of *Historia de una escalera*, the play is also a statement of hope, in accordance with Buero's view that in the very depths of despair there is always hope for mankind. It lies, in effect, in the indisputable fact, often emphasized by Buero, that man's will is free and that he is, to that extent, the architect of his own destiny.¹³ Such a view of human responsibility in relation to tragedy lies, of course, at the heart of the drama of the Golden Age, strongly coloured as this is by Catholic doctrine, but it is equally true to say that it is an important aspect of Greek tragedy. When, for example, Oedipus kills his father, he does so in an impetuous act he is capable of avoiding. Similarly, the mistakes of Fernando and Urbano are mistakes which could have been avoided, and hope for the future is seen to lie both in their recognition of that fact — the *anagnorosis* — and in the capacity of those who follow them to avoid their errors through a greater prudence and awareness. In the last scene of *Historia de una escalera* the young couple, Fernando and Carmina, express their feelings for each other, repeating the words and promises of their parents thirty years before. The ending is not, as has been suggested, an indication that the children will, according to some predetermined pattern, share their parents' fate. Rather it points to the fact that, controlling their destiny and conscious of their parents' errors, the children will avoid them and fashion a better future for themselves. And in the sense that they mirror the lives of other young people, there is hope too for them and for a future Spain that can escape the mistakes of its tragic past.

As to literary influences, *Historia de una escalera* reveals the clear imprint of the Spanish *género chico* — the one or two Act *sainetes* and the *zarzuelas*, the musical comedies which were enormously popular at the beginning of the century. The *género chico* was concerned, as has been pointed out before, with the portrayal of popular types and customs from middle or low-life society and was characterized by its realistic settings and characters and its down-to-earth, colloquial language. A tradition of so-called realism can, of course, be traced a long way back in the history of Spanish drama and is exemplified in the Golden Age, for example, in the short plays — the *pasos* and *entremeses* — of Lope de Rueda and Cervantes. In the eighteenth century the *sainete* had been the particular province of Ramón de la Cruz, while in the years preceding Buero's appearance on the theatrical scene these short, witty and essentially light-hearted pieces had achieved enormous success and popularity in the hands of the Quintero brothers. It is also important to remember, though, that from about 1910 Carlos Arniches began to develop the *género chico* in a different way, investing it with a tragic-comic note, and that this pattern was continued in the *esperpentos* of Valle-Inclán, whose debt to the *sainete* and other forms of popular literature can hardly be doubted.[14] Thus, *Luces de Bohemia*, set in the tenement buildings, the streets and cafes of Madrid and peopled by down-and-outs, tramps and prostitutes, is a perfect example of popular literature endowed with a serious and even tragic tone. It is precisely the tradition to which *Historia de una escalera* belongs. There is no mistaking the popular origins of Fernando, the handsome gallant, Elvira, the pampered coquette, Pepe, the idle sponger, or Paca, the down-to-earth gossip. Nor, indeed, is it difficult to perceive the source of the squabbles, the love-affairs and the gossip that give the play its distinctive, popular quality. On the other hand, this aspect of the play never conceals either its serious issues and concerns or its deeply tragic character. Like Valle-Inclán before him, Buero has transformed the tradition of the *sainete* into an instrument of serious drama.

In the dramatization of serious issues, in particular those which touch on the nature of human destiny, Buero is influenced to a large extent by Unamuno. Together with Lorca, Unamuno was clearly one of the twentieth-century Spanish sources to whom a writer of similar ideological concerns would turn when it came to the writing of tragedy.[15] In novels, philosophical works and plays Unamuno gave expression to the powerful conflict between reason and faith which constantly racked him. *El sentimiento trágico de la vida (The Tragic Sense of Life)* is a powerful statement of his existentialist philosophy. The novels, *Niebla (Mist)*, of 1914, and *La tía Tula (Aunt Tula)*, of 1921, as well as many others, present in and through the characters those questions relating to the extent of human freedom, the gulf between reality and human aspiration, the possibility of life after death, and the ultimate meaning of the universe which preoccupied Unamuno throughout his life. And similarly the plays, such as *Sombras de sueño (Dream Shadows)* and *El otro (The Other One)*, both of 1926, are the exploration in dramatic form of personal dilemmas. Given the fact, moreover, that Unamuno's style and manner is more sobre and in that sense more appealing than Lorca's to a man of Buero's attitude and temperament, it seems logical that Unamuno should be the greater influence. As far as Lorca is concerned, it is less the poetic theatre of *Bodas de sangre* than the symbolic realism of *La casa de Bernarda Alba* that may be discerned in *Historia de una escalera.*

Of European dramatists Ibsen is a particularly important influence, as Robert Nicholas has stated.[16] *Historia de una escalera* can be said to reflect Ibsenian concerns both in relation to its emphasis upon socio-moral problems and the more fundamental question of human existence. Characteristic of Ibsen too is Buero's preoccupation with the conflict between illusion and reality, personified in the idealist's striving in vain to realize his deepest desires. The latter gives rise in turn to another favourite Ibsen theme — the extent to which man, failing to achieve his objectives, is truly free and, in conjunction with that, the degree to which he is obliged to live within a predetermined order within which he must fashion his own destiny. The experience is one which allows Buero, as it did Ibsen, to portray man's struggle against the odds as noble and heroic. And finally, of course, Buero's dramatic method, combining realism and symbolism in a way that is suggested by the very title of *Historia de una escalera*, is highly reminiscent of Ibsen. Not only has Buero openly acknowledged the influence of the Scandinavian dramatist, he has also written articles about him. Robert Nicholas concludes:

... for Buero, the revitalization of the Spanish theatre presupposed the re-discovery of its most authentic roots — the theatrical vision and means of the Masters of Realism. Like them, Buero's realism entails a critical view of everyday life, a concern for the problem of man's ultimate destiny, and the strict observance of what has come to be known as realistic technique — natural dialogue, humble characters and settings, psychological motives of action, the development of character in consequence of that action, etc.[17]

An examination of the dramatic technique of *Historia de una escalera* reveals the extent to which the play is distinguished, for all its apparent realism, by a striking degree of symbolism. The stage settings, as is suggested by the stage direction for Act One, contain to all appearances the kind of naturalistic detail we would expect to find in a play by Eugene O'Neill:

> *Un tramo de escalera con dos rellanos, en una casa modesta de vecindad. Los escalones de bajada hacia los pisos inferiores se encuentran en el primer término izquierdo. La barandilla que los bordea es muy pobre, con el pasamanos de hierro, y tuerce para correr a lo largo de la escena limitando el primer rellano . . .*[18]   (p.31)

> *A flight of stairs with two landings, in a modest tenement house. The stairs that descend to the floors below are situated downstage left. The handrail that runs alongside them is very shabby, made of iron, and it bends and runs the length of the stage, enclosing the first landing.*

Despite its realistic detail, the scene is markedly symbolic and particular aspects of it are sharply highlighted. The prominence of the stairs themselves points to the significance of climbing and descending in a sense that quickly becomes metaphorical, and 'subir' ('to climb') and 'bajar' ('to descend') become in effect key words in the play's dialogue. The drab and monotonous colour of the settings is also suggestive in a more than literal sense. Thus, the stage direction for Act Two reinforces the earlier effect:

> *. . . la escalera sigue sucia y pobre, las puertas sin timbre, los cristales de la ventana sin lavar.*   (p.56)

> *. . . the stairs are still dirty and shabby, the doors without bells, the glass of the windows has not been washed.*

The stage setting is itself an image of the drabness of the characters' lives and, inasmuch as the settings are repeated throughout the play, they suggest too that the men and women who inhabit them are subject to the same unchanging drabness. Furthermore, the way in which the handrail twists and extends across the stage, enclosing the landing where the characters meet, is a very effective method of suggesting that their lives are contained and limited by the circumstances in which they find themselves. Finally, the handrail twists and turns back on itself on both landings in a kind of repetition which evokes the way in which within the action of the play the lives of the characters are distinguished by repeated patterns and circular events from which they seem unable to escape. In short, the stage settings of *Historia de una escalera* reveal the stylization and richness of symbolic meaning that are equally evident in the realistic settings of Lorca's *La casa de Bernarda Alba.*

The characters of Buero's play are highly realistic in many ways. Their actions and conversations, embracing the cost of living, the daily shopping and the deaths of neighbours, are precisely those of people who live in daily contact with each other. On the other hand, for all their realistic qualities, the characters are also types presented in broad outline: Fernando, the good-looking dreamer; Urbano, the strong, resolute Union man; Pepe, the sponger. And in the sense that they are types, they have, clearly, a symbolic dimension, a fact underlined by the extent to which they are all to a greater or lesser degree concerned with their lot and thus part of the play's central theme of success and failure. In addition, the characters range from young to old, embracing the whole spectrum of man's allotted span. At the outset Fernando and Urbano are young men. In the course of the action they become old. In Act Two Señor Juan laments the death of a neighbour. In Act Three Señor Juan's widow laments his death. At the end of Act One Fernando and Carmina express their love for each other. At the end of Act Three their children, thirty years later, do exactly the same. The idea of rising and falling, is, indeed, relevant to the play in more than the narrow sense of social success, for it has to do with the flow of life itself and the ascent or descent on which we are all embarked in the course of our journey through it. The range of *Historia de una escalera* is thus far greater than is suggested by its actual physical location, for the characters can be seen to be part of the rite and ritual of life in its constant flow. As they enter or leave the doors to their various dwelling in a process of almost unbroken movement throughout the play, they evoke the exits and entrances of man in general.

As stage settings are repeated throughout the play, so the repetition of certain actions creates a sense of duplication and of the circle or cycle of activity within which the characters are confined. The constant comings and goings, the opening and closing of doors, the passing on the stairs, provide numerous and relevant examples. At the very beginning of Act One the old man knocks on the door of the flats, takes the money, gives a receipt and touches his cap, as he has done hundreds of times before:

> COBRADOR: Está bien.
> *(Se lleva un dedo a la gorra y se dirige al IV.)*   (p.33)
>
> COLLECTOR: That's fine.
> *(He touches his cap and goes to No.IV)*

A little later the incident is repeated:

> COBRADOR: Está bien.
> *(Se lleva la mano a la gorra.)*   (p.35)
> COLLECTOR: That's fine.
> *(He touches his cap with his hand)*

In Act One Urbano and Pepe come into violent conflict over the latter's involvement with Rosa, and the confrontation is repeated in Act Two, gestures and actions echoing the earlier incident. Similarly, as Act One concludes with Fernando and Carmina sitting and expressing their hopes for the future, so Act Three ends with their children repeating the earlier action. In the first case the stage direction states:

Con un ligero forcejeo la obliga a sentarse contra la pared y se sienta a su lado. Le quita la lechera y la deja junto a él. Le coge una mano.		(p.54)

With a gentle insistence he compels her to sit against the wall and he sits beside her. He takes the milk-jug from her and puts it down close to him. He takes her hand.

In the case of the children, the following occurs:

Después, él la lleva al primer escalón y la sienta junto a la pared, sentándose a su lado. Se cogen las manos . . .		(pp.97-8)

Then he leads her to the first step and puts her to sit close to the wall, sitting down himself at her side. They hold hands . . .

In a stage performance due attention must be accorded to repeated and parallel actions of the kind described above, for through them is suggested the extent to which the lives of the characters are inescapably and endlessly the same. In addition, repeated actions give to the individuals who perform them — the collector touching his cap — the character of puppets or automatons, suggesting their lack of freedom and their enslavement by their circumstances. In turn, this gives to the play a sense of life's triviality, of its ordinariness, and of the smallness and insignificance of human beings.

Repetition is also a prominent feature of the play's dialogue. In Act One Fernando gives vent to his fears of time's remorseless march, and the highly stylized form of the speech, emphasizing key words by repetition, effectively conveys its central concerns:

. . . *Ver cómo pasan los días, y los años . . . Y mañana, o dentro de diez años que pueden pasar como un día, como han pasado estos últimos . . ., ¡sería terrible seguir así! . . .*		(pp.41-2)

. . . To see how the days pass, and the years . . . And tomorrow, or in ten years that will pass by like a day, as these last few years have passed by . . . it would be terrible to go on like this!

Towards the end of the Act Generosa, complaining about her husband's enforced retirement, repeats almost identically to Paca the words she had spoken to Fernando shortly before (pp.47, 52). It suggests, indeed, how individuals endlessly pursue the same topics of conversation. In Act Two Señor Juan reflects on the inevitability of death:

¡A todos nos llegará la hora!   (p.57)

The time will come for all of us!

Shortly afterwards he returns to the same topic:

Ya nos llegará a todos.   (p.58)

It will come for us all.

And finally, as we have seen in relation to the play's ending, the words of the young people, Fernando and Carmina, virtually duplicate those of their parents thirty years before, suggesting once again that individuals share the same dreams and voice the same aspirations (pp.55, 98). The dialogue of the play, to all appearances naturalistic, is seen on closer examination to be distinguished by its studied stylization, and this, as has been suggested, extends too to the stage settings and the gestures and movements of the characters. In short, *Historia de una escalera* works less on the level of naturalism than on the level of symbolic realism, a fertile fusion of styles which Buero would continue to explore.

To illustrate symbolic realism further it is useful to consider *En la ardiente oscuridad (In the Burning Darkness)* written in 1946, revised considerably, and finally performed in 1950, a year after the performance of *Historia de una escalera.* The action of the play takes place in a school for the blind where the pupils are encouraged to believe that they are normal people and refuse in consequence to acknowledge the reality of their situation. The arrival of Ignacio, a new student, confronts them with the truth, for his blindness fills him with a deep sense of anguish and he seeks to convince the other pupils that they too are abnormal. Ignacio succeeds in persuading some of them of his own point of view and succeeds too in winning the affections of Juana, the girlfriend of Carlos who, at the opposite extreme from Ignacio, represents the *status quo*. It is finally re-established when Carlos kills Ignacio, but by that time he is himself filled with the anguish previously experienced by the dead boy.

The theme of *En la ardiente oscuridad* is truth and freedom.[19] The physical blindness of the characters is, of course, symbolic of their spiritual blindness, for the pupils of the school, Ignacio apart, are satisfied with their lot and pretend that the misery in which they find themselves is, in fact, happiness. Ignacio himself, longing for physical sight, yearns in effect for something more than that, for he is, paradoxically, the true seer, the man who is aware of his limitations and who strives to go beyond them, denying the simplistic, complacent and self-deluding attitudes of the pupils and the administrators of the school. In many respects Ignacio, affected by the physical and even emotional constraints of his blindness, is a typical Buero character, and blindness, deafness and degrees of madness are prominent in many plays. Blind or semi-blind characters distinguish *El Concierto de San Ovidio (Concert at St Ovid)*. Deaf individuals are prominent in *Hoy es fiesta (Today is a Holiday)*, *La doble historia del doctor Valmy (The Double History of Doctor Valmy)* and, of course, *El sueño de la razón* in which Goya is both deaf and subject to attacks of madness. The physical defects of many of these characters, and Ignacio is a case in point, are accompanied and in part explained by their extraordinary powers of perception, for the limitations from which they suffer transform them into visionaries, *contemplativos* who are aware of and aspire desperately to a greater freedom. In the sense that this is denied them and that their fate is either death or disappointment, they are, of course, tragic characters, and Ignacio is no exception. But in their visionary qualities and in their vigorous struggle to achieve that vision there is also that fundamental note of hope which for Buero is an integral part of tragedy.

En la ardiente oscuridad has too a strong social and even national dimension which, as in the case of *Historia de una escalera*, has to do with the aftermath of the Spanish Civil War. The Franco dictatorship encouraged in its own interests the Spanish people's acceptance of its lot, in the same way that the pupils of the school for the blind are persuaded to accept their affliction as normal. Ignacio, expressing Buero's own attitude, speaks out against the evils both of deceit and self-delusion, acting as a clarion call to a future that seeks to overcome the evils of the past. It is a message of hope both for the individual and society. Less overtly social than *Historia de una escalera*, *En la ardiente oscuridad* has, nonetheless, that deep layer of social implication which is a constant feature of Buero's theatre.

As far as influences are concerned, Ibsen and Unamuno must again be singled out. Ignacio's striving for the impossible is typically Unamunian, but once again, as in the case of *Historia de una escalera*, it is the influence of Ibsen that is thoroughly pervasive. Indeed, in contrast to the somewhat simplified and one-dimensional characters of the latter, those of *En la ardiente oscuridad* reveal much greater psychological penetration. But the debt to Ibsen lies in particular in the degree to which our insight into and understanding of the characters is deepened by the play's surface realism. While this is also true of *Historia de una escalera*, *En la ardiente oscuridad* greatly enriches the process.

Throughout the play realistic settings, costumes and actions point to its deeper meaning. In Act One, for example, the happy frame of mind of the pupils at the school is symbolized in the trees outside the recreation room, for the leaves grow rich and green. In Act Two the branches are stark and bare. In realistic terms this points to the fact that autumn has arrived. Symbolically it means that Ignacio's presence has stripped the boys of their former happiness. Act Three takes place at night in a room in the residence and the stars can be seen through windows at the back of the stage. In symbolic terms the blackness of night is, of course, Ignacio's anguish and the light of the stars the object of his restless search, but the darkness also becomes Carlos's troubled state of mind after the murder of Ignacio, while his hands, touching the glass of the window, point to the beginning of his own anguished search for the freedom represented by the stars. Costume and dress are also an important pointer to states of mind, for initially the pupils are tidily dressed, in accordance with their happy and unruffled mood. The appearance of the somewhat untidy Ignacio strikes a discordant note:

> ... viste de negro intemporalmente, durante toda la obra.[20]   (p.106)

> ... he is constantly dressed in black, right through the play.

His disruptive influence is, moreover, reflected in the sense that in the course of the play many of the other pupils appear unkempt. In Act Three Carlos, who will soon assume Ignacio's desperation, is described as having 'la camisa desabrochada y la corbata floja' ('his shirt unbuttoned and his tie loose') (p.140). As for actions, they are again revealing of psychological states. In Act One, when Carlos is ignored by Juana, he gropes at the air in a way which expresses his uncertain state of mind, and in Act Two his stumbling against the furniture points to the fact that he is not the confident person he claims to be. After the murder of Ignacio, Carlos's clumsy movements further underline his agitation.

These examples of the way in which the realistic surface of the play becomes a kind of chart or mirror to the psychological journey of the characters of En la ardiente oscuridad may be compared to many similar episodes in the theatre of Ibsen. Robert Nicholas has appropriately drawn attention to The Doll's House in which Nora's secret eating of macaroons indicates her child-like and undeveloped nature, as indeed does her wearing of an Italian party dress.[21] The fact that she later discards the dress suggests that she also discards her childishness and moves towards a greater maturity. In addition, the beautiful Christmas tree that in Act One is a symbol of her happiness is by Act Two stripped of its vegetation and symbolic of her misery. The design of Ibsen's play, as is the case in much of his theatre, is one in which settings, dress, objects, movements and gestures combine and interact in an almost unobtrusive way to create a rich texture of symbolic meaning. Amongst Buero's early plays En la ardiente oscuridad is a good example of the Ibsenian method.

Las Meninas, together with *Un soñador para un pueblo (A Dreamer for a People)* (1958) and *El concierto de San Ovidio* (1962), form a historical trilogy and denote a second stage in Buero's dramatic career. The first performance of *Las Meninas* took place on 9 December 1960 at the Teatro Español in Madrid to even greater critical acclaim than had greeted *Historia de una escalera* eleven years earlier. It ran, in fact, for 260 performances, was finally withdrawn because of the theatre's other commitments and was generally acknowledged as Buero's finest work to date.

The action of *Las Meninas* portrays the circumstances surrounding the painting of the famous picture. Part One introduces the various characters: Velázquez; the beggars Martín and Pedro; Doña Marcela de Ulloa, a lady of the Court; Juana Pacheco, Velázquez's wife; José Nieto Velázquez, the painter's cousin; Angelo Nardi, an Italian painter; El Marqués, an adviser to Philip IV; the princess María Teresa; King Philip IV; and the palace dwarfs, Mari Bárbola and Nicolasillo Pertusato. The action, shifting constantly from one group of characters to another, is far less linear than kaleidoscopic, for it is concerned with revealing the relationships between them and, in particular, Velázquez's attitude towards his art and the Court society in which he lives. As far as the painting of *Las Meninas* is concerned, Velázquez has completed a preliminary version of it and awaits the King's approval for work to begin on the finished picture. Part Two, in contrast to Part One, pinpoints in a tense and dramatic courtroom situation the envy and resentment to Velázquez already suggested in Part One. He is accused by the Inquisition of having painted an obscene picture — the nude Venus. Nardi argues that his paintings of soldiers, saints and kings lack sufficient dignity and that his style lacks detail and precision. El Marqués advances the argument that, in harbouring in his house the criminal Pedro Briones, Velázquez has been disloyal to the crown, and the King himself, pointing to the painter's friendship with the princess, María Teresa, implies an impropriety between them. Velázquez's response to the accusations made against him consists of a vigorous exposure and denunciation both of individual motives and of the corruption of the Court, an appropriate breeding ground for hypocrisy and mendacity.

As far as history is concerned, Diego Rodríguez de Silva y Velázquez was born in Seville in 1599, went to Madrid in 1622 and a year later, at the age of twenty-four, was appointed Court painter, a post which he retained until his death in 1660. In 1652, after a visit to Italy in the course of which he was charged by the King to acquire paintings for the royal collection, he applied for and was appointed by Philip IV to the post of *Aposentador* or Royal Chamberlain, a position normally occupied only by noblemen and which made Velázquez responsible for the royal household and its furnishings, as well as for the arrangements for foreign visits. In 1658 he was, on the recommendation of Philip IV, made a member of the famous Order of Santiago. He died two years later after an arduous journey to the French border where Philip's daughter, María Teresa, was delivered in marriage to Louis XIV. Velázquez was thus, for almost forty years of his life, not merely close to the King himself but also a witness to the intrigues of palace life and the sad, even tragic spectacle of Spain's increasingly rapid decline in the seventeenth century. The country was beset by political and economic problems. From the time of Philip III at the end of the sixteenth century Spain had been governed not by its kings but by often unscrupulous noblemen, in consequence of which bribery and corruption were rampant. Concerned more with amusing themselves than with the welfare of their country, they presided over a Spanish Empire in rapid decline. Danger abroad, in the form of religious opposition to Spain's intolerant Catholicism, was matched within by growing dissatisfaction with ever-increasing taxation and religious persecution. Such was the national picture over which Velázquez cast his painter's eye.

Buero Vallejo's *Las Meninas* is sub-titled, interestingly enough, 'Fantasía velazqueña en dos partes' ('A Velázquez Fantasy in Two Parts'), a clear pointer to the fact that his play is not a faithful copy but an interpretation of history. It is indeed doubtful, for example, that Velázquez would have spoken to King Philip in reality with the bluntness that distinguishes his conduct in the play. In the latter he is denounced to the Holy Office by his cousin, Nieto, while history neither confirms that fact nor suggests that Nieto was a member of the Holy Office. In reality, Velázquez's wife, Juana, is thought to have posed for him as a young woman though in the play she denies having done so. More importantly, the whole of Part Two, consisting of Velázquez's interrogation by the King, appears to have no basis in reality. Buero's play is, in the sense that it reinterprets history, a 'fantasía', but in so doing he is also offering us the truth. To appreciate that point, it is essential to bear in mind, as Ricardo Doménech has pointed out, the Aristotelian view that fiction contains a greater truth than history, for while the historian relates the facts, the artist draws from those facts essential and universal truths.[22] In writing his play Buero interprets the events of Velázquez's life in his own way but not in an arbitrary manner. His Velázquez is his own Velázquez but built and constructed on what is known of him — even if the facts concerning other people are altered — in a way which crystallizes his integrity and truthfulness. As is the case in the Golden Age dramas of Calderón, the theme and message of the play is all-important.

The key theme of *Las Meninas* is 'la verdad', 'the truth', and it can be seen in different ways and on different levels. In an important scene in Part One involving Velázquez and the princess María Teresa, the painter observes:

> La verdad es una carga terrible: cuesta quedarse solo. Y en la Corte, nadie. ¿lo oís?, nadie pregunta para que le digan la verdad.[23]   (p.146)

> The truth is a terrible burden; to be alone is such an effort. And in the Court, nobody, you understand, nobody asks to be told the truth.

Later, when the King questions Velázquez about the meaning of *Las Meninas*, he replies:

> ... Representa ... una de las verdades del Palacio, señor.
> EL REY: ¿Cuál?
> VELÁZQUEZ: No sé cómo decir ... Yo creo que la verdad ... está en esos momentos sencillos más que en la etiqueta ...   (p.169)

> ... It represents ... one of the truths of the Palace, your Majesty.
> THE KING: Which?
> VELÁZQUEZ: I don't know how to express it ... I think that the truth is to be found much more in those simple moments than in etiquette ...

Finally, in the play's concluding scene, Velázquez, faced with the alternative of offering the King either a pleasing lie or an unpalatable truth, opts for the latter:

> Es una elección, señor. De un lado, la mentira una vez más. Una mentira tentadora: sólo puede traerme beneficios. Del otro, la verdad. Una verdad peligrosa que ya no remedia nada ...   (p.232)

> It is a matter of choice, majesty. On the one hand, another lie. A tempting lie: it can do me only good. On the other, the truth. A dangerous truth that will now remedy nothing ...

For an individual like María Teresa, the young eighteen-year-old princess, the truth consists of the simple fact of discovering the extent to which her father is a philanderer and of recognizing the hypocritical facade of Court life for what it really is. The latter is symbolized, of course, in most of the play's characters, who are synonymous, therefore, with un-truth, who conceal the reality of their motivations beneath an elaborate armour of appearance. Thus, El Marqués, an apparently loyal adviser to Philip, is in reality a proud, inflexible and self-centred man. Doña Marcela de Ulloa, proclaiming herself as a morally upright woman and the watchful guardian of her female charges, is driven by a deep and obsessive physical passion for Velázquez. José Nieto Velázquez, denouncing the lasciviousness of his cousin's painting for apparently religious reasons, is exposed both as a hypocrite and as an envious and ambitious man. The dwarfs, Mari Bárbola and Nicolasillo, who seem to be harmless clowns, are in reality malicious gossips, the careful, self-interested observers of palace life, the spies who profit from the misdemeanours of others. Even Doña Juana, Velázquez's wife, his supposedly loyal companion of many years, is filled with irrational fears and jealousy of her husband, the product to that extent both of a narrow upbringing and of direct experience of the deceit to which, living in the Court ambience, she is constantly exposed. In short, in contrast to the truth which María Teresa seeks so inspiringly but so naively, the world of the Court of Philip IV is presented as a fabric of closely interwoven lies. Velázquez himself penetrates beneath the surface appearance of things in many ways. When, for example, he observes to the King that truth lies in one of those 'momentos sencillos' ('simple moments'), which is what is portrayed in the unguarded informality of Las Meninas itself, he offers an interpretation of it which sweeps away the rhetoric, the pomp, the ceremony, the ritual and the mannered posturing of Court activity, together with all its other forms of pretence. On a broader front the truth is to be found too in Spain's sad and rapid decline, ruthlessly exposed by Velázquez in the play's concluding scenes:

> ... El hambre crece, el dolor crece, el aire se envenena y ya no tolera la verdad, que tiene que esconderse como mi Venus, porque está desnuda. Mas yo he de decirla.   (p.233)

> ... Hunger grows, pain increases, the air is foul and will not tolerate the truth, for this must be hidden like my Venus because it is naked. But I will state it.

And finally, of course, there is the central question of truthfulness in Velázquez's painting, in the aim and achievement of his art, crystallized above all in the trial scene in the important exchanges with the painter, Nardi. The latter attributes Velázquez's 'manera abreviada' or impressionistic style to the fact that his sight is failing and he cannot therefore perceive details. Velázquez's reply is unequivocal, though Nardi fails to understand it:

> ... Vos creéis que hay que pintar las cosas. Yo pinto el ver.   (p.221)
> ... You believe that one must portray things. I paint what I see.

Prior to this the beggar, Pedro, has observed that on one occasion Velázquez had drawn attention to the shifting, changing appearance of things and that truth therefore lies in the painter's capacity to capture fleeting, momentary impressions:

> Un día dijisteis: las cosas cambian ... Quizá su verdad esté en su apariencia, que también cambia.   (p.156)

> One day you said: things change ... Perhaps the truth lies in their appearance, which also changes.

The truth, then, is not to be found in the stilted and inflexible ritual of the Court, be this a matter of stylized gesture or carefully chosen word, for these are the things that are designed to conceal that truth and reality that shows through only in unguarded moments, the 'momentos sencillos' during which human beings are revealed to us in all their unadorned truthfulness.

When Velazquez observes to Nardi 'Yo pinto el ver' ('I paint what I see'), the words have a relevance beyond painting itself, for they relate to his more general role in the play as that of seer and visionary. In other plays — *En la ardiente oscuridad* and *El sueño de la razón* — it is the blind or the deaf man who has the special gift of truth, while those around them are deaf or blind to it. Here it is the artist, another kind of special person (the same is true, of course, of Goya) who sees things for what they are. In a bitter confrontation with his wife, Velázquez speaks of his need for an understanding companion:

> A alguien que me ayuda a soportar el tormento de ver claro en este país de ciegos y de locos. Tienes razón: estoy solo.   (p.124)

> Someone who will help me endure the torment of seeing clearly in this nation of the blind and the mad. You are right; I am alone.

But he is not quite alone, for, as we have seen, María Teresa too is a seeker of truth. And, in addition, closely associated with Velázquez throughout the play is Pedro Briones, the half-blind beggar whom he takes into his house. It is not without significance that many years before Pedro should have posed for Velázquez's painting of Aesop, for in his observation of the defects and the degradation of Spanish life Pedro is himself an Aesop figure, a perceiver and purveyor of the truth. At the end of Part One Pedro provides Velázquez with a grim and detailed account of the hunger and suffering of Spanish troops in Flanders, a situation which is now reflected in Spain itself:

> El país entero muere de hambre, don Diego. Y, como en Flandes, le responden con palos, con ejecuciones . . .   (p.178)

> The whole country is dying from hunger, don Diego. As in Flanders, they retaliate with beatings and executions.

Prior to this he has observed Velázquez's sketch for *Las Meninas* and, despite his semi-blindness, perceived in it an expression of sadness which is the essence of the Spanish nation:

> Un cuadro sereno: pero con toda la tristeza de España dentro . . . (p.174)

> A calm picture: but in it there is all the sadness of Spain.

At the beginning of Part Two his companion, Martín, mocks him for his obsession with the painting, and Pedro's paradoxical reply is again significant:

> MARTÍN (*Irritado*): ¡No sé cuántas simplezas te tengo oídas ya de ese cuadro! ¿Qué sabes tú de él, si ves menos que un topo?
> PEDRO: Pero lo veo. (p.185)

MARTÍN: (*Annoyed*): I don't know how much nonsense I've heard already about that picture! What do you know about it when you can't see any better than a mole?
PEDRO: But I see.

His words are, indeed, reminiscent in their visionary implications of Max Estrella's observation in Scene One of *Luces de Bohemia*:

> ¡Espera, Collet! ¡He recobrado la vista! ¡Veo! ¡Oh, cómo veo! ¡Magníficamente![24] (p.11)

Wait, Collet! I have regained my sight. I see! Oh, how I see! Magnificently!

Pedro, a man of the people, has seen the squalor of Spain as a whole. Velázquez, a man of the Court, observes the same squalor barely concealed beneath a cloak of refinement. They complement each other in the role of seer. Moreover, the economic decline, the general poverty of the people, a tyrannical censorship and an authoritarian rule is no less true of post-Civil War Spain than it was of the seventeenth century. And in that sense, Velázquez, the painter of *Las Meninas*, has his twentieth-century counterpart in Buero Vallejo, the writer of the play of the same name.

While Ibsen is a key influence in Buero's dramas of social realism, the historical plays reveal the decisive imprint of Bertolt Brecht.[25] The earlier examination of Alberti's *Noche de guerra en el museo del Prado* has revealed clearly enough the principal characteristics of Brechtian epic theatre and a brief resumé is therefore quite sufficient here. Brecht's theatre is associated above all, of course, with *verfremdungseffeckt*, the 'alienation effect' whereby the illusion that the theatre is life is broken down. The principal aim of the play is not escapist entertainment but the inculcation of truths both social and moral, for the apprehension of which the spectator of the play's action should not be drawn emotionally into the action but kept apart, distanced from it, capable thus of exercising his critical faculties in an objective manner, able to form judgements on the characters and their behaviour. The distancing effect was achieved by Brecht, as we have seen, in a variety of ways: by the use of commentators on the action, addresses to the audience, the use of placards to announce a scene, and songs to disrupt the flow of events. On the other hand, it would be wrong to assume that, in consequence of the above, the drama of Brecht is devoid of emotional impact. As far as Buero is concerned, his frequent insistence on audience involvement in his theatre appears to run directly counter to the theory of 'alienation'. It is interesting to see, therefore, how in *Las Meninas* he attempts to reconcile apparent irreconcilables.

The stage directions are, as described in the long account which precedes Part One, both detailed and realistic and thus in the tradition of *Historia de una escalera*. The central section of the scene — a room in the Royal Palace which Velázquez used as a studio — is, indeed, reproduced authentically:

> *Salvo la ausencia de techo, reproduce fielmente la galería del llamado Cuarto del Príncipe . . .*   (p.103)

> *Apart from the absence of a roof, it depicts faithfully the gallery of the so-called Prince's Room . . .*

On the other hand, while a concern with authentic detail is very evident, the room reminds the audience of the setting for Velázquez's *Las Meninas*, recreates history, distances us from the events on the stage and transforms the stage setting into a picture frame which, in consequence of its stylization, we view more objectively. In addition, the central area is flanked on either side by the Casa del Tesoro, where Velázquez has his rooms, and the Alcázar, where the Royal Family is housed. The geographical arrangement of the buildings is thus telescoped in a way which serves to remind us that this is a theatre set. The effect of a theatre is created too by the frequent use of a curtain across the middle of the stage which, when it is drawn, reveals a room in Velázquez's house and creates a stage within a stage:

> *. . . Entretanto las cortinas del centro se descorren y dejan ver un aposento de la casa de* VELÁZQUEZ . . .   (pp.112-13)

> *. . . Meanwhile the centre curtains open up to reveal a room in the house of* VELÁZQUEZ . . .

Used throughout the play the technique is less obtrusive than one involving changes of stage furniture, but it serves, nevertheless, to destroy the illusion of the stage as life. Finally, in relation to staging, the two balconies play an important part, one over the entrance to the Casa del Tesoro, the other over the ground-floor window of the Alcázar. In the course of the action characters appear on the balconies to observe the action elsewhere on the stage, as though they, like us, are the spectators of it. Thus, in Part One Doña Marcela observes Velázquez:

> *. . . Entretanto D*ª MARCELA *sale al balcón de la derecha y otea la calle, mirando con disimulo a la Casa del Tesoro.*   (p.125)

. . . Meanwhile, Dª MARCELA *appears on the balcony at stage-right and looks down at the street, sneaking a glance at the Casa del Tesoro.*

Just after this María Teresa observes the encounter below between Doña Marcela and Velázquez:

La infanta MARÍA TERESA *reaparece en el balcón y sin salir a los hierros los observa con recato . . .* (p.127)

The princess MARÍA TERESA *reappears on the balcony without coming outside and watches them carefully . . .*

The examples throughout the play are numerous, and while they undoubtedly contribute to the theme of Court intrigue they also have the effect of transforming the watching characters into spectators who, as they observe others, are in turn observed by us, reinforcing the idea of the play within the play or, more appropriately perhaps, the picture within the picture.

The sense of distancing is achieved too, in a typically Brechtian manner, by the use of Pedro Briones and Martín as commentators on the stage action. At the beginning of Part One both characters are spotlighted at either side of the stage in a highly stylized and theatrical manner:

La escena se encuentra en borrosa penumbra, donde sólo se distinguen dos figuras vigorosamente iluminadas, de pie e inmóviles en el primer término de ambos laterales. (p.106)

The stage is in deep shadow and only two strongly spotlighted figures can be seen, standing motionless down-stage on either side.

They are, moreover, figures from two of Velázquez's famous paintings — of Aesop and Menippus — or at least the models for the paintings, and are intended, through their appearance and immobility, to bring the paintings to mind, creating thus the necessary distance between the audience and the stage action. And if we do not recognize them, Martín makes the point, though negatively:

MARTÍN (*Al público*): No, no somos pinturas.

MARTÍN (*To the audience*): No, we are not paintings.

The direct address to the audience, a favourite Brechtian technique, establishes a clear gulf between us, the observers of the action, the two characters at the front of the stage, and the setting and events immediately behind them about which they proceed to give us information. Martín informs us that the year is 1656, he tells us that in the past he and Pedro were models for Velázquez, and, in a series of exchanges with Pedro, explains the nature and function of the various buildings which we see behind them. In short, Pedro and Martín frame the action of Part One for us, like guides in a picture-gallery. The beginning of Part Two repeats the process, they appear from time to time breaking up the action of the play, and at the end Martín acts as commentator once again. The use of costume is also significant in terms of distancing, for we are constantly reminded through the dress of the characters that we are observing both the figures from Velázquez's famous painting and, in consequence, from Spanish history. Early in Part One two ladies-in-waiting appear on the Palace balcony:

> *Son dos damiselas muy jóvenes:* Dª AUGUSTINA *tal vez no pase de los dieciséis años,* y Dª ISABEL, *de los diecinueve. Visten los trajes con que serán retratadas en el cuadro famoso.* (p.110)

> *They are two very young ladies:* Dª AUGUSTINA *is perhaps no more than sixteen, and* Dª ISABEL, *no more than nineteen. They wear the dresses with which they will be portrayed in the famous picture.*

When Velázquez makes his first appearance, the stage direction is quite specific:

> *Viste el traje negro, de abiertas mangas de raso y breve golilla, con que se retratará en el cuadro famoso.* (p.114)

> *He wears the black costume, with wide satin sleeves, and the small ruff with which he portrays himself in the famous painting.*

Later still, Don José Nieto Velázquez appears:

> *Viene vestido de negro de pies a cabeza, con golilla y capa, tal como lo vemos en el cuadro de Las Meninas.* (p.129)

> *He is dressed in black from head to foot, with ruff and cloak, exactly as we see him in the painting of Las Meninas.*

And finally, there are the dwarfs, Mari Bárbola and Nicolasillo:

> *Vienen lindamente vestidos, tal como los vemos en el Prado.* (p.149)

> *They are elegantly dressed, just as we see them in the Prado.*

The characters who perform the action of the play seem thus to have stepped directly out of the frame of *Las Meninas* in order to play their parts within another picture, the frame of the play itself. At the end, moreover, the stage setting is transformed back into the picture of *Las Meninas*, a brilliantly effective tableau:

> *A la derecha de la galería, hombres y mujeres componen, inmóviles, las actitudes del cuadro inmortal* . . . (p.237)

> *At the right of the gallery, men and women adopt, motionless, the postures of the immortal picture* . . .

We are forcefully reminded here that in the course of the play as a whole our role has been that of observer. Consequently, we are made to think and ponder on the thoughts and attitudes of the characters as they have been revealed to us during the action, and to draw for ourselves the conclusions and lessons of that action.

Like costume, lighting has an important function. It is used at the very beginning of the play to spotlight Pedro and Martín, to separate them from the setting as a whole and thus to pinpoint their role as commentators: *'dos figuras vigorosamente iluminadas'*, *'two strongly spotlighted figures'* (p.106). On other occasions lighting is used to illuminate particular areas of the stage, as in the case of a room in Velázquez's house:

> ... *un aposento de la casa de* VELÁZQUEZ, *que se va iluminado por el balcón de la derecha.* (p.113)

> ... *a room in the house of* VELÁZQUEZ, *which is lit by the balcony to the right.*

Elsewhere it is Velázquez's workroom in the Palace:

> *Al tiempo, la luz general decrece y aumenta en la zona central, donde desaparecen las cortinas para mostrarnos el obrador del cuarto del príncipe* ... (p.134)

> *At the same time the general lighting effect dims and is intensified in the central area, where the curtains disappear and we see the workroom in the quarters of the prince.*

In Part Two the lighting is again focused on the workroom, on this occasion in order to concentrate on the dramatic scene of Velázquez's trial:

> *La luz general decrece y se concentra sobre las cortinas dejando las fachadas en penumbra. Las cortinas se descorren y dejan ver el obrador.* (p.207)

> *The general lighting of the stage fades and focuses on the curtains, leaving the façades in shadow. The curtains are drawn and we see the workroom.*

As the last two stage directions suggest, the lighting is uniform for much of the play, 'luz general', and the effect is therefore naturalistic. When, however, the lighting changes in the manner suggested by the examples given above, it has the very important consequence of drawing attention to moments of high theatricality, and in so doing it forcibly reminds us that we are watching not a slice of life but a work of theatre, with all its artifice and stylization.

In relation to the behaviour of the characters, including their movements and gesture, Buero's technique is for the most part naturalistic, but to this it must be added that in *Las Meninas* there are, in fact, two kinds of behaviour: private and public. The latter involves, of course, an element of ritual that is part and parcel of Court life and, though in its context realistic enough, it does introduce into the visual aspect of the play a significant element of stylization. Thus, whenever the King appears, the characters bow or kneel before him:

Cuando aparece, EL MARQUÉS y NARDI se arrodillan.   (p.159)

When he appears, THE MARQUIS and NARDI kneel.

When Velázquez appears before the King, he displays due reverence:

VELÁZQUEZ se arrodilla. EL MARQUÉS se detiene junto al primer balcón. EL REY llega junto a VELÁZQUEZ, que besa su mano. (p.168)

VELÁZQUEZ kneels. THE MARQUIS stops near the first balcony. THE KING approaches VELÁZQUEZ, who kisses his hand.

Given that Buero's technique, especially in the province of private behaviour, is predominantly realistic, those moments of formality and etiquette observed in the presentation of Palace life have the clear effect of presenting the play as history and thus of distancing the action.

Distancing effects do not, however, alter the fact that the outstanding feature of *Las Meninas* is its warmth and humanity, and the extent to which emotionally we identify with its characters. In Velázquez's picture the stillness of the figures caught in a moment of time within the frame of the picture does nothing to diminish their warmth and human sympathy. In this respect Buero's method and achievement are very similar, for, given the distancing or framing effects already described, the play abounds with scenes of powerfully expressed human passions, including love, grief, disdain and anger. Doña Juana's irrationally jealous outbursts against Velázquez are especially moving, as are, indeed, his attempts to convince her of her error (pp.121-4, 200-3). In Part One the otherwise narrow-minded and puritanical Doña Marcela reveals in no uncertain terms her powerful feelings for Velázquez (pp.127-9). Velázquez himself displays his undisguised scorn for El Marqués (pp.138-9) and his immense compassion for the beggar Pedro (pp.173-83). In Part Two the scenes between Velázquez and the King betray great warmth and mutual affection (pp.191-2). The trial scene is remarkable for Velázquez's dignity and anger, as well as his burning honesty. And finally there is the moving spectacle of Velázquez's grief on the receipt of the news of Pedro's death (p.231). The revelation throughout the play of the range of passions and emotions described above involves the audience directly, drawing it into the play in a way which contradicts effects of distancing. Buero's achievement is, as was Alberti's, to balance involvement and detachment, to express passion within a frame in such a way that the observer of the action can identify with the characters, feel for them, yet learn from the observation of the experience. As a worthy precedent he had, indeed, not only Brecht but also the great dramatists of Spain's Golden Age, who knew full well how to combine teaching with entertainment. In terms of structure there is a marked difference between Parts One and Two. Part One has a loose structure, consisting of a series of scenes in which the various characters are introduced, their motives are hinted at, and the focus changes constantly from one set of figures to another and from one area of the stage to another. Part Two, on the other hand, has an altogether tighter structure, for its action is anchored firmly to the cross-examination of Velázquez, and the motives of the characters, previously hinted at, are clearly exposed. At the end of the play, moreover, the figures are frozen into the position they have in Velázquez's famous painting. In general terms the technique of the play reflects Velázquez's style of painting in *Las Meninas*, for the group of figures, though tightly organized and immobilized, is seen to be composed on closer examination of fluid, impressionistic details, of swift and inspired brushstrokes that, in relation to each other, build the picture. Buero's impressionistic Part One, building to the firm structure of Part Two, is thus a stage equivalent of the painter's art which he, as a student of painting, understands. It is yet another example of Buero's tribute to Velázquez in what is one of his finest plays.

The point has been made in the preceding pages that one of Buero Vallejo's principal aims in the theatre was to involve the audience emotionally in the stage action, be it through the Ibsenian presentation of the play as life or the Brechtian notion of the play as history. These two European giants of the theatre have in their different ways had a profound effect on Buero, but now it falls to us to consider a third whose impact is also great and whose theatre is deeply concerned with the relationship between stage and audience — Luigi Pirandello. The aim of Pirandello's major philosophical plays — *Cosi è (se vi pare) (Right You Are, If You Think So)*, *Sei personaggi in cerca d'autore (Six Characters in Search of an Author)*, and *Enrico IV (Henry IV)* — written between 1916 and 1922, was, as J.L.Styan has put it, 'to question whether the truth could ever be known about other people.'[25] In *Six Characters in Search of an Author* Pirandello, in order to throw the audience into doubt about the stage characters and itself, deliberately breaks down the traditional barriers between stage and auditorium. When, for example, the characters enter, they do so from the auditorium, as though from the real world, and when at the end the stepdaughter makes her exit she does so by running down the aisle and out into the street. To what extent, then, are the people on the stage actors, to what degree is the play a piece of theatre? To what degree are we, watching them, sure either of them or ourselves? Pirandello's drama, extending the traditional boundaries of theatre, sought at its best to make the audience itself experience the nature of self-deception and the relativity of truth. This was the task which Buero Vallejo set himself in three plays written in the sixties: *La doble historia del doctor Valmy (The Double History of Dr. Valmy); El tragaluz (The Skylight);* and *Mito (Myth).*

La doble historia del doctor Valmy was, interestingly enough, performed in English in Chester in November 1968, to mark the opening of the Gateway Theatre. As its title suggests, the action of the play is concerned with two stories. The first of these deals with a married, middle-class couple who immediately appear on stage and address the audience, informing them that the action about to be performed is not to be believed. This, the second story and the real action of the play, concerns Daniel Barnes, a member of the secret police. In the course of one of his interrogations he has castrated a political enemy and, in consequence of his feelings of guilt, become impotent. As a direct result of her husband's sexual inadequacy, Mary Barnes develops an intense sexual frustration, is driven out of her mind and finally kills him. At the end of the play the original couple appear again to remind the audience that it should not believe what it has just been told. They are then led away by a male nurse, the final implication being that their allegation is not to be believed either.

Given the element of theatricality that is so fundamental to Pirandellian theatre, the technique of *La doble historia* is vitally important. It is characterized above all by Buero's very deliberate concern to present the Daniel Barnes action in particular as theatre and not as life, thereby underlining its element of incredulity. Firstly, his story is not presented directly or in a linear manner but through Dr. Valmy's narration of the case to his secretary. For this reason the stage is divided into separate areas: downstage right Dr. Valmy's office; downstage left a park; downstage centre the living-room of the Barnes household; and up-stage centre, on an upper level, the police-station where Daniel Barnes works. Secondly, the stage setting is presented not realistically but in a simplified and stylized way: a neutral background; a couple of chairs for the doctor and his secretary. The doctor's narration of the events surrounding Daniel Barnes has the effect, moreover, both of shifting the focus of the action from one area of the stage to another and, given the leaps in time from present to past and past to present, of placing Dr.Valmy, as Barnes's medical adviser, in different phases of the action. In the stage presentation of *La doble historia* Buero has moved a long way from the representation in *Historia de una escalera* of the stage as life.[27]

The evident theatricality of the Daniel Barnes story is designed to make us doubt its authenticity and thus to place our faith in the couple who, both at the outset and the conclusion of the play, warn us to that effect. On the other hand, the manner of presentation of the Barnes action in no way diminishes the human and totally credible dimension of its themes and situations, and when the accusing couple are themselves exposed as mental patients, doubt is cast on the veracity of their claims that the Barnes story is false. Dr. Valmy reveals, in fact, that they are neighbours of the Barnes who have come to him for advice about their own anxieties. In the end the implication is that their claim to be telling the truth is itself a piece of make-believe, a theatrical gesture designed to win our sympathies. In other words the apparently incredible story of Daniel Barnes is, for all its theatricality, the true story which we, the audience, have been led to believe is false.

The theme of *La doble historia del doctor Valmy* is, quite simply, the theme of truth and the attitudes that individuals adopt towards it. The couple, distorting the reality of things, pretend that they do not exist. Daniel Barnes himself, in consequence of his refusal to admit to the truth of his own cruelty, is rendered impotent. His wife, Mary, becomes insane because she cannot face the truth of her husband's guilt and of her own inability to have another child. Daniel's mother looks at his body as though refusing to accept the fact of his death. She will certainly not reveal the truth to her grandson, nor in the past has she been entirely honest with Daniel about his father. In one way or another all the characters of the play are thus distinguished by their unwillingness or inability to come to terms with the reality of their lives.[28]

In relation to the questions posed by the play, where does the audience stand finally? Buero has, quite simply, disconcerted us, leading us to regard the truth as false, showing us that the lie is what we assumed to be the truth. In standing us on our heads and exposing us for the simple and gullible people we are, Buero has, moreover, awakened in us feelings of guilt and inadequacy related to ourselves. To what extent do we, indeed, close our eyes to the truth, be it the truth about ourselves or the world in which we live? To what degree do we, when we see wrong, oppression, injustice, tyranny, pretend that it is either not there or a piece of make-believe? In this process Dr. Valmy himself is a key figure, for he observes that, though a doctor and a man of science, his attitude is less scientific than one of grief: 'Yo prefiero mostrar el dolor del hombre . . .' ('I prefer to reveal man's grief . . .') (p.102). This clearly, is Buero Vallejo's own intent: to awaken compassion and grief for those who suffer, to identify us with their suffering. If, in *La doble historia del doctor Valmy*, he has adopted the

Pirandellian stance of confusing illusion and reality, stage and audience, he has done so to make us more conscious of our own shortcomings.

A consideration of *La doble historia* leads directly to an examination of *El tragaluz,* first performed on 7 October 1967 at the Teatro Bellas Artes in Madrid, though in certain respects the play evokes too the social world of *Historia de una escalera.* At the outset the audience is addressed by two futuristic characters, El and Ella (He and She), who reveal that current technology makes it possible to reconstruct the past and who propose the presentation of events from the second half of twentieth-century Spain. The events, which the audience is called upon both to observe and judge, involve a Madrid family and span a period of thirty years, commencing at the end of the Spanish Civil War. It is revealed that in the family's efforts to return to Madrid, only Vicente, the biggest and strongest of the three children, succeeded in forcing his way onto the train, taking with him the family provisions and ignoring his father's command to disembark. As a consequence of his actions, his sister, Elvirita, dies of malnutrition, for she is already weak, and his father is reduced to a state of madness.

The action of the play itself reveals that, since the events described above, the mother and father and their other son, Mario, have lived in a shabby basement, deprived of all material comforts, the only natural light coming from a skylight through which no more than the legs of passers-by can be seen. The father, oblivious to those around him, cuts figures from newspapers, journals and postcards and repeatedly poses the question: 'Who is this?' Mario, a virtual recluse, devotes his time to intellectual pursuits, writing articles and correcting proofs. Vicente, in contrast, has prospered. He lives alone in a splendid apartment and has become an important figure in a publishing house. From time to time he visits the other members of the family and during one of his visits is killed by his father who fails to recognize him.

The themes of *El tragaluz* are largely exemplified by the two brothers, Mario and Vicente, who are in turn reminiscent of opposing characters in other plays: Urbano and Fernando in *Historia de una escalera* and Ignacio and Carlos in *En la ardiente oscuridad.*[29] For Mario the world outside his basement home is a world of 'dog-eat-dog', of pure materialism, self-advancement and the inhumanity of man to man, a world which, through his quiet dedication to his intellectual activities, he steadfastly rejects. At the same time, though, Mario is, like many other of Buero's characters, a *contemplativo,* pondering on and seeking an answer, in Unamunian fashion, to the why and the wherefore of human existence. When he and Vicente were children, they observed the legs through the skylight and wondered about the identity of the passers-by. In adult life Mario repeatedly hears his father ask of his paper cut-outs the very question which he, Mario, now asks himself: 'Who is this?' He seeks, like Ignacio in *En la ardiente oscuridad*, an answer to the mystery of his own and others existence, but in the posing of the question knows that there is no answer, for in the end reason is defeated.

Vicente, in total contrast to Mario, is the pragmatist, aware of his objectives and of what is needed to achieve them. As a man who pursues and obtains material success, he is, moreover, unconcerned with the meaning and purpose of human life. And yet, given the fact that he is essentially a wheeler-dealer, he has a deeper dimension, for while he has the power to manipulate and dominate the lives of others, he too is the victim of the kind of life he has chosen for himself. He is, indeed, the victim of the 'dog-eat-dog' society in which he operates, paying for, as well as benefiting from, his *modus vivendi*. On the other hand, it is important to remember, as is the case in Buero's plays in general, that Vicente, enjoying freedom of choice and action, has chosen his way of life and is thus responsible for his destiny.

The second part of *El tragaluz* is concerned with the judgement and punishment of Vicente's opportunism and is thus Buero's comment on the society which shares Vicente's attitudes. Firstly, Mario denounces as an act of pure self-interest his brother's refusal many years ago to leave the train on which he had found a foothold. It is the kind of action which he has repeated throughout his life, profiting at the expense of others. As for Vicente himself, part of his nature seeks forgiveness, especially from his father, and motivates his visits to the basement-flat, while another part of him, recognizing the way of the world, encourages him to pursue still his chosen path:

> Pero, ¿quién puede terminar con las canalladas en un mundo canalla?[30]
>
> (p.354)
>
> But who can refrain from dirty tricks in a dirty world?

Believing that he can escape the consequences of his actions, he fails to do so, in the end bringing upon himself the punishment effected by his father. His fate, stemming from his own self-interest, illustrates his folly.

The father, el Padre, is a key figure in the action and the meaning of the play. He is portrayed, in the first place, with considerable skill and insight, a man obsessed with the traumatic events of the past. The cutting out of figures, the concern with their identity, the recurring memory of the train, the confusion of the skylight with the window of a train — all are consistent with the experience of a man damaged and haunted by his past experience. But, as in Mario's case, the father has a deeper significance which serves to enrich the play's meaning. When, for example, Vicente confesses before his father, he does so as though before God:

> Le hablo como quien habla a Dios sin creer en Dios, porque quisiera que El estuviese ahí . . .   (p.353)
>
> I speak to you like someone who speaks to God, without believing in God, because I wish He were here . . .

And the punishment Vicente is made to suffer is, though partly self-induced, a kind of divine punishment, a bolt from a wronged and avenging divinity. In addition, the father's manipulation of the small cut-out figures invests him with a superhuman significance, reminiscent of Valle-Inclán's god-like omnipotence in relation to the characters of his *esperpentos.* And when he addresses the figures with the question, 'Who is this?', he invariably claims to know the answer to the question, while others remain mystified. In short, like other characters in Buero's plays who are distinguished by their blindness, deafness or madness, the father of *El tragaluz* has about him a sense of mystery and ambiguity, an extra dimension which adds significantly to the play's levels of meaning.

Though dealing with the tragedy of a single family, *El tragaluz* is also, of course, the depiction of Spain's tragedy and suffering in the years that followed the Civil War. At the end of the play Ella observes:

> El mundo estaba lleno de injusticia, guerras y miedo.   (p.355)
>
> The world was full of injustice, wars and fear.

But the ending, while stressing suffering, suggests too that element of hope which, emanating from tragedy, we always associate with Buero. The mother, la Madre, opens the skylight and Mario and his girl friend, the pregnant Encarna, observe the passing figures to the accompaniment of Mario's remark:

> Quizá ellos algún día, Encarna . . . Ellos sí, algún día . . . Ellos . . . (p.357)
>
> Perhaps them someday, Encarna . . . Yes, them someday . . . Them . . .

While the words are ambiguous, they seem to indicate a hope for mankind, a hope which is embodied too in the child which Encarna is soon to bear, for the child, unblemished by the errors of the past, signifies a new beginning, a new phase of life and, inasmuch as the child has a broader symbolism, a new Spain.

The point has been made already that, in terms of its social background and characters, *El tragaluz* brings to mind *Historia de una escalera.* In terms of technique, on the other hand, Brecht and Pirandello are the principal sources of inspiration. In relation to the former, techniques of distancing are clearly important. In relation to the latter, as in *La doble historia del doctor Valmy*, Buero succeeds, despite effects of distancing, in creating a confusion of identity between the audience and the stage whereby they mirror each other. Indeed, as is his practice elsewhere, his purpose is to involve his public on a critical and emotional level, as is suggested by his observation on the function of the two narrators:

> ... creo que me permiten... sobrecoger aún más a ese público y, por qué no, tal vez a un público universal de hoy, ya que no se trata de un problema específicamente español... Es al público de nuestro tiempo, de los años oscuros que vivimos al que trato de sobrecoger sirviéndome de esos investigadores... La funcíon de sobrecogimiento emotivo es, para mí, fundamental en estos personajes... Esta combinación de reflexión y temor es la esencia de la función de esta pareja de personajes...[31]

> ... I believe that they allow me... to surprise that audience even more and perhaps too — and why not? — a wider contemporary audience, for we are not dealing with a specifically Spanish problem... It is the public of our time, of the dark years in which we live that I seek to surprise, availing myself of those investigators... The function of emotional shock is, for me, fundamental in relation to these characters. This combination of reflection and fear is the essence of the function of this pair of characters...

The linked concepts of reflection and fear neatly embody the paradoxical fusion of Brechtian detachment and Pirandellian involvement achieved by Buero in *El tragaluz*.

A consideration of the stage setting suggests initially the naturalism of *Historia de una escalera*, for the stage, divided into two main sections, presents a basement and an office realistically furnished. Thus, the basement:

> *Los muebles son escasos, baratos y viejos. Hacia la izquierda hay una mesa camilla pequeña, rodeada de dos o tres sillas ...*   (p.289)

> *The items of furniture are few, cheap and old. To the left is a small table, with a heater beneath it, surrounded by two or three chairs ...*

Similarly, the office furniture is realistically described — a filing-cabinet, a table, a chair, a typewriter, books, photographs on the walls. On the other hand, there is also about the whole an imprecision, a kind of blurred effect which detracts from its solidity and gives it instead a dream-like, floating quality, the effect, in short, of belonging to another world, distanced from us:

> *El experimento suscita sobre el espacio escénico la impresión, a veces vaga, de los lugares que a continuación se describen.*   (p.289)

> *The experiment invests the stage area with a frequently vague impression of the locations which are as follows.*

In this respect the role of the two narrators, El and Ella, is vital, for throughout the play they control the way in which the action is presented to us and the degree, therefore, of our proximity to or distance from it. When they appear, they themselves are distanced from us by their dress, their movements and their speech, for they are space-like beings, machine-like, the inhabitants of a future age:

> ... *una joven pareja vestida con extrañas ropas, propias del siglo a que pertenecen. Un foco los ilumina. Sus movimientos son pausados y elásticos. Se acercan a la escena, se detienen, se vuelven y miran a los espectadores durante unos segundos. Luego hablan, con altas y tranquilas voces.*(p.291)

> ... *a young couple dressed in strange costumes, appropriate to the century to which they belong. A spotlight illuminates them. Their movements are slow and languid. They approach the front of the stage, stop, turn and face the audience, gazing at it for a while. Then they speak in voices that are soft and high-pitched.*

Lit by the spotlight, standing downstage between the audience and the action that takes place behind them, they frame it for us, as do Martín and Pedro in *Las Meninas*. But there is also more to it than this in terms of distancing effects. Firstly, the two narrators, bringing the audience forward in time, recreate an action from the past, from the time to which the audience really belongs but from which it has now been removed. That action, moreover, is recreated mechanically, by means of scientific aids, and at given moments has a distinct quality of unreality in terms of lighting, movement and sound.

At the very outset, in the directions that precede the action, Buero clearly indicates that the lighting of the stage in relation to the events involving the family will be characterized by its unreality:

> *La luz que ilumina a la pareja de investigadores es siempre blanca y normal. Las sucesivas iluminaciones de las diversas escenas y lugares crean, por el contrario, constantes efectos de lividez e irrealidad.*   (p.290)

> *The light which illuminates the pair of investigators is always white and normal. The subsequent lighting of the different scenes and locations creates, on the other hand, constant effects of pallor and unreality.*

When, indeed, scenes commence, they are bathed in a flickering light, reminiscent of the flickering light of a magic lantern, which gives to the figures an insubstantial quality, like the images of a silent film, before they assume a greater solidity:

> *El telón se alza. En la oficina, sentada a la máquina, ENCARNA. VICENTE la mira, con un papel en la mano, sentado tras la mesa de despacho. En el cuarto de estar, EL PADRE se encuentra sentado a la mesa, con unas tijeras*

en la mano y una vieja revista ante él; sentado a la mesita de la derecha, con un bolígrafo en la mano y pruebas de imprenta ante sí, MARIO. *Los cuatro están inmóviles. Ráfagas de luz oscilan sobre ambos lugares.* (pp.292-93)

The curtain rises. In the office, seated at her typewriter, ENCARNA. VICENTE, seated at his desk and holding a paper, looks at her. In the living-room, THE FATHER is sitting at the table, with a scissors in his hand and an old magazine in front of him; and sitting at a small table to the right is MARIO, holding a pen and with some page-proofs in front of him. The four figures are motionless. Waves of light flicker over both settings.

The device is one which is used frequently. In addition, in order to further underline the element of play and theatricality, as opposed to a realistic action, areas of the stage are lit separately, while the rest is left in darkness or semi-darkness:

Las ráfagas de luz fueron desapareciendo. En la oficina se amortigua la vibración luminosa y crece una viva luz diurna. El resto de la escena permanece en penumbra. (p.293)

The waves of light disappear. In the office the flickering light fades, to be replaced by bright daylight. The rest of the scene remains in shadow.

The movements of the figures are also conceived unrealistically. In a stage direction given above Encarna, Vicente, Mario and el Padre are seen to be motionless prior to the commencement of the action (pp.292-3). In the action itself the figures come to life only when the attention is focused on them. El, controlling them, makes the point:

. . . actuarán a ritmo normal cuando les llegue su turno. (p.293)

. . . they will move at normal speed when it is their turn.

That speed is, moreover, achieved only slowly, as though a piece of film is being made to acquire its normal pace:

EL *y* ELLA *salen por ambos laterales. El ritmo del tecleo se vuelve normal, pero la mecanógrafa no parece muy rápida ni muy segura. En la penumbra del cuarto de estar,* EL PADRE *y* MARIO *se mueven de tanto en tanto muy lentamente.* (p.293)

HE *and* SHE *exit at either side of the stage. The speed of the typing becomes normal, but the typist does not seem very quick or certain. In the semi-darkness of the living-room,* THE FATHER *and* MARIO *move at times very slowly.*

In conjunction with the degree of normality achieved in the lighting of individual scenes, the characters begin to move normally, as though a process of winding them up or investing them with life has been completed.

The speech of the characters is, in the words of El, superimposed:

Como los sonidos son irrecuperables, los diálogos se han restablecido mediante el movimiento de los labios y añadido artificialmente. Cuando las figuras se presentaban de espaldas (o su visualidad no era clara), los calculadores electrónicos . . . han deducido las palabras no observables . . .

(p.292)

Since sounds are irrecoverable, speech has been recreated according to the movement of lips and added artificially. When the characters have their backs to us (or cannot be seen clearly), the electronic machines . . . have deduced the words that cannot be observed . . .

The effect of superimposition, like the effects of flickering light and slow-motion movement, is evidently heightened at the beginning of scenes and subsequently disappears, but its presence is sufficient to give to the action a clear sense of distance and remoteness.

In this respect the frequent reappearance of the two narrators, in conjunction with their didactic and moralizing role, is also important, for, in typical Brechtian manner, it sharpens our critical faculties and underlines our role as observers of the action. Thus, at one point Ella takes advantage of a delay in the action to comment on what has been observed so far:

Lo aprovecharemos para comentar lo que habéis visto.   (p.307)

We will take advantage of this to comment on what you have seen.

Elsewhere, in an extended conversation, they observe that material from the past may be interpreted by machines but also by a perceptive mind, thereby encouraging us, in the role of observers, to judge the events set before us:

EL: Cada suceso puede ser percibido desde algún lugar.
ELLA: Y a veces, sin aparatos, desde alguna mente lúcida. (p.312)

HE: Each event can be perceived from some place.
SHE: And at times, without machines, by some alert mind.

In Brechtian theatre effects of distancing are acheived in a variety of ways, ranging from the use of placards and commentators to episodic, deliberately disrupted action. If anything, *El tragaluz,* particularly in relation to lighting, movement and speech, extends the possibilities of distancing effects.

The Pirandellian influence in *El tragaluz* is to be sought in two principal areas, neither of which is really alien to Brechtian practices: firstly, in the kind of issues posed by the play; and secondly, in the degree of our own identification with those issues. As to the first point, the father's question, 'Who is this?', a question of a particularly Pirandellian character in terms of its emphasis on identity and relativity, echoes through the play, inducing us ultimately to ask of ourself the question which the father puts to his paper and cardboard figures and which, by extension, Mario begins to ask both of himself and others. The skylight, the play's central metaphor, plays its part in the process too, for by the end of the play the skylight can be interpreted as a kind of mirror and the anonymous legs perceived in it or through it — the legs of a bustling world outside the basement — can be seen to be our own, the audience watching the play synonymous with the passers-by observed by the characters. In addition, despite effects of distancing and alienation, there is one important aspect of the play's technique which enables characters and audience to identify with each other: its strong element of naturalism. Not without reason has a parallel often been drawn between *El tragaluz* and *Historia de una escalera*, for, within the scenes involving members of the family, conversations, quarrels and confrontations have an authenticity and a degree of realism to which we can easily approximate. In short, as in *Las Meninas*, Brechtian devices constitute a framework whose purpose and effect are clear, but the framework does not exclude scenes of warmth, passion and humanity which, though not destroying the sense of distance between the audience and the stage, allow us to bridge it in such a way that the process of contemplation and judgement of others becomes in effect the process of self-analysis. *El tragaluz* is a play which reveals very clearly the European dimension of Buero's experimentation, but more than that it reveals him mastering those techniques in a way which allows him to communicate powerfully his own deeply felt and highly personal message.

El sueño de la razón, premiered on 6 February, 1970, at the Teatro Reina Victoria in Madrid, deals with the life, times and work of another painter, Francisco de Goya, and is one of Buero's truly outstanding works, not least in terms of its technical innovation and experiment. Although both naturalistic and Brechtian elements are still in evidence, the play is distinguished above all by Buero's ambitious use of the so-called immersion technique — already commented on in relation to *En la ardiente oscuridad* — whereby the audience is made to share fully in the emotional and mental experiences of a character on the stage, in this case Goya.[32] His deafness occasions strange and terrible noises, while his tormented mind breeds imaginary monsters. That the audience is made to share Goya's experience means in effect that the role of actor and spectator is fused, and that the stage and auditorium becomes an immense theatre. Robert Nicholas makes the point that if Buero's early *Historia de una escalera* was characterized by its realistic illusion, *El sueño de la razón* creates in the audience itself a theatrical illusion.[33]

The action of the play is set in December 1823, at a point in time when, about five years prior to his death, Goya was deaf and ill. The beginning of Part I focuses on the King, Fernando VII, whose reign has been one of tyranny and terror, and reveals his preoccupation with Goya, a liberal who has rejected the Court in favour of a solitary existence in the Quinta del Sordo, his home outside Madrid. The action then moves to the Quinta del Sordo where we learn that Goya, now seventy-six years of age, is occupied primarily with the 'Pinturas negras' (the 'black paintings'), the terrible representations of witches and monsters which he paints on the walls of his house, and which his mistress, Leocadia, sees as a symptom of his insanity. Dr. Arrieta, a friend of the painter, attempts to explain the noises heard by Goya and discusses the 'Pinturas negras' with Father Duaso, another friend who is also a representative of the King. At the end of Part One the 'Voluntarios realistas', an anti-liberal group, paint a cross on the door of Goya's house and throw a stone through his window.

Part Two of the play is concerned with the King's persecution of Goya and with the painter's increasing fears, partly motivated by his realization that the authorities have intercepted a letter of his, critical of the King. Fernando, indeed, instructs his 'Voluntarios realistas' to visit the Quinta del Sordo. There Goya is seen asleep, his dreams filled by the phantoms and monsters of his paintings, including Leocadia, who attempts to decapitate him. The imagined attack is immediately succeeded by a real attack when the 'Voluntarios realistas' burst into the house, tie up and beat Goya and proceed to rape Leocadia in his presence. Subsequently Goya seeks refuge in his son's house but in vain. Overwhelmed by his experiences, as well as by old age, he is finally obliged to ask the King for forgiveness and to seek permission to leave Spain for France.

As far as its themes are concerned, *El sueño de la razón*, is preoccupied very largely with the clash between liberal ideals and the tyranny of absolute power, the one embodied in Goya, the other in Fernando.[34] In a sense the conflict between the painter and the King is reminiscent of a similar opposition in *Las Meninas*, though in that play the monarch is a much more sympathetic character. At all events the two contrasting ideologies are, of necessity, mutually exclusive, distanced from each other, though at the same time inter related, and these two aspects of the theme are cleverly suggested and projected throughout the play, especially in the two very different worlds of the Quinta del Sordo and the Palace. Goya and Fernando never meet in the course of the action, a fact which suggests that the gulf which separates liberalism and dictatorship cannot be bridged. On the other hand, the one constantly impinges on the other. Thus, at the beginning of the play the King observes the Quinta del Sordo through a telescope, while from the window of his own house Goya observes the Palace. Similarly, the King embroiders in the Palace while Goya paints in the Quinta. Parallels in the action point both to distance and overlapping. Indeed, though not in the Palace physically, Goya is very much in the King's mind and in his conversations, not least through the intercepted letter, while the fears of the painter are much to do with the danger represented by the King. When Fernando's agents enter the Quinta, assault Goya and rape Leocadia, the incident marks the point in the play where the two conflicting ideologies of freedom and authoritarianism meet head on, even if the two men who embody them are still physically separated.

Ricardo Doménech has drawn attention to the inextricable link in the play between the theme of absolute power and the emotion of fear, which is experienced both by Goya and the King.[35] Fernando, though his power is absolute, is afraid, like all dictators, of the forces opposed to him, and fear in turn increases both his watchfulness and his cruelty. As far as Goya is concerned, his fears are bound to increase as Fernando's opposition to him grows and are reflected more and more both in the loud sound of his heartbeats — audible to the audience — and in the terrifying visions which assault him. In short, the theme of tyranny and the emotion of fear are inseparable, both in the tyrant and in the victim of tyranny, and the close interrelationship is a key element in the play.

Another important theme is that of the world of Goya's Spain as madhouse. It is a unique feature of *El sueño de la razón* that the dramatist obliges us to see Goya's world as he himself sees it, and to experience too the terrible sounds that fill his head and the terrifying monsters that dominate his fevered imagination. In short, through a process of identification with the painter, the audience is made to observe a world that is distorted and grotesque, in which people open their mouths but speak no words, gesticulate wildly and frantically, and move about the stage as though they are demented. This, moreover, is the world not of Goya's fearful phantoms but of the human beings who surround him, yet the link between the two, as well as the link with the hideous paintings that deform the painter's walls, is quite clear. It is worth recalling at this point the observation of Max Estrella in Valle-Inclán's *Luces de Bohemia:*

> . . . El esperpentismo lo ha inventado Goya. Los héroes clásicos han ido a pasearse en el callejón del Gato.[36] (p.106)

> . . . Esperpentismo was invented by Goya. The classical heroes have gone for a stroll through Cat's Alley.

Inasmuch as the world of Goya is seen by him as hideous and distorted, and Buero communicates that vision to us, the dramatist has, in effect, written his own *esperpento*, and in terms of theme as well as technique very useful comparisons can be made with Valle-Inclán's theatre.

Although *El sueño de la razón* focuses so much on Goya as a unique individual, he can also be seen, as is so often the case in Buero's drama, in a much more universal sense — both as the embodiment of Spanish liberalism and as the personification of the universal aspiration to freedom. In addition, Goya represents an eternal problem which the liberal intellectual, living in a tyrannical regime, is forced to confront. Unable to tolerate the nature of the society in which he lives, he withdraws from it in horror. To that extent Buero embodies in the figure of Goya both the impossible circumstances and the isolation of the liberal intellectual in an alien society. Goya assumes a broader significance too in the sense that he is Buero's characteristic 'visionary'. Cut off from the world around him, not by blindness as in Ignacio's case in *En la ardiente oscuridad*, but by deafness, Goya sees the world with an insight with which 'normal' people do not see it, and his paintings, appearing to portray a deformed and distorted version of the world, actually depict it as it is. Fernando complains that Goya has rarely painted him and never painted his wives. The truth of the matter is that Fernando has not the insight to realize that he and his Court are constantly present in the 'Pinturas negras'.[37]

Buero's portrayal of early nineteenth-century Spain evidently has its relevance to the Spain of the early 1970s, a fact which, as in *Las Meninas*, cannot be ignored. Making use of double meanings and allusions to contemporary events which are unmistakable, the dramatist is much concerned with communicating to his audience those problems which preoccupied Goya and which are equally appropriate to them. On the other hand, the social and political implications of *El sueño de la razón* constitute but one of the levels on which the play works. It is true to say that Buero's theatre, be it 'historical' or not, is equally concerned with man on a much more universal plane — with man's concern with his own identity and meaning in the scheme of things, as the questions posed by *En la ardiente oscuridad* and *El tragaluz* suggest. In the end, indeed, justice is only done to Buero's art when the metaphysical as well as the social dimension of his theatre is duly recognized.

In terms of its dramatic technique, *El sueño de la razón* is Buero's most striking and innovative play, a culmination, in effect, of the different experiments already considered here in relation to other plays. An examination of the stage setting — two rooms in Goya's house — suggests initially, for example, the naturalism of *Historia de una escalera*, for considerable emphasis is placed on the furniture, as well as on the painter's tools. There is certainly less stylization than is the case in *La doble historia del doctor Valmy* or *Las Meninas.* On the other hand, both Parts One and Two of the play commence with a scene involving the King and an adviser which is distinguished by its stylization. These scenes are enacted downstage, in front of the main set, which is left in darkness, and only the bare essentials of furniture are suggested — a chair, the King's embroidery frame. In short, from the very outset the two strands of naturalism and stylization are interwoven. The subsequent action is often naturalistic, but, given this, by no stretch of the imagination can *El sueño de la razón* be considered a naturalistic play. This assumes far less significance when we take into account the way in which Buero uses the 'Pinturas negras', for their effect is quite simply to transform the play's naturalism into the grotesque.

Buero uses the 'Pinturas negras' in a cinematic fashion. The walls of Goya's house are not used, therefore, to display in a naturalistic way two or three of the pictures which Goya painted on them. Rather, the backcloth presents the 'Pinturas negras' as a series of constantly changing images: 'Judith', 'Saturn Devouring One of his Sons', 'The Fates', 'The Pilgrimage of San Isidro', dissolving one into the other in an almost surrealistic manner. Thus, at a given moment the background is dominated by 'Saturn Devouring One of his Sons':

> ... *Las pinturas del fondo se borran lentamente y sólo reaparece la de 'Saturno'...*[38]   (p.36)
>
> ... *The pictures on the backcloth slowly disappear and only 'Saturn' reappears...*

The effect of this is two-fold. Firstly, the pictures changing constantly before us come to dominate our attention and imagination. Secondly, since the pictures represent humanity in a grotesque, deformed and monstrous form, it is not the naturalistic but the grotesque aspect of the play which imposes itself upon us.[39]

Consideration of the 'Pinturas negras' leads us to a consideration of the presentation of the characters of the play itself in terms of the grotesque nature of the paintings. Fernando, the King, is dressed in black, his eyebrows are thick, his nose large and his chin prominent:

> ... *Bajo las tupidas cejas, dos negrísimas pupilas inquisitivas. La nariz, gruesa y derribada, monta sobre los finos labios, sumidos por el avance del mentón...*   (p.10)
>
> ...Beneath the thick eyebrows, two very black and searching eyes. His nose is thick and prominent and descends over his thin lips, which are pulled in by the thrust of his chin...

When Goya himself appears, he is seen to be short, with white hair and sideboards, and his painter's smock is covered in paint stains (p.16). Doctor Arrieta, a friend of Goya, is described in the following way:

> ... *Es hombre vigoroso, aunque magro; de cabellos rubios que grisean, incipiente calvicie que disimula peinándose hacia adelante, cráneo grande, flaca fisonomía de asceta ...* (p.18)

> ... *He is an active but thin man; his fair hair is going grey and he is beginning to go bald, which he conceals by combing his hair forward; his head is large and he has the lean features of an ascetic ...*

In Part Two Leocadia enters the room dishevelled and dressed in rags (p.69). In short, in terms of physical appearance the human characters of the play have something of the grotesque nature of the figures of the 'Pinturas negras'. It is an aspect of them that is bound to be heightened by the fact that they move about the stage against the background of the 'Pinturas negras'.

The grotesque character of the human figures is further heightened by their exaggerated movements and gestures, which in part at least stem from the fact of Goya's deafness. In order to make themselves understood, the characters are obliged to exaggerate, particularly with hands and arms, what would otherwise be normal movements. In addition, since we see and hear them from Goya's standpoint, they mouth silent words. The effect, inevitably, is to render them comic and absurd. In an early scene, for example, Goya himself furiously rings a bell and it makes no sound (p.17), while Leocadia, answering his call, tries to make him understand, gesticulating furiously and shouting inaudibly:

> LEOCADIA *forma rápidos signos y grita al tiempo inaudiblemente, enfadada.* (p.17)

> LEOCADIA *makes quick gestures and at the same time shouts inaudibly, angrily.*

Presented in this way, the human figures acquire the character of puppets and much of the action takes on the appearance of a puppet-show. The quarrel between Leocadia and Gumersinda is a particularly good example. Throughout the argument they indulge in wild gesticulations, while Goya hears their words as the cackling of a hen and the braying of a donkey:

> *Por boca de ambas señoras, los cacareos y los rebuznos se alternan ...* (p.144)

> *In the mouths of both women, the cackling and the braying alternate ...*

In another incident Goya shakes Leocadia like a rag-doll, reminiscent of Friolera's shaking of his wife in *Los cuernos de Don Friolera*. An argument between Goya and Leocadia reveals her twisting her hands while Goya rushes across the stage to grab his gun — the action significantly accompanied by an off-stage voice which mockingly refers to Goya as a puppet:

VOZ *(Entre carcajadas de los otros)*: ¡Asómate, fantoche...!   (p.61)

VOICE *(Amidst the laughter of the others)*: Come out, you puppet!

Again, Leocadia collapses hysterically onto a chair while Goya observes her exaggerated gestures:

LEOCADIA *estalla en inaudibles gemidos y se derrumba sobre un asiento ... GOYA mira un instante sus aspavientos...*   (p.80)

LEOCADIA *launches into inaudible moans and collapses on a chair ... GOYA observes for a moment her exaggerated gestures.*

Exaggerated movement and the often grotesque appearance of the characters is frequently accompanied too by certain sounds, notably raucous laughter, or shouting and screaming, as some of the examples quoted above have already shown. Thus, the King, in conversation with an adviser: *Ríe a carcajadas (Guffaws loudly)* (p.11). Goya similarly, despite his despair, is pesented in the same way as he observes the quarrel between Leocadia and Gumersinda:

Inquieto y oprimiéndose los oídos, GOYA *ríe a carcajadas.*   (p.44)

Restless and covering his ears, GOYA *guffaws loudly.*

The cackling and braying of the two women have already been alluded to. Leocadia herself is often given to unrestrained moaning, weeping or shouting:

Convulsa, LEOCADIA *grita.* ARRIETA *intenta calmarla.*   (p.52)

Overcome, Leocadia *screams.* ARRIETA *tries to calm her.*

The human characters of the play are, indeed, puppet-like, *esperpento* figures. In this respect Goya's remark to Leocadia and Gumersinda is significant in relation to the play as a whole:

¡Y no quiero ver más muecas! Parecéis monas!   (p.43)

I don't want to see more grimaces! You look like monkeys!

By creating links between the deformed figures of the 'Pinturas negras' and the human characters on the stage, Buero makes the point that the society in which Goya lives is, in effect, the 'Pinturas negras' come to life. The pictures shown on the backcloth are important, clearly, for the element of visual distortion. On the other hand, there are also the pictures conjured up by Goya's fearful imagination — pictures which move and speak — in which sound is very important. He is, for example, frequently assaulted by mocking laughter, *carcajadas*, by the miaowing of cats and the barking of dogs: in short, by grotesque and often animal or non-human sounds which we have seen to be associated with the human characters. The link between the two is clearly established. In addition, the fact that the paintings constitute Goya's vision of the world as it really is is established by observations both by Goya and the other characters. Thus, almost as the play begins the King refers to the punishment imposed on one of his adversaries in terms of a Goya engraving:

> CALOMARDE: ... Todo Madrid aclamaba vuestro augusto nombre al paso del reo, arrastrado en un serón por un borrico ...

> EL REY: Se diría un grabado de Goya.   (p.12)

> CALOMARDE: ... The whole of Madrid acclaimed your illustrious name as the criminal passed by in a basket pulled by a donkey.
> THE KING: One might refer to it as a Goya engraving.

Goya himself refers to the Inquisition in strictly non-human terms:

> Son insectos que se creen personas.   (p.26)

> They are insects who regard themselves as human beings.

When Goya observes the Palace through his telescope, the background is dominated by the huge and monstrous figure of Saturn — in effect, by an image which evokes the real nature of King Fernando. Indeed, Goya makes the point that the horrific world of his picture is the reality he has seen and experienced:

> He pintado esa barbarie, padre, porque la he visto.   (p.56)

> I have painted that savagery, father, because I have seen it.

One cannot study *El sueño de la razón* without being aware, in terms of dramatic technique, of the profound influence of Valle-Inclán and the *esperpento*, though at the same time, bearing in mind Buero's knowledge of European theatre in general, the impact of the Theatre of the Absurd is not to be discounted.

The preceding discussion of the play's technical features suggests the kind of distancing seen already, for example, in *Las Meninas* and thus a continuing Brechtian influence. The historical nature of the subject, the projection of the pictures and the puppet-like nature of the characters all have the effect of separating stage and auditorium. On the other hand, that separation is also bridged by the involvement of and the identification of the audience with Goya himself in consequence of the immersion techniques already alluded to. In addition, despite the fact that Goya often has the character of a puppet, this does not prevent his assuming truly touching and even tragic dimensions, which further facilitates our identification with him. His often agonized speeches, effectively communicating his frustration and despair, are important in this respect. Again, in relation to his defects Goya does not exclude himself from the generality of men, including ourselves, and we therefore begin to see his defects as something that we share. In a highly significant moment Goya makes the point that the grotesque figures of the paintings stare at him in ignorance of their own ugliness:

Nos miran sin saber lo feos que son ellos.   (p.26)

They look at us without knowing how ugly they are.

The same is true, of course, of us, the audience, as, from the other side of the stage, we observe both Goya and the pictures in ignorance of our own moral and spiritual ugliness. In short, the 'Pinturas negras' and the stage action that takes place in front of them is transformed in the course of the play's evolution into a huge mirror in which we perceive our own reflections.

This discussion of the theatre of Buero Vallejo allows us to make a very positive assessment of the dramatist in relation both to his themes and dramatic technique. As far as the former are concerned, the social dimension of Buero's drama — his deep concern with post-Civil War Spain — is obviously a significant and serious element. But if that were all, the appeal of the plays would inevitably remain, for all their seriousness, narrow and restricted. That this is not so is due to the fact that Buero, like all great dramatists, is interested in man not merely as a social entity but as a being confronted by and often aware of the complexity and the mystery of his own existence, whose meaning, if not revealed, is constantly probed and questioned. Moreover, this deeper, more universal level of Buero's theatre is one which is consistently made meaningful and relevant to the audience itself in a way which erodes the barriers that so often separate art and personal experience. As for technique, Buero's drama is one of the most striking examples in the history of both Spanish and European twentieth-century theatre of constant experiment and innovation, employed not merely for its own sake but as a means of communicating more effectively a play's meaning. Only in one area, the area of language, can the plays be said to disappoint a little. The striking technique of the plays — El sueño de la razón — often stylized and poetic, demands the kind of inspired poetic language that so often characterizes the work of Valle-Inclán, Lorca and

Alberti. To that extent Buero's adherence to a basically naturalistic language must be regarded as a weakness.[40]

1 Francisco Ruiz Ramón, *Historia del teatro español, siglo XX* (4th ed.) (Madrid, 1980), 337. This important book contains an important section on the theatre of Buero. See 337-84.

2 Such is Francisco Ruiz Ramón's conclusion. See 384.

3 Robert L. Nicholas, *The Tragic Stages of Antonio Buero Vallejo* (Valencia, 1972), 14.

4 Ricardo Doménech, *El teatro de Buero Vallejo* (Madrid, 1973), 84.

5 *Historia del teatro español, siglo XX*, 338.

6 *The Tragic Stages of Antonio Buero Vallejo*, 15. On the question of tragedy in Buero's theatre, see too the following: Martha T. Halsey, 'Buero Vallejo and the Significance of Hope', *Hispania*, LI (1968), 57-66; 'Light and Darkness as Dramatic Symbols in Two Tragedies of Buero Vallejo', *Hispania*, L(1967), 63-8; 'The Dreamer in the tragic Theater of Buero Vallejo', *Hispanófila*, 7(1959), 51-8; Kessel Schwartz, 'Buero Vallejo and the Concept of Tragedy', *Hispania*, LI (1968), 817-24.

7 See *El teatro: enciclopedia del arte escénico*, ed. Guillermo Díaz-Plaja (Barcelona, 1958), 66-7.

8 *El teatro: enciclopedia del arte escénico*, 74-5.

9 *El teatro: enciclopedia del arte escénico*, 71.

10 On the influence of Brecht on Buero Vallejo, see, in particular, Robert L. Nicholas, *The Tragic Stages of Antonio Buero Vallejo*, 58-60.

11 There is a detailed study of this aspect of Buero's theatre by Victor Dixon, 'The "Immersion-Effect" in the Plays of Antonio Buero Vallejo', *Themes in Drama*, 2(1980), 113-37.

12 The point is made very strongly by Jean-Paul Borel, *El teatro de lo imposible*, translated by Gonzalo Torrente Ballester (Madrid, 1966), 231-32.

13 See, for example, Ricardo Doménech, *El teatro de Buero Vallejo*, 88.

14 See Pedro Salinas, 'Del género chico a la tragedia grotesca: Carlos Arniches', in *Literatura española siglo XX* (Madrid, 1970), 126-31. Also, Vicente Ramos, *Vida y teatro de Carlos Arniches* (Madrid, 1966).

15 The influence of Unamuno is discussed by Richard Doménech in his introduction to the edition of *Historia de una escalera* and *Las Meninas*, (5th ed.) (Madrid, 1981), 11-12.

16 *The Tragic Stages of Antonio Buero Vallejo*, 19-22. See too Robert E. Lott, 'Scandinavian Reminiscences in Antonio Buero Vallejo's Theater,' *Romance Notes*, VII (1966), 114; Martha Halsey, 'The Rebel Protagonist: Ibsen's *An Enemy of the People* and Buero's *Un soñador para un pueblo*, *Comparative Literature Studies*, VI (1969), 462-71; 'Reality versus Illusion: Ibsen's *The Wild Duck* and Buero Vallejo's *En la ardiente oscuridad*', *Contemporary Literature*, II (1970), 48-58.

17 *The Tragic Stages of Antonio Buero Vallejo*, 22.

18 Page references are to the text of the play published in Selecciones Austral, Madrid, 5th ed., 1981. There are studies of the play, in addition to those of Doménech and Nicholas, by Farris Anderson, 'The Ironic Structure of *Historia de una escalera*,' *Kentucky*

Romance Quarterly, XVIII (1971), 223-36; Robert Kirsner, *'Historia de una escalera:* A Play in Search of Characters', *Homenaje a Rodríguez Moñino,* I (1966), 279-82; Mariano de Paco de Moya, *'Historia de una escalera,*veinticinco años más tarde' — *Estudios literarios dedicados al Profesor Mariano Baquero Goyanes* (Murcia, 1974), 375-98. For more general studies, see William Giuliano, *Buero, Sastre y el teatro de su tiempo* (New York, 1971); Martha Halsey, *Antonio Buero Vallejo* (New York, 1973); José Ramón Cortina, *El arte dramático de Antonio Buero Vallejo* (Madrid, 1969); Catherine Elizabeth Dowd, *Realismo transcendente en cuatro tragedias sociales de Antonio Buero Vallejo* (Valencia, 1974).

19 See Ricardo Doménech, *El teatro de Buero Vallejo,* 51-71; Antonio Buero Vallejo, 'Comentario', *En al ardiente oscuridad,* (2nd ed.) (Madrid, 1952).

20 Page references are to the text of the play in *Teatro español: 1950-51* (Madrid, 1951).

21 *The Tragic Stages of Antonio Buero Vallejo,* 31. Nicholas makes some very interesting comparisons between the dramatic technique of Ibsen and Buero.

22 Doménech's study, in *El teatro de Buero Vallejo,* 149-77, is the most useful in terms of the play's themes. See too Robert Nicholas, *The Tragic Stages of Antonio Buero Vallejo,* 64-9; Francisco Ruiz Ramón, *Historia del teatro español, siglo XX,* 361-4; and the relevant sections on the general studies of Buero's theatre mentioned in n.18.

23 All page references are to the text published, together with *Historia de una escalera,* in Selecciones Austral, 5th ed., 1981.

24 The page reference is to the text published in Austral, 11th. ed., 1980.

25 On this point see Robert Nicholas, *The Tragic Stages of Antonio Buero Vallejo,* 58-60. Buero Vallejo has himself written on Brecht, as in 'A propósito de Brecht', *Ínsula,* Nos. 200-20 (July — August 1963), and translated *Mother Courage,* presented in Spain in 1966.

26 J.L. Styan, *Modern Drama in Theory and Practice, II, Symbolism, Surrealism and the Absurd* (Cambridge, 1981), 79. On Pirandello see too Ronald Gaskell, *Drama and Reality: the European Theatre Since Ibsen,* 117-27.

27 On aspects of staging Robert Nicholas, *The Tragic Stages of Antonio Buero Vallejo,* has some perceptive observations. See 77-80.

28 For a thematic study see Ricardo Doménech, *El teatro de Buero Vallejo,* 222-40. Page references to the play are to the text published in *Artes Hispánicas,* I (1967).

29 There are numerous useful studies of the play: Ricardo Doménech, *El teatro de Buero Vallejo,* 107-25; Robert Nicholas, *The Tragic Stages of Antonio Buero Vallejo,* 80-6; Angel Fernández Santos, 'Una entrevista con Buero Vallejo sobre *El tragaluz', Primer Acto,* 90 (1967).

30 Page references are to the text of the play in *Antonio Buero Vallejo, Teatro: Hoy es fiesta, Las Meninas, El tragaluz,* (3rd ed.) (Madrid, 1980). This volume also contains a number of interesting essays on Buero's theatre.

31 Angel Fernández Santos, 'Una entrevista con Buero Vallejo sobre *El tragaluz', Primer Acto,* 90 (1967), reprinted in the volume refered to in n.30, 64-78.

32 See Victor Dixon, 'The "Immersion-Effect" in the Plays of Antonio Buero Vallejo', *Themes in Drama,* 2 (1980). See in particular, 128-9.

33 *The Tragic Stages of Antonio Buero Vallejo,* 94.

34 In terms of theme see Ricardo Doménech, *El teatro de Buero Vallejo,* 178-203; 'Notas sobre *El sueño de la razón', Primer Acto,* 117 (1970), 6-11; Angel Fernández Santos, 'Sobre *El sueño de la razón.* Una conversacion con Antonio Buero Vallejo', *Primer Acto,* 117 (1970) 18-27.

35 *El teatro de Buero Vallejo*, 186-9.

36 The page reference is to the text published in Austral, 11th ed., 1980. In relation to the influence of Valle-Inclán and the *esperpento* on Buero Vallejo, it is important to bear in mind Buero's essay on Valle-Inclán in *Tres maestros ante el público: Valle-Inclán, Velázquez, Lorca* (Madrid, 1973).

37 Richardo Doménech, *El teatro de Buero Vallejo*, 197.

38 Page references are to the edition published by Escelicer: Madrid, 1970.

39 If the link with Valle-Inclán is striking, so, in relation to the projection of pictures on the backcloth, is the link between *El sueño de la razón* and Alberti's *Noche de guerra en el Museo del Prado*.

40 See Robert Nicholas, *The Tragic Stages of Buero Vallejo*, 120. Mention must be made here of Buero's most recent plays, though they have not been his most successful. *La detonación (The Explosion)* received its first performance at the Teatro Bellas Artes in Madrid on 20th September, 1977, and *Jueces en la noche (Judges in the Night)* at the Teatro Lara in Madrid on 2nd October, 1979.

CHAPTER VI

Alfonso Sastre

Alfonso Sastre is, with Antonio Buero Vallejo, the most significant Spanish dramatist of the last thirty years. Born in Madrid in 1926 and commencing his career as a dramatist in the late 1940s, Sastre, like Buero, has produced most of his work under the constraints of the Franco dictatorship. In more than twenty plays he has also, like Buero, revealed both a constant concern with the predicament of Spain and with the need to revitalize Spanish theatre. On the other hand, Sastre has shown himself to be a much more politically aggressive dramatist than Buero and his difficulties under the Franco regime — notably in relation to the performance and publication of the plays written in the 1960s — have therefore been much greater. In addition, Sastre's burning desire to transform the Spanish theatre is much more closely related to a political ideology than is the case with Buero, and to that extent there is a link between Sastre's theatre and the political plays of Alberti written in the 1930s, as well as, of course, with European political drama in general. Taken as a whole, Sastre's theatre falls into three periods: the short plays written between 1945 and 1950; the socially committed, full-length works performed and published between 1950 and 1960; and the plays written since 1960 which, during the Franco domination of Spain, were neither performed nor published. Attention will be given here to three plays. *Escuadra hacia la muerte (The Condemned Squad)*, written in 1952, looks back in certain respects to Sastre's earlier period but in its social implications belongs to the socially committed plays. *La mordaza (The Gag)* (1954) falls firmly within this second period. *Asalto nocturno (Night Assault)*, written in 1959, belongs chronologically to the second period but, especially in terms of technique, looks forward to the plays of the 1960s in which, above all, the influence of epic theatre is very strong.[1]

The first period of Sastre's dramatic production must be related to the experimental theatre group, Arte Nuevo (New Art), with which he was associated from 1946 to 1948. Together with other similarly-minded young men — Alfonso Paso, Medardo Fraile, José Franco. José María de Quinto, José Gordon and José María Palacio — Sastre objected strongly to the commercially orientated, superficial, escapist and bourgeois theatre that, as has been mentioned previously, thrived in Spain after the Civil War. The aim of Arte Nuevo was thus to provide an alternative theatre which both dealt with serious themes and issues and revitalized theatre technique. For the group Sastre wrote four short plays: *Cargamento de sueños (Cargo of Dreams)*, *Uranio 235 (Uranium 235)*, *Ha sonado la muerte (Death Has Sounded)*, and *Comedia sonámbula (Sleepwalker's Comedy)*, the last two in collaboration with Medardo Fraile. In terms of theme these plays present man as the victim of forces which he cannot combat and which he does not understand; man, in short, is a helpless, lost creature in an absurd world. Thus, in *Cargamento de sueños* the protagonist, man, relates his life to a strange interlocutor called Jeschoua. He describes the torment and the meaningless of his own existence as well as that of men in general, destroys Frau, the only person who has meaning for him, and in the end loses a game of chess to Death. It is no coincidence, given both the symbolism and the pessimism of Sastre's pre-Beckett theatre, that it has often been compared to Beckett's drama. As far as technique is concerned, these plays are characterized by such devices as flashback, dreams and violent transitions in time and space. But while they reveal Sastre to be an innovator in the Spanish theatre of the late 1940s, they lack the social concerns and perspective of his later theatre. In this, as Farris Anderson has observed, Sastre would 'present characters who are not only creatures of anguish but also men of action: human beings in their historical, social function as well as their timeless existential predicament'.[2]

Sastre's views on the purpose and function of theatre, notably on the relationship between art and socio-political questions, have been expressed over many years in both articles and books, beginning with the student magazine, *La hora (The Hour)*, in 1948. In 1950, in collaboration with José María de Quinto, one of his associates with Arte Nuevo, Sastre founded a new theatre group, Teatro de Agitación Social (Theatre of Social Agitation), reminiscent in some respects of the *agitprop* groups of the 1930s, and in an accompanying manifesto, published in October 1950, set out its principal aims.[3] Stressing that the Teatro de Agitación Social was not intended to represent the viewpoint of any single political party, Sastre and María de Quinto nevertheless argued that theatre should strive to involve its audience in social and political issues. The social aims of the theatre, which current Spanish drama ignored almost completely, were, Sastre argued, more important than purely aesthetic considerations, and for that reason the Teatro de Agitación Social should become an integral part of Spanish life:

> ... pretende incorporarse normalmente a la vida nacional, con la justa y lícita pretensión de llegar a constituirse en el auténtico teatro nacional. Porque a un estado social corresponde como teatro nacional un teatro social, y nunca un teatro burgués que desfallece día a día ...

... it seeks to integrate itself normally into the life of the nation, with the just and lawful intention of becoming a part of the true national theatre. For a social state must have a social theatre as its national theatre, and not a bourgeois theatre which grows more infirm day by day ...

As part of their programme, Sastre and María de Quinto proposed to produce the plays of socially orientated foreign dramatists whose work would hopefully awaken the social consciousness of Spanish audiences — among them Ernst Toller, Bertolt Brecht, Jean-Paul Sartre, Eugene O'Neill and Arthur Miller. In the event, the proposals of the T.A.S. were strongly resisted by a regime opposed to left-wing activities and Sastre's project died almost in the moment of conception. Nevertheless, the dramatists mentioned above point to the dramatic background against which Sastre's concerns and theatre technique should be considered.

Despite the failure in practical terms of the T.A.S., its manifesto represents an important moment in the history of twentieth-century Spanish theatre: a protest and the assumption of a position which did not fall entirely on stony ground or on deaf ears. Sastre has himself observed that 'el Manifiesto resonó en España y fuera de España' ('the Manifesto reverberated inside and outside Spain').[4] At all events, his exposition of his aims is but one example of a continuing process in which Sastre has been involved now for more than a quarter of a century and in the course of which he has vigorously propounded his theories on theatre, sought to involve the Spanish public in the examination of the theatre and the society of the period in question, and in a more general sense invited it to ponder on the nature and purpose of art. In short, if Sastre's plays have often been banned, his voice has not been silenced.

Sastre's first book, *Drama y sociedad (Drama and Society)*, published in 1956, contains important essays written between 1949 and 1956 and is an effective statement of his views on theatre during that period.[5] Above all, Sastre demands of the dramatist commitment and responsibility. On the other hand, the writer's *engagement* should not be tied to any particular political ideology but should be concerned with involving the public in the questioning of accepted values and with stirring its conscience. The aim of the theatre, then, should be to agitate and disturb, and with this in mind a certain kind of theatre should be cultivated. Avoiding both purely aesthetic considerations and specific propaganda, the dramatist's aim should be the cultivation of 'detached penetration', which is to say that the play should document reality, employing 'realism' to do so, and should thereby allow the observer of the play to understand, to 'penetrate' the conditions and circumstances of his existence. To this extent, in the sense that Sastre is concerned with the reality of man in his social environment, he argues for a theatre of Social Realism.

At the same time, Sastre states that man's social circumstances should always be seen as part of a broader framework, in consequence of which the theatre should also be concerned with the tragic reality of human existence in general. For Sastre himself the tragedy of human existence lies in the fact that man finds himself in a closed situation in which his search for happiness and the meaning of life is invariably defeated, a fact which provokes both horror and pity. Reflecting Aristotelian notions of tragedy, as well as the views of twentieth-century writers like Sartre and Unamuno, Sastre sees tragedy as posing the questions: Why do men suffer and who is responsible for their suffering? In this sense tragic drama is, for Sastre, a kind of investigation with profound metaphysical implications, but, as has already been pointed out, such an examination must not be separated from the consideration of man in his particular, social setting. In relation to the tragic emotions, the spectator should be moved to feel for man on both levels, and if he is prompted to seek the causes of human suffering on a metaphysical plane, he must also do so on a social plane. Finally, in terms of its form, Sastre states that tragedy, in order to move and disturb people, must have a documentary quality which presents contemporary life, as in his view do the plays of Toller, Brecht, Sartre and Miller.

Between *Drama y sociedad* and another important book, *Anatomía del realismo (Anatomy of Realism)* (1963), Sastre continued to produce a stream of essays, many of which defined more clearly his earlier ideas. Of particular interest is an essay on Beckett's *Waiting for Godot*, published with the text of the play in the journal, *Primer Acto*, in April 1957. On the one hand, Sastre saw *Waiting for Godot* as the perfect expression of man's existential situation, of the failure of communication and the pointlessness and triviality of human existence. On the other hand, he was bothered by the play's pessimism for the simple reason that pessimism is the negation of committed theatre and committed action and thus of the social activity and reform that Sastre wanted his own plays to inspire. It is not surprising, given this fact, that Brecht should ultimately become a greater influence on Sastre than Beckett.

Anatomía del realismo both includes previously published essays and introduces new material.[6] Sastre rejects some of the ideas expressed in *Drama y sociedad* and extends and states with greater clarity some of its most important arguments: notably, that the writer should have a sense of social responsibility; that aesthetic literature serves no useful purpose; that tragedy is an important and relevant form; and that realism is the only acceptable mode of expression. In the course of the book Sastre often refers to Brecht, whose theoretical writings he had begun to study around 1960, while other important influences are Engels and George Lukács. As far as the purpose and function of literature is concerned, Sastre consistently argues not in favour of dogma and propaganda but of revelation and illumination, in which respect realism is the key, for realism for Sastre is the means whereby the artist makes his work relevant. To this extent Sastre shares the view of Lukács that realism allows the writer to depict man as a complete entity, both in relation to the society in which he finds himself and to existence as a whole. Realistic theatre is thus less a particular style or mode of expression than a form of theatre which is grounded in the reality of men's lives.

The ideas expressed in Sastre's articles and books published since 1950 are, of course, put into practice in the plays written since that time, and in this respect there is a marked shift away from the emphasis of the work written for Arte Nuevo. There Sastre had presented man in relation to a hostile environment that lacked a truly historical or social perspective. Subsequently, as the manifesto of the Teatro de Agitación Social suggests, he became much more aware from 1950 of the theatre's potential as an instrument of social change and of its capacity for denunciation. In certain respects some of the plays of the 1950s still contain elements of the nihilistic vision so evident in the earlier work. Such are *Ana Kleiber* and *La sangre de Dios (The Blood of God)* (both 1955), *El cuervo (The Raven)* (1956) and, as we shall see, *Escuadra hacia la muerte* (1952). On the other hand, most of the plays of the fifties, including *Escuadra hacia la muerte*, cease to be the 'dramas de frustración' ('dramas of frustration') characteristic of the Arte Nuevo period, and become instead 'dramas de posibilidad' ('dramas of possibility').[7] One of the key characteristics of the 'dramas de posibilidad', as the phrase itself suggests, is that the characters, even though they cannot escape suffering or even death, can to a certain extent at least control their circumstances. Moreover, the forces against which they struggle are not those of an inexplicable and hostile universe but those of an unjust society which destroys individuals in a variety of ways. At the same time, although the social perspective of these plays is extremely important, the human dimension is never lost, for Sastre investigates precisely those human conflicts that are the consequences of social pressures.

The dramas of social realism are twelve in number and span the years 1950 to 1962. They are *Prólogo patético (Pathetic Prologue)* (1951); *El cubo de la basura (The Rubbish Bin)* (1951); *Escuadra hacia la muerte (The Condemned Squad)* (1952); *El pan de todos (Bread for Everyone)* (1953); *La mordaza (The Gag)* (1954); *Tierra roja (Red Earth)* (1954); *Guillermo Tell tiene los ojos tristes (William Tell Has Sad Eyes)* (1955);

Muerte en el barrio (Death in the Neighbourhood) (1955); *En la red (In the Net)* (1959); *La cornada (Death Thrust)* (1959); *Asalto nocturno (Night Assault)* (1959); and *Oficio de tinieblas (Office of Darkness)* (1962). All twelve plays, given the differences between them, present human beings in their historical and social setting and in one way or another are deeply concerned with men's struggle for social liberty without the sacrifice of individual integrity. Needless to say, the plays are uneven in quality, sometimes because the link between individual characters and their social background are not sufficiently firm, and sometimes because the individual character himself does not elicit sufficient sympathy. *El pan de todos* is a good example of the former, *Guillermo Tell tiene los ojos tristes* of the latter. The best of the dramas of social realism are, very clearly, those plays which succeed in relating the individual to his social background, in portraying the individual in a manner which allows us to identify with his predicament, and which, above all, manage to see man in relation to his existence as a whole, thereby broadening and deepening the frame of reference. Such is Sastre's achievement in *Escuadra hacia la muerte, La mordaza, Muerte en el barrio* and *La cornada*.

While these 'dramas de posibilidad' correspond to what might be broadly described as a 'realistic' phase in Sastre's theatre, the plays written after 1960 point to his growing interest in epic theatre and reveal very clearly the influence of the theory and practice of Brecht, though, as *Anatomia del realismo* suggests, epic does not exclude Sastre's definition of realism. *Asalto nocturno*, though written in 1959 and belonging to the second phase of Sastre's dramatic production, can also be regarded as Sastre's earliest experiment in epic drama. In the sixties and early seventies he produced, in accordance with his new enthusiasm for Brecht, *La sangre y la ceniza (Blood and Ash)* (1965), *El banquete (The Banquet)* (1965), *La taberna fantástica (The Fantastic Tavern)* (1966), *Crónicas romanas (Roman Chronicles)* (1968), *Ejercicios de terror (Excercises in Terror)* (1970), and *El camarada oscuro (The Dark Companion)* (1972). In contrast to the plays of the second period, many of which were performed in Spain, the six plays mentioned above were neither performed nor published under the Franco regime. They appeared instead only in typescript, entitled *Teatro penúltimo (Penultimate Theatre)*, and represent in that respect what has been described as theatre in a void, excluded both from the stage and the printed page.[8]

In terms of technique, the epic character of Sastre's drama of the sixties can be succinctly described. Firstly, the play is characterized now by a looseness of structure, for it consists of a number of scenes and episodes linked in a manner that is often arbitrary. Secondly, Sastre adopts the characteristic Brechtian 'narrative' method: characters speak directly to the audience, and ballads, slogans and titles announce the events about to take place. Thirdly, actors step outside their parts; the dialogue is used to comment on the action; and parts of the action overflow from the stage into the aisles of the theatre. Fourthly, the stage action is frequently interrupted by a variety of noises, from screams to sirens, and by sudden changes in the lighting of the stage. And finally, even though the action of a play may be fictional, parallels are drawn between it and real events, from Nazism to Francoism, with which the spectator will be familiar. In short, Sastre's aim in his epic theatre is to create a distance between the stage action and the spectator, to reduce the degree of audience involvement to the point where the observer of the play can form more objective judgements about it and can leave the theatre convinced of the need to change society. At the same time it must be emphasized, as Farris Anderson has stated, that even if Sastre's epic theatre does involve greater distancing, he 'relies more heavily on suggestion that on argumentation; he is more concerned with exposing the spectator to provocative images of revolution than with convincing him rationally of the urgency of transforming society.'9 It would be difficult to expect less of a dramatist as committed as Sastre.

Escuadra hacia la muerte, on which Sastre began work in 1951, deals with five soldiers who, as a punishment for their crimes, find themselves involved in a suicide mission at the outbreak of World War Three. The five men are commanded by Corporal Goban, a man who, despite their hopeless and absurd predicament, imposes upon them the strictest military discipline. Increasingly incensed by Goban's tyrannical treatment of them, the soldiers finally turn on him and murder him in the course of their Christmas Eve celebrations. Goban's death marks the climax of Part One of the play. In Part Two the soldiers, liberated from one tyranny, are made to realize that they are now the prisoners of the consequences of their action — of their guilt and fear — as well as of the hopeless nature of their military situation. Two of them wander off seeking vainly to escape, a third hangs himself, and the remaining two await their death.

When Sastre began work on *Escuadra hacia la muerte*, the intention was that the play should be performed in London by a Spanish theatre group. He therefore approached the subject with a London performance and his theatre colleagues of Arte Nuevo very much in mind. Given both these factors, and especially the experimental nature of Arte Nuevo, Sastre wrote the play with a sense of freedom, uninhibited by the strictness of censorship and of the Spanish stage of the 1950s.

In the event the London performance did not materialize and the first performance of *Escuadra hacia la muerte* took place in Spain on 18

March 1953, presented by the Teatro Popular Universitario at the Teatro María Guerrero in Madrid and directed by Gustavo Pérez Puig. Although the play was officially banned after three performances, it had the effect of establishing Sastre as a young dramatist of great promise.

In terms of its broad themes, *Escuadra hacia la muerte* is concerned with frustration and despair on the one hand, and on the other with positive action and hope. In this sense the play expresses Sastre's own ideological struggle and the evolution of that struggle at the time of composition: a consideration of man's predicament, of the possibility of action in relation to that predicament, and of the consequences of that action. In Part One, therefore, the dramatist presents the oppression of soldiers, and in revealing their final rebellion against it, suggests the possibility of revolutionary action as an instrument of change. The liberation of the soldiers from Goban's repression does not, though, as we have seen, do anything more than expose them to their own emotional conflicts. Sastre expresses, in effect, his views of the need for revolution without losing sight of the fact that revolutionary action brings with it its own problems. While Part One of the play ends on a note of hope with Goban's death, Part Two concludes pessimistically, suggesting a sense of imprisonment that is no less strong than it was at the very outset.

Precisely because the themes of *Escuadra hacia la muerte* are of a broad nature, the play has lent itself to a variety of interpretations. In relation to a specifically Spanish context, it is not surprising that Corporal Goban should often have been seen as a symbol of the dictatorship imposed by Franco, and the rebellion against Goban as the reaction of an oppressed people against such tyranny. Neither is it surprising, given the possibility of such an interpretation, that the play was banned in Spain after only three performances, for the military saw it as a direct attack upon them. There can be no doubt, of course, that Sastre intended the play to be an indictment of the post-Civil War political situation, but even within a Spanish context it has deeper resonances. As has been pointed out already, the soldiers' murder of Goban offers only a partial solution to their problems. In other words, Sastre's intention was not merely to advocate revolution but to draw attention to the problems that stem from such activity.

Looked at in another way, the play has also been interpreted within a broader European context. Seen in this way, Goban becomes the embodiment of the Fascism which plunged Europe into the Second World War, while the soldiers represent the forces that overcame Hitler. The freedom which they achieve through Goban's death parallels the European situation of the post-War years, a time in which, having overthrown Fascism, men were confronted instead by the terrors of the Cold War and nuclear destruction. Juan Emilio Aragonés has described *Escuadra hacia la muerte* in the following terms:

> ... un drama en el que no se dan respuestas. Un drama construido sobre trágicas y alucinadas preguntas. El drama de esta Europa desconcertada e incierta en la que todos estamos ...[10]

> ... a play in which no answers are provided. A play built around tragic and haunting questions. This drama of the disturbed and uncertain Europe in which we all live ...

Sastre has himself also spoken of the play's European dimension:

> No vale, ahora, soñar vagamente con una Europa unida y con el enrolamiento en esa fantasmal tercera fuerza. Entre dos fuegos, la juventud europea trabaja. Aprende oficios, hace oposiciones, cátedras.¿Qué sentido tiene todo eso bajo la amenaza de una guerra? En *Escuadra hacia la muerte* no se dan respuestas, pero, al menos, se busca en las raíces de las trágicas preguntas.[11]

> There is no point now in dreaming vaguely about a united Europe or about involvement with that shadowy third world. Caught in the middle, the youth of Europe work. They learn trades, sit examinations, prepare themselves for professorships. What sense is there in all this under the threat of war? In *The Condemned Squad* there are no answers, but at least there is some probing into the sources of agonizing questions.

These words have a very clear parallel in the play in the anguished soliloquy of Javier, the intellectual, as he questions the purpose of his existence:

> Han pasado dos horas y más. ¡Un, dos! ¡Un, dos! Una escuadra hacia la muerte. ¡Un, dos! Lo éramos ya antes de estallar la guerra. Una generación estúpidamente condenada al matadero. Estudiábamos, nos afanábamos por las cosas, y ya estábamos encuadrados en una gigantesca escuadra hacia la muerte. Generaciones condenadas ...[12]   (p.95)

> More than two hours have passed. One, two! One, two! A condemned squad. One, two! We were already that before the war started. A generation senselessly condemned to the slaughterhouse. We spent our time studying, struggling to achieve things, and we were already assigned to an enormous condemned squad. Generations of us condemned ...

The third level of meaning of the play is, of course, neither merely Spanish nor European, but universal, for Sastre's ultimate concern is the predicament of man in general. At one point in the play, Pedro likens his situation and that of his four companions to the predicament of others elsewhere:

> Os advierto que hay muchas escuadras como ésta a lo largo del frente ...
> (p.79)

> I tell you there are many squads like this, all along the front ...

Towards the end of the play, as the soldiers agonize about a possible course
of action, Javier draws their attention to the pointlessness of it all:

> Todos son . . . caminos de muerte. ¿No os dais cuenta? Es inútil luchar. Está
> pronunciada la última palabra y todo es inútil. En realidad, todo era inútil . . .
> desde un principio . . .   (p.122)

> All roads . . . lead to death. Don't you realize? To resist is useless. The last
> word has been said and everything is useless. To tell the truth, everything was
> useless . . . from the beginning . . .

In addition, there are frequent suggestions in the play both of man's sinful
nature and of his consequent abandonment. In the final scenes of the play
Javier speaks of his fate and that of his companions as a preordained
punishment:

> Formaba parte de un vasto plan de castigo.   (p.124)

> It was part of a great scheme of punishment.

Later in the same scene he develops the idea:

> . . . Hay alguien que nos castiga por algo . . ., por algo . . . Debe haber . . ., sí, a
> fin de cuentas, habrá que creer en eso . . . Una falta . . . de origen . . . Un
> misterioso y horrible pecado . . . del que no tenemos ni idea . . .   (p.125)

> . . . There is someone who is punishing us for something . . ., for something . . .
> There must be . . ., Yes, in the end, we must reach that conclusion . . . a
> mistake . . . long ago . . . A mysterious and terrible sin . . . that we are unaware
> of . . .

Again, in the play's very final scene the two remaining characters express
very clearly their sense of isolation, puzzlement and abandonment:

> LUIS: Pedro, y todo esto, ¿por qué? ¿Qué habremos hecho antes? ¿Cuándo
> habremos merecido todo esto? ¿Nos lo merecíamos, Pedro?
> PEDRO: ¡Bah! No hay que preguntar. ¿Para qué? No hay respuesta. El único
> que podía hablar está callado . . .   (p.130)

> LUIS: Pedro, why did all this happen? What did we do? When did we do
> anything to deserve all this? Do we really deserve it, Pedro?
> PEDRO: There's no point in asking. Why ask? There's no reply. The only one
> who could explain it isn't speaking . . .

Looked at in this way, *Escuadra hacia la muerte* becomes at its highest
level Sastre's presentation of man as a whole, abandoned by God because
he has himself abandoned God, and cast adrift in consequence in a world
which has no meaning or order.

A consideration of the play's technique illustrates very clearly the way in
which the action functions on different levels.[13] Ten of the twelve scenes are
set in or around a hut in a forest, where the soldiers have installed
themselves, and the setting is characterized by a certain realism:

Interior de la casa de un guardabosques, visible por un corte vertical. Denso fondo de árboles. Explanada en primer término. Es la única habitación de la casa. Chimenea encendida. En los alrededores de la chimenea, en desorden, los petates de seis soldados. En un rincón, ordenados en su soporte, cinco fusiles y un fusil ametrallador. Cajas de municiones. Una barrica de agua. Un teléfono de campaña. Una batería eléctrica. Un gran montón de leña. Una caja de botiquín, con una cruz roja. Puerta al foro y ventana grande en muro oblicuo a la boca del escenario. (p.65)

The interior of a gamekeeper's hut, seen through a vertical cut-out. A background of thick trees. A slope in the foreground. It is the only room in the hut. The fire has been lit. Around the fireplace, in some disarray, are the sleeping-mats of the six soldiers. In a corner, placed in orderly fashion in a rack, five rifles and a light machine-gun. A box of ammunition. A cask of water. A field telephone. An electric battery. A great pile of wood. A first-aid box, with a red cross. A door leading out from the back and a large window in the wall that runs at an angle from the front of the stage.

The numerous objects give to the setting solidity and definition. On the other hand, the actual location of the hut is far from precise, for the forest background creates a certain vagueness and, taken in conjunction with subsequent allusions to woods and mountains, has the effect of placing the hut and the soldiers in a much more timeless, less precise context. In addition, the setting as a whole is highly suggestive of enclosure, for the forest encloses the hut and the hut the soldiers, creating thereby a sense of claustrophobia and imprisonment which reinforces the sense of the soldiers being trapped in a situation from which there is no escape. Beyond its realistic level, the symbolic meaning of the play is very evident.

This symbolic meaning is reinforced by the settings for the two scenes that take place away from the hut. In Part One, Scene Five, Javier is on guard:

Un proyector ilumina la figura de Javier, en la guardia. Capote con el cuello subido y fusil entre las manos enguantadas . . . (p.94)

A spotlight picks out the figure of Javier, on guard. He wears a great-coat with the collar raised and holds a rifle in his gloved hands . . .

The effect of the spotlight, silhouetting Javier, is to transform the individual into the universal soldier. In Part Two, Scene Eleven, Adolfo and Andrés, attempting to escape, appear in the darkness:

En la oscuridad, ruido de viento. Hay — pero apenas pueden ser distinguidas — dos sombras, entre árboles, en primer término. Suenan, medrosas, como en un susurro, las voces de Adolfo y Andrés. (p.126)

In the darkness, the sound of the wind. There are — though it is difficult to perceive them — two shadows, between the trees, in the foreground. The voices of Adolfo and Andrés can be heard, whispering fearfully.

The presentation of particular individuals as vague shadows, the shapes of the trees, the sound of the wind, have the effect, very clearly, of universalizing both settings and characters. In terms of characterization, Sastre's technique also combines realistic and symbolic elements. In the case of Corporal Goban, the emphasis falls very firmly on the extent to which he is a type, the very epitome of military discipline and inflexibility. In Part One, Scene Two, Andrés observes: 'Ese hombre es un bruto' ('That man is an animal') (p.77), and it is, indeed, the violence and brutality of Goban, reflected in word and deed, that is constantly emphasized, to the exclusion of all human feeling. In the play's first scene Goban kicks Javier and hits Luis across the face. Later, he punches Andrés in the stomach and kicks him in the chest. The man's harshness is revealed too, of course, in his words, which are often like his blows, assaulting the ears of those under him. The one-dimensional, puppet-like presentation of Goban is, to a certain extent, reminiscent of the characterization so typical of *agitprop* plays, and in this sense *Escuadra hacia la muerte* is highly reminiscent of the propaganda plays of Piscator, Brecht and, as an earlier chapter suggests, Alberti.

To a certain extent, the five soldiers are also types, their individuality subordinated to their military role and its requirements. In addition, there is between them an essential sameness in the sense that they share a common and unseen enemy. In short, the five soldiers assume a single role, which is that of man as victim. On the other hand, Sastre is careful to allow the individuality of the five men to shine through, for our ability to identify with them as feeling and suffering human beings, to feel their anguish, determines the extent to which we come to see their imprisonment and its attendant despair as our own. Each of the soldiers, in the course of the play, is given a history, a background in which unhappiness and suffering loom large. In addition, at given moments the terrible doubts and fears of the characters reveal themselves in a particularly powerful form, as in the case of Javier in Part One, Scene Five, when a growing awareness of his loneliness and isolation reduces him to the level of a whimpering child calling for its mother:

... Yo no quiero caer prisionero. ¡No! ¡Prisionero, no! ¡Morir! ¡Yo prefiero ... (*Con un sollozo sordo.*) ¡morir! ¡Madre! ¡Madre! ¡Estoy aquí ... lejos! ¿No me oyes? ¡Madre! ¡Tengo miedo! ¡Estoy solo! ¡Estoy en un bosque, muy lejos! ¡Somos seis, madre! ¡Estamos ... solos ..., solos ..., solos ...!(p.95)

... I don't want to be taken prisoner! No! Not a prisoner! I prefer to die! (*With a muffled sob.*) To die! Mother! Mother! I'm here ... far away! Can't you hear me? Mother! I'm afraid! I'm alone! In a forest, far away! Mother, there are six of us! We're alone ..., alone ..., alone ...!

In many ways Sastre's presentation of the soldiers is, at key moments, expressionist — in its emphasis on man as victim and martyr of war, in its revelation of the inner man, and in the staccatto and highly charged nature of its language.[14]

The example quoted above reveals very clearly that, far from being naturalistic, the language of the play is often characterized by certain structures and patterns — repetitions, parallelisms, even pauses — which communicate powerful feeling. There are other occasions too when the highly patterned nature of the dialogue reflects Javier's despair, as in Part Two, Scene Seven (p.122). In total contrast, Pedro's decision to disclose the facts about Goban's death and face the consequences is expressed in language whose terse phrasing and abrupt rhythms fully reflect his positive attitude:

> ... Ya sabéis cual es mi actitud. Interpretadla a vuestro gusto. Yo voy a entregarme al Consejo de Guerra. El que no quiera seguir mi suerte puede irse ...   (p.117)

> ... You know my view already. Interpret it as you like. I'm going to let myself be court-martialled. If you don't want to follow my example, stay here ...

An examination of the dialogue as a whole makes it clear, indeed, that it revolves far less around the normal chit-chat of soldiers than around their reaction to their circumstances. Reflecting different and often opposing attitudes, the dialogue assumes, especially in the second half of the play, the character of a fiercely contested debate. True to his view of the function of theatre, Sastre raises the dialogue of soldiers, which in so many plays of this kind is coarse and lacking in substance, to the level of dialectic.

Finally, Sastre's use of lighting is highly effective. When the curtain rises on Part One, the light of day is fading fast. When the play ends and the soldiers' end is inevitable, darkness engulfs the stage. In both cases physical darkness suggests the soldiers' imprisonment, firstly at the hands of Goban, secondly in relation to their circumstances, and on both counts darkness reflects too their despair. In addition, in certain scenes the lighting is stark and harsh, and in this sense evokes the harshness of the soldiers' existence. Such is the case in Part One, Scene Six:

> Se oye — sobre el oscuro — una canción de Navidad cantada con la boca cerrada por varios hombres. Se enciende la luz. Lámparas de petróleo ...
> (p.96)

> In the darkness a Christmas carol can be heard, hummed by a number of men. A light appears. A number of oil-lamps ...

Furthermore, in many instances, as has already been suggested, the effect of lighting, or its virtual absence, is to blur and even eliminate realistic detail and thereby create broad effects which universalize both individual figures and whole scenes. In short, like the dramatists discussed in previous chapters, Sastre uses the different elements of stage-performance to achieve an integrated effect which is powerful in both thematic and dramatic terms.

Sastre began work on *La mordaza* in 1953 and completed it in 1954 during his military service. The play was performed on 17 September, 1954, at the Teatro Reina Victoria in Madrid, directed by José María de Quinto, and, given the fact that *Escuadra hacia la muerte* was performed by a student group, represents Sastre's first professional production. *La mordaza*, as its title 'the gag' suggests, was written by Sastre as a specific protest against repression — the kind of repression which under the Franco regime militated against freedom of action and speech — and in his *Obras completas (Complete Works)* he has stated very clearly: 'Vivimos amordazados. No somos felices. Este silencio nos agobia' ('We live as though gagged. We are not happy. This silence weighs upon us') (pp.283-4).[15] It is ironic, given Sastre's purpose in *La mordaza*, that the play was performed without any kind of opposition.

The action of *La mordaza* centres on Isaías Krappo and his family: his wife, Antonia; his sons, Juan, Teo and Jandro; and Luisa, Juan's wife. Isaías is guilty of the murder of a stranger, whose body has been found on his property, but intimidates his family into keeping his secret — especially Luisa, who had accidentally witnessed the crime. It is Luisa who first breaks the gag of silence by revealing to Teo and Juan that their father is the murderer, but it is not until the final scene of the play that the family as a whole break free from his tyranny when Luisa informs the police inspector of her father-in-law's guilt. In the epilogue to the play Juan brings news that Isaías has been killed while attempting to escape from prison.

In writing *La mordaza*, Sastre was influenced in no small measure by a real-life event: the murder in 1952 in France of an English family, the Drummonds (mother, father and daughter), and the eventual indictment for that murder of Gaston Dominici, an old, well-known and powerful farmer in the village of Lurs. In the case against the old man his children's testimony played a significant part, and the general similarity between this affair and the circumstances of *La mordaza* is quite striking. At the same time Sastre has emphasized that the Dominici case merely gave him the idea for the play and that its events are totally fictitious.[16]

As far as its themes are concerned, the central concern of *La mordaza* is that of tyranny and oppression, though this has both a particular and general significance. In the first place, while there is no specific reference to Franco's Spain, the play comments very clearly on certain conditions, notably the ruthless suppression of truth, that prevailed in Spain at the time of its composition and which had led, for example, to the banning of *Escuadra hacia la muerte* after only three performances. Secondly, though, precisely because there is no specific reference to Spain, the examination of tyranny becomes much more general, and in this respect there are important similarities between *La mordaza* and *Escuadra hacia la muerte*. In the figures of Goban and Krappo, Sastre embodies the essence of tyranny — debilitating, will-sapping, even daemonic — whatever its object. Thus, just as in *Escuadra hacia la muerte* the soldiers accept without protest a situation imposed upon them, so in *La mordaza* the family of Krappo — itself evocative of a family in a broader sense — accepts in silence a similar state of affairs. Both Goban and Krappo are depicted as believing implicitly in brute force and as exercising a fiendish hold on those under them, and in the end both tyrants reveal a marked resistance to those who seek to destroy them. In short, Sastre creates in both individuals an image of tyranny that expresses concisely and powerfully its different facets.

The similarities between the two plays do not, of course, obscure the important differences between them.[17] Above all, *Escuadra hacia la muerte* looks back to Sastre's earlier plays, written for Arte Nuevo, and retains much of their fatalistic attitude. In contrast, *La mordaza* falls very firmly within the second period of social realism and, as the term suggests, is concerned less with unseen and inevitable forces outside the world of the play than with a particular society, with individuals within it, with the pressures placed upon them, and with their reaction to those pressures. Furthermore, *La mordaza*, being a 'drama de posibilidad', focuses much more on positive answers and on the way in which society can escape from the oppression imposed upon it. The soldiers of *Escuadra hacia la muerte* have only a very limited choice, and after the positive act of their rebellion against Goban the range of options open to them is progressively closed, the second half of the play consisting of a descending movement into individual and collective despair. In *La mordaza*, on the other hand, the movement of the play is an ascending one, for with the arrest of Krappo — and more so with his death — there is a sense of freedom from an earlier oppression that is totally absent in *Escuadra hacia la muerte*. Despite the fact that memories linger on and to that extent disturb their peace of mind, the members of the family of *La mordaza*, having removed the 'gag' of fear, begin to breathe again, and their situation at the end of the play is fundamentally altered for the better.

This important difference in direction can be illustrated by key questions posed by characters toward the end of both plays. In the last scene of

Escuadra hacia la muerte, Luis, alone with Pedro and confronted with inevitable death, appeals to Pedro:

> Pedro, y todo esto, ¿por qué? ¿Qué habremos hecho antes? ¿Cuando habremos merecido todo esto? ¿Nos lo merecíamos, Pedro?[18]   (p.129)
>
> Pedro, why all this? What can we have done in the past? When can we have brought all this on ourselves? Did we deserve it, Pedro?

In Scene Five of *La mordaza* Juan puts to Teo what appears to be a similar question:

> ¿Y qué hemos hecho nosotros para merecer este castigo?   (p.175)
>
> And what have we done to deserve this punishment?

In both cases the question can be taken to suggest the dilemma in which human beings find themselves and their search for an answer to or for the cause of human suffering. In the two cases in question the answer is, though, fundamentally different. *Escuadra hacia la muerte*, far from giving a specific answer, suggests that man may seek to find the reason for his anguish but, given the meaningless nature of his existence, will never find it. In *La mordaza* the answer is provided by Teo:

> Nada. No hemos hecho nada.   (p.175)
>
> Nothing. We haven't done anything.

Moreover, in putting the question to Teo, Juan is not really alluding, as did Luis, to a general situation or condition in which man finds himself — even if it is still possible to interpret the question in this more general way — but to the specific family situation of fear and silence imposed upon them by their father. Teo's answer to the question is also specific, for it refers to the lack of resistance to Krappo of which they are guilty and which has allowed his tyranny to continue. In addition, by alluding to their failure to do anything in the past, Teo is also suggesting a positive way forward, a course of action whereby oppression, be it individual or collective, may be opposed and overcome.

The differences between the two plays suggest, quite clearly, the way in which the world of *La mordaza*, while not losing its more general and symbolic significance, has become more particularized and human as opposed to universal and generic. Krappo and his family are, indeed, part of a community whose character and history are firmly drawn, so that the action of the play acquires a solid base. In addition, the characters themselves are more rounded and thus more recognizably human than is the case in the boldly presented figures of *Escuadra hacia la muerte*. An examination of Sastre's dramatic technique serves to illustrate the point.[19]

As in the case of *Escuadra hacia la muerte, La mordaza* is distinguished for the most part by a single set:

> *Habitación que sirve de cuarto de estar y comedor en una casa rural de grandes proporciones, de sombría y pesada arquitectura. Hay una gran lámpara encendida: una lámpara que no consigue iluminar todos los rincones de la habitación. Las ventanas están abiertas. La gran chimenea, apagada. Es una cálida noche de agosto.* (p.133)

> *A room which is used both as a sitting-room and a dining-room in a large country house whose design gives it a gloomy and heavy atmosphere. A large lamp has been lit but it does not illuminate the corners of the room. The windows are open. The great fire-place is empty. It is a warm night in August.*

Despite the fact that the play as a whole is less overtly symbolic than *Escuadra hacia la muerte,* the symbolic suggestion of its setting can hardly be denied. The oppressive nature of the house reflects perfectly the tyrannical character of its owner, Isaías Krappo, and the idea is sustained too in the non-visual aspects of the stage setting: in the suggestion of suffocating heat and in the silence of the family as they eat their meal:

> *El viejo Isaías Krappo preside la mesa en que la familia está cenando. Antonia, Luisa, Juan y Jandro terminan de cenar silenciosamente . . .*(p.133)

> *The old man, Isaías Krappo sits at the head of the table where the family is having dinner. Antonia, Luisa, Juan and Jandro finish eating in silence . . .*

The symbolic implications of the initial setting are subsequently developed throughout the play, notably through allusions to the oppressive heat. Thus in Scene Four:

> . . . Esta noche hace más calor que nunca . . .   (p.162)

> . . . Tonight it is hotter than ever . . .

Here, moreover, the storm which breaks overhead is suggestive both of the contained passions of the family, which now explode, and of a divine punishment executed on Krappo. Thus Teo observes:

> . . . Es que de pronto me parece que Dios nos va a castigar destrozando la casa con un rayo. *(Se ve a través del ventanal un relámpago vivísimo que ilumina todas las caras.)* . . .   (pp.166-7)

> . . . It seems to me that God is about to punish us by destroying the house with lightning. *(Through the window there is seen a brilliant flash of lightning which illuminates all their faces.)* . . .

The play's very clear symbolism is, nevertheless, balanced by a significant degree of realism. There is evoked, for example, beyond Krappo's country house, a village, its inhabitants and its history. In the very first scene Krappo himself refers to the villagers and to their envy of him on account of his wealth and power (p.141). In Scene Two Krappo informs the police officer of the part played by the villagers in the Resistance, of their suffering, and of their hatred of collaborators:

> ... Esta fue una de las comarcas más castigadas, comisario Roch, y los campesinos tienen buena memoria. (p.151)
>
> ... This was one of the areas that suffered most, Inspector Roch, and the peasants have long memories.

Within the broad picture of opposition to the enemy, Krappo's role was, indeed, an important one, his own history, which is described in Scene One by the man he murders, part of the history of the village and the area. In short, while the action of the play works very suggestively on a symbolic level, it is also firmly anchored within both a recognizable social background and a specific period in history in a way in which *Escuadra hacia la muerte* is not.

As far as characterization is concerned, the individual figures of *La mordaza* are generally more rounded and thus more human than those of the earlier play, given the fact that the five soldiers of *Escuadra hacia la muerte* do have their own individuality. Krappo, for example, though pedominantly forceful and domineering, is not the one-dimensional, archetypal tyrant embodied in Goban, for there are other facets to him. Thus, in the opening scene, his initial bullying of the family gives way to a much more ironic treatment of Juan. Furthermore, Krappo has very recognizable weaknesses which, if they do not make him any the more appealing, certainly make him more human. Such is his attention to his daughter-in-law, Luisa. As for Luisa herself, she emerges in the course of the play as a thoroughly convincing human being. Particularly revealing in this respect is Scene Three when she unwillingly informs Juan that his father is the murderer, for though she detests Krappo for his advances towards her, it is not her hatred of him but the difficulty of bearing the burden of her secret which leads to her exposure of him:

> LUISA: Tengo miedo de hablar.
> JUAN: No tengas miedo. Habla.
> LUISA: Sé que voy a hacerte mucho daño, pero soy egoísta y no puedo llevar esta carga yo sola. *(Con lágrimas en los ojos.)* Ayúdame. (p.156)
>
> LUISA: I'm afraid to speak.
> JUAN: Don't be afraid. Tell me.
> LUISA: I know I'm going to hurt you, but I'm selfish and I can't carry this burden alone. *(With tears in her eyes.)* Help me.

Spirited on the one hand, vulnerable on the other, Luisa is a figure of true flesh and blood. In addition, Krappo's two eldest sons, Juan and Teo, are portrayed with conviction, the one very different from the other. Juan is presented as somewhat weak, overwhelmed by his father's domination of him and even unwilling to accept the truth about him. Teo, in contrast, even though he too has silently endured his father's tyranny, hates him for a variety of very credible reasons, not least for his unfeeling treatment of his wife, Antonia:

> Trata mal a nuestra madre. No puedo sufrir el tono en que le habla.
>   (p.159)
> He treats our mother badly. I can't bear the way in which he speaks to her.

Clearly, these are people with whom we can identify — with whom, indeed, we must identify if we are ourselves to feel and thus react to the tyranny to which they are subjected.

The dialogue of *La mordaza* is particularly striking both for its power and its economy. In Krappo's case, of course, the language is terse and forceful, marked by repetitions and strong rhythms that reflect his domination of the members of his family. Thus he complains about Teo:

> ¿Por qué no ha venido a cenar a su hora? Eso es lo que quisiera saber. Eso es lo único que me preocupa en este momento.   (p.134)
> Why hasn't he come to eat at the proper time? That's what I want to know. That's the only thing that bothers me at this moment.

In this sense Sastre uses language to convey the crushing, overwhelming force of tyranny. As far as those who suffer from it are concerned, the dialogue is used to suggest in one way or another their sense of oppression. Thus, in the early stages of the play the lines spoken by Juan and Teo suggest both their fear and lack of resolution, and contrast markedly with Krappo's tirades against them. Similarly, Krappo's wife, Antonia, physically almost blind and emotionally drained by constant family conflict, expresses her weariness in repeated allusions to the overwhelming heat, allusions which both in their frequency and their heavy, monotonous rhythms convey her sense of hopelessness. Gradually, of course, the characters of the play, especially Luisa, Teo and Juan, shake off the gag of fear, albeit with considerable effort, and the dialogue therefore reflects both their conflict and their liberation. Indeed, by the end of Scene Four Teo can confront his father and express himself as resolutely as had Krappo previously in relation to his son. Thus, in the course of the play the tone and the rhythm of the language of those who were oppressed acquire the momentum of rebellion and, to the extent that we identify with the individuals, sweep us along with it. The language of *La mordaza* is, when analyzed, seen to be carefully orchestrated and is in many ways far from naturalistic. Sastre, indeed, uses the language of the play as much for its emotional effect upon an audience as for its informative purpose, but he does so almost without our being aware of it — ideology transformed into art.[20]

The third phase of Sastre's theatre, as has been stated previously, began around 1960 and involved a growing interest in the theories and practice of Brecht. Nevertheless, in an essay written in 1960, Sastre expressed certain reservations about the Brechtian approach to drama.[21] On the one hand, he shared Brecht's view that the theatre should be concerned with much more than the creation of a naturalistic illusion. On the other, it also seemed clear to Sastre that the distancing and alienating techniques of epic theatre ran the considerable risk of failing to engage the spectator sufficiently in matters of concern and conscience which by their very nature demanded a response that was as emotional as it was intellectual, for, as far as Sastre was concerned, the need to transform society must be passionately felt as well as grasped. Sastre's epic theatre, though it owes much to Brecht, is thus rather different from Brechtian drama in its emphasis. Above all, argumentation is less important than suggestion. While the stage action presents a revolutionary ideology, and at times does so in a fairly direct and unambiguous manner, Sastre is on the whole, as Farris Anderson has indicated, 'more concerned with exposing the spectator to provocative images of revolution than with convincing him rationally of the urgency of transforming society'.[22] The various 'epic' techniques employed by Sastre must clearly be considered within this context.

Asalto nocturno, written in 1959, represents Sastre's first genuine experiment in epic theatre and anticipates in many respects, therefore, the six plays written between 1965 and 1972, none of which were either performed or published. Farris Anderson is of the opinion that *Asalto nocturno* is 'a relatively unimportant piece of work, suffering from the same imbalance characteristic of the less successful dramas of social realism'.[23] Ricardo Doménech, in contrast, has observed that for him the play is one of Sastre's very best works and, in particular, one of the most 'relevant' Spanish plays of the late 1950s and early 60s.[24] What cannot be denied, at all events, is its key position in Sastre's theatre as a whole.

Asalto nocturno presents in its very first scene the murder in his New York home of Professor Marcelo Graffi by Harry Müller, a professional killer. Thereafter, the action of the play takes the form of an investigation in the course of which Inspector Stephen Orkin traces the events that led to Marcelo Graffi's death. In Scene Four, for example, the latter is seen ten

years earlier when he is visited by Angelo Bosco, a man who is guilty of a
crime against the Graffi family in the past and who is now in fear of his life.
Angelo Bosco's death at the hands of Tonio Graffi is his punishment for
that crime, and it is this event which subsequently leads to Marcelo Graffi's
murder, the event carried out on the instructions of Ugo Bosco, Angelo's
son. These violent events are related as well to other incidents even further
back in time which slowly emerge through Stephen Orkin's investigation.
Carlo Graffi, a rich and powerful man, had ruled tyrannically over an island
in the Mediterranean, taking advantage of those who lived there. On his
death he had been replaced by his son, Sandro, but the son had merely
continued his father's dictatorial rule and had been killed by Angelo Bosco.
Thus, the violence of the past is seen to be the source of violence in the
present. Stephen Orkin, moreover, consistently frames his account of the
enmity between the Graffi and the Bosco family with a description of the
violent events that have continually disrupted civilization in the twentieth
century.

As in the case of *Escuadra hacia la muerte* and *La mordaza*, *Asalto
nocturno* is concerned with the theme of violence, repression, tyranny and
its inevitable consequences, and the theme is developed on two levels, the
particular and the general, both of them closely interwoven. On the first
level, as the preceding account of the play suggests, the murder of Marcelo
Graffi, with which the action begins, is the most recent act of violence in a
long chain of events which has its origin in Carlo Graffi's violent and
tyrannical domination of the lives of the inhabitants of the island. Sastre is
clearly concerned with portraying man as both the agent of violence and the
victim of its repercussions. The story of the Graffi and the Bosco families is
suggestive, indeed, in its more particularized sense, of the Spain in which
Sastre is writing his play, and especially, in this connection, of the two
camps — the pro and anti-Franco factions — into which the country was
divided both during and after the Civil War. To this extent the rebellion in
the play against the dictatorship of Carlo Graffi which is continued by his
son, suggests Sastre's advocacy of a possible course of action against the
Spanish dictatorship, or at least points to the inevitable consequences of
systematic repression. On the other hand, if positive action is recommended, Sastre is also very much aware, as both *Escuadra hacia la
muerte* and *La mordaza* indicate in their different ways, of the often
counter-productive nature of such action or, at least, of the price that has to
be paid. Thus, in the play itself the innocent party of long ago — the Bosco
family — becomes the instigator of murder, while the original guilty party —
the Graffi — becomes the victim. The oppressed can easily assume, in short,
the very characteristics which occasion their revolt. Such is man's tragedy

— to find himself in an ever-widening circle of violence from which there is no escape.

The play's broader, more general meaning is suggested by the way in which the incidents involving the Graffi and Bosco families are placed by Stephen Orkin within the context of world events in the twentieth century. The murder of Marcelo Graffi is thus described as having taken place in 1956, the year of Suez and the Russian invasion of Hungary. Elsewhere at this time people are dying still from the effects of nuclear radiation at Hiroshima, the Cold War threatens the peace of the world, racial disturbances disrupt the United States, and the Americans are experimenting with flights into outer space. On other occasions in the play Orkin takes us further back in time, as in Scene Four where he refers to the end of the Second World War, the destruction of Hiroshima and Nagasaki, the Nuremburg trials, and efforts to rebuild from the chaos of war. In Scene Five he evokes the First World War and the events which followed it: in the United States the rise of Al Capone, in Italy and Germany the growing power of Fascism, and, of course, the appearance on the scene of Hitler. Finally, in Scene Six we are transported by Inspector Orkin to the turn of the century, when, in conjunction with scientific discoveries of a constructive nature, the slow but inevitable advance towards the First World War is already evident. In *Asalto nocturno* the traditional forward movement of the play becomes instead a movement backwards in time, an exploration and revelation in the manner of *Oedipus Rex*,[25] whereby the whole of the twentieth century up to the year of the play's composition is seen to consist of constant explosions of violence and destruction, each more terrible than the previous one and in relation to which the forward march of civilization seems almost insignificant.

The ending of the play lacks the optimism of *La mordaza*. While Stephen Orkin expresses the hope that man will not be destroyed by nuclear war, that hope must clearly be set against his earlier account of the violence of twentieth-century history, and when, finally, he looks at a newspaper to see what has happened in the world, he does so with evident anxiety:

> . . . ORKIN *mira la primera página con inquietud. Pero, por fin, sonríe. Dice al público:*
> ORKIN: Todavía nada . . .; Yo deseo que nunca![26]   (p.237)

> . . . ORKIN *looks anxiously at the first page. But finally he smiles. He says to the audience:*
> ORKIN: So far nothing . . . And I hope it will never happen!

The implication is that at any moment the specific night assault of the play — the killing of Graffi — could become a monstrous, totally destructive nuclear night assault of world-wide proportions. While we share Orkin's hope that we might be spared a nuclear holocaust, we share too his uncertainty. At the beginning of the play, Professor Marcelo Graffi, fully aware of the presence of the assassin, awaits his arrival with evident terror. By its conclusion Sastre has, in effect, placed us in Graffi's shoes as we wait for the bomb to fall.

The point has been made already in relation to Sastre's 'epic' phase that, while he inherited much from Brecht, he was also very much aware of the dangers of distancing techniques. For Sastre, a 'committed' dramatist, it was essential that the spectator of the play be not merely intellectually stimulated by the issues set before him, but emotionally moved by them. A consideration of *Asalto nocturno* reveals quite clearly how Sastre employed dramatic technique in order to achieve this delicate balance.

An analysis of the play's first two scenes shows that, far from being epic, they are largely naturalistic in character. Scene One, for example, located in Professor Marcelo Graffi's house in a district of New York, has a setting which contains numerous items of furniture and suggests, in effect, a real room. Thus, when Graffi first appears, he lights a lamp and then takes a book from the many within reach:

> ... *El profesor enciende la luz de una lámpara discreta y se despoja de un abrigo ligero* ... *Coge algún libro que está a mano — desde cualquier sitio de la habitación hay libros a mano* ...   (p.163)

> ... *The Professor lights a small lamp and takes off his lightweight overcoat* ... *He picks up a book that is within reach — in every part of the room there are books within reach* ...

Just afterwards, Graffi takes a glass and a bottle from a cupboard:

> *Abre un mueblecito y saca de él una botella y una copa* ...   (p.163)

> *He opens a small cupboard and takes out a bottle and a glass* ...

Through the evocation of a real room and, in conjunction with it, the introduction of a character who, on entering, behaves in a way we immediately recognize and can identify with, Sastre creates the illusion of the stage as life and thus immediately involves the audience in the stage action.

Secondly, through the portrayal of strong emotion — both Graffi's and the servant's — Sastre engages his audience even more deeply. From the moment of his first appearance, Graffi is shown to be in a state of fear, which is communicated to us by his movements, his voice and his words. Thus, the glass trembles in his hand, he wipes his brow, his voice shakes, and he refers with fear to the fact that his life is in danger. His fear is, moreover, communicated to his servant, Margarita, as the following exchange suggests:

> PROFESOR: Es preferible. Tengo que ofrecer la menor resistencia, Margarita. No lo entiende, ¿verdad? *(Un silencio. Enciende, tembloroso, un cigarillo.)* Tengo . . ., tengo razones para hacerlo. Pero además es que me ahogaría si todo estuviera tan cerradaa . . . Abra esa ventana, por favor . . . Hace calor aquí. (MARGARITA, *asustada, vacila.*) Hágame caso, se lo ruego. (MARGARITA *abre y mira con terror hacia la noche.*)
> MARGARITA *(Grita)*: ¡Me da miedo! ¡Permítame que cierre, profesor Graffi! (p.170)

> PROFESSOR: It's better. The least resistance, the better, Margarita. You don't understand, do you? *(Silence. Trembling, he lights a cigarette.)* I've . . ., I've got my reasons for doing it. In any case, I'd suffocate if everything were closed . . . Open that window, please . . . It's so hot in here. (MARGARITA *is frightened and hesitates.*) Do what I say, I beg of you. (MARGARITA *opens the window and looks out into the darkness fearfully.*)
> MARGARITA *(crying out)*: It frightens me! Let me close it, Professor Graffi!

Throughout the scene the fears of the characters become greater and the atmosphere of terror is further underlined by sounds from outside the house:

> *Un silencio. Se oye a lo lejos la sirena de un barco. Es como un prolongado lamento . . .* (p.168)

> *A pause. The siren of a boat is heard in the distance. It is like a long lament . . .*

By the time the assassin finally arrives, announcing himself with a loud knocking on the door, his still, faceless form outlined ominously in the doorway when Graffi opens the door, Sastre has intensified the mood of fear to the point where the theatre audience is able to share Graffi's terror at the prospect of imminent annihilation. Far from distancing the spectator, Sastre deliberately involves him in order to make him feel to the full, as Graffi feels it, the terror of the unseen threat, the invisible assassin.

For most of Scene Two, as the murderer is questioned by the police, the technique is similar, but then, as Stephen Orkin prepares to play to Graffi's widow a tape of her husband's last message, Sastre brilliantly moves from audience involvement to alienation. The sense of distancing is achieved firstly by the obliteration of the naturalistic stage picture and the transformation of Stephen Orkin from someone involved in the events we have been witnessing to someone who now begins to talk about them, directly addressing the audience:

> *. . . Empieza a hacerse el oscuro sobre las demás figuras y, por fin, sólo la de* ORKIN *queda iluminada. Entonces retira la mano del resorte, enciende un cigarillo y se dirige al público.* (p.182)

... The other figures fade into darkness and finally only the figure of ORKIN
remains lit. He withdraws his hand from the start-button, lights a cigarette and
addresses the audience.

The key factor here is, firstly, Orkin's shift of position in relation to the
murder of Graffi, for suddenly he advances from the time in which he was
investigating the case to a time in which the investigation has been
completed and he is looking back, no longer the involved detective but the
much more detached commentator. Similarly, as far as we, the spectators of
the play, are concerned, our own identification and involvement with the
Graffi affair, so marked in Scene One, is rudely disrupted, and we are
made, in consequence of Orkin's shift of position, to observe that affair in a
much more objective way. Furthermore, Orkin's address to the audience
does more than put the Graffi affair at a distance: it also places it within the
context of world events of that time which are recounted to us in a factual
manner:

Estamos en 1956 y se respira un mal ambiente.

....

Guerra de nervios y desembarco anglofrancés en
                                        [Suez. Bombardean Port Said.

....

Se derrama sangre en Hungría. Y los partidos comunistas
viven las consecuencias de la muerte de Stalin y
                                        [del XX Congreso.   (p.183)

We are in 1956 and the air one breathes is bad.

....

A war of nerves and the British and the French
                [invade Suez, bombarding Port Said.

....

Bloodshed in Hungary. And the Communist parties
suffer the consequences of the death of Stalin and
                [of the twentieth Congress.

Having felt with Marcelo Graffi the full terror of imminent extinction, our
emotional reaction to violence and danger is transformed into an
intellectual perception of violence as an integral part of the history of the
twentieth century.[27]

This pattern of involvement and detachment is sustained very effectively
throughout the play. Scene Three, for example, focusing on the assassin,
Harry Müller, and his wife, Ana, presents him to us not as the faceless
murderer, but as a man fond of his wife, nervous of the contract he is hired
to carry out, and anxious to begin a new life. Later in the same scene Ugo

Bosco discusses with Harry Müller the plan for Marcelo Graffi's murder as
a punishment for his own father's death, and his feelings of hatred and
vengeance are powerfully suggested:

> Es preciso que horas antes sienta la amenaza. ¡Que se dé cuenta de que va a
> morir! ¡Que le haga temblar el terror de lo que va a ocurrir! ¡Que se
> estremezca de pensar . . .!   (p.193)

> It is essential that he should feel the threat hours in advance. That he should
> know he is going to die! That the terror of what is going to happen should make
> him tremble! That he should shake with fear just by thinking about it . . .!

Here, as in Scene One, the spectator of the action, having been distanced
from it at the end of Scene Two, is drawn into it once more and made to
share the emotional conflicts and tensions of the characters. In total
contrast, Scene Four begins with Stephen Orkin again addressing the
theatre audience, taking us even further back in time to events that
preceded and led to Marcelo Graffi's murder, and once more placing those
events against a broader picture of world violence:

> *A telón corrido aparece el inspector* ORKIN *y se dirige al público.* (p.195)

> *When the curtain rises Inspector* ORKIN *appears and addresses the audience.*

In the course of the scene, though, immediately following Stephen Orkin's
discourse on the state of the world at the end of the Second World War, we
become the highly involved witnesses of the murder of Angelo Bosco by
Tonio Graffi, an event which is not only the source of Marcelo Graffi's
death on the orders of Angelo Bosco's son, Ugo, but which in its suggestion
of sheer terror is a precise emotional parallel to Marcelo Graffi's situation
in Scene One. Thus Angelo Bosco, seeking the forgiveness of Marcelo
Graffi for a crime committed in the past, expresses his fears of imminent
death:

> *Su voz ha tenido un acento de gran espanto.*
> *Ahora guarda silencio, como asustado de las palabras que acaba de*
> *pronunciar . . .*   (p.200)

> *The tone of his voice has suggested great fear.*
> *Now he is silent, as though frightened by the words he has just uttered . . .*

Similarly, the feelings of Marcelo Graffi and his wife, suddenly confronted
by a figure from their past, are projected with power and immediacy:

> MARY *mira a* MARCELO *con inquietud. . .* MARY *sigue con angustia sus*
> *palabras . . .*   (p.204)

> MARY *looks uneasily at* MARCELO . . . MARY follows his words with
> deep concern . . .

And the emotional graph of the scene reaches its peak when Tonio Graffi, confronting his old enemy, murders him in an adjoining room:

> ... *De pronto un grito ahogado, algo como:*
> VOZ DE ANGELO: ¡... por mi hijo ..., la paz! ¡Usted ...!
> *(Un gemido. El ruido de un cuerpo que rueda por los suelos.*
> MARY *ahoga un grito y se separa con horror de la puerta ...)*   (p.206)
>
> ... *Suddenly a stifled cry, something like:*
> THE VOICE OF ANGELO: ... for my son's sake, ... no more violence!
> You ...!
> *(A moan. The sound of a body hitting the floor.* MARY *stifles a cry and moves away from the door in horror ...)*

The effect of Sastre's constant switching from close-up to distance, from specific to general, and present to past, is undoubtedly disconcerting. In the first place, it keeps us on our toes, for after the first occasion — Scene Two — on which our involvement with the characters is unexpectedly destroyed, we are never again sure of our own position in relation to the stage action. Secondly, having been made aware of the broader world of violence in which the Graffi-Bosco feud is set, we are made not merely to react emotionally to violence but to think about it in relation both to ourselves and other men — to ponder on its causes and its consequences. And thirdly, though we are made to think, we are never allowed merely to think, for the technique of the play, combining or alternating involvement and distancing, constantly makes us feel the full horror of violence and tyranny. The ending of the play illustrates the point well. Orkin, having completed his account of the investigation of the Graffi case, refers again to the broader picture:

> Por lo demás, la gran historia continúa. Las noticias de los periódicos de hoy nos hablan de una posible suspensión de las pruebas atómicas ... (p.236)
>
> As for the rest, the flow of history continues. The newspapers inform us at present of a possible suspension of atomic tests.

As the action comes to an end, Orkin, in his role as narrator, reinforces a factual, objective level. On the other hand, he admits that he is filled with terror at the prospect of world destruction and looks anxiously at the newspaper in search of reassurance. The distanced narrator is thus simultaneously the involved participant. Orkin feels precisely that terror experienced by Marcelo Graffi in the play's first scene. And what is true of him is also, of course, true of us. The ending of the play, in strict accordance with Sastre's desire to avoid effects of excessive alienation, obliges us not merely to think about the way in which we are threatened but also to feel it.

Alfonso Sastre's theatre, as this discussion has attempted to show, is both serious in terms of its aims and striking in terms of its achievement. As far as Sastre's preoccupations are concerned, he has to be considered against the background of the particular Spanish political situation of the years 1939 to 1975, a situation of repression and tyranny from which his 'committed' theatre springs directly. On the other hand, Sastre is clearly more than a Spanish dramatist and his plays consistently have a broader dimension, as in Buero Vallejo's case, in consequence of which the particular violence assumes universal proportions, and its subject becomes not Spanish man but man in general. Secondly, the earnestness and vitality of Sastre's viewpoints are accompanied by a constant search for a means, an instrument, a technique whereby that viewpoint may be communicated. An examination of the three plays considered here reveals, in short, a conclusion which can be applied to the whole of Sastre's theatre: the vitality of his ideology is accompanied by the vitality and boldness of his experiments in theatre technique. And in this respect, clearly, Sastre fully deserves to be grouped with the other major dramatists considered in the preceding pages.[28]

1   For studies of the theatre of Alfonso Sastre, see Farris Anderson, *Alfonso Sastre* (New York, 1971); F. Ruiz Ramón, *Historia del teatro español, II: Siglo XX* (4th ed.) (Madrid, 1980), 384-419; C.C. de Coster, 'Alfonso Sastre', *Tulane Drama Review,* V(1960), 121-32; D. Pérez Minik, *Teatro europeo contemporáneo* (Madrid, 1961), 399-406; G. Torrente Ballester, *Teatro español contemporáneo* (2nd ed.) (Madrid, 1968), 332-38; Victoria Urbano, *El teatro español y sus directrices contemporáneas* (Madrid, 1972), 210-15.

2   *Alfonso Sastre,* 84.

3   See 'Manifiesto del T.A.S.', in *Alfonso Sastre,* ed. José Monleón (Madrid, 1964).

4   See F. Ruiz Ramón, *Historia del teatro español, II* . . ., 387.

5   *Drama y sociedad* (Madrid, 1956).

6   *Anatomía del realismo* (Barcelona, 1965).

7   In this respect see the introduction by Farris Anderson to *Alfonso Sastre: Escuadra hacia la muerte; La mordaza* (Madrid, 1975), 22.

8   F. Ruiz Ramón, *Historia del teatro español, II* . . ., has made the point very strongly. See 411-19. Of the plays in question *El camarada oscuro,* together with *Askatasuna!* and *Análisis espectral de un comando al servicio de la revolución proletaria (Ghostly Analysis of a Commando in the Service of the Proletarian Revolution),* has appeared in *Teatro político de Alfonso Sastre* (Donostia, 1979).

9   *Alfonso Sastre,* 117.

10 'Alfonso Sastre y las trágicas preguntas', *Alcalá,* 25 March, 1953.

11 Sastre's note for the first performance of the play. See too J.E. Aragonés, 'El teatro profundizado de Alfonso Sastre', *Punta Europa,* VIII (1963), 28.

12 Page references are to the edition by Farris Anderson, see note 7. Anderson's introduction contains useful and perceptive observations. See too A.M. Pasquariello, 'Alfonso Sastre y *Escuadra hacia la muerte*', *Hispanófila*, 15 (1962), 57-63; Juan Villegas, 'La sustancia metafísica de la tragedia y su función social: *Escuadra hacia la muerte* de Alfonso Sastre', *Symposium*, XXI (1967), 255-63; Leonard C. Pronko, 'The Revolutionary Theater of Alfonso Sastre', *Tulane Drama Review*, V (1960).

13 Most critics have concentrated on discussion of the play's themes, or on the the relationship of *Escuadra hacia la muerte* to the rest of Sastre's theatre. There is some consideration of the play's dramatic technique in Farris Anderson's introduction to his edition of the play, 36-40.

14 It is worth recalling in this respect that in 1950, just a few years before the composition of *Escuadra hacia la muerte*, Sastre had proposed producing, as part of the programme of the Teatro de Agitación Social, foreign plays which included those of the German expressionist dramatist, Ernst Toller.

15 *Alfonso Sastre, Obras completas*, preface by Domingo Pérez-Minik, notes by Alfonso Sastre (Madrid, 1967).

16 Sastre has himself commented on his use of the Dominici case in *Obras completas*, 284-85.

17 In this respect see Farris Anderson, *Alfonso Sastre*, 96-100, and the introduction to his edition of the play, see note 7.

18 All page references are to the edition by Farris Anderson to which reference has already been made.

19 The similarities and differences between the two plays are discussed in some detail by Farris Anderson in the introduction to his edition of the play, 40-52.

20 As in the case of *Escuadra hacia la muerte*, the dramatic technique of *La mordaza* has been almost entirely neglected.

21 See 'Primeras notas para un encuentro con Bertolt Brecht', in *Primer acto*, 13(1960).

22 Farris Anderson, *Alfonso Sastre*, 117.

23 Farris Anderson, *Alfonso Sastre*, 119. Chapter 7 of Anderson's study contains useful comments on Brechtian epic theatre but has very little to say on *Asalto nocturno*. F. Ruiz Ramón, *Historia del teatro español, II . . .*, 405-6, has some interesting observations on *Asalto nocturno* and discusses the third phase of Sastre's drama in some detail. See 411-19.

24 See 'Tres obras de un autor revolucionario', in *Alfonso Sastre: Cargamento de sueños, Prológo patético, Asalto nocturno* (Madrid, 1964).

25 F. Ruiz Ramón, *Historia del teatro español, II . . .*, 406, makes the very pertinent point that in *Asalto nocturno* Sastre has used in a very original manner Greek tragedy and Brechtian epic theatre — which is to say, the two apparently opposing modes of theatre which demand, respectively, emotional involvement and alienation.

26 All page references are to the text in *Alfonso Sastre: Guillermo Tell tiene los ojos tristes, Muerte en el barrio, Asalto nocturno* (Madrid, 1978).

27 See note 25 above.

28 The general critical neglect of Sastre's theatre is both surprising and unjustified. Given the fact that, in consequence of the Spanish political situation between 1939 and 1975, Sastre's plays had significantly less exposure than those of Buero Vallejo, the lack of critical attention is, perhaps, understandable as far as Spanish critics are concerned. On the other hand, few critics outside Spain have given Sastre's work the attention it deserves.

Conclusion

The preceding pages have concentrated very largely on the work of five dramatists — Valle-Inclán, Lorca, Alberti, Buero Vallejo and Sastre — and for the most part on two broad periods in the history of twentieth-century Spanish theatre: 1900 to the end of the Civil War in 1939; and the post-Civil War years to the death of Franco in 1975. If little has been said about the current decade, it is merely because little of significance has happened. What conclusion can be reached, then, about the five dramatists in question in relation to (a) the originality and merit of their dramatic work, and (b) its importance in European drama? And what opinion can be formed of Spanish theatre as a whole in the twentieth century?

As far as the general picture is concerned, the pattern has remained constant throughout the period under discussion. Since the turn of the century the theatre-going public has consisted very largely of the middle classes who for the most part have wanted to be entertained rather than be made to think. To that extent audiences have, in effect, shaped the kind of theatre that has emerged: a theatre characterized by its lack of true seriousness, its conventionality of themes and form, and its dedication to material profit. As for dramatists, those who have sought success — in terms of public acclaim and financial reward — have been prepared to sacrifice originality to conformity, or at least to compromise. In the early years of the century the process is exemplified by Jacinto Benavente, whose initial biting of the hand that fed him quickly became passive acquiescence. After the Civil War, dramatists such as José María Pemán, Joaquín Calvo Sotelo and Víctor Ruiz de Iriarte illustrate the continuation of the process, all of them writing well-made plays mostly devoid of either social criticism or speculation on human existence. And today the situation remains virtually unchanged, for a visit to Madrid or Barcelona will reveal the predominance of light comedies, musicals and — a recent development — shows of a sexually titillating nature, patronized almost exlusively by the middle classes.

In this respect Spain is not, of course, essentially different from most Western European countries, and the pattern described above is certainly true of the British commercial theatre, exemplified by the West End. If, for example, an attempt is made to account for the emergence of 'significant' plays at a given time in the British theatre, it quickly becomes clear that they are very often associated with non-commercial organizations — using the term in a broad sense — and subsidized institutions. Thus, John Obsborne's

Look Back in Anger, initiating a new wave of serious, thought-provoking plays in the late fifties and early sixties, made its appearance at the Royal Court Theatre under the intelligent and committed direction of George Devine. Today, the new work of dramatists such as Howard Brenton and David Hare is often commissioned by the National Theatre, proving the point that only in an atmosphere of largely economic freedom can writers dare to ignore the pressures placed upon them by the demands of theatre impresarios, themselves subservient to the god, money. As far as Spain is concerned, such freedom has been difficult to come by, certainly to the extent enjoyed by British writers. Only during the Second Spanish Republic, in the years immediately preceding the Civil War, did Spanish writers and artists have the opportunity to express themselves freely, and Lorca, for one, availed himself of it. For the most part, Spanish dramatists of true merit and importance have in one way or another been obliged to seek their own freedom: by rebelling against the system, as in Valle-Inclán's case; or by cunningly working within it, as in the case of Buero Vallejo; or even by writing plays which were unlikely to be performed, a course of action adopted by Alfonso Sastre. Spanish dramatists of real note are thus men of considerable courage and independence, not to mention talent.

The achievement of Ramón del Valle-Inclán is by any standards quite remarkable — firstly, of course, on account of the originality and the visionary, forward-looking character of his theatre; and secondly, because his work was realized very largely in ignorance of developments taking place in the theatre outside Spain. As has been suggested, Valle-Inclán opposed almost from the outset the commercialism, the superficiality and the lack of imagination of the Spanish theatre of his time, so much so that he wrote many of his plays to be read rather than performed. In doing so, he achieved, of course, the artistic freedom which allowed him to experiment, and the whole of his dramatic output bears witness to this fact. The *Comedias bárbaras,* for example, two of which were written in the first decade of the century, reveal clearly Valle-Inclán's revolutionary conception of theatre: his fervent rejection of Naturalism in favour of an approach to drama based on the close interdependence and interaction of its different elements of action, scenery, costume, movement, lighting and speech. In short, Valle-Inclán's intuitive efforts to create in Spain a new kind of theatre paralleled the work of such visionaries as Adolph Appia and Edward Gordon Craig in other European countries. Moreover, Valle's influence in this particular area on the other Spanish dramatists of significance, such as Lorca and Alberti, was probably considerable, even if at the same time they responded more directly to European influences.

In addition to the above, Valle-Inclán's major contribution to twentieth-century Spanish theatre, was, of course, *esperpentismo*. The concern here is not so much with the technique of drama as with the more fundamental question of the perspective from which the dramatist views the world, and in this respect Valle-Inclán's observations both in *Luces de Bohemia* and in *Los cuernos de Don Friolera* must be amongst the most interesting and important in twentieth-century theatre in general. The concept of grotesque distortion, of men and women stripped of tragic grandeur even though their plight be tragic, of life presented as a comic, mocking and absurd spectacle, is so central to much of theatre of our time. It is as though we are describing here the essential features of the work of Ionesco, Beckett, Pinter, Arrabal and others, when in reality this theatre of the absurd is the work of a Spaniard in the early 1920s, more than thirty years before the celebrated Absurdists were writing their plays. To what extent Valle-Inclán's theory and practice directly affected later European dramatists, other than Arrabal, is questionable, but no one can deny either the visionary nature of Valle's ideas or their highly imaginative expression in his plays. *Luces de Bohemia, Los cuernos de Don Friolera* and *Divinas palabras (Divine Words)* merit a place in the repetoire of any self-respecting national theatre.

As in Valle-Inclán's case, Lorca's approach to dramatic art was synonymous with his rejection of the commercial theatre of the 1920s and 30s, dominated still by those same dramatists — Benavente, the Quintero brothers, and others — against whom Valle-Inclán had himself rebelled. From his very first play, *El maleficio de la mariposa* with its insect characters, Lorca followed Valle in setting his face against Naturalism. In terms of dramatic style and technique, the whole of his theatre reveals his constant desire to seek new and arresting non-naturalistic ways of expressing the issues that preoccupied him most. The tradition of puppet-theatre proved in this respect to be a fertile source of inspiration, and in *Los títeres de Cachiporra* and *El retablillo de Don Cristóbal* Lorca employs its broad effects both to expose human views and weaknesses and to enable us to laugh at them. Farce too was an effective, non-naturalistic vehicle, and in such contrasting pieces as *La zapatera prodigiosa* and *El amor de Don Perlimplín* Lorca reveals its capacity to express serious themes and his own ability to see in farce the darker shadows of tragedy. In these comic plays there is a strong Spanish influence, especially that of Golden Age drama, but Lorca is also very much a European dramatist and the impact of European theatre movements can be discerned in most of his work. Surrealism, given that in Buñuel and Dalí it had its Spanish champions, is one European movement that shaped the writing of both *Así que pasen cinco años* and *El público,* on the one hand in their power to shock, on the other in their expression of the inner lives of the characters. And Symbolism, its imprint strong throughout Lorca's theatre and achieving its finest expression in the rural tragedies, enabled Lorca to suggest the universal truths, forces and impulses that lie beneath the surface appearance of human existence. To this extent, then, the European tradition is highly significant in relation to Lorca's theatre, but in absorbing it and adapting it so masterfully to his own ends, his own contribution to the theatre of Europe is unquestionably very great. In terms of technique Lorca put into practice the ideas on theatre performance, already mentioned in connection with Edward Gordon Craig, with which he was directly familiar. Fusing the different aspects of theatre, be the work a farce or a tragedy, he achieved that mixture and synthesis of art forms which is so recognizably 'modern' and which we now accept as the norm. It is this modernity which in part explains the appeal of Lorca outside Spain.

Technique, though, cannot be divorced from content, and Lorca's success and importance as a dramatist lie as well in the universality of his themes. In one respect the issues of all his plays are those which obsessed him personally, born of his own experience and anguish: the concern with instinct and the individual's freedom to express his feelings; the repression of the latter by convention and tradition; the frustration and destruction wrought by passing time; and the terror and inevitability of death. But if they were issues deeply felt by Lorca, they are also concerns which affect us all and which therefore have an inbuilt universality. Lorca's particular genius lies, firstly, in his response as an individual to the central problems of human existence, and, secondly, in his capacity as a writer to express that response in a style and a language which other human beings can recognize and be moved by. The broad appeal of Lorca's theatre can thus be explained in terms of both content and form. His plays often have, clearly, the timeless quality of myth, the ability to encapsulate the essential issues of human experience. The fact that no one else followed in his footsteps is explained by the simple fact that no one else had the necessary gifts to do so.

Rafael Alberti, is, as a dramatist, less well-known than either Valle-Inclán or Lorca, yet his achievement is considerable. Sharing with them a detestation of the intellectual sterility and the lack of innovation of the commercial theatre, Alberti set out to remedy such deficiencies in his own plays. Here, then, is another dramatist who deliberately rejected out-dated Naturalism in favour of a more imaginative and expressive technique, often influenced by the visual arts, and in this respect Alberti's models were both Spanish and European in general. His acquaintance with the Residencia de Estudiantes in Madrid brought him into contact with European developments in literature, theatre, ballet and cinema and inspired him to develop that fluid style of theatre already mentioned in connection with Valle-Inclán and Lorca. Alberti thus contributed greatly to the modernization of dramatic technique in Spain. Furthermore, mention must be made of the direct influence on Alberti of Brecht, and consequently of Alberti's contribution to the development of epic theatre in Spain, notably through *Noche de guerra en el Museo del Prado*. As well as this, Alberti came into contact at a fairly early stage in his dramatic career with the political theatre of Erwin Piscator and with the possibilities of a politically commited theatre. The European dimension of Alberti's work is thus of great importance, but it is essential also to recognize his debt to the Spanish dramatic tradition: to Lorca and Valle-Inclán, of course, but also to the puppet-plays, the farces and, in the case of *El hombre deshabitado*, to the religious drama of the Golden Age.

As far as subject matter is concerned, Alberti's theatre is designed to make its audience think: firstly, about the political situation of the Spain of the 1930s; and secondly, about the issues confronting man in general. In an overtly propagandist play such as *Radio Sevilla* Alberti's primary purpose is to mock the Fascists and rouse Republican supporters, but even here the theme of the inhumanity and hypocrisy of men in general is clear enough. It is developed more strongly in the full-length play, *El adefesio,* written after the Civil War, and a consistent technique of grotesque distortion, highly reminiscent of Valle-Inclán, allows Alberti here to portray human beings as predatory monsters. What is especially striking about both plays is his delicate balancing of intellectual and emotional impact. On the one hand, effects of distancing oblige the spectator to think about the events placed before him; on the other, those events also involve him emotionally, for they elicit strong reactions. The process is illustrated perfectly in *Noche de guerra en el Museo del Prado* where historical perspective and grotesque distortion compel the spectator to judge the spectacle of man's inhumanity to man, while highly emotional episodes of an expressionist character allow him to feel the anguish of the characters on stage. Alberti can be said, in short, to have borrowed from European dramatists — especially Brecht and Piscator — the techniques whereby he could express more forcefully the issues which preoccupied him most. Certainly, his own theatre possesses a unique voice and includes some of the most original and moving plays written in the twentieth century.

The drama of Antonio Buero Vallejo takes us into a different era and set of circumstances as far as theatre in Spain is concerned: the years of the Franco dictatorship, a time in which the dramatist was confronted by increasing limitations in producing a body of work whose importance is two-fold. Firstly, following Valle-Inclán, Lorca and Alberti, he is an experimenter and innovator, strongly opposed to the dull, unexciting and well-worn formulae of the commercial theatre. Secondly, he is an essentially serious dramatist in terms of theme, questioning the moral and social problems of post-Civil War Spain. In contrast to a writer such as Alberti, Buero does not, though, adopt an open, antagonistic stance. Instead, he works within the system to which he is opposed, often writing obliquely in order to communicate his message.

In terms of dramatic method and technique, Buero Vallejo has been strongly influenced by a number of European dramatists, and his plays reveal at different times the imprint of such significant figures as Ibsen, Pirandello and Brecht. *Historia de una escalera* and *En la ardiente oscuridad* both reveal, for example, the influence of Ibsen, for the apparent realism of the action and the characters can be seen on closer examination, as in Ibsen's *The Doll's House*, to have a much deeper, broader, symbolic significance. In contrast, *Las Meninas* shows Buero's masterly use of a wide range of Brechtian distancing techniques, and the same is true of the even more technically dazzling play, *El sueño de la razón*. Again, such plays as *La doble historia del doctor Valmy* and *El tragaluz* are clearly Pirandellian in influence, designed through the use to which the stage is put to confuse in our own mind the nature of illusion and reality in order to make us ponder on their relationship in our own lives. It is undoubtedly true to say that in terms of dramatic technique Buero Vallejo is one of the most inventive Spanish dramatists of the twentieth century.

Buero is, in addition, a highly intellectual dramatist who is constantly concerned with examining both the society in which he lives and the nature of man in general. In the plays mentioned above the social and moral questions affecting post-Civil War Spain are closely analyzed, be it more or less directly, as in *Historia de una escalera*, or indirectly, through historical parallels, as in *Las meninas* and *El sueño de la razón*. At the same time, all these plays have man in general at their very centre, and examine the nature of his existence and destiny. It is therefore no accident that Buero should be so interested in tragic drama and that he should present human beings as the victims of a chaotic and hostile universe, though it must be said that the pessimism implicit in such a view does not obliterate in these plays the hope for man's ultimate salvation. There can be no doubting, then, either the seriousness of purpose or the technical innovation of Buero Vallejo's theatre, and he remains one of the most important and interesting figures in Spanish drama since 1950. His considerable qualities are, though, somewhat offset by the rather flat, unpoetic character of his language, a weakness highlighted by comparison with Valle-Inclán, Lorca and Alberti.

In contrast to Buero Vallejo, Alfonso Sastre has refused to work cunningly and subversively within the Franco dictatorship. He has, instead, opposed and confronted it, and written his plays as a form of protest, in consequence of which many of them have been forbidden in Spain. It is hardly surprising, given the political character of Sastre's plays, that he should have been strongly influenced by European political theatre, notably by that of Brecht whose theoretical writings Sastre began to study around 1960 and whose ideas he has put into practice in many subsequent plays. His contribution to the development of epic theatre in Spain has therefore, like Buero's, been significant, though it is important to recognize too that Sastre's plays are in certain respects very different from those of Brecht. In particular, argumentation is less important for Sastre than the exposure of his audiences to images of revolution that will inspire them to wish to transform society. In this sense Sastre's theatre is essentially his own, a modified form of epic, and one of its principal characteristics, which cannot fail to impress, is its burning intensity. At the same time, Sastre's strongly felt committment does not mean that his plays are merely about Spain or that they are in any way undisciplined. As to the first point, the ultimate concern of Sastre's drama is man, and his plays constantly relate man both to the society in which he finds himself and to human existence as a whole. As to the second point, plays like *Escuadra hacia la muerte* and *Asalto nocturno* are impressive not merely for what they have to say but also for the way in which they say it — their dramatic technique highly effective in relation to the ideas they have to communicate. Like his view of the purpose and nature of theatre, Sastre's method is constantly evolving and changing. In the second half of the century he is, with Buero Vallejo, the most significant figure in Spanish theatre.

This study of twentieth-century Spanish drama has attempted to isolate those dramatists who, judged by content and form, seem to be the most important. On both counts Valle-Inclán, Lorca, Alberti, Buero Vallejo and Sastre merit special attention, though others, like Max Aub, clearly deserve more than they have been given. All five dramatists studied here have made a notable contribution to Spanish theatre by giving it a broader, European character, and some of them, in particular Valle-Inclán and Lorca, have made an impact on European theatre itself. In a final analysis it is probably true to say that Lorca remains the best-known and the most important modern Spanish dramatist, for his work, though so Spanish in many respects, has a true universality, and his technical facility is remarkable both for its variety and quality. But all five dramatists have invested the Spanish theatre with a high degree of seriousness and artistry which merit recognition wherever plays are performed.

Selected Bibliography

A. General

Borel, J.P. *El teatro de lo imposible*, translated by G. Torrente Ballester (Madrid, 1966).

Brown, G.G. *The Twentieth Century. A Literary History of Spain*, Vol. 6. ed. R.O. Jones (London 1972).

Craig, Edward Gordon. *The Art of the Theatre* (London, 1980).

Díez-Canedo, E. *Artículos de crítica teatral: el teatro español de 1914 a 1936*, 4 vols. (Mexico, 1968).

Esslin, M. *The Theatre of the Absurd* (revised ed.) (London, 1969).

García Lorenzo, L. *Documentos sobre el teatro español contemporáneo* (Madrid, 1982).

García Pavón, F. *Teatro social en España* (Madrid, 1962).

Gaskell, R. *Drama and Reality: the European Theatre since Ibsen* (London, 1972).

Gorelik, M. *New Theatres for Old* (London, 1940).

Guerrero Zamora, J. *Historia del teatro contemporáneo*, 4 vols. (Barcelona, 1967).

Marqueríe, A. *Veinte años de teatro en España* (Madrid, 1959).

Pérez Minik, D. *Teatro europeo contemporáneo: su libertad y compromisos* (Madrid, 1961).

Rodríguez Alcalde, L. *Teatro español contemporáneo* (Madrid, 1973).

Ruiz Ramón, F. *Historia del teatro español, II: Siglo XX* (4th ed.) (Madrid, 1980).

Styan, J.L. *Modern Drama in Theory and Practice, II, Symbolism, Surrealism and the Absurd* (Cambridge, 1981).

Modern Drama in Theory and Practice, III, Expressionism and Epic Theatre (Cambridge, 1981).

Torrente Ballester, G. *Teatro español contemporáneo* (2nd ed.) (Madrid, 1968).

Urbano, Victoria. *El teatro español y sus directrices contemporáneas* (Madrid, 1972).

Worth, Katherine. *The Irish Drama of Europe from Yeats to Beckett* (London, 1978).

B. Individual
RAMÓN DEL VALLE-INCLÁN

Alberich, J.M. 'Cara de plata, fuera de serie', *Bulletin of Hispanic Studies*, XLV, (1968), 299-308.

Bermejo Marcos, M. *Valle-Inclán: Introducción a su obra* (Salamanca, 1971).

Brooks, J.L. 'Valle-Inclán and the Esperpento', *Bulletin of Hispanic Studies*, XXXIII (1956), 152-64.

'Los dramas de Valle-Inclán', in *Estudios dedicados a Menéndez Pidal*, (Madrid: Centro Superior de Investigaciones Científicas, 1957), 177-98.

Buero Vallejo, A. *Tres maestros ante el público (Valle-Inclán, Velázquez, Lorca)* (Madrid, 1973).

Cardona, R. (With Zahareas, A.N.). *Visión del esperpento* (Madrid, 1970).

'*Los cuernos de Don Friolera:* estructura y sentido', in *Ramón del Valle-Inclán. An Appraisal of His Life and Works*, ed. A. N. Zahareas (New York, 1968), 636-71.

Dagum, D.E. 'Una incursión: *Divinas palabras* de Valle-Inclán', *Cuadernos Americanos*, CLXX, (1970), 205-23.

Edwards, G. 'Valle-Inclán and the New Art of the Theatre', *Neophilologus*, LXVIII (1984).

'*The Comedias bárbaras:* Valle-Inclán and the Symbolist Theatre', *'Bulletin of Hispanic Studies*, LX, (1983), 293-303.

Gatti, J.F. 'El sentido de *Los cuernos de don Friolera'*, in *Ramón María del Valle-Inclán* (Universidad Nacional de la Plata, 1967), 298-313.

Gillespie, G. (With Zahareas, A.N.) 'Luces de Bohemia: tragedia y esperpento', in *Ramón del Valle-Inclán: An Appraisal...*, 615-21.

Gómez Marín, J.A. *La idea de sociedad en Valle-Inclán* (Madrid, 1967).

González, P.A. 'Los cuernos de Don Friolera', *La Torre*, II, (1954), 45-54.

Greenfield, S. '*La reina castiza* and the Esthetics of Deformation', in *Ramón del Valle-Inclán: An Appraisal...*, 541-52.

Herrero, J. 'La sátira del honor en los esperpentos', in *Ramón del Valle-Inclán: An Appraisal...*, 672-85.

Lyon, J. 'Valle-Inclán and the Art of the Theatre', *Bulletin of Hispanic Studies*, XLVI, (1969), 132-52.

Lyon, J. *The Theatre of Valle-Inclán* (Cambridge, 1983).

March, María Eugenia. *Forma e idea de los esperpentos de Valle-Inclán* (Madrid, 1969).

Matilla, A. '*Las comedias bárbaras:* una sola obra dramática', in *Ramón del Valle-Inclán: An Appraisal...*, 289-316.

Las 'Comedias bárbaras'. Historicismo y expresionismo (Salamanca, 1972).

Phillips, A.W. 'Sobre *Luces de Bohemia* y su realidad literaria', in *Ramón del Valle-Inclán: An Appraisal...*, 601-11.

Risco, Antonio. *La estética del Valle-Inclán en los esperpentos y en 'El ruedo ibérico'* (Madrid, 1966).

Salper de Tortella, R. 'Don Juan Manuel Montenegro: the Fall of a King', in *Ramón del Valle-Inclán: An Appraisal...*, 317-32.

Sánchez, R. 'Gordon Craig y Valle-Inclán', *Revista de Occidente*, 4, (1976), 27-37.

Smith, Verity. *Ramón del Valle-Inclán* (New York, 1973).

Speratti-Piñero. 'La farsa de *La cabeza del dragón*, pre-esperpento', in *Ramón del Valle-Inclán: An Appraisal...*, 374-85.

Zahareas, A.N. ed. *Ramón del Valle-Inclán. An Appraisal of His Life and Works* (New York, 1968).

'Friolera: el héroe visto con "la perspectiva de la ribera"', in *Ramón del Valle-Inclán: An Appraisal...*, 630-5.

Zamora Vicente, A. *La realidad esperpéntica. (Aproximación a 'Luces de Bohemia')* (Madrid, 1969).

FEDERICO GARCÍA LORCA

Adams, Mildred. *García Lorca: Playwright and Poet* (New York, 1977).

Alberich, J.M. 'El erotismo femenino en el teatro de García Lorca', *Papeles de Son Armadans,* XXXIX, (1965), 9-36.

Allen, R.C. *Psyche and Symbol in the Theatre of Federico García Lorca* (Austin and London, 1974).

The Symbolic World of Federico García Lorca (University of New Mexico Press, 1972).

Babín, María Teresa. 'García Lorca, poeta del teatro', *Asomante,* IV, (1948), 48-57.

Estudios lorquianos (Puerto Rico, 1976).

Barnes, Robert. 'The Fusion of Poetry and Drama in *Blood Wedding', Modern Drama,* II, (1960), 395-402.

Berenguer Carisomo, A. *Las máscaras de Federico García Lorca* (Buenos Aires, 1969).

Busette, C. *Obra dramática de García Lorca: Estudio de su configuración* (New York, 1971).

Byrd, Susanne. *'La Barraca' and the Spanish National Theatre* (New York, 1975).

Cannon, C. 'The Imagery of Lorca's *Yerma', Modern Language Quarterly,* XXI (1960), 122-30.

'Yerma as Tragedy', *Symposium,* XVI, (1962), 82-93.

Cano, J.L. 'De *El maleficio* a *Mariana Pineda', Cuadernos Americanos,* XXIII (1962), 201-13.

Carrier, W. 'Poetry in the Drama of Lorca', *Drama Survey,* II, (1963), 297-304.

Correa, G. 'Honor, Blood and Poetry in *Yerma', Tulane Drama Review,* VII (1962), 96-110.

La poesia mítica de Federico García Lorca, (2nd ed.) (Madrid, 1975).

Devoto, D. *'Doña Rosita la soltera:* estructura y fuentes', *Bulletin Hispanique,* LXIX, (1967), 407-40.

Doménech, R. *'La casa de Bernarda Alba', Primer Acto,* L (1963), 14-16.

'A propósito de *Mariana Pineda', Cuadernos Hispanoamericanos,* LXX, (1967), 608-13.

Durán, M. 'El surrealsimo en el teatro de Lorca y Alberti', *Hispanófila,* (1957), 61-66.

Lorca: A Collection of Critical Essays, ed. M. Durán (Englewood Cliffs, N.J., 1962).

Edwards, Gwynne. *Lorca: The Theatre Beneath the Sand* (London and Boston, 1980).

'Lorca and Buñuel: *Así que pasen cinco años* and *Un Chien andalou', García Lorca Review,* IX, (1981), 128-43.

Frazier, Brenda. *La mujer en el teatro de Federico García Lorca* (Madrid, 1973).

Gaskell, R. 'Theme and Form: Lorca's *Blood Wedding', Modern Drama,* V (1963), 431-39.

Greenfield, Summer M. 'Poetry and Stagecraft in *La casa de Bernarda Alba', Hispania,* XXXVIII, (1955), 456-61.

'The Problem of *Mariana Pineda' Massachusetts Review,* I, (1960), 751-63.

Guardia, Alfredo de la. *García Lorca: Persona y creación* (Buenos Aires, 1944).

Halliburton, C. Ll. 'García Lorca, the Tragedian: An Aristotelian Analysis of *Bodas de sangre', Revista de Estudios Hispánicos,* II (1968), 35-40.

Higginbotham, Virginia. 'Bernarda Alba — A Comic Character?', *Drama Survey,* VI, (1968), 258-65.

The Comic Spirit of Federico Garcia Lorca (Austin and London, 1976).

Honig, E. *Garcia Lorca* (New York, 1963).

'Lorca to Date', *Tulane Drama Review*, VII, (1962), 120-6.

Knight, R.G. 'Federico García Lorca's *Así que pasen cinco años'*, *Bulletin of Hispanic Studies*, XLIII, (1966), 32-46.

Laffranque, Marie. *Federico García Lorca* (Paris, 1966).

Lázaro Carreter, F. 'Apuntes sobre el teatro de García Lorca', *Papeles de Son Armadans*, XVIII, (1960), 9-33.

Lima, R. *The Theater of Garcia Lorca* (New York, 1963).

Lott, R. 'Tragedy of Unjust Barrenness', *Modern Drama*, VIII, (1965), 20-7.

Martínez, M. 'Realidad y símbolo en *La casa de Bernarda Alba'*, *Revista de Estudios Hispánicos*, IV, (1970), 55-66.

Monte, A. del. 'Il realismo di *La casa de Bernarda Alba'*, *Belfagor*, XX, (1965), 130-48.

Morla Lynch, C. *En España con Federico García Lorca: Páginas de un diario íntimo, 1928-36* (Madrid, 1958).

Morris, C.B. 'Lorca's Yerma: Wife without an Anchor', *Neophilologus*, LVI (1972), 285-97.

García Lorca: Bodas de sangre, Critical Guides to Spanish Texts (London, 1980).

Nadal, R.M. *Lorca's 'The Public'* (London, 1974).

Newberry, Wilma. 'Aesthetic Distance in *El público'*, *Hispanic Review*, XXXVII (1969), 276-96.

Oliver, W.I. 'Lorca: The Puppets and the Artist', *Tulane Drama Review*, VII (1962), 76-96.

'The Trouble with Lorca', *Modern Drama*, VII, (1964), 2-15.

Palley, J. 'Archetypal Symbols in *Bodas de sangre'*, *Hispania*, L, (1967), 74-9.

Ramsden, H. (ed.). *Federico García Lorca: Bodas de sangre* (Manchester, 1980).

Riley, E.C. 'Sobre *Bodas de sangre'*, *Clavileño*, VII, (1951), 8-12.

Rincón, C. *'Yerma* de Federico García Lorca: Ensayo de interpretación', *Beiträge zur Romanischen Philologie*, V, (1966), 66-99.

'La zapatera prodigiosa de Federico García Lorca', *Iberoromania*, IV (1970), 290-313.

Río, A. del. *Vida y obras de Federico García Lorca* (Zaragoza, 1952).

Rubia Barcia, J. 'El realismo "mágico" de *La casa de Bernarda Alba'*, *Revista Hispánica Moderna*, XXXI, (1965), 385-98.

Sánchez, R.G. *García Lorca: Estudio sobre su teatro* (Madrid, 1950).

Sharp, Thomas, F. 'The Mechanics of Lorca's Drama in *La casa de Bernarda Alba'*, *Hispania*, XLIV, (1961), 230-3.

Skloot, R. 'Theme and Image in Lorca's *Yerma'*, *Drama Survey*, V, (1966), 151-61.

Smoot, Jean J. *A Comparison of Plays by John Millington Synge and Federico García Lorca: The Poets and Time* (Madrid, 1978).

Sullivan, Patricia, L. 'The Mythic Tragedy of *Yerma'*, *Bulletin of Hispanic Studies*, LXIX, (1972), 265-78.

Touster, Eva K. 'Thematic Patterns in Lorca's *Blood Wedding'*, *Modern Drama*, VII, (1964), 16-27.

Valle, L.G. del. *La tragedia en el teatro de Unamuno, Valle-Inclán y Garcia Lorca* (New York, 1975).

Young, R.A. 'García Lorca's *Bernarda Alba:* A Microcosm of Spanish Culture', *Modern Languages*, L, (1969), 66-72.

Zdenek, J.M. 'La mujer y la frustración en las comedias de García Lorca', *Hispania,* XXXVIII, (1955), 67-9.

Zimbardo, R.A. 'The Mythic Pattern in Lorca's *Blood Wedding', Modern Drama,* X, (1968), 364-71.

Ziomeck, H. 'El simbolismo del blanco en *'La casa de Bernarda Alba* y en *La dama del alba', Symposium,* XXIV, (1970), 81-5.

Zuleta, Emilia de. 'Relación entre la poesía y el teatro de Lorca', in *Cinco poetas españoles* (Salinas, Guillén, Lorca, Alberti, Cernuda) (Madrid, 1971).

RAFAEL ALBERTI

Alberti, R. *La arboleda perdida* (Buenos Aires, 1959).

Beardsley, T.S. Jr. 'El sacramento desautorizado: *El hombre deshabitado* de Alberti y los autos sacramentales de Calderón', *Studia Iberia: Festschrift für Hans Flasche* (Bern and Munich, 1973), 93-104.

Berns, Gabriel. *The Lost Grove* (Berkeley and Los Angeles, 1976).

Cardwell, R. 'Rafael Alberti's *El hombre deshabitado', Ibero-romansch,* Munich, 122 II-33.

Couffon, C. *Rafael Alberti* (Paris, 1966).

Doménech, R. 'Introducción al teatro de Rafael Alberti', *Cuadernos Hispanoamericanos,* 259, (1972), 96-126.

León, María Teresa. *Memoria de la melancolia* (Buenos Aires, 1970).

Marrast, R. *Aspects du Théâtre de Rafael Alberti* (Paris, 1967), 29-31.

'Essai de bibliographie de Rafael Alberti', *Bulletin Hispanique,* LVII, (1955), 147-77.

'Essai de bibliographie de Rafael Alberti (addenda et corrigenda)', *Bulletin Hispanique,* LIX, (1957), 430-5.

'L'esthétique théâtrale de Rafael Alberti', *La mise en scène des oeuvres du passé,* ed. Jean Jacquet and André Veinstein (Paris, 1957).

'Le théâtre à Madrid pendant la guerre civile', *Le théâtre moderne: hommes et tendances,* ed. Jean Jaquot, (2nd ed.) (Paris, 1965).

'Situation du théâtre espagnol contemporain', *Théâtre Popularie,* XIII, (1955), 15-23.

McCarthy, J. 'The Republican Theatre During the Spanish Civil War: Rafael Alberti's *Numancia', Theatre Research International,* V. No. 3, (1980), 193-205.

Morris, C.B. *Rafael Alberti's 'Sobre los ángeles': Four Major themes* (Hull, 1966).

Popkin, Louise B. *The Theatre of Rafael Alberti* (London, 1975).

ANTONIO BUERO VALLEJO

Anderson, F. 'The Ironic Structure of *Historia de una escalera'*, *Kentucky Romance Quarterly*, XVIII, (1971), 223-36.

Dixon, V. 'The "Immersion-Effect" in the Plays of Antonio Buero Vallejo', *Themes in Drama*, II, (1980), 113-37.

Doménech, R. 'Notas sobre *El sueño de la razón'*, *Primer Acto*, 117, (1970). *El teatro de Buero Vallejo* (Madrid, 1973).

Dowd, Catherine Elizabeth. *Realismo transcendente en cuatro tragedias sociales de Antonio Buero Vallejo* (Valencia, 1974).

Fernández Santos, A. 'Una entrevista con Buero Vallejo sobre *El tragaluz'*, *Primer Acto*, 90, (1967), 4-15.

'Sobre *El sueño de la razón*. Una conversación con Antonio Buero Vallejo', *Primer Acto*, 117, (1970).

Giulano, W. *Buero, Sastre y el teatro de su tiempo* (New York, 1971).

Halsey, Martha T. 'Light and Darkness as Dramatic Symbols in Two Tragedies of Buero Vallejo', *Hispania*, L, (1967), 63-8.

'Buero Vallejo and the Significance of Hope', *Hispania*, LI, (1968), 57-66.

'The Dreamer in the Tragic Theater of Buero Vallejo', *Revista de estudios hispánicos*, II, (1968), 265-85.

'The Rebel Protagonist: Ibsen's *An Enemy of the People* and Buero's *Un soñador para un pueblo'*, *Comparative Literature Studies*, VI, (1969), 462-71.

'Reality versus Illusion: Ibsen's *The Wild Duck* and Buero Vallejo's *En la ardiente oscuridad'*, *Contemporary Literature*, II, (1970), 48-58.

Antonio Buero Vallejo (New York, 1973).

Kirsner, R. *'Historia de una escalera:* A Play in Search of Characters', *Homenaje a Rodríguez Moniño*, I, (1966), 279-82.

Lott, R.E. 'Scandinavian Reminiscences in Antonio Buero Vallejo's Theater', *Romance Notes*, VII, (1966), 113-16.

Magaña Schevill, I. 'Lo trágico en el teatro de Buero Vallejo', *Hispanófila*, 7, (1959), 51-8.

Nicholas, R.L. *The Tragic Stages of Antonio Buero Vallejo* (Valencia, 1972).

Paco de Moya, M. de. *'Historia de una escalera*, veinticinco años más tarde', in *Estudios Literarios dedicados al Profesor Mariano Baquero Goyanes* (Murcia, 1974), 375-98.

Ramón Cortina, J. *El arte dramático de Antonio Buero Vallejo* (Madrid, 1969). Schwartz, K. 'Buero Vallejo and the Concept of Tragedy', *Hispania*, LI, (1968), 817-24.

ALFONSO SASTRE

Anderson, F. *Alfonso Sastre* (New York, 1971).

Aragonés, J.E. 'El teatro profundizado de Alfonso Sastre', *Punta Europa*, VIII, (1963), 28.

Coster, C.C. de. 'Alfonso Sastre', *Tulane Drama Review*, V, (1960), 121-32.

Pasquariello, A.M. 'Alfonso Sastre y *Escuadra hacia la muerte*', *Hispanófila*, XV, (1962), 57-63.

Peréz-Minik, D. *Teatro europeo contemporáneo* (Madrid, 1961), 399-406.

Pronko, L.C. 'The Revolutionary Theater of Alfonso Sastre', *Tulane Drama Review*, V, (1960).

Ruiz Ramón, F. *Historia del teatro español, II, Siglo XX* (4th ed.) (Madrid, 1980).

Sastre, A. *Drama y sociedad* (Madrid, 1956).

'Primeras notas para un encuentro con Bertolt Brecht', *Primer Acto*, 13, (1960).

Torrente Ballester, G. *Teatro español contemporáneo* (2nd ed.) (Madrid, 1968), 332-38.

Urbano, Victoria. *El teatro español y sus directrices contemporáneas* (Madrid, 1972), 210-15.

Villegas, J. 'La sustancia metafísica de la tragedia y su función social: *Escuadra hacia la muerte* de Alfonso Sastre', *Symposium*, XXI, (1967), 255-63.

Index